Troubled by Truth

Troubled by Truth

Biographies in the Presence
of Mystery

Kenneth Cragg

The Pilgrim Press
Cleveland, Ohio

Originally published
by The Pentland Press Ltd., Durham, England,
as *Troubled by Truth:*
Life-Studies in Inter-Faith Concern,
© 1992 by Kenneth Cragg

Pilgrim Press edition published 1994
The Pilgrim Press, Cleveland, Ohio 44115

Printed in the United States of America on acid-free paper

99 98 97 96 95 94   5 4 3 2 1

Library of Congress Cataloging-in-Publication Data
Cragg, Kenneth.
Troubled by truth : biographies in the presence of mystery / Kenneth Cragg.
p.   cm.
Originally published: Durham, England : Pentland Press, 1992.
Includes bibliographical references and index.
ISBN 0-8298-1005-6 (alk. paper)
1. Religious biography.
2. Religious pluralism.
I. Title.
BL72.C73   1994
200'.92'2—dc20
[B]   94-6906
CIP

CONTENTS

PREFACE

Do we have what it takes? is a frequent yet curious question. 'Have' and 'it' and 'takes' are all so imprecise. Is 'taking' active or passive, efforts we make or submission required of us? Or both? 'Trouble', either way, will be the word next on our lips. And trouble is certainly what we have to take in positive intent, as well as what we undergo in being subject to its forms.

This book aims to explore the trouble with truth as it exacts both sorts of taking in the deepest areas of human experience – those that have to do with the interpretation and management of life, with the reckonings that occupy the faiths of the world. Biography has always been the first clue to theology, and in Christian tradition the reality of God is believed to have been biographised in Jesus as the Christ – the divine Word expressed in human terms and engaged with just those issues of wrong and mysteries of meaning which most bewilder and oppress the human self. That 'Christ-clue', however, to all that we mean of God and say of ourselves is not taken by other old and contrasted versions of the human scene.

Yet all who care are comparably troubled by truth. Because we differ, all are in danger of letting the easy idea of allegiance do duty for the hard idea of truth, allowing our mutual relation to go by default. There are, however, those who let their private trouble with truth engage them with the diversity of plural worlds of anxiety, perception and worship. The studies that follow have thirteen such in review. Six were/are known personally to the writer. The introductory chapter explains the choice and sets the context, while a concluding chapter attempts to summarise the logic of the stories examined.

Such biographies of mind – they are no more – may serve to focus what is at stake in contemporary pluralism and do so the more effectively for being intimate and personal. Despite wise old Francis Bacon, we may well doubt that Pilate was jesting when he asked: What is truth? still less so when he cried: *Ecce Homo.*

Kenneth Cragg
Oxford, Christmas 1991

'I trouble thee too much, but thou art willing.
'Tis my duty, Sir.'

William Shakespeare.

'..somewhat beyond our reach but yet no less a truth for lack of our perspective . . . unless we have a soul gentle enough and spacious enough to contemplate what is true love.'

John Milton.

'He is the Truth:
Seek Him in the kingdom of anxiety.'

W. H. Auden.

Introduction

COMING TO TERMS

i

'And now, O Lord, why hast Thou delivered up the one unto the many . . . and scattered Thine only one among the many?' The anxious question of 4 Ezra 5:27 over the desolation of Jerusalem has an insistent Jewish ring but has within it something of the puzzlement and disquiet all religions feel in the situation of being 'one among many'. No doubt there are multitudes in most faiths who never reach a genuine or disconcerting consciousness of plurality. Their lives are sufficiently engaged in the business of sheer survival. Or if not exhaustion in poverty, then apathy, illiteracy, tradition or cultural confines of mind and society, effectively absolve them from relating to diversity. There are others, however, whose numbers increase in pace with global awareness between cultures and continents and a common sense of the earth, who discover religious contrasts and comparisons either as a riddle or as a fascination which they may not dismiss or ignore. That by which they live as an interpretation of the world has alternates, rivals, aliens to it, excluders from it. They come to see 'the one' as other than 'the many'. How, then, should they respond?

Asian faiths would not, of course, broach the matter in the words of Ezra. His language derived from a premise about ethnic identity and sacred place which they do not share and he wrote out of a desperate tragedy shaped by a logic they would disallow. But even the faiths that seem most amenable to the multiple situation and most congenial to diversity are, none the less, equally as capable as the Semitic faiths of self-assertion and self-vindication.[1] All such postures are clearly an index to something problematic to them, perhaps even prejudicial to their peace of mind, in what is other than they. Such sentiments are often reinforced

by the fact that what divides has long history within it of consanguinity in
a far past, or of physical conquest and communal tension, the distant
'scatterings' that have made them many.

We are familiar, in recent decades, with an instinct on all sides, if in
limited reaches of participation, to open out the singular to the plural, the
particular to the universal, the one to the many. Dialogue has come to be
a familiar word to denote the desire, and the propriety, intending such
mutual encounter, abating prejudice, elucidating meanings and eliciting
trust. It is seen as no more than a due recognition of the single habitat:

> . . . common mother, thou,
> Whose womb immeasurable and infinite breast
> Teems and feeds all.[2]

This urge is the more pressing inasmuch as religions have so long, and so
bitterly, contrived to divide mankind, or to sanction human confrontations
with the mandate of divine warrant abetting the passions of bigotry or
conspiring with the lusts of power. Whatever the limits of what dialogue
can achieve, at least the will to it, in the view of many, is a long overdue
recognition of the crimes of religions. If repentance within them is a clue
to their honesty, then the humility which dialogue, when it is right, must
pre-suppose, will serve such penitence well. It calls in question those
premature conceits of certainty in which all faiths have, at times, indulged.

We have by now numerous studies of the nature and conduct of
inter-religious relationship. But what does coming to terms with plurality
really mean in the actual experience of persons in their believing inside
their relating? Genuinely 'delivered up, the one unto the many', we will
not, in Ezra's anguish, be at odds with destiny. For we have conceded
what is seen as vocation, and we are not banished into exile. In exploring
we are continuing. It is with identity and roots, not divorced from them,
that we undertake to recognise the diversity that is. In forfeiture of self
there is no friendship; in abandonment of home there is no being
hospitable. But what do the guests we entertain mean in our hospitality?
Do we not speak, in a happy quirk of vocabulary, about 'entertaining
ideas'? Relationships are only authentic when both parties are authentically present in them.

Yet are we there, authentically, unless we are there as 'the one'? Can
we rightly relativise, even by implication only, what is ultimate and can
only be religious when it is so? Can commitment ride with optionality? Is

conviction honest if it is not honestly commended? Is faith not inherently witness? 'That which we have seen and heard declare we ...' (1 John 1:3). 'Compare we' seems an improper substitution. What, in short, is the significance of inter-faith for inner faith? How is inner faith both loyal and transactable in inter-faith?

There is no doubt that biography is the right field in which to trace the tensions and examine the issues. Indeed, biographical theology has better claims to legitimacy than systematic or speculative theology. It might be claimed that, far from being a threat to inner convictions, the will to relate outside them has an entirely tonic quality. Too much Christian theology has been too long domesticated within its own interests, its internal debates about Christology or its controversies about justification and atonement. All these, confined as they were within 'givens' that were not at issue, would have gained immensely from full exposure to the puzzlements that other faiths must bring to them. Islamic theology, likewise, has long been inhospitable to its urgent obligation relating to the role of Muhammad and the event within it of Quranic revelation. All theology, if not hitherto, has now to be inter-theology undertaking non-theology most of all.

Such readiness, however, entails awareness, exposure, width of sympathy and access. Indeed, it entails mission. For there is no surer tribute to common humanity than the will to mission, no larger educator into universality – given a right mind – than the vocation to translate one's particularity into new dimensions. Certainly Christian theology, within and beyond the New Testament, was unmistakably a missionary theology. They know less of their faith who have no will to tell it. It has often proved that those most ardent to express have been most ripe to understand. Faith has been refined precisely in not being private. Or, mission apart, those of ambivalent or tentative beliefs have best explored them, sifted and discerned them, in encounters where their doubts might be suspected, contrasted or resolved. Such apprenticeships of faith are by no means confined to formal scholarship. They are pursued in literature, in the themes of imagination, in the stresses of international affairs, and in the interpretation of experience and tribulation in the world.

All these are within the personal equation. It has long been a commonplace that dialogue cannot obtain between faiths; it can only be an enterprise of people. Even if it be a 'Thus saith the Lord', it is always a human voice speaking. And if we are exchanging agnosticisms it is only in their being ours that we do so. It is important, of course, for persons in meeting not to imagine themselves in any formal sense representatives, and they are certainly not negotiators. How adventurous their thoughts may be is for their own discretion. But they will best serve their faith and their friends outside it, if they keep patiently in view the debtors they are within their own tradition together with the actualities of the faith's history in the past and its turmoils in the present. Even so, dialogue will foster inner perceptions of meaning and invitations of hope which mere soliloquy would never have aroused. It is only biography which holds such disclosures. It is from life stories that we can take their measure. If we are saying: 'Let there be light', it will be well to add: 'Let there be windows'.

ii

These chapters, therefore, aim to take for windows a group of personal experiences in which encounter with pluralism proved a school of mind. In every case there had to be a coming to terms with faiths one did not share, of letting the non-sharing investigate its reasons and so discovering what it was that had, of necessity, to be shared whether by virtue of a common, human predicament, of a mutual indecision, or of the mandate of mission. The implications of such varied meetings will only be understood if the net is cast widely enough. Yet it can only be selective in its catch. And 'catch', some will suspect, is nicely ambiguous here. Why these here chosen, and not others, readers will properly ask. Reflection would have been differently occupied if other figures had been present. For the most part we concentrate on the Abrahamic faiths – a common designation which itself begs many questions. But India is also here and three thinkers are included whose instincts freed them to roam surmisingly over the entire field of religion. Let plain apology be made for the omission of names any reader is urgent to insert but no apology to critics who complain only by first ignoring – as reviewers often do – the author's own acknowledgement of incompleteness.

Six of the thirteen personalities here were – or are – known individually to the writer and all but one could be said to be contemporary. By the logic throughout here of personal nexus, that might be thought to be an asset, if also a factor subjectively deciding choice. Is there any will to be objective which is not subjectively reached? Eight Muslim thinkers have been treated elsewhere.[3] Four others, of sharply differing perspectives, are included, with three Christians broadly engaged with aspects of Islam. There are three who grapple with things Judaic, two from within Jewry and one Christian. What might be called the Christian/Indian dialogue has two perceivers of its meaning. In most contexts the pressure of the secular is either latent or lively and, in several cases, the burdens of mind are more inward than relational. The debate is then more about what the inner faith is, or needs to be, rather than how it might align with inter-faith. Yet such turning inward, under the weight of tragedy or the forfeiture of confidence or the perplexity of identity, is everywhere the mark of sincerity – the sincerity which alone has integrity in relating to others.

If, therefore, more celebrated names are not included, the content need be no less significant, and no less satisfactory for the purpose in hand by being the more ordinary. Had Martin Buber, or Louis Massignon, or Franz Rosenthal, or Ninian Smart, been present, or a throng of other names which readers might suggest, the essential issues would have been the same.

The absence of professional theologians and of mystics needs to be noted. The former are unlikely to be so alerted to inter-cultural realities as, for example, linguists, anthropologists, bi-nationals, novelists and even lawyers, contrive to be. It is sometimes true that the more deeply devout, the more anxiously perplexed, are liable to be found outside the sanctuaries rather than within them. This is not to say, however, that they may not be widely conversant with Scriptures and rituals about which they are healthily inquisitive. Mystics, when it comes to dialogue, tend to be a law unto themselves. For if they are of the more rigorous sort, they live with ineffables that cannot be related in conscious study or transactable terms. Even the less rigorous distrust rationality and prefer mystery to elucidation. Nevertheless, subject to the constraints of careful study and ascertainable criteria of belief, there are at least seven in our chosen number who could readily enter into the distinction some mystics make between elucidation and illumination.

Including one now notorious novelist and one comparatively obscure (outside his own country) playwright serves to underline the role of imaginative literature in encounters of belief and doubt across traditional frontiers of either. The elusiveness of narrator in character, hint in plot, and imagery in language, or the flux of conjecture and intention between reader and author, exactly suit what has to be tentative or ambivalent in experience between faiths. Moreover, poets and dramatists of the human condition can escape the censorships, formal or internal, which often govern the formulations of conscious debate and official theology. The *personae* of imaginative writing are portrayals at once awaiting and eluding identification – a situation which equips them both to affirm and to conceal.

In English villages in the months of spring there has long been the honoured custom of 'beating the bounds'. It consists of frolicsome processions around the confines of the parish, beating the bushes, blessing the dividing ditches and fences and scattering flowers around the borders. It is a seasonal affirmation of parochialism in the conviction that, as the New England poet has it, 'good fences make good neighbours'.[4] Rustic territoriality is, or was, emotional security. Have the ancient landmarks been removed? Is there some encroachment to reverse? Do we still know where we are and do our neighbours know? For does not 'who' belong with 'where'?

'Beating the bounds' has long been an instinct of the religions. 'Premises' have to be secure whether they are places where we dwell, notations where we sing, or truths from which our logic argues. Even where boundaries have been purposefully crossed the resulting controversies have often resembled a more energetic beating of the bounds. Encounter has stimulated vigorous self-assertion, either way. For boundaries, after all, are reciprocal. Ensuring mine is ensuring his, staking ours is staking theirs, and neither see how trespassers might be welcome.

> Before I built a wall I'd ask to know
> What I was walling in or walling out...

For the most part the walls are of our inheritance and of our maintaining. The analogy could well deceive us. How far it might not is what we have to study. Our mentors have at least met on frontiers. They have come to terms – speaking, enquiring, thinking terms with one another. What do they find? Is there a way in which ancient landmarks may still be noted yet distrusted, revered for what they define but no longer for what they confine?

iii

Coming to terms with diversity and with the will to relate means also coming to terms in themselves, with words as the vocabulary of faith. Here the very counters with which we might reckon in mutual recognition are themselves ambivalent or opaque, if not wanting altogether. United by a common humanity we are divided by uncommon languages, the ideas these transact and the emotions they arouse. Non-intercourse is liable to be dictated by the very means, in speech and symbol, which exist to overcome it. These, serving so well inwardly, for that very reason fail to serve outwardly. The very terms of religion, when we come to them, impose a kind of exclusion zone or, perhaps, a confusion zone, in which we exchange incomprehension.

When George III of England wrote to his equally long-reigning contemporary Emperor Ch'ien Lung, the serene majesty of China, requesting diplomatic and commercial relations between such unequal powers, he received a lofty answer:

> This request is contrary to all usage of my dynasty and cannot possibly be entertained ... Our ceremonies and code of laws differ so completely from your own that, even if your envoy were able to acquire the rudiments of our civilization you could not possibly transplant our manners and customs to your alien soil ... I set no value on objects strange or ingenious, and have no use for your country's manufactures.[5]

'Contrary to all usage ...' is how translators have frequently found the words they brought, the terms they owned. 'South Sea barbarians' – so Ch'ien Lung described the western sailors of whom he heard, nibbling at his southern shores. Uncouthness and barbarity have always been first identified and then registered in language.[6] 'Hearsay' is, in that sense, the guarantee of prejudice. Language is, therefore, quite literally where religions have to negotiate.

It is this fact which makes so apposite the presence in Chapter 1 of Henry Martyn, our only representative outside this twentieth century. For his brief career in missionary translation is as telling as any concerning the problematics of words and terms in the transactions of faith. Martyn encountered the 'x into y will-not-go' situation and faced it with a strong equipment of scholarship sustained by steady anguish of spirit. The mathematical analogy would have suited him, had figures of speech which abound in belief not been far more intractable than figures in fractions. 'Grace', 'truth', 'redemption', 'church', 'hope', and other vital words in his New Testament currency struggled to fulfil themselves in Indian idiom. It is evident in Martyn how he was more vitally in encounter with theology-in-philology than any academic professor. For he was made to feel, via his robust *munshis*, or local scholar-aids, the full strain, and even the venom, of the resistance to meaning implicit in the otherness of words. In that sense his 'mission' was the deepest tribute to otherness – unlike academic abstraction – in that it truly reckoned with what was there. The common notion that mission impedes real encounter because it speaks out of a conviction and intends communication, needs to be treated with the scepticism that critics frequently bring to mission itself. What cherishes its terms is more likely to discover what their translation takes than the complacence which merely trades them.

The very stress of this language situation makes it necessary that dialogue itself should, somehow, create its own terms of transaction. This might be said to be the very task itself. What is at stake within words must negotiate with what may be made to avail to take it. What from the nature of faith found itself in words, only did so because it found words for itself. So the familiar that is inward on one side must find its way into what is familiar on the other side by engagement between the reciprocal unfamiliars until they suffice as carriers or, otherwise, cease to be cyphers in opaqueness. The venture is adventurous. For trusted words and symbols are invested with security and hold assurance of identity. But, if the soul is moving into participation, vocabulary must somehow do the same.

There is stamina to help achieve this in the realisation that in each religion words and symbols have themselves acquired their connotation through elastic reckoning within their own tradition and have also coined themselves out of encounter. Terms crucial in the monotheistic faiths, for example, have been shared, revised, or enlarged by transmission between them, or have been domesticated from external sources through mutual shaping of significance. The same can happen in contemporary deliberation so that, in some measure, the given in meaning is also the received.

If dialogue is to attain terms in its exchange rather than merely bring them, there must be care lest inventiveness does not simply enshrine, and not unravel, ambiguity. Some dialogicians, among whom Raimundo Panikkar may be numbered, prove adept in neologisms which intend to escape the disservice in traditional language but leave vital matters either unclear or unresolved. The substitution of 'theandric' from 'trinitarian' is a case in point. The one has a definition which makes man as 'necessary' to God as God is to man, whereas the doctrine of the Trinity has long been understood as confession of that divine 'beyondness' from which creation could credibly arise.[7] If we are speaking, for example again, of 'tempiternity', it must be more than a formula disguising the riddle of time and eternity.

While new mintings need critical treatment if they are to serve the need, old coinage demands it more. Multiple misconceptions have arisen from partial or distorting translation of such pivotal terms as Torah, Dharma, Karma, Nirvana, Advaita, Dukkha, Taqwa, Shalom, Messiah, Pleroma, Hamartia and many more. If we cannot well penetrate all that insiders mean by their language, we can at least be alert to the misconstruing outsider supposition brings, as the first step to knowing and being known. It is well, too, to restrain the temptation to denote what we think the other means in ways which unwittingly, or intentionally, debase the currency we have thereby undervalued – as was the case with Isma'il al- Faruqi.[8] We do not well elucidate if we seem also to deride. Positively, it is necessary to look for how words can be elasticized to undertake new dimensions within their existing usage, so that by interpenetration shifts of perception may occur by an awareness which receives while it retains. Many intriguing instances of this potential emerge in the biographical studies that follow.

iv

There is, however, a crucial factor in the right relating of religious language, namely the centrality to each of its own Scripture. Indeed, the phenomenon of Scriptures, with the status they enjoy and the role they play, not only determines in large measure what dialogue must undertake but also conditions the mentality brought to it. All the major faiths are mysteriously endowed with sacred writings. They may have been possessed by their possessors in a variety of histories of origin and of theories of inspiration but they exercise a controlling aegis over the minds and wills of their adherents. They complicate comparison and mediation of religious vocabularies by sanctions of authority, familiarity and the strange prestige which belongs with their mystique. It has often been noted, for example, how the very sequences of the Qur'an through the sacred practice of *tajwid*, or loving, scrupulous recitation, shape the very logic of the Muslim mind. Jewish and Christian piety, in distinctive ways, lives from and with the feel of the Bible. The poetry of the Bhagavad Gita and the aphoristic wisdom of the Dharmapada enter pervasively into the soul of the devout Hindu and the quest of the Buddhist. The Rabbinic mind, it would be fair to say, is the mental transcript of the Talmud. The copious margins of the Qur'an give the lie to the notion of the marginal being marginalised. For they frame the very text itself in their own prison and those who write them believe themselves free only there. For the Sikh the holy Granth and, after the death of Gobind Singh, the writings themselves came to be seen as the eternal, spiritual Guru of all Sikhs.

The definitive role of Scriptures is familiar enough. Our first biography is at once into the issue it presents. For Henry Martyn believed that Scripture translation was the primary duty. He had a total confidence in the efficacy of the Scriptures that had convinced him. His inner faith required him to hold that, once suitably rendered, they would mediate the same conviction everywhere. In deep pain he discovered the formidable pre-possession, by other Scripture, of the minds he sought to reach. His tragedy deserves its prior place here in that it belongs so crucially with the heart of things. Others, sensing the quandary of Scriptures in other Scriptural territory turn, like C.F. Andrews, to common action or, like Constance Padwick, to patterns of theological devotion. Yet none escape the actual status, the potential tyranny, of multiple 'words of the Lord', diversely comprehended and competitively hallowed, imbuing all relationships. They hold the criteria for all encounters among their custodians and yet somehow preclude these from engaging without them. For there is that about their status which forbids their being laid aside. Thus they must necessarily preside over the courts in which they are themselves at issue. As themselves the theme of what needs to be examined they nevertheless reserve their own jurisdiction.

This situation is clearly critical for all that inner faith has in hand in the will to inter-faith. To what extent are Scriptures capable of being shared? Wilfred Cantwell Smith may say, boldly, that 'Islam is what Muslims say it is'.[9] Why only Muslims? Are Scriptures like 'mother tongues', so that no one can be 'bi-scriptural'? Was not Muhammad 'a mercy to the worlds'? Should other than Muslims, then, be warned off the holy Quranic ground?[10] Does one need to 'own' a Scripture credally in order to possess it intelligently? Can one belong with a text in sympathy if not in dogma? If Christians find and welcome truth in the Gita or the Granth are they thereby committed to underwriting all that those 'native' to these texts believe about their origin or status? Can we belong selectively with other Scriptures? Or how will such a liberty ride with the authority they are deemed to possess and require to impose? What of the claim all possessors of their own are liable to make that only they truly understand it and only they are its due interpreters? Yet, given such a 'trespassers prosecuted' stance, how will faiths ever relate, seeing that Scriptures document them?

The questions multiply. Plainly, Scriptures must be foremost in any inter-situation. The will to have them for criteria without the status that inwardly makes any the sole criterion must surely operate. The necessity is bound to be painful on all hands. For it demands a radical shift of mentality, at least for purposes of conversation. It therefore becomes a focus of what all relatedness must be, as a readiness to think oneself other than one is, and to do so without any final sense of compromise, still less of betrayal, inasmuch as one has sensed the vocation as the only honest loyalty. There cannot well be inter-faith which does not get to the heart of the inner conviction and 'inter-Scripture' is where it is most likely, and most proper, to happen.

When, and as, it does, a further perspective is likely to emerge. The exercise inter-faith-wise will become not only a reverent reckoning with mutual authorities but a reckoning with authority itself. Scriptures avail for multitudes of believers as 'the final court of appeal', the tribunal which is itself in no sense on trial. Much of religion lives in that situation. Once we have been alerted to the fact of it there lurks the question of why it should be so. Or, indeed, should it be so? Why do, how could, Scriptures have this final say? May I not go behind them and ask this? Indeed, if I am counting them to be that which I will not go beyond, nor interrogate as if they were not final, surely that is itself a decision I have taken. Being thus so crucial, should it not be itself assessed? 'Dogmatic slumbers' may have prevented the question from arising but once it has come into the mind it will not rest until it is faced. Facing it may well bring me back to a Scriptural ultimacy I freely opt to trust but it will be a different quality of trust from the unexamined faith I had before. Or I may wonder how, for so long, I relied on what I had never thought to interrogate, on what I assumed to need no interrogation.

One of the fruits of the inter-faith situation is that it is liable to have this sequel, if only in making us aware of finalities as options: or in moving us to ponder how other minds can be so entrenched we realise tellingly our own entrenchments. Muslims, in the heyday of their expansion in the seventh and eighth centuries, used to wonder how continuing Christians could be so crass as to persist in a plainly superseded doctrine which lacked both credibility and the power to preserve them from total conquest. For the one the experience was a vindicating triumphalism, for the other a purging paradox. Faiths do not have their equations in that form now. But in any circumstance, not least that of current secularity, their natural inquisitiveness about each other raises for each of them radical questions about why they are what they are and whether they remain so. There is no genuine dialogue except in steady self-interrogation.

Nor is the question of final authority merely relational within religions as diversely 'given'. Why should any of them obtain? In some sense all depend on the theme of revelation, of the mediation and sanction of meaning through divine agency of prophethood, illumination, or intuitive wisdom. But how does 'revelation' convince us of its being so? If we can identify it of ourselves, do we really need it? For we presumably know what we should be looking for if, in fact, we are able to say: 'Here it is:

this is the Word of the Lord.' If we know enough to have the criteria to recognise what as 'revelation' we receive, how was it necessary, or 'from beyond'?

The questions are familiar enough. The fact of them in no way excludes revelation as both urgent and authentic. But they do require us to acknowledge that it must be somehow reciprocal to our receptivity, an enabling of our capacity to receive, a colloquy with our self-awareness.[11] That it requires our cognisance does not mean that it is not wholly given. There is comfort here – even in the stresses of inter-faith – in the fact that, so understood, no revelation can be categorical to the point at which it, or its custodians, can be absolutists who only assert, and do not minister, what they have apprehended. For it was not as absolutists that they received it. Whether the *Iqra'* that breathed the Qur'an, or the Dharma speaking in the Dharmapada, or the God breathing into the Sruti Scriptures of the Hindu, or 'Thus saith the Lord' to the Hebrew prophets – all are so received, credited, sacrilised, by human cognisance and live in human currency. The divine that is beyond is always articulate in the human that is within.

This inclusive fact does not resolve our perplexities about the manifoldness of purported revelation. Indeed, diversity begets plural exclusivity. Yet it does so precisely for the reason we have explored. Revelation could not proceed except in finality; that is its nature. For it is a human cognisance of the divine mystery and, as such, occurs in a particular locale of time, of culture and of people. These, with other mysterious factors, diversify both its incidence and its content. Thus it yields a plurality of finalities.[12] These in their origin and their perpetuation are a contemporary inheritance which inevitably divides. But the sense for which we have argued, of a necessary and crucial human-ness about their genesis, can assist us in awareness of the relativity they must own – albeit in their finality inwardly received – to the alternatives they now humanly confront.

But have we been disloyal, even treacherous, in adopting here a stance which seems to validate as revelatory whatever purports to be such and to have religious currency? In one sense, No! For this is the *de facto* situation we face, in which we must positively recognise that diversity exists. There is no transactable monopoly of truth. In another sense, Yes! if the sense of the revelatory in the plurality obscures or disserves the distinctiveness which decisively belongs to Christian apprehension of truth. Acknowledged pluralism would seem to require of every faith a reverent, irenic identification of that within it which requires that it persist in emphatic particularity as the bearer of that 'than which there is no other'. We will defer to a final chapter the theme of a Christian decisiveness, leaving to any and every other faith the occasion to show its own cause why it must be, and remain, what it is. The decisive thing for the Christian, 'God in Christ reconciling', the loving, self-expending Lordship, 'the God with wounds', will always be distinctive. But it will share much else with every faith and, therefore, hold its decisiveness inclusively with questions and answers everywhere as far as it consistently can. Ultimacies elsewhere will have their perspectives on the shared world. With these, for its own sake and for theirs, it will always be related in articulate hope by warrant of its own decisive ground.

V

It follows that if this is what we mean by 'coming to terms' it has to happen within the actualities of politics, of social issues and religious adversity. Its intellectual demands cannot be confined to the academies nor its spiritual tensions to the theologians. There were significant biographies of dialogue in the trauma for Indian Muslims of the partition of the sub-continent, and their exclusion from that statehood which Pakistan insisted was a *sine qua non* of survival. Hence the presence of a voice from that situation in the person of Asaf Fyzee. Or inner faith inevitably becomes inter-faith in the anguish of Jewish reflection on the Holocaust, as in the novels and essays of Elie Wiesel. It belongs, from the same context, in the self-examination of Christianity over the meaning of Judaic tragedy and Judaic continuity and their bearing on Christian conscience and Christian claim. James Parkes is here a notable case in point. In Rabbi Abraham Heschel we find an almost unique Jewish reckoning with inheritance and destiny, with the Hasidic tradition of Polish Jewry fulfilled in the American scene and the inter-faith repudiation of the Vietnam War.

No less revealing biographically, within Islam, are the deeply contrasted lives of Isma'il al-Faruqi and Salah 'Abd al-Sabur, the former a sharply dogmatic figure forever trying to escape intellectually from any necessity for paradox yet caught tragically in its toils; the other musing as a play-wright and poet on the tribulations and temptations of the martyr and on the martyrizing of ordinary folk by the injustices and indignities of daily life. These in their different ways were in steady dialogue with their own Islam and, the one controversially, the other tangentially, in converse with Christian and Jew.

And who would not concur with the painful dialogue, overtones and undertones, precipitated by publication of *The Satanic Verses*? Salman Rushdie's fantasies certainly intended provocation, if not the one they achieved. For they were provoked first within him by a conscious, rejectionist engagement with what he saw as the futility and the anachronism of religion in general and of Islam in particular. Here was an author in passionate inward dialogue with himself over the meaning of human experience, deliberately inciting Muslims to self-scrutiny but only accentuating their defensiveness by the crude tactics he employed. The resulting furore only served to bolster, rather than to interrogate, the bland assumptions of western liberalism. Dialogue sometimes provides its liveliest themes when it is effectively at its worst.

All the more reason, then, to include three deeply self-critical, acutely self-conscious practitioners in the persons of Raimundo Panikkar, Arnold Toynbee and Wilfred Cantwell Smith – writers whose breadth of sympathy and acumen of mind enable them to reach below the particularities, where less ambivalent writers rest and stay, to undertake what timidity would exclude. Their different versions of how dialogue may, or can, eventuate will usefully bring us to a final chapter intended in retrospect as 'a lantern on the stern'.

Chapter 1

HENRY MARTYN
(1781 – 1812)

'I long to know what I seek after'

i

The words are an entry in the Journal of 31 July 1809, three years and three months after Henry Martyn's arrival in India in 1806. A youth of twenty-five, his ardour foresaw what he called 'the expanding circle of action'. It proved instead a contracting cycle of disease. He was a consumptive before he came to India, His tenure fell short of five years in the sub-continent. His last two were spent on the road through Persia towards Europe carrying with him, for publication there, the fruits of his work on New Testament translation. He died at Tokat in Armenia on 16 October 1812. Translation had been his central concern, not only because Christian Scripture was crucial to his mission, but because his infirmity left him little voice for vigorous preaching. Study may conjecture what India might have done with him and he with India, but for the tragic brevity of his dialogue of soul. For 'dialogue' indeed it was – and all the more vital for the fact that his intention was always 'mission'. It was precisely the gentle quality of his earnestness which made dialogue the more engrossing both in spirit and in theme. There is no more emphatic reminder than the short career of Henry Martyn that if either is to be authentic the two are inseparable.

To be sure, he intended 'conversion'. But he knew that the patient commendation of Christ which might achieve it had to overcome the enmities of politics and wrestle with the ambiguities of cultures. Nowhere was the effort more exacting than in the field of words, of sacred writings and the taxing vocabulary of contrasting faiths. Whether immersing himself in dictionaries, consulting with vexing or querulous *munshis* or

15

pundits, or resolving the nuances of the parables and the mysteries of Paul and John, he was in converse with faiths as he met them precisely because he was the bearer of his own. His few and tragic years had an intensity of feeling that no lengthening time could have made more penetrating and entire. His story represents encounter between religions at its most anguished and, for that same reason, its most radical. Its intellectual content was wholly consecrated to the business of communication. Its considerable academic prowess was saved from exotic indulgence or erudite complacency by the sheer quality of his inner concern with Christ.

His mind and character were shaped in a Cornish childhood. He was the third child of a modest family, the Martyns of Truro, where Methodist influences were strong. Small of stature and unprepossessing in appearance, and orphaned of his mother in his third year, his maturing was slow and uneasy. He was liable to moods of withdrawal, sharpened by his eagerness to love. He came to St. John's College, Cambridge in the autumn of 1797, where uncertain beginnings quickly blossomed into academic success. He emerged as something of a prodigy in mathematics, and a keen devotee of Isaac Newton. It was the sudden death of his father in 1800 which aroused him to explore the mysteries of life. All the relevant factors, as Cornwall and Cambridge shaped them in his mind, conduced him to prayer and to the study of the New Testament. The evangelical experience of need, of grace, of forgiveness and the call to discipleship, crowned his search and settled his career. Charles Simeon, Fellow of King's College and in full flow as Vicar of Holy Trinity Church, Cambridge, became his mentor, together with John Sargent, another Fellow of King's. Martyn emerged with the most brilliant of mathematical degrees and became a Fellow of St. John's. In 1803 he was ordained as Simeon's curate and, to the bewildered reproaches of his academic colleagues, dedicated himself to the humdrum pastoral duties of a village in the Fens.

With all the fervour of an instinctively ardent soul he was already probing further, looking to Asia and to mission. He had come to grace in the stirring days of William Carey whose famous *Enquiry into the Obligations of Christians* (1786) became the symbol of an awakening to the world-dimensions of faith, made the more urgent by the commercial and political ambitions currently pursued by the East India Company. Fired by the *Life of David Brainerd* of Connecticut, an apostle to Amerindians, Martyn knew himself summoned to a vocation mirrored in the ever self-scrutinizing, self-defining pages of his *Journal* which, begun in these Cambridge years, and continuing almost to his travels' end, ranks as a superb document of what obtains between religions in one soul's transactions of inner meaning and outward yearning. Martyn's introspective honesty, total compassion and genuine anxiety for integrity, make of autobiography itself a dialogue concerning truth – truth within and truth beyond. For there is not only the truth of proposition such as doctrine purports to be. There is also the truth of character, like the 'true' of bells, or music, or diamonds.

That latter truth, in Henry Martyn's case, was made complex – as such truth ever is – by the fact that he came to India in the capacity of a chaplain to the East India Company. He had his sisters to support in Truro and the salary was urgently needed on their account. But was it not also vital to undertake those 'evidences of Christianity' which are only present – or confoundingly absent – in the persons of the 'factors' in commerce, the personnel of British merchants and officials? Martyn's contacts in London made him keenly alert to the tensions of the Company connection which would dog him to the end. His dialogue with India had the perpetual sub-plot of his disquiet with the mercantile auspices which, for all they entailed of dismay and dejection, had to be endured with patient hope. The psalmist's prayer: 'Let not those that seek Thee be confounded through me[or: "us"]', lay close to the heart of his anxieties. There is no inner faith which can be absolved from the cultural company it is required to keep. The need to be embarrassed is constantly present in the intercourse of all faiths. Only by their own lights can they make it genuine. Before we come to Martyn's engagement with what he found in the India of her faiths, it is well to appreciate his dialogue with his own kin.

ii

His long voyage out was a bitter induction to its painful features. On the one hand he believed deeply in the providence of power. *En route*, at the Cape of Good Hope, in January 1806, he was aware of the fluctuating fortunes of the Cape Territory and how European rivalries in the throes of the Napoleonic Wars dominated the setting in which his fragile task was set.[1] Even so he registered delight in the notion of William Carey that 'there should be an annual meeting, at the Cape of Good Hope, of all the missionaries in the world'.[2] In a sermon in India the next year he said: 'How marvellously is India put into the hands of a Christian nation for a short time – may we lay a lasting foundation for the Gospel in it.'[3]

He was wrong about any imperial brevity. But he knew it precarious on

other grounds. He was well aware of the disdain and disfavour with which
the East India Company regarded mission and all its works. When he was
still at school in Truro, its Directors had minuted its view that

> ...the sending of missionaries into our eastern possessions
> is the maddest, most extravagant and most unwarrantable
> project...ever proposed by an enthusiastic lunatic.[4]

It was in such terms that his 'parishioners' deplored and derided his
'interest' in 'the natives', his bother with their languages, his compassion
for their tribulations, his concern for their souls. Indians, illiterate,
caste-ridden, poor, alien, were the centre of his 'chaplaincy' for whom the
ministry to 'people of the Company' was occasion. The Gospel, he
believed, enabled him to counter hostility with a divine logic. 'If our
Lord,' he told the cavillers,'had always travelled about in a palanquin, the
poor woman who was healed by touching the hem of his garment might
have perished.'[5] To be accessible is at once the hallmark of love and
therefore also the instinct of faith.

Martyn's integrity wrestled hard with the other side of his role, when
Indians alleged, or whispered, that by taking his salary he was sharing in
plunder. He thought long on his liabilities, lived with inner unquietness of
mind and searched for patience. He wrote:

> I know not how to decide...thoughts occur to me.... A
> man who has unjustly got possession of an estate hires me as
> a minister to preach to his servants and pays me a salary:
> the money wherewith he pays me comes unjustly to him,
> but justly to me. The Company are the acknowledged
> proprietors of the country and the ruling power.[6]

'Acknowledged' begged more questions than it resolved. Yet it was a holy
pragmatism and his inner faith lived with the unease as only integrity can.
It was consoling too that his salary supplied the means for those *munshis*
who had the verbal clues to his precious translation. Philology was in the
reckoning as well as conscience.

The New Testament apostles, whom Henry Martyn aspired to emulate,
had no such problems. But Martyn's was not their world. At the very
moment of his venture into India, Lord Wellesley, as Governor, had
defeated the Mahrattas and extended the Company's control into the
Princely States. And whatever the facts of the times, Martyn himself had

very little time. Conscience had to live with destiny.

It was not, however, to Britain in India that Martyn had come, except as the circumstance of his coming to Indians. It was they he sought for because his inner faith assured him that they were included in a divine embrace of suffering love and must, therefore, be encountered, as they truly were, in the reach of his trust with that conviction. He quickly discovered that there was an inter-faith logic in the hospitality of his Christianity. How he followed it is our prime concern.

iii

When his ship, oddly named *Union*, touched at Madras his first impressions of India were sombre and daunting. Behind him lay nine months of tedious voyage and alternating moods of ardent anticipation and acute depression. He believed he had left England behind for ever and, with it, the gentle hope of marriage he had blissfully indulged and firmly countermanded. Welcomed by officialdom at Madras, he characteristically confided to his diary:

> While the turbaned Asiatics waited upon us at dinner I could not help feeling as if we had got into their places.[7]

He went on to Calcutta to be greeted by William Carey, already some years into his long saga with Indian languages and his enterprise of philology, printing and translation. They were kindred spirits. Already at Cambridge and on shipboard Martyn had been digesting the linguistic prerequisites for the converse of religions. They were to preoccupy all his calculations and to absorb all his skills and energies. It was in the setting of Scriptures that he located what his inner faith had to achieve.

There was a sense in which this assumption took over all that was at stake and, so doing, deferred the larger issue of popular comprehension. Henry Martyn's implicit faith was that once readers had the Christian page before their eyes, the reading mind would understand. For him, the translator's work – given the right diligence in seeking out the 'conveyance' of the Word – would turn the key of comprehension. Was there not inherently in the text the open face of meaning? Did not the sacred writing offer with its content a kind of sacrament of transmission effectual in its own right? He was sure that once the Hebrew and the Greek had passed into the Urdu, the Hindi, the Sanskrit, the Bengali by devoted labour, the text would be its own perfect advocate. There could be no culture gap to perpetuate the distance the Scriptures had the power to bridge. In any event, his physical condition and all his personal endowments shaped his vocation in those terms. Whatever the otherness of ethos, of symbol, of society, he, for his part, would serve and set all meeting within the sacred Christian page. He would engage with India sufficiently in giving it, as far as in him lay, his sacred Book, his New Testament. Grammar and the dictionary would be the tools of his theology. To 'rescue a word' would be to 'discover a universe'.[8]

Whatever the dimensions of encounter which this left fallow, it was a veritable 'inter-ness' in its own right and a genuine pioneering. It required rigorous converse with Hindu and Muslim 'consultants', taxing, and often teasing, the Christian 'initiate' who was, at once, ardently primed with his meanings in Christ and necessarily pupilled to sons of India. Martyn was thus discovering in elemental form the very basics of encounter.

His first and lasting impressions of India gave no pause to his conviction of the utter urgency of what he brought. It is wise, in understanding him, to remember that he learned India long before those stirrings within Hinduism which moved Mahatma Gandhi to repudiate the caste system as truly non-Hindu.[9] Everywhere he saw oppressive evidence of apathy, superstition, suffering and human tragedy, religiously unrelieved if not religiously contrived. What 'dialogue' may be able to sense and hope in our time is no right yardstick by which to measure – still less to condemn – the reckonings of the past. Hindu self-reform lay far ahead of Martyn and the spiritual ventures of the great Moghul, the Emperor Akbar, far behind. And he, for his part, was in a distressingly different world of incongruity from that of the first Christian apostles in their congenial Mediterranean orbit of 'Hebrew, Greek and Latin'.

Many times his mind went to those models of his purpose. 'I endeavoured to think,' he wrote, 'how St. Paul would act in my condition'.[10] But, as T.S. Eliot has the Magi say: 'There was no information.' For Paul was always between the Jordan, the Orontes and the Tiber, never by the Ganges. 'Above all,' with the New Testament before him he pleaded, 'tell me where . . . I may find India.'[11] This was certainly 'dialogue'–intense, meticulous and sustained. Often his local mentors proved tormentors in respect of his struggle for the expression of meaning. The right terms were often so elusive and his interlocutors fractious or wearisome. 'The idioms,' he wrote of Urdu,

> . . . are so numerous, perverting the most innocent phrases
> into obscurities and giving another meaning to the simplest

expressions that nothing but very long acquaintance with the
natives can give you any power in it.[12]

The impatient hint there of vexation indicates that the problems were
alive. His frustrations were reciprocated by the *munshis* whom he re-
imbursed from his private purse, of one of whom he wrote:

> He said with dreadful bitterness and contempt that after the
> present generation . . . a set of fools would perhaps be born
> such as the Gospel required . . . who would believe that God
> is man and man is God . . . He sometimes cuts me to the very
> soul.[13]

Most of the basic terms of Christian faith were liable to be opaque or
repulsive to Hindu mentality and Muslim dogma. Jesus's conversation
with Nicodemus invited the notion that transmigration was its meaning.
He studied the poet Sa'di for clues to illuminate the parables but remained
lost in his quest for them. The pressure led him at times to near despair
and perhaps a touch of human petulance, as when, in a Sermon, he told
his chaplaincy folk:

> God is not at all anxious to accommodate Himself to the
> prejudices of proud men, nor will He new-model His
> scheme to make it more agreeable to their views.[14]

His constant habit of prayer restored his vision and returned him to his
longsuffering. He was only discovering that his task was unremitting, a
struggle in which 'there was no discharge'. 'Church', for example, was an
awkward quantity:

> A word for 'Church' I have not yet found, as *munshi* knows
> no word in Arabic or Persian to express it: but no doubt
> there is some word in one of the oriental versions . . . I have
> written 'the company of the chosen' which comes most near
> to the *ekklesia*. If the single word which may occur should
> not readily express this idea, I would rather use a phrase,
> explanatory as above, than leave such a word as 'church' is
> in English, to which very few English affix the right idea.[15]

The last comment is a telling one. For the translator is always in some measure the theologian. It is clear that he sensed how his immediate lexical problems belonged in a still broader field and that the very possibility of meaning-in-transmission was at stake. He wrote on 14 March 1807:

> I wait first to see the effect of the distribution of the Scriptures in India: if that is not efficacious, there will be some marvellous exhibition of divine power made here, whether in a way of judgement or grace I do not know.[16]

What could only be awaited his life-span did not encompass, nor – bye and large – have the succeeding centuries.

iv

That fact does not make Henry Martyn's biography the less creatively 'dialogical'. Pioneers are not, by definition, attainers. In retrospect, it may be asked by some whether Martyn was ever in dialogue at all? Was he not essentially evangelist? Should we apply to him the pathos of R.S. Thomas's lines:

> They listened to me preaching the unique Gospel
> Of love, but our eyes never met.

By no means. There are clear indications in Martyn's anguish of spirit – for such it was – that he had more than an inkling of the issues that lay within and beyond the sufficient task he had set himself and which was all his years allowed. In the sermon earlier quoted for its hint of irritation he declared:

> The minister of the Gospel will make use of all the variety of methods which the topics of religion or the feelings of men will supply...For the minds of men may require certain preparation for the want of which the Gospel may be unintelligible.[17]

A lively sense of the 'unintelligible' is the beginning of wisdom in an inter-faith situation where to be 'minister of the Gospel' sharpens the need for it. Otherwise inner faith is not present and dialogue lapses for lack of parties. It is clear that Henry Martyn knew this well. His ready contact with 'common folk' was the surest proof of his will to belong. While formal Hindu religion and Muslim pride aroused his reproaches, in contrast to other missionaries like Marshman he was painfully sensitive to bewilderment, the lack of which is the mark of the sheer dogmatist. Martyn's instinct was to take his perplexity and despair back into spiritual self-reproach rather than into exploration of doctrine. Purely devotional reassurance did duty for intellectual query. It was in his soul rather than in his creed that he faced his doubts. If we, now, do otherwise and allow ourselves a different sanction, that gives us no warrant for an arrogance that discounts what governed him, namely his commission in Christ.

For he certainly knew what it meant. He wrote:

> What surprises me is the change of views I have here from what I had in England. There my heart expanded with hope and joy at the prospect of the speedy conversion of the heathen. But here the sight of the apparent impossibility requires a strong faith to support the spirits.[18]

He was being made aware of how disparate his task was from that of Paul and Barnabas in Cyprus or Iconium. He was faintly grasping the geographical partiality of the Scriptures he trusted, the confinements of their precedents for mission to spheres of cultural affinity so far from what met a Cornishman in Cawpore. He 'repeated the farewell discourse of St. Paul' to the Ephesian elders, but it only proved a measure of how different was his own journey forward. 'I confuted all their errors as plainly as possible from the Word of God, and they had nothing to reply, but they did not seem disconcerted.'[19]

We find him dubious about the very necessity of argument.

> For myself I never enter into a discussion without having reason to reflect that I mar the work for which I contend by the spirit in which I do it ... I wish a spirit of enquiry may be excited but I lay not much stress upon clear arguments. The work of God is seldom wrought this way.

Even so, he continues in the same entry:

> I am preparing for the assault of this great Muhammadan Imam. I have read the Qur'an and notes twice, for this

purpose, and even filled whole sheets with objections, remarks, questions, etc. But, alas! what little hopes have I of doing him or any of them good in this way.[20]

Like Jeremiah, he was committed to that from which there could be no release either in success or in escape. But precisely by holding to it and documenting it so tellingly he biographised for all successors the very elements of inter-faith. He knew the Christian onus for what it had to be, in what he called 'my sorrowful reflections at night, occasioned by everything I see of the enmity of men against Jesus the Saviour.'[21]

It was an 'enmity' others might mitigate in the sort of discourse which present perspectives have made possible, or which its bearers, in less solicitous mind, might attenuate in a looser will to comprehend. But to know it then for what it was makes Henry Martyn a prince of genuine relationship fulfilled in a paradox of perplexity and consecration.

V

However, two important qualifiers which Martyn's inner faith imposed upon his encounter in the inter-situation need careful reflection, if his significance is to be understood. The one lay in the finality – as it was for him – of the Scriptural denominator. Relying on the authority of his Bible, and of the New Testament in particular, he clearly expected 'rival Scriptures' to be ousted from the reckoning. He thought, for example, that 'the Qur'an would pale into insignificance'.[22] This was not to register the role of its contents in the emotions and the loyalties of Muslims, aside from its textual themes. It was to focus all issues in terms of the status of Scriptures – Christian, Hindu, Islamic or Buddhist. It was to formulate things at stake almost exclusively as items of competing authority. It did not go behind the meanings within such authority to sift them on grounds other than the warrant they had by virtue of being 'Scriptured'. So doing, encounter in those limits precluded the ventilation of the respective contents of Scriptures on their own merits, as these might be separated from the claim made for their identity.

In the given atmosphere perhaps no other such course was viable. But 'truth in . . . ' is a different formula from 'truth out of . . . ' if the former can be seen with 'in' denoting meaning, not sacrosanct source. For if truth *has* a 'where', it *is* also a 'what'. Dialogue has to go, ultimately, behind what the faithful can invoke *qua* textual ground, to what they present *qua* truth which can itself 'find' people in their whole context, rather than merely be found in sacred document.

This is not to disavow the reach, or the mystique, of such sacred document, nor to neglect the enormous sanction it commands over cultural identity. It is, rather, to allow of that quality coming over into the ken of minds and wills culturally versed in other texts which require to be honoured and do not consent to be displaced. Such counsels are no doubt easier in our time than they could have been in Martyn's but that fact does not diminish their point.

Aside from setting up rivalries of 'inspiration' and status, the enthronement of the Scripture category tends also to conceal how the Scripture 'native' to Christians in fact holds its meanings available. This matter lurked, of course, beneath the surface of Martyn's devoted labours with dictionary and vocabulary. For the text as we have it – and as textual research can refine it – came into being by a process which has to be central to the reckoning by which we possess it in its finality. The text is the climax – and also the deposit – of an inter-play of historical, liturgical, communal and editorial factors. It was garnered from oral memory, corporate tradition, lectionary usage, and developing belief. How all these contributed belongs with its right exegesis and needs to be in sound perspective when it is commended to other, and highly contrasted, Scriptural constituencies of faith.

Here, doubtless, we are back in the theology which has to be more than textual translation but which all textual translation has to serve, as the indispensable handmaid of the Word. There is a sense in which such commendation necessarily demands the living mediation that carries the text into living conversation where, as text alone, it cannot go. 'Do you understand what you are reading?' as in the story in Acts 8: 26-40, elicits the answer: 'How can I unless some man gives me the clue?' – the clue which the text holds latent and the friend makes plain. Henry Martyn knew this well enough. In time and place it was not given to him to have the twin roles in ideal harness.

This suggests another reflection. Those *munshis* on whom he had to rely – how could they be 'Philips' either to Martyn's would-be readers of his monumental labours, or to Martyn himself? Translators today in 'mission-dialogue' strongly believe that the situation has to be reversed. Translators should all be 'natives' of the receiving language. If there are to be 'informants', let them be western scholars in the theological 'know'. Then the 'alien' factor is no longer primary but subordinate and the local authenticity is in final control. This, however, presupposes what Henry

Martyn painfully lacked, namely, a fellowship of 'Indians in Christ' who
might let him be the subordinate his will to humility would have eminently
qualified him to be. He had once written: 'A missionary is apt to fancy
himself an Atlas', carrying the weight of the world.[23] Yet the lonely burden
was his glory. 'A thing finds itself in words', it has been said of literature,
'by finding words for itself.' It is a dictum which would fit what Christianity means by 'the Incarnation' of 'God in Christ'. In Henry Martyn,
translator, the Christian 'thing' was finding itself in words, which – as a
diligent linguist – he was translating into character.

vi

For that reason it remains to trace the course of Martyn's biography.
We left him with Carey in Calcutta to plunge into his immediate labours.
But if biography is the clue we think it to be, his significance deserves
more than the foregoing in analysis. Chafing at delay in Calcutta and
resisting the temptation to remain in the society it afforded, he finally
received a posting to Dinapore, in the Patna district, six weeks journey
up-river. *En route* he busied himself with languages: Hindustani, Bengali,
Sanskrit and Arabic. His appetite was voracious and his memory retentive. His pastoral activities among all sorts in the station – merchants,
officials, soldiers, illiterate camp women, children and a medley of visitors
and transients – drew down the resentment of the élite or the ruffianly but
endeared him to the needy and the wistful. But his parallel work on
translation was unremitting.

He was commissioned in June 1807, from Calcutta, to undertake an
Urdu New Testament and to supervise a Persian and an Arabian translating the New Testament into their languages. He found endless fascination
in holding half a dozen languages within his care, relishing the nuances of
vocabulary and fired with a tireless zeal to relate them effectively to the
treasured truth of the New Testament. After two years in Dinapore he was
transferred to Cawnpore where, increasingly, his health deteriorated and
his pastoral exertions drained him of energy to the point where it was
tribulation to attempt to preach. He returned to Calcutta in November
1810. As a concession to old Charles Simeon, his portrait was painted
there and sent to England, where Simeon received it with shocked
disquiet. The Martyn he had farewelled five brief years before seemed to
him a gaunt and worn shadow of his former self, still patently the
scholar-saint, but tempered in adversity.

His purpose was clear. He would travel overland to Europe carrying his Urdu New Testament and his unfinished scripts in Arabic and Persian and make his way through Persia first and then, perhaps, to Damascus, to test and finalise these versions. His Cambridge days had given him a love of the Persian story and the Persian poets. William Carey's pioneer printing press at Serampore, destined to be destroyed in a devastating fire in 1812, was still intact and would later serve.[24] However, there was a preference for founts only available in Europe. And Martyn, with his questing mind and his genius for personal friendships was anxious to learn a traveller's way, his eager spirit ready to defy the gathering awareness of physical deterrence.

British officialdom gave him leave and Christian Armenians in Calcutta, according to New Testament usage, gave him letters of introduction to their community in Persia. His ship rounded Cape Comorin and touched at Goa and Bombay, where he transferred to an East India vessel, which gave him the opportunity to set foot on Arab soil at Muscat and later set him ashore at Bushire on the southern coast of Persia. There the Arabic New Testament he had superintended under the hand of the volatile Arab, Sabat, was readily approved by Muslim Arabs, but the Persian draft was roundly criticised. Both verdicts heartened Martyn to pursue his way into inland Persia where, it was believed, Arabic Christian Scriptures were to be unearthed, and where he hoped to correct and complete the Persian draft. Drained by fever and fatigue in the heat of June, he made his strenuous way in a caravan from Bushire to Shiraz, famed city of the great poets, where he remained for a whole year, eagerly accepting the offer of Shirazi savants to translate the New Testament with him into Persian.

> The Martyn who moves among the doctors of Shiraz is clothed with an almost magical calm, with the serenity of a man who has forgotten himself in the service of a Greater.[25]

In the garden close by the Qur'an Gate of Shiraz there ensued the final and perhaps the most taxing dialogue of all with the haunt of the poets and the high and low of the city's people – Muslim, Indian, Jewish, Armenian, Sufis and pundits. He realised that Sabat's flowery and exotic Persian draft must be jettisoned and a new beginning made. As winter drew on the place became astir with comment. Everything about Martyn was intriguing to the Shirazis – his youth, his charm, his versatility in languages, his competence with their poets and, most of all, the fervour of his faith in the Jesus of his precious Scriptures where all his interests centred. Correspondingly, there was the age-long Islamic habit of debate in public, when the prowess of learning and language could be on display for the delectation of the pundits and the amazement of the wordless. Inevitably Martyn was drawn into responding to the Muslim will to engage him and courtesy, not to say prudence, demanded that he should react. He had a lively confidence in his own case, with an instinctive recoil from the likely futility of purely argumentative situations. It is fair to believe that he was emotionally constrained where he sensed dishonour to his Master rather than disposed to undertake controversy with dogma and logic.[26]

He preferred what he called 'the very recesses of the sanctuary' to the often crude, or merely disputatious, 'choppings of theology'. Yet it was the latter his presence aroused in the minds of learned Shirazis who believed themselves mandated to undertake the defence of Islam. An old mullah named Mirza Ibrahim confronted Martyn with a treatise, to which he replied in a tract. The exchange was followed by a dinner party which ended inconclusively. Great circumspection was needed since the danger of fanatical arousal was always present.

A similar situation obtained when, the Persian New Testament complete and handwritten copies ready, Martyn made his way north from Shiraz, to Isfahan and thence to Teheran, where he lay patient siege to the Vizier in the hope of a means of audience with the Shah, to whom he wished – according to revered custom – to present his work. Disappointed of that hope, he pressed on to Tabriz where, mercifully, Sir Gore Ouseley, the British Ambassador, was able to secure presentation to the Shah, not of Martyn himself, who was now a desperately sick man, but of the all-important Book.

He sensed that his end might be near and wrote farewell letters to his friends in Truro and in Cambridge where sometimes, in semi-delirium, he found himself wandering again.[27] On 2 September 1812, he departed from Tabriz, abandoning his dream of Damascus, to try to cover the 1,500 miles to Istanbul in the hope of reaching Europe. Plague was raging in that far-off city. Martyn's own mortality was near at hand. Befriended by Armenian Christians via Erivan and Etchmiadzin, 'wanting still the years of Christ', he died on 16 October at Tokat ten days after the last entry in his tireless Journal, and two days after he had sent an Armenian named Sergius, with a bundle of his listed papers and documents, for safe delivery in Istanbul.

vii

There is no chronicle of his dying. His years, few and crowded, made living exegesis of an inner faith kindled and fulfilled in love to Christ responsively to a Christ perceived and loved as the open secret of God. His three *Persian Tracts* which the Cambridge Professor of Arabic, Samuel Lee, published in 1824 certainly conceded the necessity of controversy and the tradition of 'disputing' inherited from the medievalists. Much of what is in them became the stock-in-trade of nineteenth century exchanges about Sonship in Jesus, the Trinity, the 'corruption' of Christian Scriptures, 'abrogation' in the Qur'an, 'being prophesied' as a test of 'founders of faiths', what is meant by 'sin' and what are the pre-requisites of forgiveness.[28] It was perhaps too early a stage in the modern encounter between two faiths for the participants to find a mutual awareness of imponderables belonging to both, or for the Christian 'side' to think to enlist the great positives of Islam about creation, creaturehood, man's *imperium*, gratitude, and divine accountability for the world; to interpret by help of these the authentic reality of Incarnation and redemption. It takes controversy a long time to overhear the import of its own undertones.

But the salient fact about the inner faith of Henry Martyn in the inter-pursuit of its vocation is his dialogue with himself. Possessed of 'the pearl of great price', purchased with 'all that a man has', he found himself in an Indian/Persian market where that supreme treasure was, somehow, no pearl at all. It was quite devalued and yet, the 'market' aside, 'pearl' chemically and emphatically it remained. There lay the puzzling paradox. Are pearls only priced when they are prized? Can their worth be only a market value? How was he to reconcile the invaluable with the unwanted? To have lived the pain and perplexity of this paradox and never to have relinquished or retreated into forfeiture of love and of vocation was his true glory and the full significance of his biography.

What, to pursue the metaphor, was he expecting of a purchaser, inasmuch as the 'commodity' on offer was compromised simply by belonging where it was to be acquired? Henry Martyn was never in doubt about 'conversion'. But his very concern for it made him aware also of the 'sales resistance' to who he was, whence he came and where he belonged, an Englishman 'in Christ'. There was the problem of the 'merchant' as well as of the 'merchandise'. It is part of the greatness of Henry Martyn to have captured in his own travail the essence of this issue. When reproached by

Company personnel about the schools he set up for Indian children in
Dinapore and Cawnpore, he told them that

> ...what they understood by making people Christians was
> not my intention: I wished the children to be brought to fear
> God and to become good men and that if, after this declara-
> tion, they were still afraid, the fault was not mine but
> theirs.[29]

Trying to set Company apprehensions at rest about 'meddling' unnecessarily and troublesomely with 'natives', was he also labouring with his own
inner questions? There could be for him no doubt about what 'fear-
ing God' and 'being good men' required. But perhaps the Christian
prerequisites – as they were to him – could be deferred, left implicit, not
needing to be avowed in being, nevertheless, crucial. At least his gentle
initiatives were challenging the privacies of culture and mere conformity
precisely in moving out of them. The fault must lie, not with ventures of
conditional inclusiveness such as the Gospel inspires, but in the complacent exclusiveness which parochialises its beliefs. It is the ventures
which incur the tensions inseparable from a faith for which integrity means
being intended for – and so intending – the world.
     Henry Martyn was in the van of the modern discovery of this onus of
faith. Dialogue has not resolved it. He was also, tentatively, close to
another aspect of what a will-for-the-world Christianity discovers: namely,
the constricted geographical forum within which its founding apostles
moved – the forum which alone is documented in the sacred text of its
(allegedly) 'sufficient' Canon.[30] His meditations were deeply Scriptural
and so he found himself seeking sustenance in the precedents supposedly
available in Paul and John. He did not find them, except in the quest for
purity of heart. He was acutely aware that, for the rest, he was not facing
the first apostles' situation, nor were they ever facing his. Their Epistles
knew nothing of India and would have found Hinduism as baffling as he
did himself. But if they had no direct light to shed on his task, how were
they adequate to his need? The thought of their inadequacy would have
been anathema to him, a subtle deflection of his mind from doctrinal
rectitude. For he was ever aware of the presence of temptation. Yet the
struggling discipleship that made him so deserved better of its apostolic
models than they were able to fulfil.
     His quality of spirit made him the first of modern missionaries to know
the painful perplexity of registering the sheer otherness of faiths. For he

did not academicise the experience and seek refuge in study for its own sake. Gifted scholar as he was, he did not escape his burden by forgoing the convictions that shaped it. Nor did he allow the philology he loved to suffice him as in itself an end. He therefore exemplified the truth that the full measure of dialogue – as we now intend the term – is known only where something more than dialogue is consciously at stake. Beyond agreement, disagreement, recognition, non-recognition, proximity and distance, attraction and repulsion, there has to be always present that yearning for the other which Henry Martyn knew as alone consistent with relationship itself. He knew his inner faith as somehow vicarious. Its meaning moved among other meanings for their meanings' sake. In that ambition it could expect no education but the intention to fulfil it. Could this ever be complete however long the years?

> Who is sufficient for these things? . . . Truly love is better than knowledge. Much as I long to know what I seek after, I would rather have the smallest portion of humility and love than the knowledge of an archangel.[31]

Chapter 2

CHARLES FREER ANDREWS
(1871 – 1940)

'India in the Portraiture of Christ'

i

'Christian-Faith Andrews' was how many Indians came to read the initials C.F.A., as one to whom they were greatly endeared, who symbolised in heart and action the very gist of being Christian as outsiders might perceive it. Their conclusion was the more remarkable transpiring, as it did, in a period of deepening tension between the aspirations of Indian nationalism and the retentive, self-esteeming habits of British imperialism. The man who came to epitomise for Indian opinion the quality of heart and mind by which Christianity might be expected to belong in imperial politics was himself the frequent victim of British ostracism and suspicion. Indian ill-will could suppose him a spy in the liberation camp serving the ends of an establishment which was itself, at times, spying on his suspected treacheries to Empire and its necessary devices of control and suppression. By sheer integrity of spirit and transparency of soul, Andrews availed to undeceive them all – but only in the grace of what his vigorous Anglican Christianity came to be, in response to the experience of India, as India came home to him, disturbing, refining, interrogating and steadily fulfilling the Christianity he brought. He came in March 1904, when he was thirty-three. India re-shaped what Cambridge had earlier fashioned out of his family heritage. It did so by the temper it evoked within him and by the summons which its present history brought to his conscience. On both counts it made him the Christian he became as the realised logic of the Christian he always was.

It is necessary to put the matter this way. For there is a sense in which C.F. Andrews' biography has to be read as a disavowal of dialogue rather than a study in it. His Christian instincts were served by rigorous classical scholarship, tempered by a strenuous – and successful – search for intellectual honesty in the things of faith. But they were prompted by the primacy of compassion and the criteria of the heart. He experienced India as somehow disallowing the subtleties that were credal by the authority of the impulses that were spiritual. Christ became ever more compellingly the referent of all his discipleship but via 'the reasons of the heart' which precluded abstract controversy. He was capable of what he called 'insurgent thoughts' but they were aroused in him by moral issues that demanded action rather than by niceties of dogma which might neutralise the will. One could better 'act out silently the Christian faith' than discourse comparatively about its doctrinal claims, in the confidence – which perhaps he too readily assumed – that such 'silent witness' was 'easily understood'.[1]

The contrast with Henry Martyn is immediately evident. The impulses of yearning and devotion were one and the same. But the 'faithful argument' on which Martyn relied gave way in Andrews to 'the argument of faith', released and exemplified by a reciprocal love – exchanging positive relationship wherever it could be found without staying to resolve what, in purely mental reservation, might give it pause. Where Martyn met the Hindu and the Muslim mind in the exigencies of the laborious task of translation in which he spent his soul, C.F. Andrews was constrained by India to rely on the person and the story of Jesus widening, by inherent right, into the consciousness of other faiths as already correspondent to their souls' desire.

This confidence, which we must explore and illustrate, means that Andrews represents a distinctive quality of inter-faith relationship. It is one in which the 'inner' and the 'inter-' almost fuse. The descriptive 'Christian', as it belongs in C.F. Andrews, becomes a loving pre-possession extendable to other faiths in the sense that he believes them already susceptible of its inner meaning by virtue of their own spirituality insofar as this is truly alive with human compassion realistically directed to human tragedy and suffering out of a pure conscience. It was this that made him resist mere controversy in order to engage a mutual encounter with injustice and wrong. The inner dimension was always for him resolutely Christian, painfully ripened by sharp experiences of re-definition. But, as such, it was ardent for inter-faith vocation fulfilled, not in discursive reasoning and comparative theology, but in discovering how divine love in Jesus and the Cross would verify itself in every living, active conformity to the principle it enshrined in its marvellous eventfulness. The assurance which might seem to some the very abeyance, if not avoidance, of dialogue was, for C.F. Andrews, the only authentic form of it. Religions, for him, should rendezvous in Gethsemane rather than on the Areopagus. The complexities of a Raimundo Panikkar might not have eluded his intelligence; they would certainly have dismayed his soul. His meeting-point with religions was in the contagions of the love of which, for him, 'God in Christ' was the ground and the theme and the pledge. Such was the 'portraiture', the 'drawing-out' of Christ, which India evoked in him.

ii

Almost a century separated C.F. Andrews' 'passage to India' from that of Henry Martyn. They had a Cambridge nurture in common but in quite contrasted terms. Charles Simeon had left his durable legacy, but for Andrews at Pembroke College the influence of Lightfoot and Westcott, the great bishop-scholars of the day, and of the orientalist, E.G. Browne, was paramount. It was the untimely death in Delhi of Westcott's son Basil, C.F.A.'s close Cambridge friend, which decided Andrews' Indian destiny. Loyalty required that he should take his place. But the antecedents of that conviction are far back in the family history and the shaping of his personality. The second son in a very large family, Charles Freer was born to John E. and Mary C. Andrews, in Newcastle-on-Tyne on 12 February 1871. When he was six years old the family moved to Birmingham where he was to find lively occasion for his developing awareness of urban poverty, but also a delectable savouring of the local countryside. The Andrews were devoted members of the Catholic Apostolic Church in which a moving spirit had been the Scottish divine, Edward Irving (1792-1834). It was an intriguing amalgam of strong puritan probity of character, eschatological expectation of the near return of Christ, a zeal of revivalism and – perhaps incongruously – a rigorous hierarchy officiating in a deeply sacramental sense of liturgy and ritual. The last stemmed, in part, from its missionary-minded contacts with Eastern Orthodoxy and continental Catholicism. Andrews Senior was an 'evangelist' of the Church, within its 'apostolic' pattern of 'angels', 'apostles', 'evangelists', and 'deacons'. For long he coveted C.F.A. as a potential 'ordinand' within the Church.

An 'Irvingite' upbringing (as the sect was often called) played a vivid part in the younger Andrews' imagination. It was an intense, colourful, dedicated world, impressive with vestments, incense and ritual, yet shot through with rigorous discipline and infused with that half-defiant, half-exalted attitude characteristic of sects which know themselves to be an idiosyncrasy on behalf of God. But perhaps most critical of all in the emergence of Andrews' personality was the shape in which it posed the issue of authority. The Catholic Apostolic Church had an implicit faith in the text of Holy Scripture, with a special penchant for the Book of Revelation with its mysterious numbers, its dire warnings and its ardent triumphalism 'before the throne of God'.

For, with his lively intelligence and the fostering it found in King Edward VI School, Birmingham as a prelude to Cambridge, he encountered strongly the tensions implicit for questing minds between devout family loyalty and the sifting demands of truth. They were heightened in Andrews' case by experiences of mystic ecstacy which came to him from time to time, notably in Lichfield Cathedral (that tripled steeple-house which George Fox in his ecstacies had so despised) and in the Court of Pembroke College, Cambridge. It was to these he owed the utter consecration of soul which always undergirded and sometimes over-rode the findings of his mind.

Soul and mind together under the impact of Cambridge discovered and embraced the Church of England and, with it, the pain of parents and son in the family strain it caused. Theology at the University bore the imprint of Brooke Foss Westcott, Regius Professor of Divinity from 1870 to 1890 when he became Bishop of Durham. It had close personal links with the School at Birmingham and Andrews was well served by College tutors and able friends. There was a love of India in the air via the recent formation of the Cambridge Mission to Delhi. Scholarship in the Biblical text, personified in the work of Westcott, Hort and Lightfoot, was scrupulous, perceptive and devout. It was corroborated by vigorous social conscience which found expression in the Christian Social Union. The *Lux Mundi* theologians in 'the other place', notably J.R. Illingworth, Charles Gore, H. Scott Holland and W.H. Moberly, were pioneering new understandings of how the event of 'God in Christ reconciling the world' should be interpreted in the world of Darwin, Carlyle and Tennyson, and how due response might be made to the challenge of David Straus, Leslie Stephen and the many other exiles from belief.[2]

Underpinning all this heartening experience of liberation and commitment was an 'incarnational theology' and what Westcott called 'the kinsmanship of peoples'. 'The Christ-event' had consecrated all life, all society, all experience and become the measure not only of the love in God but the dignity in man. Andrews might have adapted the phrase of John Wesley about 'exchanging the faith of a servant for the faith of a son', yet owning that a filial service was his life's destiny.

The future, however, was to prove that he had not yet arrived where a Christ-integrity needed to be – the future, that is, as India was to unfold it. Andrews was still resolutely Anglican. He had not emerged from the rigorism of the Irvingites to submit to the Biblical tenets or the denominational vagaries (as he saw them) of the Cambridge Inter-Collegiate Christian Union. He disapproved non-, or improper, sacramental patterns and the ways of dissenters. When he saw in Pembroke Court his strange vision of an oncoming radiant figure from the Chapel door, it was of one carrying the sacramental vessels in a priestly Christ-likeness. Yet it was a priestliness which reached into ministries for human poverty to which Andrews turned, on Wearside and in South London, when his Cambridge studies ended. They had brought him far on the way to an inner faith, ready to be alert to the role of mind and given to the tasks of love.

His Ordination in 1896-1897 sealed his integrity to Christ – and to Church – as he then perceived them, though at some point prior to India misgivings began to bring him disquiet over the 39 Articles and any linking of anathemas with creeds. His soul-intensity was liable, then and later, to take physical toll. He was briefly back in Cambridge as a Fellow of his College (a due reward for his 'Double First') before his India-destiny began.

His initiation there had the happiest auspices – happiest in the sense of being at once a welcome and a revelation. To both aspects of the new experience his generous and sensitive spirit responded with the zealous imagination of a ripened readiness, receiving in being received. His first mentors were S.S. Allnutt, Principal of St. Stephen's College, Delhi; Susil Kumar Rudra, its Vice-Principal; and Maulvi Shams al-Din, his Urdu teacher in Simla. He had brought Christ as the theme of his presence. He was surrogate for the dead Basil Westcott. His intention was through and through missionary, serving institutions of prayer, education and compassion. Had it been otherwise India would never have educated him in the reach of what he intended in coming. Such is the paradox of mission in hands like his. The convictions that gave it urgency also gave it pause, in the sense of requiring of it steady self-examination.

For C.F. Andrews this happened in three broad areas and by dint of the gifts of character with which grace and nature had endowed him. He discovered the depth of Indian Christianity in the persons with whom he served,[3] so that he could never disown the meaning, and therefore the objective, of conversion, as Mahatma Gandhi was to urge him to do. For to repudiate conversion into Christ would be to deny the reality of truth and freedom. But, further, he discovered the depth of Hindu saintliness, found – and remaining – outside the forms of Christian belief and practice. Rabindranath Tagore, his *Gitanjali* and other poems,[4] seemed to Andrews self-authenticating participation in grace and holiness. He had, therefore, to ponder in what sense his Christian 'mission' served them. Was Christ already theirs in some way – the Church apart? The question was not to be crudely banished, nor hastily resolved. Further again, he came to have to reckon with old and new forms of Christian obduracy – as it seemed to him – or disloyalty to the way of Christ, fortified, as it often was, by credal orthodoxy. His confident Anglicanism began to sit less readily on his shoulders as he realised the different dimensions India gave to allegiance, seeming to require of both faith and church a greater hospitality between, within, and beyond themselves.

His Englishness was quickly felt to be embarrassing to his faith as he came to appreciate the ambiguities of the British Raj. His sympathy with Indian nationalism and Arya Samaj steadily grew at the expense of his pride, his equanimity and his relations with some fellow missionaries and with the generality of British India. From both groups he came under suspicion as a dubious quantity whose loyalties were insecure.[5]

These several discoveries were deeply intertwined. There was nothing fickle or wayward about them. They were the reckoning of his inward faith with the context it had entered. They were the very pulse of mission. And they were made in the pursuit of that concern for compassion which the Christian Social Union had inspired, now translated into Indian terms. Andrews began to register the claims of Indian poverty and to realise its implications for politics and for the churches. Social justice obviously entailed urgent demands on Hinduism, its doctrines of life and society. But was it not more appropriate for a foreigner to leave that criticism to Indians and take issue instead with the liability of British power and the onus of the imperial presence? If there were to be 'kinsmanship of peoples', it could only be in the bearing, not the shifting, of accusation and responsibility. Andrews found himself recruiting what he saw to be the positive heart of English identity and tradition, namely, the will to be free, as the legitimate right also of Indian nationalism. He was among the first to realise the necessity – only conceded after his death – of complete independence.

Steadily, through the first decade of his life in India, he began to move

out from the immediacies of College teaching, in visits wider afield,
aiming to recruit, or convert, mission personnel to his vision and to align
Indian Christians wisely with Indian liberty. Moral issues moved him to
break out of the Anglican prerequisites of Christian participation on
which he had earlier insisted, as itself a prerequisite of demonstrating his
conviction that Christianity itself could help resolve the chronic an-
tipathies of Indian religions. Could Christ not be a genuine fosterer of a
right Indian nationalism? Political realism, it seemed, argued a de-
antagonising of religions, with Christ as the peacemaker and friend. In a
paper, *Christ in India*, written in 1910, he declared:

> Because Christ is 'the Son of Man' Christianity must be all
> comprehensive, larger far than the Church of the baptised.
> The Christian experience must be one of an all embracing
> sacrament in which Christ is seen and revered in all men.[6]

iii

The 'must' in that resolve related surely to the Christian community,
since others would have their own terms on which potential 'comprehending' of 'the Son of Man' might obtain. There lay the issue which Andrews
instinctively assumed to be negotiated in the heart, whatever might be the
quandaries of the doctrinal mind. Ardour took care of the latter when he
called, in the same year, in *India in Transition* for

> ...the union of the English and the Indian, as Christians:
> the union of the Brahmin and the Pariah, as Christians: the
> union of the Hindu and Muslim, as Christians. Then and
> then only will the heart of India respond fully to the
> Christian message and a new Indian nation arise.[7]

There is clouded logic here in the sense that there is a 'message' yet to be
received. But is its 'reception' only in zealous action? For 'as Christians' in
his phrasing can only mean 'as if they were...' – given the categories he
lists. And what of 'an Indian nation arising' on the impulse of a faith of
only a tiny minority of its peoples and against the grain of cultural identity
and anti-imperial struggle? Moreover, he still wanted, in the same essay,
to root Christian meanings in baptized membership, since they could not
'rove unattached'. Perhaps he meant to say that what needs to be
confessionally attached somewhere can, nevertheless, be practised by

the unattached, perhaps even by those who, like Gandhi, not only avoid attachment but emphatically abjure it – in the name of that very nationalism which Andrews saw as in urgent need of the ethics of the truly baptized.

All faiths in some measure are free to speculate on a moral emulation of them from outside their faith-community, and to view with varying degrees of tolerance its alien doctrinal context. Much dialogue has come to be concerned with just this situation, compelled as honest observers are to recognise that their system has no monopoly either of saints or rogues, of well-doing or evil-doing. It is, however, painfully evident that what is 'inter-faiths' cannot be confined to issues having to do with the effectiveness of conscience, private or public. Nor can it dissociate all that pertains to conscience, its guiding and its guarding, from the themes we call doctrine and the habits we call ritual. These always need scrutiny that is more than pragmatic.

The transition through which Andrews was passing is clear from the sequence of his writings. His intellectual disquiet about Hinduism was very real to him before it partially receded under pressure of his social imperatives of compassion. His lively sense of Christian personhood made it difficult for him to sympathise with Advaita Vedanta and its evacuation of personal significance in the totality of transience. He held that 'the West' (presumably here 'Christianity')

> will never accept as finally satisfying a philosophy which does not allow it to believe that love between human souls may be an eternal reality.[8]

It was right to recognise a 'law of renunciation' but as the clue to eternal life, not as the 'non-self' of the anatta doctrine.

Even so, Christianity was not 'the enemy of Indian religious thought'; it was its 'fulfiller', seeing that the Spirit of God was manifestly at work in the Indian sages. Did not the Sikhs' Granth Sahib counsel:

> If you long for the Lord of all, become as grass for men to tread on. If a man beat thee, beat him not in return but bend to kiss his feet.

Did not the Buddhists' Dharmapada enjoin that anger should be overcome by love and evil by good?[9] Yet the incarnational theology he had loved in Cambridge, the influence of the Oxford idealist, Thomas Hill

Green via *Lux Mundi* and his cherished Westcott – these held him in two minds.[10] At this period he wrote a missionary manual: *The Renaissance in India* in which, in tabulated contrast, he set down the incompatible teachings of Hinduism and Christianity on: God; the World; Human Life; Salvation; Social Order; The Past; and The Goal. He saw their 'fundamental concepts' as altogether contradictory. He deplored the absence in Indian faiths of a 'true and clear moral doctrine of sin and redemption, based on a worthy and historic Gospel of Incarnation and Resurrection'. But he believed that 'the longing for this had been latent in all the better elements of Hinduism'. He concluded that

> When Hinduism and Islam are examined in the light of this
> need [i.e. Indian nationhood] they are found to be inex-
> tricably bound up with the very evils from which India must
> be set free.[11]

He reviewed favourably the several Reform movements in Hindu society and the Aligarh initiative in Islam. But 'if Christ were to satisfy the longing soul of India' there was 'much in Hinduism that must perish at His appearing'.[12]

Some critics would approve these strictures as a proper realism, others reprove them as contentious and ill-judged. Would it not be fairer to see them as the interior debate of Andrews in his love for India – a debate between faith as authority and faith as sympathy? He was in process of finding his Christology in 'what he owed to Christ', rather than in what he owed to doctrine – real as that debt was, letting present experience revise his retrospect. The stress of the transition was taxing to mind and heart alike. He was in the midst of the truth that dialogue about relationships can only be within them. He was moving to the decision that took him from Delhi to Santaniketan.

iv

It was a cumulative decision and could perhaps be studied by a biographer around the dilemma of 'conversion'. We have seen Henry Martyn inwardly struggling with the puzzle of how to be truly in the steps of the New Testament in a world so different – a world for which that supreme New Testament had no precise directives except the duty to 'make disciples', which was exactly where its cultural limits least satisfied its 'loyalists' in the India they found. That central issue was urgent for a born translator whose whole faith was in the wonder, the authority, of his Scripture. C.F. Andrews – as he himself confessed – was 'a bad linguist'.[13] But he was a winsome befriender, a ready listener, an ardent admirer. It was natural that, for him, the central problem would be whether to dissociate an evident Christ-likeness from any necessary Christian allegiance when its presence, otherwise, seemed to him self-evident. In other words, how mandatory was 'conversion'? What did 'making disciples' mean if, in effect, they were already made? Perhaps he could only reserve any transaction of 'conversion' as a reservation to old loyalty and as recruitment to the *locus standi* of Christ-likeness in the Christ-history which need to be identified, by some on behalf of all, in the Christian institutions of faith and church.

To this problem we will return. For it accompanied Andrews all the way. His first decade brought it into focus. As he was drawn by conscience more deeply into the cause of Indian liberation and began to contribute articles to various journals, his political sympathies opened up to him a variety of Indian friendships beyond those available to him in college education. He became convinced that 'far beyond the direct ministry of the Christian Church Christ's personal presence was found and in that presence is the fulness of spiritual life.'[14] Hindu associates fell more readily into this rubric than others.

Muslims, however, were in no way exempt. One of his great mentors was Maulvi Zaka Ullah, then a venerable octogenarian in old Delhi, whose influence on Andrews was memorable enough to inspire – years later – an affectionate biography, in which he identified a tolerant, courteous, refined and dignified Islam movingly personified in a character in which he had no mind to induce 'religious' change. Admittedly, Zaka Ullah was old-fashioned in some of his ways. He found Queen Victoria 'wholly good', and wrote a book, *Victoria Namah*, to say so. Gladstone was the paragon of political probity. Victoria had replaced Akbar as Akbar had replaced Asoka. The British were a third dimension with Hindu and Muslim and vital to the future of India. English was the key to liberating education but not to the eliding of Urdu which Zaka Ullah insisted in speaking at all times. To lose the vernacular into which he diligently translated scientific and other texts would be to denationalise the young. 'A father to me,' Andrews wrote, Zaka Ullah enabled him to appreciate that 'compassion for suffering humanity was the supreme attribute of God in the Qur'an.'[15] He wrote the biography as a tribute of affection and admiration which quite revised his sense of mission – at least where such character adorned Islam.

But, revealing as this friendship was, the core of Andrews' transition from St. Stephen's College, Delhi to the Ashram at Santiniketan was the attraction of Rabindranath Tagore and his poetry, coupled with anxieties about Christian 'faith-fencing' which – in due Anglican order – had earlier been his faith-security and his mind's consent. His friends at the College had been tolerant of the loose rein on which they could hold him, but deeply regretted his final break. Bishop Lefroy, of Lahore, now Metropolitan of India, wisely refused to accept Andrews' desire to renounce his Holy Orders. Knowing his man, he sensed that some ambivalence might be right and there were occasions through the rest of Andrews' career when he ministered as if no resignation had been tendered. Yet he was also able to pursue his own vocation free of the formal obligations of Anglican ministry. His conscience was more at ease despite the sharp hostility his move engendered and he was at liberty to obey the call of political action which, in turn, deepened his commitment to interpret his mission increasingly in terms of campaigning with all and any so minded against social wrong, sustained by the meditative techniques and fellowship of Tagore's Hindu Ashram.

The first such campaign introduced him to Mahatma Gandhi in the action on behalf of indentured Indian labourers in Natal, where Andrews' intervention had a decisive impact, as it did similarly in later occasions. His Britishness made him a valuable ally in government quarters, while his tireless zeal for the cause endeared him beyond all suspicion, however much outsiders might dismiss him as a zealot or distrust him as a sinister intruder. The narratives of his political commitment in Fiji, his participation in the Indian Congress, again in East Africa and in South Africa in the twenties do not, in detail, directly concern the study of his inter-faith significance, except as focusing the issues it held for him and constantly preserving him from abstraction and pure intellectualism. The impulse to de-Europeanise his ways grew stronger. He found release in adopting the practice of stooping to kiss the feet of loved Indian mentors like Gandhi and Tagore. His visit to Japan with the latter in 1916 introduced him to Japanese religions and added a new complexity to his experience.

His very reputation, though alienating him from the traditional missionary community, enabled him to influence the Arya Samaj and other anti-Christian groups to moderate their charges against mission as no 'orthodox' missionaries could have done. Correspondingly he was, at times, able to affect the attitude of British officialdom, most notably through his personal relationship with Lord Hardinge, during his Viceroyalty.[16] The cost of the mediatorial role, its toll on his health and psyche, were heavy. But, from time to time, his vision was retrieved from depression by those visitations of wonder which had come to him in Lichfield and Cambridge and could be renewed in Pretoria and Bengal. His powerful visual imagination enabled him to translate the prosaic discipline of the Ashram at Santiniketan or Visva Bharati into vivid enlightment of soul. In South Africa in 1914, a 'Face' filled the night sky, other 'faces' of human need shining through it to be finally merged into the face of Tagore.

V

'I had a lover's quarrel with the world', was Robert Frost's poetic proposal for his epitaph.[17] Andrews would have had 'India' for 'the world' and if he had retained 'quarrel' would have meant it only of the ills of poverty, alien rule, discord and apathy. For the rest the accent was on 'lover'. From wanting to inform, to enlighten, to admonish, he came to want fully to belong. He had experienced the cycle whereby mission comes to mean mutuality, given and received. This was no mere form of dialogue. It meant an inter-fusion of soul, which – for its own sake – required a reconciliation of all that was authentic in the will to come and all that was authentic in the will to find. The two authenticities could only be known in common. The evangelist would also be the learner.

One aspect of the reconciliation had to do with the painful theme of inclusion in Christ prior to the incidence of mission. Could it be that the eternal wisdom of God delayed itself until twentieth-century Westerners arrived? Could 'the Saviour of the world' be so belated? Andrews tried to find whether there were analogies to 'the fulfilment of Judaism' in Christian faith present in respect also of Hinduism. He looked into history anxious to find sources in eastbound Nestorian Christianity in the first Christian centuries to explain 'pro-Christ' aspects in Indian religion. He was more alert than some to the subtle congratulation that might be lurking in the notion of a 'crown of Hinduism'.[18] His thoughts went further. He wrote:

> I am beginning to understand from history that Christianity is not an independent Semitic growth but an outgrowth of Hindu religious thought and life besides . . . Christ appears to me like some strange, rare, beautiful flower whose seed has drifted and found a home in a partly alien land. India, in this as in so many other ways, is the great mother of the world's

history. Christ, the Jewish peasant, lived instinctively, as
part of his own nature, this non-Jewish ideal of *ahimsa*,
which is so akin to Hinduism, He had the universal compassion, the universal charity, as marked in the agony of
crucifixion, on the sunny Galilean hills.[19]

Clearly his was a Christology of experience rather than of definition. It
centred on the personality within the gospels and on the suffering love of
the Cross. As such, given his cast of mind, it could be readily aligned with
Hindu concepts of *bhakti* devotion and the *avatar*. His Christianity made
him abjure 'negative theology', that is, the need to deny within the right to
affirm. For this reduced faith to a charade. Yet, by his reluctance to
formulate in metaphysical terms what he believed, he risked a 'negative
theology' of his own. The plea: 'Show us the Father,' (John 14:9) had been
fully granted. But the portrayal only devotion could know and only
experience could affirm.

This new consciousness of God's love came to me directly
through Christ and in no other way. What the equation was
which made God and Christ one in my innermost and
deepest thoughts I could not have explained . . . His face was
ever before me when I thought of God . . . In Christ God had
become human and personal and real. In Christ God's
infinite formlessness takes form.[20]

To abandon this conviction would be spiritual suicide. By its very nature it
was universal. It was the point where east and west were one, as a spiritual
consciousness, not an intellectual formulation. By 'the joyous movement
of the Spirit in Galilee', God was known as 'infinitely humble and forbearing', Jesus

. . . is the Son of the Father, not in any narrow, abstract,
metaphysical sense, which has no moral meaning, but in a
deep spiritual sense of Oneness – one in mind, one in will,
one in purpose, one in character itself. Herein, in the
character of God is the profoundest religious change that
Jesus offers to all human estimates and values.[21]

He could quote both Robert Browning's *Saul* and the *Ramayana* as
united in this assurance.

How should we assess this inner faith as itself the inter-faith which India had generated in the eager self of Andrews? Genuine, certainly, and deeply moving, content to contain within itself what it saw no need to reconcile? It would seem so. This divine loving, enfleshed in Jesus as 'the face of God' argues the abiding significance of personhood – in you and me and all mankind – as its very *raison d'être*. For what is 'loving' in the absence of 'beloveds'? Yet Asia reads our individuation in totally other terms as fleeting, illusory and finally inconsequential. Despite his disquiet, noted earlier, about the non-self doctrine of anatta, he could later reproach 'Tennyson's craving for individual contact and recognition after death' as 'morbid and wrong'. 'True and simple love must break these bonds before it is wholly rid of self.'[22]

Further, can we agree that the desire to understand 'has no moral meaning', or that to want metaphysical idea is 'narrow'? May it not rather enlarge worship and serve an integrity which its suppression might impair? It was entirely right and in character for him at Santiniketan to blend texts from the *Upanishads* with Christian devotion. But was his analogy of colour and whiteness proper to the points at issue in the shape of Ashram worship? In a letter to Tagore about Visva Bharati he described

> a simple, central place of worship, with its white marble pavement and its absence of all imagery and symbol...the best expression of our individual freedom of belief and our common worship of the One Supreme. Each of us may add what colour he likes to that pure whiteness.[23]

White is so helplessly vulnerable to colours. Can it do more than submit to their capture of its neutrality? Or does the 'colourless' return us to a negative theology? Are we not relying on the very 'colour' of Jesus 'on the sunny hills of Galilee'? And what of the 'darkness over all the land until the ninth hour'? Andrews did not resolve these issues; it was his honesty to live them. But the problem whether the 'inner' of his faith can take over the 'inter-' of its relations in this way remains. Had he romanticised India?

It follows that he held very loosely to the questions Christian faith incurs around the New Testament itself. Did he romanticise the unity and verve of the first apostles? Did he allow for the prism of subsequent conviction and experience through which the light of Jesus was refracted? He could write, for example, about the seventeenth chapter of John's Gospel as

> Jesus' supreme prayer fully recorded and handed down to
> us ... all the thoughts that were in the mind of Jesus at that
> solemn hour before the Passion[24]

where others might note its strange contrast to the Synoptic record and
understand it as the great 'testament' of Christ's achievement as known in
faith's comprehension and even speaking of Him in the third person (v.3).
This does not make the prayer less truly Christ's, only more perceptively
so.

Andrews' characteristic encounter with Albert Schweitzer is germane to
this context. He was thrilled by the famous conclusion of Schweitzer's *The
Quest of the Historical Jesus* about Jesus being 'one unknown' who,
nevertheless comes to us *as such*, calling us as He did the disciples of old.
We, like them, will only 'learn who He is ... in the toils, the conflicts, the
sufferings which [we] shall pass through in His fellowship.'[25] The summons
to follow and the sense of its sequel are authentic. But did Andrews
appreciate how disconcertingly far Schweitzer's Jesus was from the figure
he had recognised in Galilee and toiled to give to India? Schweitzer's Jesus
was an apocalytic visionary whose Sermon on the Mount was an 'interim
ethic' required for – and to be ended with – the brief present interlude of
eschatological suspense. For the rest, the Jesus of orthodox tradition was
'mythical', a total misconception. It was this 'unknown Jesus' who could,
nevertheless, call us paradoxically into a discipleship in which He would
reveal a 'self', other than historical, that discipleship would 'learn'.

Wrestling as he did with whether it mattered in Hinduism that Shiva and
Krishna were 'mythical', whether the Christian claim to Jesus' actuality
was crucial, Andrews always went back to what had been known, and
could still be known, on those 'sunny hills of Galilee'. He was surely right
to do so, in spite of Schweitzer's enigma of 'the quest'. For the paradox of
Schweitzer was that the New Testament records themselves were precisely
the product of 'the toils, the conflicts, the sufferings' which those first
apostles passed through in Christ's fellowship. Why should their 'knowing'
account of Him be doubted? Why were subsequent 'questers' to be found
so far strangers to history in the experience of devotion? Andrews
implicitly took the spirituality of Schweitzer, thrilled by other facets of his
missionary self-sacrifice in 'the primeval forest', without fully realising
how counter to 'what he [Andrews] owed to Christ' were the critical
'findings' of Schweitzer's scholarship.

That there is an unambiguous account of Jesus in the New Testament
we cannot well claim. But there is a credible consensus of witness if we

hold together Jesus and His consequences in their bearing on each other and, accordingly, trust the portrayal that results. It was this that C.F. Andrews lived to present to Indians in the sure confidence that India should duly claim it for her own and that, indeed, vital aspects of it were suited to her genius.

The point at issue in Andrews' devotional assurance about the Jesus of the New Testament is its compatibility with his consent, alongside Hindu friendships, 'with eager readiness to sink the temporal in the eternal'.[26] Such consent, though apposite to Hindu thought, calls in radical question the Christian significance of the Incarnation. For there, as Andrews had rejoiced to believe in his Cambridge nurture, 'the temporal' was truly the image-bearer of 'the eternal'. There was no 'sinking' but an enlisting, a dignifying, a fusing, in the meaning of lines which Andrews loved from Edmund Spenser:

> For of the Soul the body form doth take,
> For Soul is form and doth the body make.[27]

Christ's Incarnation has to be seen as no less a truth about humanity as truth about God, the validation of the whole human order in creation as being intended as – and capable for – 'the divine image'. Only by that intention do we fully measure the reach and tragedy of human sin and wrong. It is this dimension of the redemptive necessity explicit in the Incarnation which is liable to be neglected if 'the human in Christ which is also divine' is taken to be identifiable in others as 'divine beauty, truth and love'.[28] Such qualities in souls may indeed be 'related to Christ', as Andrews believes. But will it be so only in terms of discernible moral qualities dissociated from the cost, and the experience, of forgiveness?

Yet consistency is not to be expected of the generous mind of C.F. Andrews and perhaps, under Indian tutelage, it should not matter. His instinct to believe all 'goodness' 'Christian', or – better – 'Christ-related', wherever he saw it, was always counterbalanced by his central conviction about the Cross. He recalled with emotion how the great contralto, Dame Clara Butt, at Santaniketan had sung the negro spiritual: 'Were you there when they crucified my Lord?'[29] His theology of grace was perhaps the wiser for not attempting to formulate how divine compassion fulfilled itself in the obedience of Christ. It was enough for him to know it as the eternal 'moment of truth' concerning the nature of God as love.

vi

But what of the institutional custodianship of that conviction? We must return, finally, to the issue of 'conversion', or – more strictly – of the form in which such truth should affirm itself, know itself, and commend itself in the wide diversity of human time and place and – for Andrews – in the searching, straining, striving world of India in the throes of aspiration, poverty, liberation and contention?

How necessary are Church and Creed, how right or proper is recruitment to them from within faiths and cultures otherwise sanctioned and self-possessed? How should the singularity of any belong in the plurality of all? What do ventures such as Andrews' from within the 'inner' of their own allegiance into the 'inter-situation' imply for the continuity of the former? For it was only from the 'inner's' impulse that there was venture in the first place.If he had not been the Christian he was in Cambridge, Andrews would never have arrived in India. Other, and different, Christians might have thought him to be caught, even betrayed, in the paradox of surrendering his own motivation in the course of supposedly fulfilling it. Or was that situation growth and wisdom? If so, how could the new wisdom tally with the old ground that had been indispensable to it? Can, or should, 'establishments' of doctrine and faith-community (for such they are) properly consent to be – as it were – 'disestablished' by an apparent unwillingness to continue such?

We have seen how, as a student and young priest, Andrews had been restive within his Christian loyalties by credal or ecclesiastical prescripts which had become untrue for him. He had been converted to 'a wider ecumene' of Christians after an earlier rigorism against non-Anglicans. India and other factors extended the process into a hospitality for which a 'Christ-likeness' evident to him in Hindus and Muslims and others required him to acknowledge them and be, in some sense, in community with them around that recognition. But what of the visible, definable Christian 'institution'? Should he want to incorporate them into it by faith, baptism and Holy Communion? If they had the secret of the Church, should they not share its form? Was not definitive recruitment vital to the efficacy of the Gospel which was at the heart of 'Christ-likeness' and – as the whole phenomenon proved – vital to its very feasibility in the world? Could Christ do his present work in the world without the aegis of what his Scriptures called his 'body'? If one was minded to escape that question by invocation of the Holy Spirit to whom belonged 'the things of Christ', what when – as always – the ministries of the Holy Spirit moved through instruments of text and person? The Holy Spirit was never a means to evade the liability-in-trust.

The urge to a wider ecumenism has gone far since C.F. Andrews. It was part of his significance to have known it so pressingly. Openness to love, the abatement of bigotry, the will to co-operate, the search to understand, the mind to meet – all these are well transferred from church to mosque to temple, to gurdwara, to shrine, just as they are from St. Peter's to Geneva, to Kiev, to Canterbury and the rest. Yet can 'religious' serve as a satisfactory denominator of the theme or the warrant of such will to 'comprehension'? And what of the implicit religion which repudiates all 'religiousness'? How is any religious identity known, secured, affirmed, believed, renewed – or even doubted – without its structure of belief, of symbol, code and community? Does it not have to preserve identity?

Whether it must or not, it certainly does. No religion practises self-dispossession. All are tenacious of adherence, even those which have the reputation of ambiguous tolerance. Culture, race, language, usage, zeal and apathy, all combine to perpetuate the establishments that live by these. For C.F. Andrews the question was how far his Christianity should believe and practise its ordinance of baptism.

Mahatma Gandhi, to whom he was passionately devoted, as mentor, friend and ally, emphatically thought not. For Gandhi, change of religious allegiance was a near-blasphemy, a renunciation of heritage, memory, identity itself. To seek it on the part of others was the denial of love. Doubtless political factors in the stress of Indian nationalism lay behind this view. For Hindu loyalty was obviously a vital element in Indian liberation. In his inner heart Andrews could not accept this ruling. In a letter to Gandhi as late as 1937 he wrote:

> Your declaration that a man should always remain in the faith in which he was born appeared to be not in accordance with such a dynamic subject as religion. Of course, if conversion meant a denial of any living truth in one's own religion, then we must have nothing to do with it. But it is rather the discovery of a new and glorious truth for which one would sacrifice one's whole life. It *does* [C.F.A.'s italics] mean also, very often, passing from one fellowship to another, and this should never be done lightly....
> Christ is to me the unique way whereby I have come to God, and have found God, and I cannot help telling others about it whenever I can do so without any compulsion or

undue influence. I honour Paul the apostle when he says:
'Necessity is laid upon me: woe is me if I preach not the
Gospel!' . . .
I do not think it follows that we shall always be fighting as to
whose 'Gospel' is superior. There are clear-cut distinctions between Christians, Hindus and Muslims which cannot
today be overpassed. But there is a precious element of
goodness which we can all hold in common.[30]

The upshot, then, for Andrews about baptism was not whether but how.
He would, as it were, see only as baptizands those who 'could do no other,
so help me God.' He would not induce or instigate; but he would always
welcome and receive. Otherwise he would, he knew, be denying the very
hospitality of God to humanity in Christ and reducing the love in Christ to
a perquisite of Christian birth, a 'God so loved the Christians . . .' thesis,
and totally illogical inasmuch as, on that showing, there would never have
been any Christians thus to exclusify themselves. What could not be only
true for some must necessarily be true for all. The Gospel and privacy
could not co-exist.

But Andrews reached, and practised, this conclusion only after deep
and painful parallel participation in the ethos of India and the re-
education into Christ which it gave him. To the indispensability of the
Gospel he must join, in an ever-critical sense, the indispensability of the
Church and of its mandate to share its destiny with 'whosoever will'.
There is something we may see as 'apostolic' in the misgivings through
which he passed, the tense quality of his church-loyalty given the reluctance it had in him, and the pain he had from it. We have seen how Bishop
Lefroy left open a resumption of Anglican ministry for him in answer to
his disquieted surrender of his Holy Orders. Resume he did, with much
emotion, at St. James, near the Delhi Gate and in St. Stephen's. When
asked in mid-life about 'not missing Holy Communion', he might point to
small children he was befriending and say: 'These are my holy communion.' But the ordered sacrament retained its place in his mind and
spirit and finally in his practice. He attended the 1938 Conference in
Tambaram, an almost legendary figure, and gave it freely of his counsel.
Bishop Leslie Brown tells of a late occasion at Kottayam when Andrews
took special pains to express his delight and joy over a young Indian who
had just been baptised.[31]

Another factor impressed him in this context. Would not the outright
repudiation of baptism disqualify the existence of those Indian Christians

who, like Susil Rudra at the outset, had been his vital initiation into India? In Rudra's case a Christian openness to Hinduism and Islam had its antecedents in the policy of complete severance which Alexander Duff in Calcutta had enjoined upon the elder Rudra in baptism, years before. Perhaps decisiveness was a necessary factor in an ultimate openness once transition had been achieved and identity established. For there is no hospitality in the absence of a home.

So, while it might well be true that there was faith beyond the forms of faith, the forms of faith remained crucial to that possibility. Perhaps there was point in the New Testament reference to 'eunuchs for the kingdom of heaven's sake'. (Matt. 19:12.) Was there a valid vocation in those who would forego adventures into wider ecumenism, into receptive pluralism, into risks of syncretism, and the rest, for the sake of 'staying by the stuff', holding the fort, and so conserving that which gave to others 'the means of grace' for wider sympathies? It would seem that Andrews would have appreciated such renunciation of adventures, while in no way willing himself to remain unmarried to India. 'There are diversities of gifts.'

He stipulated clearly in his will that he should be buried, lest cremation be interpreted as meaning that he had not died in Christ.[32] That was the conclusion of the whole matter, the verdict of the will – interment in the soil of India but on Christian ground. The perplexity of the relationship for which he had lived would be resolved beyond the grave.

Chapter 3

CONSTANCE E. PADWICK
(1886 – 1968)

'Through Liturgy to Islam'

i

Eyebrows were raised and queries made when the Society for the Promoting of Christian Knowledge, a venerable Anglican institution, published *Muslim Devotions* in 1961. Had it lost its way? the critics asked. Was Islamic piety a fit topic for inclusion in the promoting of Christian knowledge? Its mandate had long been the nurture of Christian literacy in Asia and Africa and due education in the faith everywhere. Supporters of this enterprise would surely suspect that it had misread its brief.

Thirty years on there are different thoughts. It is readily conceded that – for its own sake and for its right 'promotion' – Christian knowledge must learn and listen outside the privacies in which it would otherwise be sheltered. If it truly belongs to humanity it must also belong with them. The world into which it finds itself commissioned is not merely continents and shores, but cultures and faiths. Geography may describe the world; it is religions which interpret it. Into these, therefore, its concern must go – and go to understand and to converse in the courtesy that counts 'nothing human alien'.

Constance Padwick's authorship was a pioneer piece, an imaginative Christian gesture towards Islam, in the form of a careful penetration into its spirituality as found in its popular Sufi liturgies of praise and penitence and petition. She would be amused to find herself in present company in these chapters. Her work was truly scholarly but in no way professorial. It was not the product of a Chair or an academy; nor was it the fruit of a sabbatical episode funded by a research grant and leading back into congratulatory retreat in job security. It was the work of the road, the harvest of long and patient garnering. Her collections of the *Awrad* and *Ahzab*, as they are called, the prayer-manuals of the Sufi Orders, were searched out in mosque courts, purchased in little bookshops by their gates, and often conjured from reluctant vendors puzzled by the strange interest in their contents of a quaint-looking *Faranjiyyah*, whose informed conversation soon reassured them as to her *bona fides*. At times the precious wares were thought too sacred to be sold. In that event a handy gift would set up the happy make-belief of an exchange of presents and due propriety would be observed.

Constance Padwick was much travelled from the Bosphorus to the southern Sudan, from Morocco to Isfahan. She noted as her collection grew where each item had been acquired, with numbers to identify the contents. The enterprise continued through many years and as the rich world of Sufi prayer became more familiar she came to know what gaps she needed to fill. The more popular ones were endlessly reprinted but others were of rarer vintage and the quest for them had to be more patient.

There was inspiration in her realisation that in this treasure trove – for such she esteemed it to be – she had access to a world within a world, a dimension of Islam where its inner meaning in ordinary souls could be truly learned. For the prayer-manuals, normally of postcard size, and squarer, were meant for daily recitation. Light and limp, they could be hidden away in the folds of the *jalabiyyah* or tucked into a little corner behind the merchandise or under the mattress or the saddle-bag. They were as ubiquitous as their devotees, and a veritable store-house of Islamic piety. Like all liturgies they carried the imprint of generations, originating as they did from revered founders of the Orders in the middle centuries of Islam. There could be no more apt occasion of an inter-attention to an inner faith than in these 'rosaries', (as the term *Awrad* has it) of the soul's devotion.

ii

The initiative behind the collection and its study was certainly an inner impulse of Christian faith. In youth, Constance Padwick had found a lively sense of Palestine through a visit there in 1910. Born in July 1886, her earliest years were spent in the Sussex countryside at West Thorney on the edge of Chichester Harbour and within sight of the English Channel. Her father was a barrister who had turned to farming. It was an idyllic childhood implanting a delight in external nature, in the artistry of birds and flowers and arousing an imagination never slow to find incentive. In 1896 the family moved to London where, in Finsbury Square, she had her education at home. She studied briefly in Paris and, responding to the appeal of Christian allegiance, took up the study of New Testament Greek prior to the pivotal journey to Palestine which sealed her sense of vocation. She edited a children's magazine and after rejection, on health grounds, by the Church Missionary Society, she eventually made her own way to Egypt and apprenticed herself to an Arabic Press engaged in Christian publication. As her skills and interests widened she qualified for a scholarship to pursue her Arabic and Islamic work at London University's School of Oriental Studies, where she specialised in Arab folklore.

On her return to Egypt, Christian literature became her driving concern. She was the mainspring of the Central Literature Committee of the Near East Council of Churches, and Editor of *Orient and Occident*, the Cairo journal founded by Temple Gairdner whose biographer she became in 1928 – a 'Life' written with great feeling and perception within a year of his death. Gairdner, himself a gifted leader, musician, playwright and author, and greatly loved within the Egyptian Churches, had been her constant mentor and inspiration.[1]

If her literary power was kindled by the acute sense of debt and sorrow in that common bereavement in Cairo, the kindling gave worthily in return. Her pen had a quality of expression, a capacity for vivid portrayal of scene and setting, and a sometimes lyrical power of vision. *Temple Gairdner of Cairo* served effectively to share a personality and invigorate vocation in the following generation. Padwick's *Henry Martyn: Confessor of the Faith*, written six years earlier and quoted in Chapter 1, had tested her skills and given ample proof of her command of the poetry of things, in turn of phrase or glimpse of pathos. Her evocation of the final days and hours of the dying Martyn, tended in delirium by unknown Armenians, was tuned to Martyn's soul. She would have scorned to be a hagiologist, but she knew how to infuse narrative with fervour.

Her biographical bent found other themes later, notably her tribute to Lyman MacCallum in *Call to Istanbul*, and an edition of the letters of Lilias Trotter, a pupil of John Ruskin and talented missionary in Algiers.[2] She saw them both as 'frontier people', and – being such herself – was able to convey the experience of being loyally one identity in the genuine awareness of another. To this dual citizenship of the spirit – which was yet not dual – we will return. It includes other figures like the renowned French orientalist, Louis Massignon,[3] in the circle of Constance Padwick's friendship. It is the central significance of her life, her study and her writing.

iii

She lived and travelled in the Arab East, mostly in Egypt and Palestine, through the troubled decades of the growth of Zionism and the Second World War. After the Arab/Israeli War of 1948 she took up an urgent project in the Nuba mountains, the Kordofan province of the southern Sudan, where the official policy of Arabicization made urgent the provision of Arabic textbooks for schools at all levels. She excelled in the writing of simple texts which drew on her sympathy with folklore and her skill with local proverbs. Earlier in Algeria she had made a study of dreams and visions among villagers.[4] With her youthful London studies she was able to conjure into life the stories and themes that could serve to new literacy among the Nuba people. There, as in North Africa, her sense of romance gave a warmth to her efforts as she recalled the lively Christianity which had once flourished among the Nuban and the Berber peoples where ruined churches and sunken baptistries could still be traced in terrain that had once echoed to their sounds. She would have shared R.S. Thomas' reverie, how

> ... here once ... a preacher caught fire
> And burned steadily before them
> With a strange light so that they saw
> The splendour of the barren mountains
> ... and sang their Amens ...
> In a way that men are not now.[5]

For every inner faith has long history in which calendars of time do not tally and the tenancies of place both ebb and flow.

Her three years in Kordofan ended in serious illness late in 1951 from which she only partially recovered in hospitals in Omdurman and Kenya. She was in her sixty-sixth year and ready for convalescence with her sister in Istanbul. Convalescence was not retirement until 1957 when the Istanbul biography could take shape in the quiet of Maiden Newton, a Dorsetshire village in the Thomas Hardy country. In Turkey Cottage (so named already) she reverted to her old love of botany and produced an index of flowers taken up and published by the British Royal Horticultural Society for use in their celebrated Wisley Gardens. Six years later, joined by her sister, she moved to Lower Odcombe in Somerset where she died in her eighty-second year. It was a blissful seclusion with long retrospects of travel and venture both with, and into, faith. In the year before her death she wrote:

> Here we have all the little wee early flowers that came on with the mild weather and are now startled with the cold... I have my head in botany books, and dim wonderings about the history of the Church today. We have a splendid country parson and it is a joy to watch him undertaking us, with such knowledge of the way of country people. I shall wait eagerly for news... *Dominus tecum.*[6]

It had been a long journey from West Thorney, criss-crossing the Arab world, via Nubia and Istanbul, back to rural Somerset, gathering *en route* through Christian curiosity of spirit an authentic index to Muslim spirituality. 'Let us be modest for a modest man,' she had noted Charles Lamb observing.[7] Her own modesty would not be because *Muslim Devotions* was something to be modest about. It was a pioneer thing, thorough, imaginative, and – as inter-faith research has need to be – ardent and sincere. What does it signify of both inner and inter-faith?

iv

From an early point in her career Constance Padwick had become aware of the two Arabics of Islam and the Christian Churches. The two faiths had settled into distinctive vocabularies, at least in areas relating to religion and themes that had most to do with mutual comprehension. In the brevity of life, Henry Martyn could only tackle vocabulary in the immediate concern of translation, and that in a variety of languages. By the twentieth century, Arab Christians of Padwick's knowledge had possessed the honoured Van Dyck (Beirut) Bible for more than sixty years.[8] It had acquired a prestige which might be likened to that of the 'King James' (Authorised) version in English. But it did not 'read' like the Qur'an. It was differentiated from that Scripture simply by being a translation and it was liable to Hebraisms and to usages which did not 'go' well into Arabic. In parts, as seriously in the Book of Job, it could be unintelligible. And even where the sense came through, the form was uncongenial to Muslim Arab eyes and ears.

It is true that pivotal words in the two faiths like *Allah* (God), *Injil* (Gospel), *Rasul* (Apostle), *Kitab* (Book), *Iman* (faith), *Rahmah* (mercy), *Tawbah* (repentance) and many more were common to both. But their usage differed sharply and some Muslims were disposed to demand, or assume, that only their Muslim import should properly enjoy currency. Christian Arabs insisted on their right to them and to their Christian connotation. But their coincidence, even when not a matter of friction, was always a source of confusion.

The issue of disparate vocabularies was psychic as well as philological. To see coincidence as a feasible clue to mediation of meaning was, for the most part, ruled out as liable to risk some forfeiture of identity. To savour and keep the different Arabic was a gesture of self-assertion, a symbol of identity and so, in turn, a proof of loyalty. Adventures with words, as generating adventures into mutuality, were thus precluded by the temper most in need of creative risk. What of the will to see minority status as sometimes apt for courage and not only for caution? Survival had been the age-long anxiety of the churches, and a brave doggedness their pride. Perhaps an 'outsider' – if sufficiently identifying with the anxieties – could serve what saw beyond them.

Instinct told her that familiarity with the daily language of Muslim piety might open out discoveries of kindred themes and of the words which might convey them, especially if these could be elasticised – together with a 'stretching' of the minds that used them. For it is in availability of words that meanings may be related. The idea of exclusifying vocabulary can only result in the isolation of significance. There are risks, to be sure, and care is proper but care with risk has always been the vocation of theology.

There had, of course, long been a Christian interest in Islamic mysticism, by those with vague ideas about transcendental unity beyond the language of all faiths, based on 'the inner light' or pleading the much ill-quoted verse concerning 'the kingdom of God...within you' (Luke 17:21), as if history and language and form had no part in it.[9] Constance Padwick meant to understand articulate mysticism as it was lived in the prayers and acts of devotion Islam had formed out of its own, distinctive history around Muhammad, the Qur'an and the several 'masters', or *aqtab*, of the Sufi Orders. She knew it bore the imprint of all these and required to be studied in the definition they had given to it. That definition, appropriately known in its own right, offered the other spirituality in which Constance Padwick had been nurtured, a language that was mutual. For it had to do with adoration, celebration, self-deprecation, yearning, hope and the submission of the will. The thing at stake was not the shared attitudes of humility, reverence, aspiration, salutation and blessedness. It was the histories, the Scriptures, the events, the sacred *personae*, where these attitudes had their ground and focus, their warrant and reward. There were the events of the Gospel and the events of the Qur'an. There was the personality and the passion of Jesus, and the personality and Hijrah of Muhammad.

Was it not a sounder instinct to locate the thing at stake, not in bald and tedious controversy, in scholastic argument, but in the warm and fervent experiences of the soul in its seeking and its finding? Would not that be the truest setting of what urgently needed to be related? Why not take the 'inner' of devotion, in either sphere, to the centre of the 'inter-' thinking between them? To have believed so and to have undertaken the purpose with such perseverance makes Constance Padwick a far-sighted exponent of the art of meeting. For *Muslim Devotions* covered almost forty years, more than half of these its patient gathering, the rest its steady composition, the manuscript being much delayed, and jeopardised, by the circumstances of war and travel. Its quality lies in the care and thoroughness with which it undertook the study of the vocabulary of Sufi liturgies and how their Islamic provenance might align with Christian parallels and contrasts.

V

Before coming to the contents of *Muslim Devotions* it will be wise to face the suspicion that the images are affected by the lens through which they are seen. Muslim reviews of the book were few, late and disappointing. Dr. Syed Valiuddin of the well and long reputed *Islamic Culture*, of Hyderabad, India, reviewing it in 1966, feared that

> ... with the idea of Incarnation always lurking in the background, it is not to be expected that the Muslim formulation of Transcendence will find any sympathy or understanding.

It was a harsh verdict, with the sinister word 'lurking' and the scepticism about a 'sympathy' so studiously present. In comment between faiths there are always emotions and moods as well as issues of mind and doctrine. He was wrong to think that the liturgies she studied had

...become relevant only in so far as they fitted into the
Christian framework and led to the Christian perspective.[10]

Unless the 'inner' of every faith is to exclude 'inter-' meaning, relevance
has to be finally assessed by *human* reference. Worship, penitence, guilt,
desire, self-awareness, longing, wonder and adoration are all shared
dimensions of the soul, before, during and after they are housed, articulated and perhaps resolved, within the forms of belief and piety which
differentiate religions. In coming to a mutual penetration of those disparate forms we need to restrain the instinct which cannot feel beyond our
own. We have to be ready for that within our human experience which
makes us all kin whatever the shape associations give to it and however
exclusive, unilateral or indisputable those associations may demand to be.
Such demand belongs to the necessary finality they must claim as purport-
ing to explain and fulfil our human predicament. Yet those finalities, in
the authority of the faith, symbol, ritual and heritage in which they
are operative, can never escape the human element which needs and
trusts them, and which makes mutual attention imperative. Simply to be
mutually dismissive, wholly imprisoned in our own frames of reference,
would be to deny their referability to the rest of mankind and so their
disqualification in respect even of ourselves. What cannot 'mean' for all
cannot 'mean' for any.[11]

What, then, were the great themes of the several, major Sufi Orders
which *Muslim Devotions* explored in the currency of their prayer manuals
in Jerusalem, Damascus, Baghdad, Cairo, Aleppo, Aden, Khartoum,
Bombay, Lahore, Istanbul, Tunis, Beirut, Sidon, Meshhed and Algiers,
where the author gathered them, with careful annotation of where and
when?[12] They can be readily comprised in five main areas: Praise of God;
Salutation of the Prophet; Penitence; Pardon; and Petition. These will
take us into the world of the practising Sufi in the *zawiyas* or 'prayer-cells',
in which the liturgies were said, and into the soul-privacies of their
individual members. Our task, like the author's, will be to learn their
inner meaning without obtruding relational issues, until these can be
rightly discerned.

Some prelude is necessary to their study. Constance Padwick was
careful to provide it in her Introduction. 'Devotion', of course, begins with
the obligatory prayer-rite, the formal *Salat* of Islam to which the *Adhan* or
call to prayer, summons the faithful five times daily. Those mandatory acts
of prayer may engage the 'intention' (*niyyah*) of the worshipper, with
which they must always begin, in further *munajat*, or more intimate

'communion', when the retrains of *Salat* are repeated and elaborated as if, by the informal, to do the formal more worthily. But it is an 'informal' only in that sense. For it relies on the Qur'an and on the pattern of words warranted by the 'Masters' to whose Order the devotee belongs. Those Masters initially may have drawn on personal inspiration, on vision and ecstacy, but their liturgies have the sanction of their saintliness and prestige. The ordinary user should not presume on personal insight beyond that which comes in the loyal discipline of the *zawiya* and the *barakah*, or 'blessed charisma', of the Master.

As anthologist, Padwick explains her care to ensure that the manuals she acquired were certified as truly 'popular' by those in the *suqs* and precincts and stalls from which they came. In that way she hoped to exclude esoteric material and be confident that it was an active and contemporary spirituality she had under study. The frequent reprinting of the manuals, their lack of date and 'copyright' (an unknown notion) as if locally reprinted where printers sensed a market, as well as traces of their currency far beyond the Arab world, confirmed that view.

This feature of the situation made for unusual difficulties in the normal apparatus of scholarship made good, however, by comprehensive listing in the Appendix of the manuals used, their vintage and place of purchase. She was not deterred by suggestions on the part of critics that aspects of the manuals could be regarded as naive or superstitious, even tending to the magical in recital or invocation. Folklore belonged with all religions. Its low-minded features should not be allowed to obscure the truly authentic and the real. 'This,' she insisted

> is not only a fairer procedure for the understanding of the
> life of devotion but it is also probable that in learning what
> devotions mean when they are carried to intensity we best
> learn also to understand the diffused and weakened religious
> ideas of the masses.[13]

There is reason to believe that the manuals were circulated and used more widely than the membership of the Orders.

vi

In exploring the five areas into which it was agreed to comprise the contents of *Muslim Devotions* we summarise a range of spirituality which Constance Padwick set out under fifteen chapters. The whole is a biography of dialogue, in the sense that the collector had a life-interest in its significance and was throughout responding to the kinships it contained to her own Christian devotion. From time to time she would note a turn of phrase or a mood of soul that brought Teresa of Avila or Lady Julian to mind. But she was not concerned in so doing to bring the manuals into explicit relation with Christian faith and liturgy. The possibility of a 'dual citizenship' in their meaning and the crucial question of its 'auspices' we will come to later as something always only latent in her study. The dialogue stays with the reader, presented with what is a collective biography of devotion from which to inform it.

Everything in Islamic piety is summed up in *Allahu akbar*, 'greater is God'. The Arabic root k b r yields the reflexive: *takbir*, the term which denotes this *Magnificat* of the Muslim. It has the sense of both to affirm and to proclaim, as in Surah 17.111: 'Make Him greatly great', (*kabbirhu takbiran*) where the verb supplies its own object from its own root, thus indicating intensity. The 'making great' of God is the confession of what already is, yet is needed because of the idolatry which disputes it. The comparative form (*akbar*) cannot admit any stated comparison, since nothing is worthy to be compared with God. Hence the proper English translation, neither simple ('God is great'), nor superlative ('God is greatest') – both of which are true but not unambiguously so. Thus the claims of all pseudo-gods, and of all supposed absolutes of more subtle modern idolatries, are repudiated. Here, we might say, is transcendence by acclaim, ultimacy demanding insistent acknowledgement as the constant duty of man and the clue to human dignity. All pretension bows in this subservience to the sovereignty with which nothing may compare and none should dispute: *Allahu akbar*, a theology and a piety denying and defying all the demonic.

The *takbir* is the fount of all praise in that, imperative as it is, it only echoes how this transcendence is 'greatly Self-aware', in the meaning of the divine name: *Al-Mutakabbir*. Devotion cannot rightly think of the divine unity, or power, or quality, only turning on the human confession of it. Such confession only aligns in humility with eternal fact – an attitude of soul which is itself a participation in the meaning and in no sense a mere statement of opinion of which the speaker is the ground. This point recurs below in relation to the divine Names. It is because these *are* God's that He is called by them.

The praise of God, then, in the formal prayer-rite and in the manuals, allows no self-congratulation as some worships might. All is awe and surrender conformably to that other great word: *Al-Rabb*, 'Lord', used in its full Semitic sense of 'Owner', 'Master', 'Disposer'. [14] *Rabb al-'Alamin* is 'the Lord of all being', of all that knowledge comprehends in 'the worlds'. *Al-Rahman al-Rahim* declare the 'mercy' or 'compassion' of 'the Lord' belonging essentially to His nature and operatively to His action. In the praise-clause both are adjectival but both may also be nounal elsewhere. *Rabb* as denoting *Allah* is reciprocal to *'abd* ('servant') as denoting man. An ascription in *Taharat al-Qulub* runs:

> It is enough of honour to me that I should be Thy slave:
> It is enough of grace to me that Thou should'st be my
> Lord. [15]

That 'exchange' between divine condescension and human wonder marks the liturgies at their most wistful. The accents of sovereignty in *takbir* are found compatible with a sort of reciprocity (if theology may so speak) between the divine and the human, implicit in *khalil-Allah*, ('the friend of God') as a descriptive, for example, of Abraham, who figures in prayers of salutation. God, having 'a friend', thereby becomes (or, rather, is) one – a truth which must make the two words *Allah* and *khalil* somehow alike. A relationality in respect of man enters, in some sense, into the being of God. Upon that conviction the whole of Sufi devotion proceeds as responsively assuming it to be so. As devotion, the humble of the Orders did not stay to debate with the scholastic theologians how such relationality, if real, could square with divine eternal self-sufficiency. [16] They simply took it to be the life-line of their own souls.

This is the central point of the *Asma al-Husna*, the 'beautiful Names of God', which are at the heart of all praise and of all petition. 'God has them,' says the Qur'an 'so call upon Him by them.' (Surah 7:180) The prayer manuals, it would be fair to say, consist in response to that command. They live in the import of the Names, in how numerous they are, and in the significance of the divine, human mutuality they express, and, in expressing, transact. The name-ability of God is the mark of all Semitic faiths. It may be well to speak theoretically about 'transcendence' as 'a humane science'. [17] But we do not know transcendence; we know dependence. We know the buds of spring, the leaves of autumn, the taste of dates and olives, the feel of water, the caress of sun, the thrust of sex, the sense of grief, the pain of death. With all these the Names have to do. They translate the transcendent into the personal. Recipience of its meaning is certainly personal. The Names affirm that its munificence is personal too.

So, in the wealth of the nounal Names, God is Creator, Provider, Nourisher, Bestower, Giver, Sustainer. Praise, then, is our reverent ejaculation of the Names, just as prayer is their invocation. They mediate between what transcends and what obtains. They 'associate' God with us.[18] In exploring the manuals Padwick was taking the Muslim pulse of that association. The descriptive Names, like 'gracious', 'kindly', 'abiding', 'rich', 'percipient', 'powerful' – if we accept the feasibility of religious language – recruit from human attributes the perception of the divine. Due reservation about the indescribable cannot obviate that situation, unless we abandon the liturgies completely and opt for silence. In that event how do we fulfil the Qur'an's command to use them?

This strange interface of meaning between God and humanity belongs even more with Names like *Al-Shakur* and *Al-Shakir* from the root sh k r denoting gratitude, which is, surely, a human offering. Since there is no indebtedness in God to call for thankfulness, these Names can only mean that He is 'cognisant of human gratitude', that there is acceptance of *our* cognisance and that, therefore, human atheism is somehow divine pain. Certainly the liturgies are ardently concerned by their repetitions and their frequencies to counter what might otherwise be a wilful or a casual neglect of God. For them *shukr* ('gratitude') is the sure antithesis of *kufr* ('unbelief'). In the manuals the practice of adoration is the habit of gratitude.

Hence reiterations like *Subhan Allah* – praise, as it were, saying 'glory'; *Al-Hamdu li-Llah*, 'the praise is God's'. The formula known as the *Basmalah* earlier quoted: *Bismi-Llahi al-Rahman al-Rahim*, brings the diversity of the Names into the singularity of 'the Name of God' possessed of the most loved of descriptives in the double sense of 'mercy'. It governs all the actions of Muslim piety and life, initiating occasions, enterprise, functions, habits, in the manifold of daily life. It invokes divine favour, protection, enablement, direction and authority in all pursuits, great and small. For things can only prosper where the malign is held at bay by the divine Name and good is induced by its mention. As Constance Padwick observes, in a point to which we must return, the *Basmalah* bears analogy with the making of the sign of the Cross in Christian devotion. It is a kind of spiritual armament against evil, a fortifier of the spirit, an antidote to sickness, even a charm against lurking ill.

Any study of the beautiful Names and their place in devotion must ponder the nature of Islamic *dhikr* and its link with *itmi'nan*. 'The recollection' of God spells 'tranquillity' of soul. So Surah 13.28. So far is the remembrance of God bound up with the phrases or the rites used in the *zawiyas* that the one term denotes both. *Dhikr* is, at once, the exercise of devotion, either in fraternity or privacy, and the awareness of the divine it means to serve. The prayer manuals are meant to focus and practise the divine 'presentness' by rhythmic recital of the Names, low chanting and swaying, and concerted, often vigorous ejaculation which concentrates all energies of voice and body, so as to 'preoccupy' the soul with God. That is *itmi'nan*, the 'at rest' of the heart and mind in the divine totality. Perhaps we should say wholly counter-occupied, since the goal is to cast off all that constricts and diverts the soul from the divine focus of its true being. Then

> Askings terminate in the presence of His goodness, and needs pass away as the soul finds her stay in Him. The need of the creature is not sufficed by the whole of created things: it is necessary that its infinite need be met by an infinite generosity and power, by none other than the Truth Himself, praised and exalted be He.[19]

Such is the experience of 'the soul at rest' – a description after which devotion aspires the more ardently for its being (in Surah 89:27) the divine address to Muhammad, the consummation of his prophethood. From the praise of God we pass to salutation of the Messenger.

vii

Next only to the *Bismillah* in the frequency of the prayer manuals is the formula: *Salla Allahu 'alayhi wa sallam*. This is the *Tasliyah* or 'calling down by God of blessing upon him and greeting in peace'. This salutation of Muhammad on the part of God, which believers must emulate, derives from Surah 33.56: 'God and His angels *yusallun 'ala-l-Nabi*. O you who believed *Sallu* upon him and greet him a greeting'. The verb here belongs with the term *Salat*, the prayer-rite performed in Islam. Its meaning when used of an activity of God is understood to be a divine celebration, authorisation and attestation of Muhammad by God, as the divinely loved, commissioned and authenticated spokesman of the divine Qur'an and the human characterisation of what God approves. Thus it expresses all that the Qur'an means in Islamic belief and all that tradition enjoins of the imitation of Muhammad in conduct and character as 'the first of Muslims'.

It is not demeaning either to Muslim or to Christian faith to surmise that there may be an analogy with the meaning, in the Gospels, of: 'This is my Son, my beloved' concerning Jesus. Its use at the baptism and the transfiguration in the New Testament brings together the twin ideas of 'son' and 'servant'. There is a service which only sonship can render by virtue of identity with the divine mind. There is a sonship (this one) which only in service will be fulfilled and realised. In this two-in-one capacity the divine will is brought to pass and this is 'the good pleasure' of God both *qua* willing and *qua* doing. There is a twofoldness here because there is eternity and time, there is divine grace and human history.

The *Tasliyah*, in the distinctive sphere of the verbal Book-intention of God which is the Qur'an, means this salute of Muhammad's status in its recipience, its mediation into time, which are the instrument of the divine intention. Both are thus 'satisfactory' to God and to His angels. To believe this divine 'satisfaction' perpetually sustained by God is the other side of the perpetual Islamic adherence to, and reception of, the Qur'an. In corroborating God's abiding 'sanctioning' of Muhammad by their own *Tasliyah*, Muslims know, fulfil and commend their Islam.

So it is that the *Tasliyah* and *Taslim*, the salute and the peace-greeting follow all pious mention of Muhammad's name. It is another, powerful form of that 'association' of God and humankind we have noted in the *Asma al-Husna* and mutual *dhikr* ('Remember Me and I will remember you' Surah 2:152) in that God and men meet via the role, office and person of Muhammad. Sometimes the *awrad* of the devout, like that of Ahmad al-Tijani, plead with God to replace them in the *Tasliyah*, so that what will be unworthy and inadequate in the human one may be righted.

It becomes clear how this steady celebration of the Prophet makes of Tradition a constant spiritual ideology, a programme of the divine favour upon the individual implicit in the divinely given focus of his piety. Worship belongs to God alone. But with that worship goes the due celebration of the Messenger as a habit of devotion as well as a fact of belief. Thus the two parts of the *Shahadah*, or confession of Islam, God and His Apostle, the Unity and the prophethood, absorb all piety.

The calling down of blessing lends itself to aspects of superstition and may become a formula for *barakah*, or charm. Or it may be elaborated by the heart's affections and perhaps occasion visions of Muhammad's presence. The 'blessings' it invokes may be extravagantly numbered with litanies that plead their otherwise inadequacy to extol the theme of their delight and duty. The *Tasliyah* of the soul is likened to a key that opens, a drawing back of a veil that conceals, an irradiating light diffusing secrets to the soul. It invites the assistance of the saints in making it. Constance Padwick thinks of it as being the 'Hosanna' of Islam.[20]

In some forms the *Tasliyah* is extended to the family of Muhammad and also to Abraham as the great *Hanif*, the founding-theist and bold iconoclast, builder of the sacred Ka'bah. The 'family' may be Muhammad's kin in the faith (for Shi'ah Islam) and the company of all the prophets from Adam to Jesus. The manuals ascribe to each in that sequence his peculiar virtue or quality – Adam the 'chosen', Abraham 'the friend', Moses 'the confidant', David 'the caliph', Jesus 'the spirit' (in every case) '. . . of God'. Patient endurance belongs with Job, exile with Joseph, homeless wandering with Jesus and poverty with Muhammad. These characteristics shape the invocations that seek the counterpart to them in voyaging, in absence from home, in anxiety about the loved at home, in tribulation and temptation.

> Subdue to us this sea as Thou didst subdue the sea to Moses, the fire to Abraham, the mountains and iron to David, the winds, the devils and the jinn to Solomon. And subdue to us every sea of Thine in earth and heaven. . . and give us favourable wind according to Thy knowledge, and be to us our travel companion and replace us in caring for our families.[21]

We have arrived at our final theme of petition, which penitence and pardon must precede.

viii

The need to 'seek forgiveness' (*Istighfar*) and to seek it 'from God' is deep in the Qur'an as a necessity alike of prophets and of men. The abiding sense of the sovereignty of God and the claims of His law has its counterpart in the awareness of wrong and guilt. One of the Names of God, *Al-Tawwab* denotes Him as responsive to *Tawbah*, or repentance. The prayer manuals dwell insistently on this theme of unworthiness before God. The body is often seen as an arena of personal crisis, a sphere of temptation where innocence is at risk, excesses threaten and desires deceive. The sense of the vigilance of God only makes this awareness the more keen, as also does the emphasis of the recited Qur'an on the fate that overtook former peoples who 'corrupted in the earth' and refused divine correction. The Qur'an has numerous terms for varieties of evil, especially *zulm* with its underlying meaning of 'travesty', the doing of injustice, the violation of right, the falsity which repudiates the true and the fair. *Zulm* against God is the sin of *Shirk*, the falsehood of plural worships, alienating from God what is His alone. *Zulm* against others denies them what is just and due. *Zulm* against the self (*Zulm al-Nafs*) opens up a whole world of 'wrong within'.

Islamic transcendence has often meant divine immunity to man and men's misdeeds. But the paradox here about the heinousness of sin and the exaltedness (beyond its reach) of God does not in any way exonerate or condone. 'There is fault,' say the manuals, in a familiar phrase, 'in that which is between me and Thee.' The self of which Joseph was aware, in Surah 12:53, as 'prone to evil', is 'the soul under its own reproach' of Surah 75:2. The 'seeking of forgiveness' in the liturgies often has the implication of protection inasmuch as evil thoughts, lustful passion and bitterness of mind, are menaces as well as evils, in the forsaking of which by penitence there is also security from their entail. Sincerity, not subterfuge, must attach to penitence itself, since the mercy it awaits is all-knowing. Sickness and disease are sometimes used as analogy for sin in its weakness of will or frailty of mind.

Another recurrent metaphor with its source frequently in the Qur'an is *ta'widh*, or 'the taking of refuge'. 'I take refuge with Thee from the evil of what I have committed,' is a prayer that recurs constantly. The need for 'refuge' is not least in the immediate context of religious acts. For it is then, in *Salat*, in Qur'an recital, in the Fast, that 'the insinuating whisperer' may be most subtly present. Again, the likely assumptions of traditional belief colour the temper of both penitence and pardon of *Munajat al-Sahifat al-Sajjadiyyah*:

> My God, my sins do not harm Thee and Thy pardon does
> not impoverish Thee, then forgive me what does not harm
> Thee and give me what Thou wilt not miss.[22]

Yet the apparent 'ease' of forgiveness – as of all things divine – does not make wrong-doing less heinous on the human side as 'separation' and 'forfeiture' of peace and truth. In forgiving, too, God is answerable to His Names: *Al-Ghafir, Al-Ghafur, Al-Ghaffar* which mean that, in some sense, pardon is inherently, not haphazardly, divine, and 'refuge' – if need be from Him – is always in Him. There could not be a command to *seek* forgiveness if the seeking was not crucial to the receiving.

In a moving and apt play on words *Taharat al-Qulub* of 'Abd al-'Aziz
al-Dirini has the penitent say:

> *Hujjati hajati*: 'My argument is my need'.
> *Wasilati faqati*: 'My poverty is all I can plead".[23]

which is the sum of the whole matter, unless we add the strange and
enigmatic saying, the source of which is unknown: 'I call upon Thee in the
Name that is written on the leaves of the olive.'

ix

Petition in the liturgies is present in all that we have studied, being
inseparable from praise, linked with *Tasliyah* and moving through
penitence. It belongs closely with the divine Names in that the simple
enunciation of them with the vocative *Ya* requests that their meaning
happens. Thus *Ya Razzaq* cries: 'O Thou Provider', *Ya Fattah* 'O Thou
Opener'. There is no need to specify what coming true to the Name will
entail. The Naming, with intention, suffices. This can lend a chaste brevity
to petitionary *ahzab* which see no need to be tediously informative, least
of all in the presence of the All-Knowing. Let God answer to His Names:
that will suffice. The habit of ascription as itself petition can be seen in
somewhat more extended, but still succinct, formulae in which God is at
once adored and users beseeching.[24]

Petition has often to do with light, guidance, security and well-being.
Most frequent of all is the plea for immunity from 'the Fire' and from
damnation at the last. A recurrent metaphor in every context is that of the
suppliant at the door, the beggar at the gate. The *Bab* which admits to the
divine presence is the proper 'station' of the lowly and the needy.
Constance Padwick cites the lines attributed to both Al-Jilani and Al-
Tijani:

> I Thy servant at Thy door, Thine abject one at Thy door;
> The captive at Thy door, the destitute one at Thy door;
> Thy client at Thy door, O Lord of the worlds.
> A weary one is at Thy door,
> O Thou helper of them that seek for help.
> Thine anxious one is at Thy door
> O Thou who dost lift away the care of all the careworn.

I, Thy rebel, O Thou who seekest for penitents,
Thy rebel who acknowledges his faults is at Thy door,
O Thou who forgivest sinners,
One who confesses his sins is at Thy door.
O most merciful of all who do mercy
He who has erred is at Thy door.
This lowly, fearful one is at Thy door.
Have mercy upon me, O my Lord.[25]

In respect of pardon and petition there is the moot question of 'mediation'. The Qur'an forbids it, 'except by leave of God' and such leave is never – or rarely – given. But the prayer manuals belong to realms of devotion where theology must give way to piety, and Surah 43:86 leaves open the possibility of Muhammad's intercession. So *Shafa'ah*, or 'intercession' with God on behalf of forgiveness or need, is sought from Muhammad as the *wasilah*, or 'mediation'. Petition may then take the form of 'O God, grant him (Muhammad) his request,' perhaps pleading the precedent of God's granting the pleas of other prophets in their histories, like Abraham and Moses. Al-Jilani has the prayer: 'And Thyself (God) plead for us with Thyself,' and Al-Shadhili: 'O God, as Thou wast my guide to Thyself, so be my mediator with Thyself.'[26] There is also the thought that the prophets, though not strictly 'intercessors', may express in petition what mortal mouths would say if dumbness had not taken them.

Through all the minutiae and the complexities where Constance Padwick takes her readers there runs a spirituality she was eager to capture and careful to document. Its salient features being now reviewed, it remains to take up what is latent throughout when subsequent dialogue is joined. In salutary preface to that task it is well to share her sense of haunting beauty in the 'Prayer of Night Communion', with which she ends her treatment of Petition.

My God and my Lord, eyes are at rest, stars are setting, hushed are the movements of birds in their nests, of monsters in the deep. And Thou art the just who knowest no change, the equity that swerves not, the everlasting that passes not away. The doors of kings are locked, watched by their bodyguards: but Thy door is open to him who calls on Thee. My Lord, each lover is now alone with his beloved, and Thou art for me the Beloved.[27]

X

There are, it was earlier suggested, two crucial but latent questions awaiting us after studying the liturgies that give rise to them and out of which alone they can be answered. Constance Padwick takes note of Christian parallels and contrasts as she presents the themes, but in incidental ways leaving the comprehensive issues for others. We are thirty years on from what was at its time a new initiative. Her studies of vocabulary serve the hope of aligning differing Arabics, or if not, of clarifying wherein they differ. The details merge into what is larger still, namely: Do the common themes of the two spiritualities leave – or not leave – them still at issue with each other? And as another form of the same question: Do the differing auspices and associations of the common themes matter, or not matter?

Muslim Devotions certainly comprehended and expounded common themes. Praise of God, celebration of revelation, penitence, refuge, pardon, invocation, gratitude, the prayer of need and hope – all are there, under God, for Muslim and Christian alike. Even attendant superstitions show a kinship of frailty. Kindred fears will 'seek refuge' with a recital of a divine Name and a formula of *ta'widh*, or with 'the sign of the Cross' over the bosom. Both, in their difference, are sacramental, drawing alike on where the vital clues are held to lie. Can we say they are the same, even in being different? Bare pragmatism might say that in their function they are one. Truth, however, is more than function. Yet it has to make its way, and be at stake, within what functions. Realism requires any truth-carer to acknowledge that the spirituality of the prayer manuals is firmly anchored in the wholeness of Islam. The exposition in *Muslim Devotions* is careful throughout to show how they belong with and in the ritual prayer itself, on the *Qiblah* to Mecca and infused with the life of the Qur'an. The *Tasliyah* which so far preoccupies their piety binds them through and through with the *Sirah* of the Prophet. On every count they are so inextricably Islamic that a prosaic assessor from outside would soon conclude that they allowed no 'bridge' into the equally idiomatic character of Christian devotion.

Moreover, those 'definitives' of Islam are not going to cease. On the contrary they abide, even intensify, and though they may adjust to times are there to stay, self-aware, self-affirming, self-perpetuating. It is with their continuity that relationship must reckon. Correspondingly, the Christian identity persists. Both are doubtless subject to the inroads of secularity – an important common, contemporary denominator, yet not one which readily mediates between their distinctive entities.

The answers to our questions would seem to be necessarily affirmative. Yes! common themes do leave the two spiritualities at issue with each other. Yes! the differing associations – Jesus and Muhammad, New Testament and Qur'an, Cross and *Hijrah*, Eucharist and *Shahadah* – do matter, despite the common themes. Alike, they have God, prayer, revelation, doxology, penitence, pardon, celebration, but only with incompatibles about them. Alike they possess the sacramental mediation of meaning and enlistment of response inseparable from all religion. But ·what unifies also differentiates. Alike they exhibit superstition, know hypocrisy and produce saints, but the criteria do not always tally.

What then is to be done? Was *Muslim Devotions* just a venture in Christian wistfulness – 'hoping it might be so' about an impossible vision of affinity? Was *Islamic Culture* right in being courteously impatient with a scholarship it saw as somehow wanting Islam to be other than itself on behalf of Christian satisfaction? Perhaps. Yet are not the common themes betrayed at heart if they refuse to associate? There can be no monopolies on penitence, no cornering of prayer, no isolating of revelations, no annexations of God and, therefore, no final self-sufficiencies of faiths. It is the merit of Constance Padwick's diligence to have left us with these conclusions which can only themselves be ongoing demands.

What, then, are these demands? Let us maximise what is akin and as far as possible possess it in common despite the different auspices by which we receive it. Let us show honest cause why distinctiveness needs to remain (if it does) within the mutual human scene, why what we cannot reconcile continues to be relevant so that we are duty bound to serve it in humility. But let us do so, as far as in us lies, for the other's own sake, and from within the other's own credentials. So to do is not mere controversy; it is appreciation as the very ground of mission. Let us inter-associate meanings and perhaps, so doing, find them more radically. So doing, let everything issue into invitation. As in hospitality the given only comes over as the received. Two examples may be offered – here, necessarily from the Christian 'house of faith' – partial, no doubt, but central and doing duty for many more.

The first has to do with penitence and God. Since the event of crucifixion, the New Testament and Christian faith have always understood that there cannot *not* be a divine 'cost' in human pardon, of which the passion of Jesus is at once sign, proof and means. Faith has differed in how that sense of things is credalized as it needs to be. The differences belong with the problematics of metaphor. But, on every count, a Christian must shrink from the prayer earlier quoted: 'My God, my sins do not harm Thee . . . forgive me what does not harm Thee and give me what Thy wilt not miss.' Must we not believe that unless 'sin' matters infinitely forgiveness is unnecessary or irrelevant?[28] Is what sinners need like a throw-away from the omnipotent?

But perhaps, behind such a notion there may be a redeemable idea. Are we being asked to think of a *largesse* ('Thy pardon does not impoverish Thee'), a magnanimity like that of the father in the story Luke believed he had from Jesus? There was there nothing niggardly about the ring and the robe, the shoes and the feast. Pardon did not impoverish those ready resources, that ardent heart. But behind them lay a long travail of suffering, of deferred hope. The love that could be lavish with the welcome had borne the pain of the exile. A Christian will have to strike out that 'does Thee no harm', but the rest is redeemable. Is it not precisely omnipotence that bears all? Otherwise, that resonant term has no meaning.

The second example must go to *Tasliyah*, and wisely, since that theme is so distinctively Islamic, so apparently antithetical to the Christian universe of discourse around Jesus and the Cross. But, as hinted in the earlier discussion of *Salla Allahu 'alaihi wa sallam*, the formula has to do with divine revelation within human agency. It enshrines the theme of a certain harmony of wills whereby a divine intention moves through a human responsiveness. God effectuates the Qur'an via Muhammad's recipience and is, therefore, believed to celebrate and bless the earthly vehicle. The resulting community of faith is called to orchestrate their reverent 'congratulation' (in the strictest sense of that word).

Christology belongs, in Christianity, to the same sphere of agency and harmony, the divine via the human. It derives from how the Gospel narratives understand and present the ministry of Jesus, especially in and from his baptism. It ensues in the post-Resurrection realisation of the inclusive significance of a Jesus, teaching, caring, resolving, suffering and overcoming, as the personal enactment of the revealing, redeeming nature of God. 'My beloved, in whom I am well-pleased,' translates into 'God was in Christ reconciling the world,' into 'Herein is love,' into 'One in being with the Father.' Doxology in Christianity compatibly unites 'We acknowledge Thee to be the Lord,' with 'Thou art the king of glory, O Christ . . .' The *Te Deum Laudamus*, we might say, beyond Hosanna, is the Christian *Tasliyah*.

Of course, we have not mediated between the two faiths. We may even have discovered how apart they are. But at least we have identified a common thread, namely a human figure in a divine enterprise, an initiative achieving what becomes a celebration. *Tasliyah* and Eucharist can at least converse. Is that the lasting significance of those many engaging conversations that attended Constance Padwick's travels around the Arab lands and her assiduous courteous purchasing of pieties for study?

Chapter 4

ELIE WIESEL
(born 1928)

'The Torment of Truth'

i

'They owe nothing to anyone but everything to the dead.'[1] So writes their most celebrated memorialist about the survivors of the Holocaust. Elie Wiesel's long, almost annual, flow of books since *Night* in 1960 has made him the most eloquent and passionate of contemporary strivers after the truth of that supreme event of modern history. No biography of dialogue could omit him or evade the reaches into which, in the utter anguish of his thought, he takes it. The agony of being, and continuing, Jewish, in sequence to what is seen as a cosmic shattering of all human perspectives, gives a quality to his writing which conveys the theme relentlessly. He is the voice of the Judaic in its most agonised appeal to humanity at large – agonised in what it desperately seeks, yet agonised also in what it despairs to find.

Here is the deep paradox. Elie Wiesel's work is burdened with a haunting suspicion of all mankind. Yet, as compelling, often poetic, prose, it awaits and stirs response. It vindicates the dictum that there is no such thing as 'a literature of despair'. For some faith is explicit in every inspired pen. Yet an existential despair is the source and motive of Wiesel's pages. Their power is born of a desperation which wants 'to dream of a world completely Jewish,'[2] and, knowing it cannot, pleads that the world, denying the dream, may yet understand and, understanding, repent, learn and share the unforgettable.

One could begin nowhere else. It is the Holocaust which determines the universe of thought, both as that which must be comprehended in all its incomprehensibility and as the unanswerable accusation which must nevertheless be answered. The survivors whose voice he makes his own are condemned to survive within a mystery they can never resolve. The capacity in which they live spells a necessity never to let die the name and fate of those who did. The future is in thrall to that past. From this necessity time brings no reprieve. For the generations to be persist only through survivors.

Thus it was right also that we should begin with debt, inexorable and unremitting, and see the writing as its partial payment, a homage to the victims and an incrimination of the world. For, 'were hatred a solution the survivors, when they came out of the camps, would have had to burn down the whole world.'[3] Even in the most overwhelming indictment of mankind there is the mute appeal to something human. Evil, in that sense, is its own witness against itself. If it were all-inclusive, it could not be accused. It is only arraigned because it defies all human meaning. The enormity of guilt can only be identified by the majesty of trust.

However utterly unmatched the Holocaust may be, however far beyond all precedents of evil, it belongs with the unity of humanity. To this unity, however shattered, appeal is made most ardently where it is most bitterly denied. Such is 'the torment of the truth' – Judaic, Christian, or any other. In 'owing everything to the dead' and 'nothing to anyone', survivors are creditors of the rest of humanity, awaiting the hope of payment of the debts of guilt, of repentance and honesty, of truth. If it were not so, there could be no literature of the Holocaust, but only the silence of the dead. From a world incapable of heeding there could be only heedlessness. The whole thrust of accusation falls away unless it is also a surge of hope. There is a will to faith in the very passion of unbelief. In all its grimness, Holocaust writing, the Wiesel achievement, has to be read as strenuous appeal. It is a seeking, as well as a searing, eloquence. It has to do with the enormous indebtedness of the world and demands to have it paid. Despair that it can be, only intensifies the claim.

This dimension of tormented truth, of hope as the paradox of despair, marks all Elie Wiesel's work and influence. It makes him a foremost protagonist of the central theme in Jewish-Christian relations in our time. He is in letters what the Yad va Shem Memorial is in architecture on the western hill in Israeli Jerusalem. The pathos of his stories, the vividness of his narratives, the tirelessness of his pen, together confront the post-Holocaust world with its own image. The arraignment is no ordinary accusation. In all its proper vehemence, there is a prosecutor's search for hope. The indictment cannot hold without the faith that can identify its ground in the truth. That truth is not only stark event; it is also human community – the more insistent in being the more violated.

Holocausts – if they can ever be thought plural – overwhelm all normal landmarks, all ordinary logic. They do so not only in what they are but in what they bequeath. Their legacies rightly perpetuate their agonies. In giving voice to this quality of things past and things present, Elie Wiesel has symbolised the pain and passion of the issues between synagogue and church. He has shared the sharp animus attending them. He has sought to make an equation between Christianity and the Nazi philosophy and policy of genocide. So doing he has broached deep-reaching questions of New Testament interpretation as well as of modern European history. His writing has recruited some Christians into indiscriminate identity with his mind where the impulse of ardent sympathy forfeits a balanced judgement of both history and theology. The resulting situation is further complicated by the partisan instinct to dub all such pleas for integrity of mind in issues of controversy as masking an evil will to evade or mitigate the Holocaust. By such taxing complexities the present biography of dialogue is beset and only a wellnigh infinite patience with each other can survive the pitfalls and truly endure the torment of truth. Jewish-Christian inter-relationship must incorporate truly the meaning of the Holocaust as it bears upon each distinctively and upon all in common. To give us both the measure of that ordeal is the achievement of Elie Wiesel.

ii

Born in Sighet in Transylvania of godly Jewish parents, Shlomo and Sarah Wiesel, in 1928, Wiesel's early boyhood coincided with the gathering shadows of Nazi persecution. The story of his lonely survival in later boyhood out of the horror of the camps of extermination is told in *Night*, his first book, written after his arrival in the United States.[4] The accumulated anguish of that degradation, orphaning and incarceration and the bewildered 'nevertheless' of life and mind and spirit, created and sustain his authorship. At the age of twenty he began his studies at the Sorbonne in Paris where he spent three years. Five years later he settled in New England and his career in educational posts and in literature began. French was his first language of authorship, many of the English versions being made by his wife, Marion Esther, whom he married in 1969. The last two decades have seen a rich sequence of essays, stories and other publications, making him an honoured celebrity across America, a household name throughout Jewry and a citizen of mankind. The Jewish Theological Seminary was the first to give him an Hon. D.Litt. inaugurating a long and distinguished list of emulating Universities, Seminaries and institutions, Jewish, Christian and secular in the western world. Since 1976 Professor of the Humanities in Boston University, he has received numerous awards, prizes and distinctions, culminating in the Nobel Peace Prize in 1986. Honours open to others have also been established to bear and celebrate his name. He has chaired the American President's Committee on the Holocaust and been a member of the Board of Directors of the National Committee on American Foreign Policy.

We must keep in mind in what follows this marked and richly deserved incorporation of Elie Wiesel into the esteem and sometimes near veneration of political and literary 'establishments' today. It goes some way to offset that inveterate loneliness, that strange 'apartness' of 'a people dwelling alone', which was the Biblical description of Jewry and which so far characterises its genius through history. With a cause like the Holocaust he cannot complain that he has no hearing. The succession, and the success, of his writings corresponds to a perception of the claims, the realities, the themes, he represents. His is not a voice crying in the wilderness; he has a hearing in the counsels of power and in the courts of culture. Jews may feel, and fear, that all this is precarious, never free from jeopardy, always by leave of others. But, however that may yet be, it is far, now, from that 'sufferance which is the badge of all our tribe'. It can be read as well-earned new assurance. Perhaps the Holocaust, as cosmic enormity, has made a cosmic difference too, so long as vigilance is not deceived. To be sure, 'there is no discharge in that war'. But Elie Wiesel's voice is not unheard. At least he is 'making connections' the Holocaust cannot preclude. For it has – through his eloquence – given them occasion. To that extent, the Holocaust is not all.

It will be useful to explore the 'inner faith' of Elie Wiesel in its dialogue with all things Judaic, so that in this context we may proceed to his sharp debate with Christians, their history and faith. This, further, will involve a study of the bearing of the State of Israel and of Zionism on all that is at issue. Throughout, we need to wrestle with the entire significance and travail of Jewish exceptionality and the vexed matter of 'the Gentiles'. We must be warned – there is pain and tension all the way. Good faith must be in constant encounter with the menace of bad faith and with the knowledge that neither of these is likely to be unilateral.

iii

'The Holocaust,' wrote Wiesel in *One Generation After*, 'defies literature,' for 'no cry is sufficiently blasphemous' with which to disown it.
There can be no other theme.[5] Yet out of it, precisely, his literature is
born. Not only literature, however, is defied. Faith is. Yet likewise
faith also finds itself in its own *finis*. Where was 'the God of Israel'
in Treblinka, Birkman, Belsen, Buchenwald, Auschwitz, Mauthausen,
Blezec, Ponar, Sobibor and Majdanek? All the place-names must be
rehearsed since the nameless millions cannot be. Everything proceeded as
if the Jews did not, should not, must not, exist. Where, then, was the
covenant, the mutual inter-necessity of Yahweh and his people? 'With all
these corpses,' he cries, 'before my eyes, I am afraid to stumble over my
own.' His urge is 'to throw away the pen, burn all bridges and start to run
and curse.'[6]

Can there be a Jewish, or any other, theology after the Holocaust? Was
there not a total treachery in that callous non-intervention from on High?
The question the Jew must pose to God becomes in reverse the question
God poses to the Jew – the enigma of betrayal interrogating the enigma of
annihilation. But for the Holocaust, Wiesel himself, he surmises, would
have been a pious student, labouring devoutly over the Talmud in his local
Yeshiva, not the present passionate searcher after the credibility of God.
But which Wiesel would have been the more ultimate believer?

To doubt may be to deny, but it is also to await and to await with the
ultimate criterion of what must be awaited – an awareness of meaning
commensurate with what has to be made to mean. This theme reverberates
through all Wiesel's books. There are times when the only option is to
conclude the ancient covenant utterly foregone, shattered in the ashes of
the crematoria. There are other times when, phoenix-like, faith must
re-make a covenantal relationship with God, if only thereby not to be
posthumously defeated by Hitler.[7] How could it be that the most noxious
Anti-Semites should be the final vanquishers of Jews? Yet, if faith in
Yahweh only persisted to give the lie to them, might it be said that it was
those Anti-Semites who were making Jews Jews again? When a student
told Wiesel in Russia, 'We are Jews for spite,' he cringed and deplored that
it might be so, 'for want of better teachers.'[8] The title of the book in which
he records the exchange, *Jews of Silence*, was intended, on the other hand,
to reproach those Jews who tried, either way, to pretend an unconcern.

The Talmud might relate that when the Temple in Jerusalem was
burning under the torches of the Romans, the priests broke off the liturgy

and ritual and, climbing on to the roof, hurled the Temple keys to heaven, protesting to Yahweh that they could no longer keep safe his dwelling-place. But what happened to the keys thereafter? How can we believe in God, Wiesel asks in *Gates of the Forest*, but how, after what has happened can we *not* believe in God?[9] The moments, the days, the years, he depicts in *Night* had 'murdered his God'. 'The act of writing,' he might tell himself, 'is for me often nothing more than the secret or conscious desire to carve words on a tombstone to the memory of a town for ever vanished.'[10] But words are a will to the intelligible. What, then, do they say? What 'name' do names invoke?

What they say to Christian theology with its allegedly easy, romantic, hollow Messianic pretensions, will be clear below. As for Jewry, Sinai and divine election, part of Elie Wiesel's retention of faith hinges on the State of Israel, though in strictly defined terms which we must later note. For the rest there would seem to be, for him, an uneasy truce between a dark inscrutability in God and an earnest yearning to have it otherwise. It is not finally as a theologian but as a man of letters, a poet rather than a dialectician, that Wiesel wrestles with Judaic history and appalling genocide. To write is to affirm, albeit gropingly, wistfully, proleptically, awaiting what remains concealed. That tradition of fidelity is long in Jewish history. 'Hope which is seen is not hope.'[11] The eclipse of God is a right imagery. There is no eclipsing what does not persist.

But there are times when the theological principle of hope is, rather, in Wiesel a yearning hope in man and in humanity. There is in all Judaism this paradoxical will to participate despite – or should we say because of – abiding otherness, to belong in, and yet be 'chosen' out of, the human whole. Throughout, emphatically, he is addressing the 'Gentile' world as well as his own Jewry. To be preoccupied with distinctiveness is to be related if only for its interpretation. At worst, anti-defamation means that we must resist, dissuade, rebut, relate. At best, it means that we must possess particularity without exemption from the whole. 'Every truth,' says the narrator in *The Oath*, 'that shuts you in, that does not lead to others, is inhuman.'[12] That must include the Holocaust. The fly-leaf in that novel cites the Talmud:

> Had the peoples and the nations known how much harm they brought upon themselves by destroying the Temple of Jerusalem, they would have wept more than the children of Israel.

Had they done so there would have been something mutual within the tears. 'To have hope in God is to have hope against God,' Wiesel says.[13] Conversely, to have hope against man, as victims did, is to have hope in man as survivors plead.[14] It is clear that all attention to particularity, such as post-Holocaust survival rigorously demands of Jews, has to belong and be pursued *within* the human whole.

> The stranger has just told us that in order to save man, one must annihilate the Jew in man, and that our people must disappear so that mankind may prosper, his mouth betrays his ignorance. Whoever opposes man to himself becomes his enemy: whoever opposes man-as-a-Jew to man repudiates both.[15]

That must be true for all identities, starting with the Canaanites. To begin with the particular is to be involved in a concern for all. That 'my neighbour is as I am', is the meaning of 'loving him as myself'.[16] A common human condition underlies every grievance of the part. Where the travesty is of Holocaust dimensions the cry has to be 'to high heaven' and, therefore, to 'the whole earth'. It has always been a tormenting truth for Elie Wiesel that there are no exemptions from these implications of Holocaust. Extermination of Jews is the genocide of man, of the *genus* mankind.

How gently, how rigorously, this truth needs to be explored. It is the crucial paradox of all Jewish-human, all Jewish-Christian relationships: the 'people apart' and 'the people among'. Is there nothing but coincidence in the fact that the world's metaphysically differentiated people (as we see, for example, in Franz Rosenzweig's understanding) are history's most tragically and wilfully persecuted or disallowed people? To ask is not to condone or mitigate, still less to justify, the crimes of persecution. It is, rather, to seek that for which Wiesel passionately yearns, namely the priceless benediction of a fulfilled Jewishness within a human whole, in peace and mutual wellbeing.

This would mean asking Jewry, not to disavow its every instinct, the entire meaning of its past and future, but so to interiorise the sense of divine covenant and warrant of election as being, like all love affairs and lovers' quarrels, an internal mystery, not essentially questioning the equal humanity of all 'those Gentiles'. It is not merely that every ethnic, cultural and territorial identity is conscious of distinction from others. 'Have not all races had their first unity from a mythology that marries them to rock and hill?'[17] It is that the Judaic version, unless radically and effectively internalized, contrasts itself not merely with this and that other identity, as Germans do from Poles, and Slavs from Turks, but with all the rest of humanity thereby made a single 'other', labelled 'Gentiles'.

When this posture is most criminally rejected, in what form does the rejection proceed? Similarly, by the construction of a single master-race, like Hitler's Germans, or Dostoevsky's 'holy Russia', ranged unilaterally against 'all the rest'. Thus, 'chosen-ness' is somehow provocative unless it can be the sort that consents *not* to be unique. The very enormity of the Holocaust underlines this mystery. For where do its dastardly impulses arise – not finally from a suffering Messiah made the hero of his vulgar partisans, but from the misconstruing of what seems like rejection of themselves to angered folk bedevilled by their anger.

Consider, for example, Vincent van Gogh's comment – no stranger he to the torment of truth, though speaking here in more casual vein:

> How petty that story is (of Joshua and his invasion): My God! only think. So there are only Jews in the world, who begin by declaring everything which is not themselves impure . . . that saddening Bible which distresses us once and for all, because we are outraged by . . . its contagious folly.[18]

Wild words, no doubt. But part of the liabilities of all faiths is with, and for, not what they really mean but what they seem, or are assumed to mean. William Blake – again no babbler he but one who could write mysteriously about meeting Isaiah and Ezekiel and dining with them – hears Jewry say: 'We so loved our God that we cursed in His Name all the deities of surrounding nations.'[19] Bitter, no doubt, and sharp, the kind of observation to invite retort in kind. But, either way, retort in kind is no response, failing to take in hand how – alone – prejudice may be corrected, namely where it springs – within ourselves.

What a strange turn of the page, it may be said, is this from the pain and passion of Elie Wiesel. But is it not to take him in his own seriousness as bound, one and all, in a situation where there is no salvation except in honest mutuality? As we note elsewhere in the study of Rabbi Abraham Heschel, there is a superb humanism, a divine anthropology – 'God in search of man' – built upon the Hebraic themes of land, law and people. But is it truly 'man', or only Hebraic man? Is the latter a monopolist, or only an exemplar? Is the triad of people, place, and posterity, folk and land and history, race and home and story, not – at least potentially – the triple thread in *every* human society, every collective and culture? Can it, or can it not, be a sacred thread, a hallowed vocation, in *every* instance of its corporate experience? This is the deep question belonging to whatever that 'Semitism' is which evokes 'Anti-Semitism'. To sense it within the long and bitter tangle of Anti-Semitic crimes and horrors is to seek where Wiesel seeks – namely into the clue of being authentically ourselves with universal debts and aspirations. 'Gentiles' are the issue that Jewishness has never yet resolved.

iv

Everything about the Holocaust requires that it be isolated in history, as unprecedented, without parallel. Yet everything demands that it be sited inextricably within history. Much Jewish writing, in line with Elie Wiesel, finds the former more congenial than the latter. Non-Jews do well to realise why it should be so. When 'the unthinkable became real, producing a mutation on a cosmic scale . . . the human condition is no longer the same.'[20] 'In the beginning was the Holocaust: we must therefore start all over again.' But what 'beginning' is this with the Treaty of Versailles behind it,[21] and around it the seventy million dead of European conflict in two decades of the century? These are in no way palliatives; but they are concurrences. Nor can the termination of the Holocaust be unhitched from a trail of sacrifice all the way via North Africa from the Normandy beaches to Berlin. Is there to be only recrimination about the tardiness of rescue and not recognition of the cost of it when it came? Nor can whatever solace the availability of America may offer, as Wiesel's career so well exemplifies, to the remaking of survivors, be detached from the tribulations Amerindians have suffered through all the ever-dishonoured treaties white Americans made with them? The exceptionality of the Holocaust is not emotionally in question. To say: 'If not all victims were Jews, all Jews were victims,' is to allow that some three million non-Jewish Poles were murdered and the entire million gipsies with them under a Hitler who conceived an elimination programme 'for the suppression of lives unworthy to be lived.'[22] The interwovenness of human tribulation and the ramifications of guilt are endless. To confess it so is not to connive with enormity. It is, rather, to scrutinise one's anguish and its proper indignation. The Holocaust has such proportions of atrocity as to overwhelm the mind.

This situation is to be seen as responding to the devious iniquity in which Nazism contrived to find a role for the victim in its warrant for the crime. There is a cunning even in insanity. Zionism could be pilloried as compromising the 'national' loyalties of multitudes of Jews who either had misgivings akin to that perception of it or who sympathised without in any way disowning good faith with their actual citizenship. Elimination of the Jews could readily present itself as salvation to perverted minds. All such prejudice feeds on its own illusions, indeed invents them to pursue its ends. It follows that when, at last, 'the tyranny is overpast', the victims' innocence of what calumny assigned to them must be emphatic. Repudiation is the counterpart of righteousness. The inner faith which sustains identity has to find integrity through what it must repudiate before it can fulfil it in what it would affirm. The post-Holocaust situation is endured and told only in a passion for truth. Without the passion the truth would be untold. The outsider who might propose to separate the one from the other must first enter into their integrity in Elie Wiesel's telling.

V

To do so, if we are mere readers, is hardest of all in respect of what the foregoing means for Wiesel's perception of Christians and Christianity. For here the stress between the truth and the passion is maximal. It is as if the inner Judaic faith in him somehow necessitates the indictment of the other and his language finds a vehemence, even a venom, which embitters the content. Even so, it is urgent to be patient with the prosecution which, in lieu of dialogue, appears to identify Christianity with Nazism and drown the Christian meaning of the Cross in the Judaic meaning of the Holocaust. With these perceptions, the only way – for either – is first to reach for the mutually human meaning of tragic evil. The will to find such meaning is implicit in every page of Elie Wiesel. If, as we have argued, Jews need to register how their conviction of a privileged position in regard to God impinges on non-Jews, there is far greater urgency for the latter to grapple with how Gentile response to them has distorted, derided and denied that privilege, and tried, perennially, to destroy it. In such derision, distortion and would-be destruction, Christian factors have played a sustained and sinister part.[23]

But we must bring a chaste discernment to the reckoning or, at least, hold in rein the excesses of accusation which the intensity of passion can arouse. It may truly be an enormous thing for Jews, both devout and secular, to de-monopolise the mystery of Sinai by the interiorising of its meaning. This would in no way deprive them of it while engaging them the more securely within a human whole where 'Gentilising' of all but themselves had become happily obsolete. It might even be proper to think that such an outcome was the truest possession of the privilege, by the very paradox of its fulfilment. Something of that order had been operative in the very origins of Christianity. The fact that it led, in the second Christian century, to a more emphatic exceptionality and, reciprocally, to a confrontational near-enmity, should not blind us to its achievement then or its significance now. The Christianity that first surmounted and would have made obsolete the Jew-Gentile divide has long since entrenched it. It is strange that some Christians today, in their very sensitivity to Jewish tragedy, want to keep it so. By parallel covenants they propose to maintain the divide.

Elie Wiesel maintains it, parallel covenants or no. Covenant status for Christians can only be their affair. The Judaic must not only reserve its privilege, it must prosecute its persecutor. The persecution may have borne the Nazi stamp but it wore the Christian image. Wiesel's satire can bite deep, but must be soberly read as coming from within the dimensions of the Holocaust. 'All I knew of Christianity,' he writes, 'was its hate for my people.' 'Unable to save Israel, Jesus ended up saving mankind.'[24] Developing that bitter comment, he reduces the 'saving' to illusion. He sees Christianity as a 'Messianism without man', in that it has isolated salvation in Jesus alone and proceeded on a facile measure of what human sin really is. In *The Oath* he insists that 'the Messiah is as dependent upon us as we upon him.' 'God asks us to share in the holy work of redemption.' The plea is familiar from within the mind of contemporary Judaism. The world remains manifestly unredeemed; to believe otherwise is crass romanticism; the Jesus role is premature, illusory and, if seen as authentic, then quite fictitious. The very symbols are abhorrent:

> Every village has its own church and pointed steeple – pass
> by quickly and avert your gaze lest you get into trouble for
> visual blasphemy.

The sharp pain of the Christian adjacence, scapegoating in all its attitudes, argues the futility of a crucified Messiah. To worship a victim is somehow to learn sadism, and at the same time to devise exoneration. This whole scheme has to be – as literary critics might express it – 'de-constructed', with Judaic fidelity to God vindicated in the process.

Christians imagine their Savior expiring on the cross. Thus

they situate him outside the circle of shame...others are made to bear his shame. The Messiah, as seen by the Jews, shows greater courage: he survives all the generations, watches them disappear one after another – and, if he is late in coming, it is perhaps because be is ashamed to reveal himself.[25]

Having Jesus as the Christ is something that Christians have decided for themselves. As far as 'Jews are concerned, he may be retroactively guilty for all the murders and massacres done in his name.'[26]

'To turn death into a philosophy is not Jewish,' Wiesel makes his *Moshe* say in *The Oath*. 'To turn it into a theology is anti-Jewish. To die for God is to die against God.'[27] What is needed is 'Messianic deeds' in the living world and, when we have these, 'we will manage without him' (*the* Messiah).[28]

In this complex of perception and passion how might dialogue proceed? Perhaps we could best invoke Elie Wiesel's own words addressed as prayer to God and apply them, each to the other, as Jew and Christian: 'I no longer ask you to resolve my questions, only to receive them and make them part of you.'[29] 'Truth', he wrote, 'for a Jew, is to dwell among his brothers.' By that test how far are we truth-brothers? For he goes on: 'Link your destiny to that of your people: otherwise you will surely reach an impasse.'[30] What if it is 'the link' creates 'the impasse'?

Elie Wiesel's writing is rarely directly theological. His concern is portrayal. His genius is in making issues wring the soul to lift them out of mere debate. For him there is something almost blasphemous in discussing Holocaust. If silence conspires against it, so also does 'commentary'. For him, narrative is more telling than theory. What is indelible in the memory cannot be discursive in the mind. Theologians, almost by definition, are irrelevant in Auschwitz.

Even so, in writing, in chronicling, in communicating, he is – by implication – 'dwelling among brothers', anticipating readers who may understand. He has truth he means to have prevail. However unwillingly, he brings us back to thought about faith, to enquiry about truth. If the Holocaust is the supreme sign in history of enmity, alienation, and the death of meaning, then only the ultimate in community can take it in – community of all in mind and spirit, each 'receiving the other's questions'.

They are not received as questions if they are pre-empted – and emptied – by answers ready made. Let us not write, or rewrite, history in the sole interest of polemic. Let us seek for the good faith within our separate themes.

vi

Nowhere is this more urgent than in the way we read the Messianic. Can concept never be event? Sinai, certainly, was – remains – both. There occurred, as it were, a historization of meaning. Nomads and a volcano, peoplehood and Torah, a futurity perpetually enacted in a single past, happening as metaphor, 'God and His people' – these hold in one a time and an interpretation. An act becomes a theme because a meaning has become a deed. 'God chose the Jews.' The cynic may allege that all this is 'subjective'. It has only an asserted objectivity. That is so with all religious truth. It is not demonstrable. Faith holds that 'what is within' is 'what was there'. Exodus and Sinai are 'God warranted' because of 'God warranting'. Judaic faith holds and is held. 'All our fathers passed through the sea...'

Christians believed, and believe, likewise, concerning 'God in Christ reconciling the world'. There *is* this suffering metaphor for God, a making concrete of divine sovereignty in fidelity to the Hebraic faith in divine yearning towards man and the divine pathos that fulfils it. That it is so may be no less assertive, no less affirmative, than that 'God is in mutual covenant with Israel' as He is nowhere else. The two 'events for faith' share something of the same finality and confidence. Such instinct, after all, is Biblical. Truth has the form of event; event becomes experience and experience witness. Witness belongs with community-in-faith and to that extent the witnesses and the thing witnessed are bound together, open to the suspicion of exclusiveness and the charge of arrogance.

The two Biblical situations differ, however, in one fundamental respect. Judaic Sinai assumes its crux to be birth, 'seed', progeny, the tribal into the ethnic into the national, as the bond and sphere of the meaning. Christian Christ-event requires the condition of penitence and faith as the sufficient criterion of its community, irrespective of birth, or race or land or culture. That criterion was implicit in the nature of the Christ-event. It was also the central factor in Judaic withholding from it, despite its initiation by Jewish leadership. The new Biblical event, Jews believed, could not be seen as fulfilling the other. Sinai, for the world's sake, must remain retentive of its own. Christians have all too rarely 'received and made part of themselves the questions' that made Jews so minded. Rather they have reacted with a long resentment as from a hospitality chagrined by its own rejection. The New Testament itself bears the marks of that reaction. But it is in no doubt about the openness and how genuine, how hopeful, how imperative it was.

Given all the blighted centuries, the two Biblical events – Exodus and Christ – remain at odds. It is 'links' that perpetuate 'the impasse', and only disloyalty can loose them. But it need not be an impasse of misapprehension. Christians do not see Messiah-Jesus as having no associates. Quite the contrary. The event which is believed to have within itself, as one epitome, what redemption means and takes, demands disciples. In them it has its future tense. Those who know themselves forgiven must become forgivers. They are enabled so to be by the very fact of what was 'once for all'. One cannot rule out at least the possibility of 'the Messianic event' and intelligibly retain 'the Messianic idea'. What cannot be identified in event could hardly be conceived in mind. It would be no Judaic principle to think that we could have no past if we were to anticipate a future. On the contrary, it is out of a past, as memory holds it, love cherishes it, and ritual rehearses it, that meaning coheres. So it is in the Christian *anamnesis* of a Cross which Jewry discounts and of an Easter they see as 'premature'.

The Holocaust has been read as utterly corroborating that discounting, that verdict of prematurity. Some Christians, like Robert McAfee Brown, expounding Elie Wiesel, passionately agree. 'Doctrines of redemption no longer work in and after Auschwitz.' Forgiveness itself becomes a weak virtue. In the light of Belsen we cannot have Easter; its triumphalism is too easy. History yields us no 'victory communiqué'. The Cross glorified a passivity in the face of death. How can the crucifix ennoble anything? It speaks a craven acquiescence in which there is no redemption.[31]

Yet, as we have seen, solidarity is a fact of the human scene. Even the Holocaust takes its place in a continuity of history. Its victims matter desperately to survivors and survivors appeal to mankind about a future. Its enormity has no meaning if its perpetrators incur no guilt. The guilt lies in the appalling violation of the human. Suffering is the experience of others' wrong. Vulnerability is the concomitant of society. The question, then, about suffering under wrong is not whether, but how. Is it possible so to bear, as to bear away? In the personal equation: Yes. And love retrieves the evil by doing so, if only in refusing the alternative of retaliation, but more – in overcoming with good. Evil is then outmatched.

It is this which Christians find Jesus doing in the manner of his suffering – and doing in respect of a coalition of evil-mindedness, political, ecclesiastical, popular, identifiable in the will to his crucifixion – what the

Gospel calls 'the sin of the world'. No one ever believed that this 'sin of the world' was inclusive as a 'quantity'. To think it had holocaust proportion in that sense would be ludicrous and wild. There were, moreover, crosses every day on numerous hills. But in its quality the cross of Jesus is capable – to the eye of faith – of enshrining what evil exacts of love and how love outlives evil. All we have then to do to have the Christian faith is to be bold enough, via the Messianic hope, to associate that character of the Cross with the economy, the sovereignty, of God. This is precisely what the first Church did and, in doing so, *ipso facto* entailed upon itself an inclusive openness to that same world in the name of that perception of God.

So to conclude does not diminish, ignore or fail to comprehend the Holocaust. Nor does it weaken the imperative to have it ever memorialised. On the contrary, it goes to the heart of 'the torment of the truth' of it. Satan cannot cast out Satan. This may not be the same question as the viability of the covenant and a theodicy of unfailing election. For these there are all the resources of Judaic fidelity to God. The Cross is a discernible answer to a different question, namely, how in an economy we can attribute to God, evil is made to yield to love via the suffering in which they meet. The other question is whether the answer can have its paradigm in a history where it is disclosed, transacted and confirmed, so that we can live in its light.

States, cultures, peoples, all collectives, will still need sinews, defences, advocates, protagonists of justice and truth, such as Elie Wiesel has eloquently undertaken to be. The historian's truth, the poet's truth, the statesman's truth, the moralist's truth – all these are to be strenuously sought and served. Otherwise, the Satans are not identified nor recognised and, therefore, not confronted. But the final truth of our solidarity in man is its meaning in suffering interpreted by the love of God.

vii

It follows that there is a further area of Wiesel's thought remaining for study within his 'inner faith', namely the role of Zionism and of Israel in his vision of truth. He is adamant that the State of Israel should not be seen as, somehow, an 'answer' to the Holocaust. The Holocaust has no 'answer' that could be said to mitigate or compensate. In *One Generation After*, he wrote:

> Each time I hear of an intrinsic link connecting the national resurrection of Israel to the era of Auschwitz, everything inside me rebels against such a juxtaposition...Israel an answer to the Holocaust?...too scandalous a conclusion.[32]

Yet there was, for him, a sense in which the will to create Israel, pursuing the case for Zionism to which Hitler had given such tragic warrant, did represent a strenuous repudiation of the nihilism to which Jews had 'every right to pledge themselves'. 'Had they instead, set fire to the whole of Europe, no one would,' he said, 'have been surprised.' Israel was 'why there was no settling of accounts.'

Thus he saw in Israel 'a determination to transform the hate imposed upon it into a craving of solidarity with the world.' He read, in the events of 1967, the vindication of that resolve but observed that somehow 'the world begrudged Israel its victory,' adding, bitterly: 'They love the Jew only on the cross: if he is not yet there, well they can oblige.'[33] He does not query how 'hate imposed' is a clue to the Palestinianism he roundly and caustically ridicules. He saw the occupation, in 1967, as necessary 'for the moment', and imagined the Israel of Arab eyes as 'a non-nation peopled with non-persons', not appreciating how a 'non-peopling' attitude to Palestinians was present in the language of such leaders as Golda Meyer, Menachem Begin and Rabbi Kahan. Israel had 'an unrelenting will not to assume a destiny other than her own.'[34]

But the reading of that destiny has to unite a sense of exaltation at the mystery of renewed Jerusalem with a radical revision of the concept of divine/Judaic covenant. Both God and man 'voided' Sinai at Auschwitz. God reneged on the old covenant and man in turn repudiated what had failed so direly. In place of Sinai there has to be a new 'covenant', forged in the fires. It is no longer sacral between heaven and Israel. It is between Israel and its memories of tragedy, desertion and death. In the State of Israel, Jews have taken their post-Holocaust fate into their own hands. This is a kind of secular waiting for a Messiah, using the old imagery and working to its vision 'while knowing full well that the hope is for nought,'[35] in its old terms. The State is the ambivalent sign of the abandonment of the covenanted past, and the means of the differently covenanted future. 'The chosen people', as David Ben Gurion used to have it, become 'the choosing people'.

Thus Israel retains a sense of mission without reliance on a God who failed in the hour of greatest tribulation. Yet this Messiahship *malgré Dieu* has the lyrical ardour of Wiesel's poetic prose. In *A Beggar in Jerusalem*, he pictures the nameless victims of the Holocaust gathering at the Western Wall 'bent with humility, or touched with ecstasy,' all the dead from Europe. From their towns and villages, rising up in their millions, they have lent their names to the battle roll and shared in the liberation of Jerusalem. Dead, they are a living presence. There 'the curse has been revoked, its reign at an end.' A character, David, inserts a note into a crevice in the Wall. Now, endowed with resurrected power, they can, if they will, requite and punish the world that betrayed them. Or they can forego vindictiveness and forgive. 'The mystery of good,' Wiesel concludes, 'is no less disturbing than the mystery of evil.'[36] 'Israel,' he says elsewhere, 'represents a victory over absurdity and inhumanity, and if I claim it for myself, it is because I belong to a generation which has known so few.'[37]

Victory over inhumanity, it could be said, has come through great tribulation, to the mind and pen of Elie Wiesel, and come via his energies repeatedly. It was characteristic to imagine reminding the dead that, thanks to Israel, they now had a genuine option to forgive, standing in their new, vicarious possession of strength. The unforgettable past has to be remembered, not as a logic of vindictive hate, sterile and stunting, frowning over the future, but as an option of forgiveness. Perhaps, after all, his plea to the dead is not far from the meaning of the Christian's Cross of Jesus. But Wiesel would insist that the option secreted in the Western Wall, is different. For it is only feasible because power is restored, statehood is achieved. Only the secure can be magnanimous, not the still vulnerable.

But the more intimate sphere of the will against inhumanity, which power is assumed to allow of, relates not to Europe, but to Palestine, not to a past of Holocaust but to a future of co-existence, not on the part of the visionary dead but in the making of the living. But, again, there is the proviso of the end of vulnerability. Israel is caught in the impasse in which peace will not be made till she is invulnerable – by no criteria but her own – and without peace with the Palestinians, and through them with the hinterland, invulnerability there can never be. A message hidden in the Wall would not be read in the Knesset. *Night* and all its sequels through three decades must surely be. There, too, 'the mysteries of good are no less disturbing than the mysteries of evil.' The enigma there is not so much that of 'God's action in history', but of contemporary Zion in the land. It is how to interpret and fulfil – in Elie Wiesel's words – 'the Messianic adventure held out by Palestine.'[38]

Chapter 5

JAMES PARKES
(1896 – 1981)

'The Pain and the Paradox of Disaffiliation'

i

Through his long and active career James Parkes consecrated all his efforts on the situation obtaining between Jews and Christians, historically considered and spiritually explored. 'Disaffiliation' is an ungainly word to describe the severance by which Judaism and Christianity parted over the destiny of an ancestry they had shared. It is apposite, none the less, for study of the thought and influence of a resolute Christian champion of Jewry and Judaism writing and campaigning through five decades with sustained devotion but in radical breach with his own Scripture.

How emergent Christianity disaffiliated from continuing Judaism in the first century after Jesus, and how Judaism was deeply affected by its self-exemption from the Messianic logic of that emergence, is familiar enough. The two decisions can only rightly be understood as complementary. What is not always so evident is how far James Parkes disqualified the Christian Scriptures[1] – and so the original Christian self-understanding – in his deeply Christian concern to reckon truly and positively with the reality of continuing Judaism. He was right, on every count, to deplore and reject the familiar thesis of the supersession of the Judaic, to insist on taking to heart the Judaic reasons for non-participation (after the first stages) in the Christian thing. But in doing so, he adopted a thesis – since his time widely approved – which virtually surrendered the reasons for the Christian decision. He disaffiliated from the apostles and their Scriptures by seeing Jewry as not intended within the meaning of the Cross, and therefore uniquely excluded from the intentions of a grace

91

alleged to be universal. His was in no sense a Christian 'solution' to the paradox of separation. For it abandoned the convictions on which Christianity rested. It could, indeed, be seen – perversely no doubt, yet logically – as yet another, if inverted, form of Jewish unwantedness in a community of faith meant for everyone but themselves. The Gospels, Acts and Epistles did not affirm a Gentile exceptionality to counter-balance a Jewish one. Because of how they saw Jesus and Messiahship, they had reconciled the two and intended that the distinction should be obsolete:'... no more strangers but fellow citizens' (Eph.2:19). James Parkes retained it with his case for 'the two covenants' mutually perpetuated, concurrent and willed in the divine economy. His intention, against the tragic background of Anti-Semitism and its dire guilt, was Christian enough; the substance of the argument was not – unless we are radically to revise what Christian 'obedience of faith' involves – the 'obedience' from which alone the issue comes to be. To find the Parkes 'solution' no resolution of it will return us sharply and painfully to a continuing Christian reckoning with the continuing eloquent significance of Judaism. That is precisely the merit of rejecting what he commends. For its acceptance is – as the prophets would have said – a 'healing slightly of the hurt'. Is not dialogue disqualified if it does not know its wounds?

This may seem a harsh verdict on a noted participant. It leaves much to be taken in hand below. Since Parkes' position on what is at stake between Judaism and Christianity has found wide, popular and highly partisan favour, it is well to propose dissent with patient firmness.[2] Clarity and compassion are the more urgent here because the dialogue is laden with the complexes of guilt heightened by the vexed ambiguities of Zionism. There is no area where the vocation to dialogue has more need of care for its own integrity.

ii

James Parkes, who hailed from the Channel Islands, studied at Hertford College, Oxford, where he was drawn enthusiastically into the activities of the Student Christian Movement, becoming its Secretary in 1923. His autobiography, *Voyage of Discoveries*, published in 1969, describes how in his – and the century's – twenties he was drawn passionately into awareness of Jewry, Judaism and Judaica. The burden of Christian relation and response and, not least, repentance, became the central theme of mind and heart. It was this he carried into his Christian Ordination, as deacon in 1925 and priest a year later. There is no record of any pastoral appointment in these capacities within the Church of England. They were fulfilled in the ecumenical context and in relative freedom from official structures. Dialogue, for many, was still below the horizon when he came to his prime. It is remarkable that, from 1932, his career was largely financed by Israel Sieff, the brother-in-law of Simon Marks, of the famous chain-store. There was integrity on both sides of the relationship. Jewish opinion, in unremitting vigilance towards unpredictable non-Jewry, had valid reason to welcome and salute a friend so clearly minded and equipped to interpret Jewry, to counter what might menace or disserve it, and voice its claims within the Christian community. James Parkes, reciprocally, saw material means justified by spiritual ends. His financial independence of the Churches and, more still, of missions-to-Jews, gave him greater rapport and symbolised the goodness of his good faith.

So began a long series of books on Judeo-Christian relations, past and present. Parkes' commitment intensified with the growing threat in the thirties of Nazi rejection of the Jews. He became increasingly involved – as he saw them – in the hopes and perils of incipient Zionism and the struggles to establish what became the State of Israel. He entered vigorously into the controversies around the legitimacy of a political resurgence of Jewish identity in Zionist form. Like many Christians he failed to identify the tensions within Judaism itself and the crucial nature of the issues concerning it which Zionism involved and which Israeli success has left not only unresolved but positively sharpened.[3]

The first of his writings was *The Jew and His Neighbour* in 1930; followed by *The Conflict of Church and Synagogue* (1934); *Jesus, Paul and the Jews* (1936); *Judaism and Christianity* (1948); *End of an Exile: Israel, the Jews and the Gentile World* (1954); and his most mature definitive work: *The Foundations of Judaism and Christianity* in 1960. As well as issues between the two faiths, but always conformably with his version of these, he wrote extensively on Jewish medieval history, the history of Palestine from 135 CE to modern times, and a review of Anti-Semitism. He shared in *Oxford Pamphlets on World Affairs* during the Second World War.

It was at the War's outset that he produced his most circulated publication, written under the pseudonym of John Hadham, drawn from the village of Much Hadham where he then lived. *Good God* aimed to be a theodicy, a justification of divine strategy in the world as determined by reference to human freedom and so, in turn, by the compassionate patience of God.[4] It had a heartening message and was written with an infectious kind of confidence that, somehow, all was in 'omnipotent hand', if only we understand the significance of 'omnipotent restraint'.

What is intriguing about *Good God* is that there is only one passing mention of the Jews and their part in divine strategy. It is an ambiguous passage in that it seems to withdraw with its conclusion what it affirms in its premise. Writing of how human verdicts misread divine strategies (which then have to allow for them), he writes:

> His [God's] plan of the world having inevitably given special responsibilities to societies in certain spots, such as the Jews in Palestine, they proclaimed that He had specially chosen people whom He treated differently from others.[5]

This would seem to imply (a) that Jewish specialness is *not* unique, though the Bible sees it so, and (b) that 'chosenness' is *wrongly* thought of as 'different treatment'. Yet different treatment is so evidently there at Sinai, for 'in Jewry, is God known'. (Psalm 73:1). All Parkes' thinking is caught up in this ambivalent understanding of what covenantal privilege means both for those within it and for those without it.

Oddly too, in *Good God*, he writes that 'God has decided that all knowledge of Himself shall be subjective.'[6] By this he seems to mean that we cannot objectify authority in saying: 'This, or that, is so,' outside things mathematical and logical and via sense experience. Yet is it not precisely such 'objectifying' which happens when 'chosen people', 'promised land', 'Sinai as destiny', 'right to return', are, in fact, asserted as objective realities behind which we may not go to interrogate their credentials? Would not so much be short-circuited in religious encounter if we all conceded that 'Israel My people', 'God in Christ', and all such faith-statements, are 'subjective' in the sense that believing made them so? Then the fact of belief becoming 'fact' would allow us to go beyond 'fact of election', 'fact of the promised land', 'fact of the Cross in the heart of God', to discover how they might tally, or not tally, with criteria from experience, reason, history, mind and soul. These might – or might not – underwrite the degree to which the 'fact of belief' could legitimately be also 'the fact of the matter' in an inclusive, worthy, just and blessed sense. Is not such legitimation, the will to it, the hope of it, the way to it, precisely what dialogue concerns? Even if that aspiration is unattainable as 'the truth', the subjective 'fact of belief' may continue, with the peace of acknowledged disparity, to be the 'truth' for those who subjectively believe it.

But this is to anticipate. In *Good God*, James Parkes set a deeply Christian *confessio*:

[In Jesus] God succeeded in fulfilling the very difficult conditions He had set for Himself [in] putting things right without violating the conditions under which He made the world.

In the Cross God was ready to accept world-responsibility and 'realised the full meaning of human opposition'.[7]

This war-time tonic theology in popular form merged after the War into a resumption of the Christian case, as he saw it, for the vindication of all things Judaic as authentic and indispensable, and for the characterisation of Christianity as a wholly 'Gentile' thing, parallel, distinctive and – its origins apart – insistently non-Jewish. Parkes lived for many years in Barley, Essex, assisting in local parishes and sustaining his unfailing concern for Jews and Judaism. He died in 1981, having bequeathed his books and papers to the University of Southampton as the nucleus of the Parkes Library for Jewish studies. His career had raised all the problems of an educationalist engaged in an enterprise of radical reconciliation long overdue, and reaching into wide areas of Biblical exegesis, liturgical usage, communal prejudice and theological discourse.

iii

Before coming to the central thesis of James Parkes' view of what should obtain between the respective faiths of Jew and Christian, it is well to take stock first of the element of guilt and reparation which underlies it and which explains, in part, his attitude to Zionism and the Palestinians. There are many Christians who, with him, affirm the crucial responsibility of Christian doctrine for the tragedy of Anti-Semitism throughout history since the time of the Gospels. At all costs, Christians must now make good – as far as in them lies – the crime that lies at their door. Any honest relationship with Judaism demands an inquisition, an incrimination, of their own past. It also argues, by way of recompense, a total commitment to the legitimacy of Jewish repossession of Palestine and a complete uncritical assent to the methods by which it was achieved.

In truth, all dialogue must entail what is inwardly accusatory if it is to be outwardly authentic. By virtue of its comprehension of sin, as well as by guilt in its history, Christianity needs self-accusation as much as any. Yet guilt does not always prove a wise counsellor. A true repentance is not served by a false penance.

In Parkes' view the land of Palestine had never been abandoned by the

Jews. This was certainly true in heart and will. But some 25,000 Palestinian Jews in the beginnings of political Zionism were a tiny fraction in
the half million Palestinian Arabs who were assuredly there and not
wanting to be dislodged or relegated.[8] Sheer strength of *force majeure*
can, of course, overturn any actual situation, as it had done in the days of
Joshua. But if contemporary Zionism was not to be a *Joshua redivivus* –
perhaps with more subtle ways – must there not be, in active Zionism and
re-possession, some effective awareness of the injustice entailed? Such
justice could, for Parkes and many like him, be outbalanced by the claim
to divine mandate and the unanswerable plea of the Holocaust. Moreover,
there were many considerations tending to obscure the end-logic of
Zionism, namely a state-establishment which would be power-based and
avowedly Jewish. That logic was not seeking to exchange 'host-nation'
precariousness in Europe for 'host-nation' precariousness in the Arab
East. It was demanding to terminate 'host-nation' circumstance for ever.

Parkes accepted, and promoted, those considerations – the potential
innocence and harmlessness of the repossession if only the sufferers
consented; the actual improvement in their situation by dint of Jewish
enterprise; the ultimate compatibility of the two peoples in the ideal
Jewish State. He argued, in the event in vain, that as the State of Israel
became more 'oriental' and less 'European' the old notion of unwarranted
'intrusion' would pass and Arab-Jew relations would become amicable.[9]
But the final case was the insistence that Palestinian non-reconciliation to
dispossession was just another form of chronic Anti-Semitism, a perverse
refusal to reckon with the Holocaust or to admit such mitigation of it as
Zionism offered. Undergirding all was the warrant of that divine election
and covenant and land-destiny, the character of which – he had urged in
Good God – could only be 'subjective', but which operated as an 'objective' fact, not to be gainsaid by considerations of ethics, equality before
God, justice or human community.

There was doubtless here, as in the 'Christian Zionism' of so many
others, before and since, a will to make reparation to Jewry, to share in
whatever retrieval of the Holocaust might be had. There was no point in
countering such belonging with victims, by allowing that other different
victims were being made, victims who had no part or lot in the original
enormity in Europe. Palestinian rights were not to be pleaded in that
context unless they were ready – as the Balfour Declaration ambiguously
implied[10] – to be docile before all the exigencies of Zionism in realisation.
Need love to Jewry have been so indifferent to love elsewhere, if the love
was to be Christian? or should that question not arise?

The issues here are dangerously fraught with emotion. There is something compulsive about some Christian *Hibbat Zion*, about the love which, at all costs, and even embarrassingly to Jews, must spare no lengths to demonstrate now how truly it has replaced the former crimes. Those lengths entangle it in dark versions of its own past. A man does not devote his whole life, as James Parkes did, to a cause without that cause determining the judgements he makes about the history which generates the motive in the reading of the cause. For 'cause' is both reason and campaign. We turn from how Parkes read Middle East history to how he read the Christian Scriptures, from his active advocacy of a politically recovered Zion to his perception of Judeo-Christian relationships and the doctrine of 'the two covenants'.

iv

It is useful to begin by asking who the Gentiles, the *goyim*, the *ethnoi*, in fact are. Do the terms tell of 'nations', 'peoples', in a sense which must necessarily be inclusive of Jewry in the Davidic, the Maccabean and the Zionist sense? Such 'nations' – broadly speaking – occupy territory, use one language, cherish memories, hallow ancestors, resent exile and desire kings and rulers. All the things that Israel did, and Judea, other peoples do severally yet comparably. The evident fact is that the triangle of God, land and people, of destiny, place and identity, of whence and where and who, belongs impartially with every corporate consciousness, while being distinctively the essentials also of everything Judaic. That truth would include the Jews among the Gentiles.

Or does *Gentiles* mean 'the outsiders', 'the others', 'the at-arm's-length-ones'? Certainly something of that sense is attached to the Hebrew plural *goyim*, despite the noble stress among the prophets of an inclusive humanity and a universal rulership by Yahweh. 'Foreigners' and 'aliens' there have to be in the 'not-us' awareness which belongs inescapably with being anyone. 'We' are not 'they'. But the usage 'Gentiles', when not translated as 'nations', carries the actual potential stigma of an otherness which is more than simply a differential in demography. That 'otherness' – to them – of all but Jews was implicit in the meaning of Sinai and explicit in the whole ethos of Jewry from 'spoiling the Egyptians' to undergoing the Holocaust.

Within the self-understanding of Jewry there were overwhelming reasons why it came to be so. It is urgent at all costs to bring from outside an enormous sympathy with what that necessity imposed upon those

whose vocation, burden and tragedy it inexorably shaped. It was just such
a sympathy for all those three aspects which made James Parkes the
dedicated advocate he was. But did his response truly take its measure?
And, in that question, the further one: Was it 'Christian'? In motive and
intention, Yes! In substance and logic, No!

To see why not, it is necessary to take in what is plainly the broad
consensus of the Christian Scriptures, a consensus which gave them being
and without which they would not exist. It was consensus that had created
'new' community, and community the consensus. The documents and
the 'churches-in-church' alone suffice to explain each other. Both were
believed to be consequential on the prior, generating fact of 'Jesus as the
Christ'.

In that 'fact' of their conviction there were two parts of one equation.
The first was that the Messianic hope had happened in the personality of
Jesus, his word and work, and – as culmination – in his Cross and Passion.
The love that suffers, and suffering, redeems, came to be recognised as
disclosing (as God's Messianic liability must be assumed to do) the nature
and the sovereignty of God. By a Messiahship of that order and of that
import, the range of its relevance had been extended beyond any privacy
of race or place or worth. In *not* being a zealot, a Maccabean, an
apocalyptic, an exclusivist Messiahship, limited by reach, or law, or
election, to *these* and not *those*, it had no less than the world for its
referent. In being a Messiahship of saving wounds and risen love it
constituted God's embrace of all mankind. In being 'the hope of redemption in Israel' it had concerned 'the sin of the whole world'. To the world,
impartially and equally, therefore, it belonged and with mankind it must
be shared.

It is vital to appreciate that this was a fundamentally Jewish decision. It
was a creative verdict on the meaning and mission of Israel itself. A thing
so radical as the sharing of exceptionality, with all its paradox, was
inevitably painful. To forego a separatism chartered, it was believed, in
the unchanging intention of God, could not but be traumatic and full of
tribulation. Sadly, tragically, the reasons for reservation from this new
meaning of themselves, won out, over two centuries, against the offered
logic of this fulfilment into open peoplehood in Messiah Jesus. Tragic
historical circumstances, as well as the inner heartaches of Jewish loyalty,
motivated the self-retention of Israel. The wide horizons were foreclosed.
The churches which had owed themselves to a supreme Jewish initiative
became increasingly Gentile communities, not so much by Gentile intention as by Jewish abnegation of the destiny they proposed. Jewry would

continue in unbroken fidelity to God and Sinai and David and the sages of Yavneh. Exceptionality must abide. Let the Gentiles have their 'God in Christ'.

The heart of James Parkes' Christian conclusion is that Jewry was right. Christianity constitutes God's grace to Gentiles. Jewry is exempt, being 'already there' in the unshared grace of 'the covenant'. There are many minutiae for study and debate within the history we have summarised.[11] The Gospels and the Epistles bear unmistakably the marks of the tensions, the mutual asperities, it aroused. But there can be no doubt that, whatever the painful encounters and the legacies they left in texts and prejudices, there *was* an inclusiveness of Jew and Gentile in the one community of faith and that, therefore, *Gentiles* in the excluding sense as 'the excluded others' had to be an obsolete term. The meaning never was, then or since, to make *Judaioi* an exempted identity. How could it be, since the new embrace where there were 'no more strangers' was itself a Jewish deed understood as Jewish truth?

To hold that it was Jewishly misguided, treacherous, invalid, is to re-write the New Testament. 'God so loved the Gentiles' we must then say, revising John 3:16. It is, then, to disavow the entire intention for the world which is so marked a feature of thought and action within the Christian Scriptures. We do not ease the pain of a bereavement by supposing that the parties never had the relation in the first place which made the loss the pain it was. To be sure, if we hold to that original quality we return our-selves to the full measure of the burden from which the thesis of the 'two covenants' frees us – the burden of positive, mutually cognisant relation-ships now. But that is precisely the reason why we must. Otherwise, the relationship is lacking all its dimensions from the Christian side. Parkes' statement of the alternative case deserves careful summary.

V

Both Judaic Sinai and Christian 'Christ', he insists, are two divine events, equally acts of God, not one displacing or precluding the other. The one is for Jews, the other for Gentiles. It would have been wrong for Jews ever to have accepted to belong with Gentiles 'in Christ'. Indeed, only by *not* doing so, did they ensure what Gentiles could only have by themselves. Christology is in Christianity what 'election' is in Israel, namely, the actual and conceptual safeguarding of the essential thing. It was right that Gentiles should not be bound by ritual law, since 'grace' was theirs, and equally wrong that Jews should be seen as needing inclusion in 'the new creation'. The Torah was never meant to provide the kind of 'justification' which Gentiles need. By means of it, Jews were already there.[12] It is as if Parkes, excluding Jews from the Church *ex hypothesi*, is at pains to find, as it were, 'Christian' reasons for doing so. The task is the more problematic, given that original Christianity[13] lived by reasons to the contrary, reasons for inclusion. It was initially Jews who were doing the including.

His case turns on the thesis that Sinai and Judaism are essentially 'societal' and 'corporate', whereas Christianity is essentially 'personal' and 'individual'. He wrote:

> The profound difference between the two religions...arises
> from their two centres in man as member of community and
> in man as person.[14]

The Church is not a natural, i.e., not an ethnic, tribal or national entity. It does not exist by birth but by 'new birth'. The latter is necessarily personal. The Church is only 'people separately converted', and means a choice of relationship. Based as a new society on this new principle, the Church could not replace a different, divinely constituted order such as Israel was and remains. Parkes believes that the two are in 'creative tension arising out of the dual inheritance of humanity.'[15]

This 'once-born', 'twice-born' distinction, in which in part Parkes follows Martin Buber, hinges on a further distinction whereby the Judaic involves 'trust in...' whereas the Christian requires 'belief that...' in respect of God and His ways in law and grace. The one covenant is a mutuality of trust, the other an acceptance to believe. The two distinctions together run into sharp difficulty which, in a measure, Parkes concedes, at least in allowing that the personal and the societal inter-penetrate in either case. One can hardly recall Maimonides and think that Judaism holds no doctrine and does not 'propose' profoundly *about* God when articulating its undoubted 'trust' *in* Him. Comparably 'Lord, in Thee have I trusted' has been the age-long chorus of the *Te Deum Laudamus*. There is no doxology anywhere without a sense of 'glory', nor of 'glory' without a modicum of concept and creed.

Furthermore, the personal – if we are to heed the Psalms – seems integral to Jewishness. There is also for Parkes' theory, the issue of 'the remnant', and of 'the faithless Jew', the renegade who remains 'once-born', and yet *as if* 'unborn'. The dilemma and the paradox are plain. Clearly, there *are* personal issues within the Judaic 'societal', if a 'remnant' needs to be distinguished from the whole. Indeed, may there not be an inclusive apostasy as indicted in Isaiah 1: 2-6? And what of the utter loneliness of Jeremiah? Walter Eichrodt makes the point:

> The 'Thou shalt...' of the categorical command is directed at the individual Israelite...full citizen or sojourner in Israel. So the punishment of the law is executed only on the guilty person...The man to whom God's demand comes is recognised as a person, an 'I' who cannot be represented or replaced by any other. Even his belonging to the nation cannot provide him with a cover behind which he might retreat from the divine demand.[16]

If 'the people of God' in the Judaic meaning, are *not* depersonalised, is not the Christian trans-ethnic community not capable of togetherness, despite diversity of place, of race and culture? It might even be possible to discern in Israel itself a people who live, not by common blood but only by trust in the divine pledge, in the *dabar*, the Word, by obedience to the will of God. Should we not then be describing something like a 'church'?[17]

James Parkes would seem to have made too patently odd a case in the societal/personal distinction to undergird his separation of the Judaic and the Christian. In the complexities of pondering all that can be meant in 'people of God' there is much in Hebrew prophetic Scriptures to sympathise with what transpired in the pastoral cares of the Epistles, just as there is much in the Christian Scriptures to sympathise with the yearnings of psalm and prophet about soul and body, self and neighbour.[18]

In the life of dialogue which James Parkes lived so ardently, it is important to take adequate stock of the reasons why one faith withholds acknowledgement from another. Among them, in respect of Israel and the Church, the foregoing about community is very relevant. The continuity of Sinai in *its* people unilaterally was felt to be necessary as the one sure prescript for purity of worship and purity of life. Had not Jewish exceptionality, its separatism throughout history, been indispensable to the preservation of true being under God, the probity which mixed marriages, alien cultures, assimilation, and laxity through contiguity, jeopardised and sullied? On this crucial count, was Christian universality not suspect, even mortally perilous? The Gentiles could surely not be risked as 'fellow citizens' in the way the new Gospel proposed. Parkes' position implied that there was point in the premise though he did not accept the conclusion. Being open to 'whosoever will may come' on the basis of faith alone he acknowledged to be feasible with Gentiles, but the society of Torah-election must abstain from it, for the sake of all.[19]

Stress on the societal/personal distinction as a ground for the necessity of 'two covenants' also left unclear how the natural, ethnic, national and cultural entities, which the 'twice-born' 'new covenant' people must obviously comprise, could understand those aspects of their corporate-ness, inside the churches. Could they – or could they not – share the sort of vocation which Judaic identity possessed? The Christian Scriptures saw them as 'bringing their glory and honour' into the new unity in Christ. To think of the churches as only collectives of individuals would be to discount both irreducible fact and the potential of being, in some measure, imitators of Israel as societal instruments for divine purposes. Indeed, the irony is that the great shame of Christian identity in 'nation' and 'politics' lies in what such people-centring of faith has meant in breeding and abetting Anti-Semitism. Christian incorporation has been all too 'socie-tal', despite the personal ground of faith. The 'twice-born' have been all too tragically the 'once-born' in their Greek, Latin, German, Anglo-Saxon, Spanish, white and other, nationality. If the Gentiles were too great a risk was it not that they would act in just those terms of place, race, memory, and language, which Israel had sacrilised in 'election under God'? Would it not have been well if there had been unity to continue what had first been glimpsed – namely, vocation-in-ethnicity for all – rather than have themselves isolated from its first and great exemplar? If only the Jew/Gentile distinction had remained transcended! But that was nineteen centuries ago and the discontinuities have been perpetuated. What, if not James Parkes' thesis, has a contemporary realism to say? Or does it matter?

Before coming, finally, to that question, we had better turn to the suspicion of many that the transcending never happened.

vi

Several issues of scholarship and exegesis attach urgently to the forego-ing and James Parkes had much to write on them. What, we try to ask, *really* happened in the genesis of Christian faith and community? The fact that before, and very much since, Parkes' work Jewish scholarship has been participating, makes it all the more thorough and exciting. Parkes accepted that there *was* a 'Christian' identification of Messiah and that there *was* community in that conviction, meant for Gentiles only. Apart from that last proviso, he is one with traditional Christian faith in what is called 'the Christ-event'. For him, 'the Messianic idea' *was* realised in Jesus but in a manner still leaving Jewry with the ever-open principle of Messianic hope, not fact. There is a puzzle here. Perpetual hope is honourable indeed – the Jewish vocation of waiting for God in a trustful 'not-yet'.[20] As we have seen, however, what brought the urge to world-openness in the first Church was that Messiah, in suffering, had 'redeemed' evil in evil's inclusive moral, and universally human, terms, *not* evil in terms of Roman oppression or Jewish servitude or Gentile hostility. It was this that fitted Jesus-Messiah to be able, and worthy, for universal reach, for undifferentiated human forgiveness. The assumptions which might have been thought valid in reserving Jews from the reach of this Messiahship were precisely the ones that the Jesus of the Church's faith had *not* followed. It would seem strange to justify that faith, as Parkes did, for all but Jewry, since – by so doing – we imply that it could not be right for Gentiles either. Or do we turn the case round and plead that Jesus was not their Messiah (but still the Gentiles') by *not* being and doing what would have been exclusively for them?

That question involves much else. Keeping in mind that Parkes has conceded an actual, authentic Messiah-fulfilment for Gentiles, we have to ask why Jews, despite initiatives which they – or some of them – had pioneered, had finally to demur and declare themselves exempt? Or was there ever such consenting – indeed inaugurating – initiative on Jewish part? Here so much turns on two issues – the Gentiles in Jesus' ministry and the role of Paul. Let us take Paul first, but precede him with the context of both issues.

By context we mean the faith *about* Jesus arising, in the there and then, from faith *in* him. The Christian Scriptures, as noted earlier, *are* community in documentation and documentation via community, and each consequential upon Jesus in some sense, however far debated. Even if we want to say that the real fact was the *kerugma*, the 'gospelling', the 'heralded', it was a *kerugma* with a content, about a person, and out of a conviction. It was not self-generated. We have, therefore, to ask what may, must, Jesus have been to have had this *kerugma*, in this community, in these Scriptures? He was at the centre of all three. We may need to reserve a scepticism about whether rightly so. We will need to try to penetrate the silences from which we do not hear. This is very necessary in honesty to Jewry and its self-exemption. The whole terrain of scholarship is mined with caveats. But, minefield or not, it exists. There *is* this kerugmatic fact of Christ. There are no minutiae which can warrant us ignoring it or disesteeming what it is.

The situation is analogous with one which obtains in Hebrew Scriptures. Sinai and covenant, chosenness and the land, have within them many comparable questions as to the long movement of interpretation which entered into the substance of the belief it transmitted. History telling is always itself a factor in what it transmits as prisms are with light. What happened is told within the significance it acquired in the will to tell at all and in the sustained sequence of the telling. It is so in both parts of the Bible. We have to be historicists in that sense whether it be the Hebrew Scriptures – in respect of which Judaism, and Parkes, certainly are – or whether it be the Christian Scriptures. Whether it be Sinai, Moses, the Deuteronomist and the Chronicler, or Jesus as Christ, Paul, Luke and John, there is a comparable 'coming to mean' which is the context and condition of any scholarship that treats of it. Believing made it what it was because what it was had generated the belief. The task of study is always with that equation.

If Jewry and Judaism, in James Parkes' phrase, rightly survived the initiatives that made Christianity, they did so by disowning the aberrations of Paul. It was Paul, according to Parkes, and not Jesus, who determined the Christian attitude to Judaism.[21] His idea of 'a new creation in Christ' could not obtain within the significance and history of Israel.[22] It was right that such 'new creation' should not continue as a sect within Israel. By the same token it could never contain or perpetuate Israel. To believe that it might was to misconstrue the whole meaning of covenant and election. 'Once he [Paul] included in one body men and women of Jewish and Gentile origin and insisted on considering them equal...a new legal situation arose.'[23]

That new legal situation, occasioned by Paul's position, concerned not only the range of ritual law but also the whole relevance of Torah and community as ground of right relationship with God. The issue here was not some misreading of Torah as sheer 'legalism'. Paul was too sensitive a Pharisee to accuse the law and its custodians of mere formalism. He knew too well its authentic concern for righteousness – as it required such righteousness to be understood, namely as contingent upon its one true and only community metaphysically at Sinai. Paul's inclusion of Gentiles in the Gospel turned not only on Torah's hereditary confinement to Jews but also, and more, on his realisation that Messianic grace and forgiveness had changed the whole rationale of what was confined to whom and who could be included in what.

Paul's often anguished dissociation from 'works of the law' was not rejection of his people as, through Christ, he had come to see them to be:

that is, 'fellow heirs' with all humanity. It was his disaffiliation from what they, and he, had known them to be, prior to this new dispensation. But he was sure that the radical sequence from the one to the other was an authentic fulfilment of what Jewry had hitherto been and which remained retrospectively valid. He was remaining a Jew in believing his Jewishness sealed, fulfilled and enlarged in what he had 'in Christ'. His arguments were often midrashic in their form and passionate in their mingled assurance and distress.

But in the reading of Parkes they were wrong. The suffering Messiah of Pauline grace had his relevance in the non-Judaic realm. Paul's mind, by contrast, was that the symptoms of human need legible in that world had to be read as Jewish also and that an inclusive salvation, not a partitioned one, had sufficed to meet it. In that conviction, for all his idiosyncrasies, Paul was one with the mind of the Church.

What, however, of this interpretation *around* Jesus and the faith *of* Jesus himself? Here the 'quest', as scholarship has long called it, for the *real* Jesus of the ministry is beset by the nature of the available sources. The Gospels – as we have argued above – are about history from faith. They came into being within the stresses of the issues we are discussing between Judaising and Gentilising and bear the marks of it. We can cite passages strongly restrictive to Jewry, others that indicate a warm perception of non-Jews. We can, if we wish, find ways of resolving these merely by forcing on them, either way, our own predilections. We can even justify what seems awkwardly to support or threaten our case by the plea that it is there because it was too authentic to be suppressed or, equally, because it is too exceptional to count. That way we only play textual games.

There was, clearly, apart from Caesarea Philippi and Tyre and Sidon, a territorial confinement of Jesus' ministry to Jews. That could be entirely consistent with a subsequent apostolic enlargement, maybe indispensable to it. Sayings about 'this Gospel being preached in all the world' might still imply Jews only. What seems evident is that Jesus is recorded as surprisingly open to Samaritans, persuadable by Phoenicians, responsive to Romans and accessible to Jewish renegades. It is by no means unlikely that he knew Greek and spoke it, in cosmopolitan Galilee. He had disciples with notably Greek names. Most important of all, his Palestinian-placed parables and his teachings in general had about them a humanity needing no labels. One does not have to ask whether 'A certain man with two sons . . .' is Jew or Gentile, or whether rich fools, wayward sons, yearning fathers, or envious neighbours are Greek or Arab, Galilean or Judean.

Further, careful of Torah as he was, there was also a refreshing freedom from tyranny in respect, for example, of the Sabbath or the sick. We may need to be reticent about how Jesus may have 'intended the Church', since we only have him in the narrative of those who believed they had rightly read his mandate in reaching for the nations. His sense of his Father and his Sonship certainly does not exclude what transpired. It seems fair to conclude that the words about 'making disciples of all nations' at the end of Mark and Matthew[24] commissioned a going that had already begun. We read them as coming from the serving Jesus only as the warrant of the risen Christ.

James Parkes would seem to occupy an ambivalent position as to the will of Jesus and its fulfilled, or falsified, issue in the Church. He disaffiliates from its fulfilment as inclusive of all, Jew and Gentile alike. In any such inclusion it was falsified. For Jesus was committed, as Parkes sees him, to the irreducible continuity of a physical, and metaphysical, Israel. Yet, received as the Incarnate Lord for Gentile relevance, the Church's mission had truly obeyed him.

The question, however, must persist whether the choice must not lie, more radically, between wholly fulfilled or wholly falsified.

vii

But why should a decision matter? In a pragmatic way James Parkes made a notable effort after reconciliation. His inner faith moved into inter-relation and contrived a solution which has found favour with many – though not among those Jews who find it patronising, nor among those Christians who find it disloyal. Parkes had certainly re-written his New Testament: 'Who himself bare our sins [Gentiles speaking]... and ours only.' The 'not ours only' of 1 John 2:2 is made restrictive. The Creed must be re-phrased: 'Who for us non-Jews came down from heaven and was made man.' Most of all, the principle of the entire accessibility of Christian faith was compromised by a declared exemption from its relevance. In effect the possibility of recognition of truth, as distinct from its presentation, seems elided except as a gesture of politeness. The rubric: 'Whosoever will may...' is at an end. For there are those for whom it was not meant.

Yet do these consequences really matter? All is well-intentioned. It is practical relationships we need. The two faiths emphatically persist and, happily, are not to be reduced either to the other. They have the sanction of their very staying power, and the older has suffered so long, so darkly, from the younger. Amity must override doctrine for the sake of the urgent things needing to be done together.[25] Why, then, should Christians be reluctant to relinquish the shape their Scriptures once gave to their debt to things Judaic, now when things Judaic have so long, so tenaciously, so courageously shown their blessed and irreducible identity?

Only because only so can we duly meet each other, neither being disaffiliated from the definition of ourselves. In all dialogue we must attain to *not* concealing what we hold to be distinctively entrusted to our inner faith and, so attaining, allow it to be our positive debt of interpretation into all relating with others. So doing, it is vital to show cause, as far as in us lies, for the necessity of its availability, whatever the pain or tension involved in doing so. The same inner fidelity is assumed on the part of each in their own ultimates. This, and no less, will be the mutual tribute of integrity and the surest contribution to it.

Why, then, is feasibly universal Messianic event the given and desired crux of Christianity? Why do its dimensions in God and man make debt to the world on its account the Christian vocation? Is there a way in which those dimensions may be seen and trusted despite the Christian institution? To that question the halfway house of James Parkes seems to take us. We can best take it further with Rabbi Abraham Heschel of revered memory.

Chapter 6

ABRAHAM J. HESCHEL
(1907 – 1972)

'God's Itinerary in History'

i

It passes through the mystery of Israel, over the ground of the covenant, and the prophets are its map-readers. So the mind of one whose personality and writings are a rich Judaic measure of inner and inter-faith in the contemporary world. Many in Jewry would doubt that he is a representative voice at all.[1] But there is witness on many sides to the impact of his always fervent, often lyrical, reflections on the nature of man and the reality of God. Perhaps it has been that very fervour which displeased dryly academic scholars suspicious of commitment. However, those who must live, as well as ponder, their faith have found his quality of mind and spirit warmly authentic. There is no recent biography of soul more relevant in content and more rewarding in character than that of this wise son of a long Polish Hasidic tradition, this perceptive voice within American religion.

Yet, in a strange way, sustained dialogue is largely wanting in his numerous works. How it is so must be a main concern in this study. Why it is so probably takes us to the assurances of his own cherished identity as Jewish and a characteristic reluctance to have issues which only pain or puzzle made explicit. For that diffidence there must be a courteous respect even – a *unio sympathetica*. Lyricism and contention do not well combine. Yet there is about his eager prose a perplexing unawareness of how close he comes to where Christians find themselves in discerning interpretation of 'God in Christ'. To the point we will return, and stay to wonder what it is about retentiveness which deters us all from the full implications of our perceived sympathies.

The two areas in Heschel to which this observation relates have to do first with the nature of the equation, or non-equation, between the human and the Judaic, between humanity and Jewishness. Heschel seems at times to be yearning, indeed meaning, to equate the two. Yet there is, for him, an insistent unilateralism about Sinai and covenant whatever the bearings it affords him for his doctrine of mankind. The second area belongs with his understanding of the centrality of prophethood and how we must conceive of the relation between revelation and personality, between divine disclosure and human vehicle in the given nature of truth. It is in these two areas that the inner faith of Abraham Heschel has to do profoundly with the will to inter-relation with him on the part of any at large, and of the Christian in particular. The story behind the thinking is our first duty.

ii

Named Abraham Joshua after his grandfather, the Rabbi of Mezbizh in Podolia in the Ukraine (which had been Polish until 1793), the grandson came from a rich patrimony of Judaic piety centred on the legacy of the Baal Shem Tov, 'the Master of the Good Name', (c. 1690-1760) and of Rabbi Menahem Mendl of Kotzk (1787-1859), of whom he wrote in *A Passion for Truth*,[2] and whom he compares with the Christian Soren Kierkegaard (1813-1855) in one of his rare ventures into explicit Jewish/Christian comparison. His own father was the local Rabbi and his mother was a Rabbi's daughter. His boyhood in Warsaw was blessedly alive in the aura of the *Tziddikim*, the saints of Hasidic Judaism, with fervent piety and spiritual lyricism cherishing covenantal identity and practising with intense vitality the fellowship of the synagogue and the benediction of the Sabbath.

Endowed with a questing intelligence and a facility with languages, Heschel reached through and with this heritage into the beckoning of the wider world. His reluctant family allowed him to proceed, at the age of twenty, to the University of Berlin. His father had died when he was ten, his talented mother continuing the *shtitl*, or 'house of prayer' after him. An old Hasid warned him: 'You, holy flesh, do not become polluted from the world.' Polluted he was not. Indeed, he found his teachers in Berlin imprisoned in a kind of philosophy which 'granted God the status of being a logical possibility. But to assume that He had existence would be a crime against epistemology.'[3] Nevertheless he completed his doctoral studies in 1933 enriching his experience and maturing that tenacious hold on holiness and the reality of God which never left him, and abjuring the kind of

scholarship which disowned enthusiasm and wonder. In 1965 he told a
Christian audience in New York of the desperate watershed of his life in
1940.

> I speak as a person who was able to leave Warsaw, the city
> in which I was born, just six weeks before the disaster
> began. My destination was New York, it would have been
> Auschwitz or Treblinka. I am a brand plucked from the fire
> in which my people were burned to death. I am a brand
> plucked from the altar of Satan on which millions of human
> lives were exterminated to evil's greater glory and on which
> so much else was consumed: the divine image of so many
> human beings, many people's faith in the God of justice and
> compassion . . . [4]

He settled initially in Cincinnati, Ohio, where he became Associate
Professor of Jewish Philosophy and Rabbinics at the Hebrew Union
College. He resigned in 1945, became an American citizen, and moved to
be Professor of Jewish Ethics and Mysticism at the Jewish Theological
Seminary of America in New York, where he remained until his death and
where his major publications were written.

He rapidly mastered the English language, acquiring the facility he had
earlier achieved in Polish, Yiddish, Hebrew and German. But there was
tribulation also in his initiation into American experience. He was ap-
palled at the indifference of US Zionist Jews to the plight of the Jews in
Warsaw. 'I had no influence on the leaders of American Jewry,' he
confessed in 1964.[5] Only patiently could he mediate to the complacent,
even brash, assurance of many whom he encountered in American Jewry,
the deep significance of the trauma through which he had passed and the
traditions of soul in which Warsaw Jewry had nourished him. He was
always inwardly the immigrant, as the condition of being so incisively the
mentor and the minister amid American Jewry.

One aspect of that mentorship was the reticence with which he always
spoke of the Holocaust. It is evident in the quotation above. It was not in
him to be a protagonist of anti-Anti-Semitism or to identify the Satanism of
the Nazis with the Christianity of the New Testament. It was, he said,
'foolish to seek finite answers to infinite agony.'[6] He would hold fast to
humility, awe and compassion, recall the words of his grandfather: 'There
are a great many holes in my heart', and fall back on a universality of
concern. The Hasidic bent, or blessed bias, of his mind, never forfeit in

the American scene, was thereby able to infuse his own quality into the width and wealth of its American occasions which never ceased to fascinate and intrigue him. Explaining to an enquirer why he had always donned his hat when he walked in the forest at Vilna, he replied that the forest was a holy place and a Jew does not enter such without covering his head.

iii

Perhaps it was this Hasidic sense of things that explains his diffidence about explicit 'dialogue' with Christians. He was always ready for co-operation in practical terms. His forthright comradeship with Martin Luther King in the campaign against the war in Vietnam and in support of those who refused the draft was staunch and passionate. His participation as a Jewish observer at the Second Vatican Council in Rome was equally wholehearted and efficacious in relation to the mind of the Council on Jewish issues. He found great satisfaction in his appointment as Harry Emerson Fosdick Visiting Professor in 1965/66 at Union Theological Seminary, New York, where he exchanged the liveliest friendship with Reinhold Niebuhr and others. His inaugural lecture there: 'No Religion is an Island', offers clues to his mind. A summary will take us into the two salient concerns which we noted at the outset.

Stressing that 'Anti-Semitism is anti-Christianity and that anti-Christianity is Anti-Semitism', he summoned Jews and Christians to active mutuality in face of all that defied the human meaning enshrined in the Hebrew Bible. Both shared the mystery of 'divine pathos', which he defined as 'a divine reality concerned with the destiny of man which mysteriously impinges upon history'. The two faiths were fellow-sufferers. The choice was 'between inter-faith and inter-nihilism'. Yet 'the community of Israel must always be mindful of the mystery of aloneness and uniqueness of its own being.' The 'long history of mutual contempt' must be outlived in tasks recognised as common, and sensed in the very 'kinship of being human' which must be truly characterised by a humility which confessed 'the tragic insufficiency of human faith'.

Disclaiming the sphere of dogma and ritual, he looked for persons with the same 'fear and trembling'. 'The prerequisite of inter-faith is faith', out of 'the unending drama that began with Abraham', and necessitating 'both communication and separation'. There was deep Jewish pain in what Heschel called 'the conscious or unconscious de-Judaization of Christianity affecting the Church's way of thinking.' 'The children did not rise to call the mother blessed: instead they called the mother blind.'[7] Vital to

Christians was 'the God of Israel'; vital to Jewish being in the western world was the life of Christianity. 'It was the Church which made the Hebrew Scripture available to mankind.' The 'chasm' remained over the divinity and Messiahship of Jesus but hands could be extended across it. Must not 'the all-inclusiveness of God contradict the exclusiveness of any particular religion?' Divergence might be seen as 'a loyal opposition'. 'Missions to Jews' by Christians were a call to 'spiritual suicide'. 'Judaism has allies but no substitutes.' None could 'pretend to be God's account-ant'. The thought of 'Jews as candidates for conversion' had been well repudiated by leading Christian thinkers and should be repudiated by all. The Gentile legitimacy of Christian faith and life had been truly affirmed by Maimonides and numerous other Jewish sages. Let there be 'a resur-rection of sensitivity, a revival of conscience.'[8]

iv

'No Religion is an Island' had dealt, very properly, with only two. There was a certain irony in its moving plea against insularity. The 'continent' of which all are part – what John Donne in the original 'No Man is an Island' called 'the main' – consisted of a single human-ness with a destiny in history under the divine reality, a human-ness lived in humility, wonder and divine pathos. But what if we are also required to acknowledge that 'each religion is a continent'? A gentle readiness to differ about doctrine, while we relate patiently in spirit, may not com-pletely serve the need and the task of being mutual. There is a liability to be carried if the mutuality is to be authentic.

A Passion for Truth, published in 1973 after Heschel's death, con-stituted a Jewish/Christian study far deeper than the inaugural lecture could sustain. Written in his aphoristic style, it mainly concerned a comparison and contrast between Soren Kierkegaard and 'the Kotzker', Rabbi Menahem Mendl, whose austerity and honest despair as 'the Ecclesiastes of his age' had been Heschel's *viaticum* throughout his youth in Warsaw. The alignment was perhaps an unhappy one, since Kierkegaard, for all the authenticity of his intense personalism and his scorn of institutional Christians, could hardly be counted a balanced exponent of Christian faith. Both figures shared sharp melancholy and perennial guilt, disengagement from the world, a sense of the final irrationality of faith and a haunting awareness of obligation under God.

It was natural for Heschel to repudiate Jewishly the 'absolute paradox' in Kierkegaard whereby, allegedly, 'God in human form' became, Christianly, a substitute for 'God in Himself'. There was contrast in the way Jewishness could truly enjoy the world which Kierkegaard must reject as, darkly, – after Kafka – 'a penal establishment'. In Judaism 'just to be is to be holy', so that there is no inherited guilt, no desperate 'Fall'. Jews were never encouraged to hate life, and 'covenant' means that there is place for merit in 'good deeds'. In *Mitzvah* there is an expectation to fulfil, not a guilt to atone. 'Only vulgar minds regarded the accumulation of merits as promissory notes.'[9]

Heschel's last major work, a two-volume study in Yiddish of Rabbi Menahem Mendl, who 'carried anger as a flint bears fire',[10] lay behind *A Passion for Truth*, and made it something of a final testament. It presents more detailed inter-theology than Heschel normally allowed himself. But it is perplexing why the actual figure of Jesus plays so scant a part in his writing, there and everywhere. He kindled to a Danish Christian existentialist as one who shared, if in imbalance, the features he most admired in the Kotzker – cryptic writing, the pedagogical device of sarcasm, the feel of faith as demand and not as consolation, the scorn of the spiritually vapid, and the quest for 'a true disciple'. We are the poorer from the fact that a superb exponent of eirenicism in faith did not significantly tell the fruits of that capacity in reflection on the New Testament, on the 'meek and lowly of heart' in Beatitudes and travail, as held in Jewish memories in the first century. Kierkegaard by all means: but why not Galilee, the wilderness and Gethsemane? There is a pain here for which, no doubt, long Christian history is liable. In being a matter of regret, it cannot well be a matter of reproach.

v

Yet, all the time, the question of Jesus and of the Christian understanding of his significance within the divine pathos, which Abraham Heschel sets so squarely at the heart of all theology, is everywhere latent and, with its latency, is the further question why it should be so. A very real inter-faith is there, but it demurs from being explicit and explored. Our best proceeding into this central feature of Heschel's inner faith will be to examine its possible origin in his perception of Judaic man and then trace it more fully in his monumental work: *The Prophets*.

Israel, as 'a people dwelling apart, not reckoned among the nations',[11] finds as moving an exposition in Heschel as anywhere in Judaica, ancient or contemporary. The divine destiny of the Jew is read as index to the human meaning *per se*. In *Who is Man?* (1965); *Man's Quest for God*

(1954); *God in Search of Man, A Philosophy of Judaism* (1955); *Man is not Alone, A Philosophy of Religion* (1951), he developed in eloquent sequence his thoughts on being human. There is no doubt of the inclusiveness of his anthropology. 'God's itinerary in history' belongs with all cultures and passes through all territory. Yet the covenantal situation that hallows all human history has its norm in that which is abnormal – in the mystery of Jewry. The humanism is Biblical and, as such, ambivalent. For, at the heart of a universal mercy, there is a privileged possession. 'You cannot find Him [God] in the answer, if you ignore Him in the question,' Heschel wrote.[12] The question of God is surely paramount in the answer of 'election'.

He writes repeatedly about 'the awareness of God's relationship to His people and to all men' (p.216). Yet he is referring to 'the Holy One of Israel', who is, at the same time, 'intimately involved in the history of man' (p.225). 'The covenant is an extraordinary act, establishing a reciprocal relation between God and Man' (p.230). But which men, if it is 'extraordinary'? He lists, in defining 'pathos', 'the relation between God and man, the correlation of Creator and creation, the dialogue between the Holy One of Israel and His people' (p.231). Are the first and the third equatable within the common mediation of the second?[13] He writes in one sequence of what is 'love of the fathers' in Deuteronomy 4:37 and 10:15, and 'God's concern for all men'.

The ardour within his conviction is deeply convincing. But what of the logic? 'In the mystery of prophecy we are in the presence of the central story of mankind' (p.409). Yet so much of the burden of prophethood has to do with where 'wisdom (uniquely) pitched its tent in Israel'. The universality of the great writing prophets is always centred in the particularity of distinctive 'chosen-ness'. 'Where else,' he asks, 'did a divine idea sanctify history?' (p.421). Yet Heschel himself is magnificently translating that sanctity into a common benediction of *all* history; there is for all mankind a divine presence. It consists in the demand to be worthy of it. 'The transcendence... in man's experience is divine expectation. God reaches us as a claim.'[14] Nature, in its power, loveliness and grandeur, is 'the silent allusion of things to a meaning greater than themselves' and man disintegrates his humanity if he fails to respond or merely 'instrumentalises the world'.[15] For humanity stands in a relation to God which we may betray but not sever.

These perceptions can only be true if they are true everywhere. Yet how do they belong with exceptionality? Does the latter exemplify? intensify? particularise? If so, may not those verbs belong wherever there is a will to them? In what does 'the mystery of Israel' consist within an inclusive theology of the human as human?

The question persists in Abraham Heschel's understanding of Zionism in his: *Israel: An Echo of Eternity*, published three years before his death. Here his lyricism reaches a telling climax. The repossession of old Jerusalem in 1967 was 'an unbelievable event in which the presence of the holy burst forth.' The air of the charismatic city is 'radiant with holiness in time'. He saw in the State of Israel what enabled Jews 'to bear Auschwitz without radical despair', 'a carrying out of a divine imperative'. Its people had been 'plucked from the corroding influence of assimilation.' In the deeds of the settlers 'God was at home in the world.' Only in 1967 had he realised how deeply Jewish he was. God had no need to 'apologise for His audacity in performing wonders in 1967.' 'Messianic redemption' was necessarily 'political redemption'. Thanks to the State of Israel 'the Messianic promise' had become 'plausible'.[16]

It is a measure of the exaltation of 1967 that a mind so alive to divine presence in pathos as Heschel's should have related to events with exuberance. For he had consistently sought to surmount Jewish labels – Orthodox, Conservative, Reform, Zionist – and belong, like a good Hasid, with Abraham, Moses, Isaiah and Jeremiah. He did not survive to ponder 1982 and Begin and Sharon in the invasion of Lebanon. But he shared, as measured in *Israel, An Echo of Eternity*, that persuasion about political Zionism which 1967 brought to pass in many who had long been unpersuaded about it, or even sensed in it a fundamental misreading of the nature of Judaism. Could he truly have meant, in the emotion of the time, that 'Amalek was Führer', aligning the ancient enmity of Exodus 17:16 ('The Lord at war with Amalek from generation to generation') with Palestinian exiles and their nationhood with the Nazis?[17] Or was he not, for the time being, forbearing to ask with his customary compassion: 'Who is Man?' To be sure, his vision of 'holiness' demanded what he called 'concreteness', such as the wells, the roads, the hoes, the spades, the watchtowers of the *Aliyah* settlers demonstrated. But the Irgun and the Stern Gang were 'concrete' too.

vi

'Being a Jew,' Heschel had insisted in *A Passion for Truth* 'is struggle.' It was 'an exclusivity intent on God', disentangling oneself from enslavement to the self,[18] for ever self-critical, as the beloved Kotzker always taught. The sacred could never be guaranteed by politics or ideology, but only in the secret places of the heart. Territory could neither ensure it nor imprison it. The very *Shechinah* could go into exile.

With those thoughts we come to the great writing prophets of Israel and, in them, to Abraham Heschel's most outstanding literary work, *The Prophets*. Leaving the particular-Judaic/universal-human theme in him unresolved, we turn to this *magnum opus*. Chapters 1 to 18 and Chapter 28 are a passionate celebration of prophethood in Israel. The more technical discussion of prophetism in Chapters 19 to 27 is an updated version of his 1933 doctoral thesis in the University of Berlin.[19] Here there is careful erudition yet it is at times overtly pleading the *à priori* from which it proceeds. It is surprising how completely he excludes the person of Muhammad from his survey of almost world-wide manifestations, in some sense, of prophetism. The Qur'an (p.468) and Muhammad (p.440) have each a single mention, while Zoroaster is dismissed as 'a spark lost in the darkness' (p.472).

The Biblical prophets he expounds are Amos, Hosea, the two Isaiahs, Micah, Habakkuk, and Jeremiah. He notes their passion against injustice and on behalf of the poor, their accusation of political expediency and faithlessness, their repudiation of 'professional' soothsayers and *nabiim*, the significance of their parabolic actions and their sense of the moral realities of history. But, for Heschel, their supreme quality is their personification, almost, of the divine compassion by virtue of their 'union of sympathy' with divine mind. It is here that – as we will argue – there is crucial relevance to the meaning of Christian faith though – sadly – the *unio sympathetica* (if we may so speak) on Heschel's part with the Christian witness of the Incarnation is always and only hidden. He would doubtless have shrunk from the implications as wholly incompatible with all his loyalties. Even so, the 'hidden Christ' is there, a discernible sequence from the role within the very being of God which Heschel finds in the nature of Hebrew prophethood. If the case can be here sustained, it may go far to explain why he is silent about 'the prophet of Nazareth of Galilee'. Jesus, in fact, finds a single mention (p.300) in a discussion of Marcion, and in two footnotes inconsequentially. But, anonymously and potentially, his is 'a real presence'. If Heschel shared the longstanding, readily understandable, reluctance of Jewish writers to reckon with Jesus because of the Christian company Jesus traditionally keeps, as seems to have been clearly the case, the unnamed presence we are arguing becomes the more impressive and grateful. If that general reluctance is now, happily, being left behind in a lively flow of Jewish scholarship on Jesus and the origins of Christianity, nowhere is it less deliberately or more unconsciously so than in Abraham Heschel. To trace the fact makes for a remarkable biography of dialogue. For life is in every page of Heschel on 'the prophets'.

That, indeed, for some readers, is part of the problem. The writer is too enthusiastic for tame scholarship. His style is often more like the *dicta* of the Hasidim than the caution of the researcher. He reads often like the preacher. He impresses the critic as being 'partisan'. He has a case to make which marshals objections only like targets to demolish. He moves at times like a poet cherishing the marriage of phrase with point and at times he is urgently persuasive in being also perplexing. What, for example, should we understand from: 'It is man who is an experience of God?' (p.419). Or is he fair to the self-abnegating quest of many mystics when he writes:

> While the ecstatic disregards consciousness in order to enrich the self, the prophet disregards the self and enriches his consciousness. (p.360).

Yet his love of the balanced sentence and of paradox can be deeply illuminating.

> The prophet does not find God in his mind as object, but finds himself an object in God's mind...To think of things is to have a concept within the mind, while to think of Him is like being surrounded by His thinking. Thus, to know him is to be known by Him. (p.485).

The conclusion there is an unconscious echo of 1 Corinthians 13:12, and Galatians 4:9.

Style apart, the reader of *The Prophets* is soon aware that Heschel does not follow the historic-critical method of exploring the text in order to uncover the various strata of editorial processes supposedly in its composition. He does not concern himself with documentary criticism, dissecting and rearranging as speculation might suggest. He takes the whole as he finds it and responds to its impact as a thing of integrity. Analysts may well quarrel with this – to them – naîveté but they have a naîveté of their own when they only conclude with bits and pieces, and conjecture. Heschel seeks 'the many splendour'd thing'.

Finding it, of course, does require a careful locating of the times and situations. He carefully relates Amos to Jereboam II, Isaiah to Uzziah and

Jeremiah to Josiah and his three successor kings in Judah. It is history which yields the clues by which prophetic insight interprets the mind and purpose of God. Even to the point of apparent treachery to national interests the prophets proclaim the innate corruptibility of power as the ever-menacing context of the priority of justice. The accountability of all nations to one God gives birth to the idea of one history (p.170). It also leads to the perpetual contingency of thrones and cultures, empires and crowns – the contingency which liberates the prophets from panic fears and informs their moral perspective.

But can we go on to say with Heschel that, for the prophets, 'history...is a record of God's experience'? (p.172). The question is a way into the central theme of divine pathos. The term needs careful definition. Since 'history is where God is defied' (p.168) it is also where God is involved. This divine engagement in and with the human scene-in-time is, by its very nature, never a neutrality and, therefore, never an immunity. Nor is it, for Hebrew faith, a mere ethical monotheism, arbitrating remotely in moral punitive judgement. It can only be understood as perpetual concern, indeed liability, on the part of God. So much is explicit in the Biblical doctrines of creation and of covenant – doctrines understood as mutually related. 'Divine ethos does not operate without divine pathos.' (p.218). 'God's intimate relatedness to man...puts all life in a divine perspective, in which the rights of men become, as it were, divine prerogatives. Man stands under God's concern.' (p.219). The being of God is 'transitive' – goes across to manhood, is active in human relatedness. 'What do we mean,' Heschel asks, 'when we employ the word "God"?' After reviewing a variety of Greek and other answers, he opts for 'a unity of conscious acts, of creating, demanding, expressing and responding.' (pp.274, 278).

Biblical religion sees in creation an intentionality, a stake in mankind. By creation God becomes a party with an interest, satisfying like a creative artist a 'want' and a 'need'. This has to been seen as 'a divine situation' rather than, abstractly, as 'a divine attribute'. It is the outward directedness of divine power and mercy, by which man is the constant divine concern, and where both love and wrath are present. On God's side it is a steadfastness of mutuality. God is understood in terms of how He acts.

Here, of course, we are on common Christian and Quranic, as well as Judaic, ground. There is, within it, a crucial question of ontology in respect of which – as critics might argue – Heschel adopts a sublime positivism. All in their philosophy, theology, or agnosticism, begin in some sense with 'being'. We all ask: 'Why?' and some will decide that the question has no answer. Or, with Heschel, we can incorporate the question 'Why?' into being itself and conclude that, within what is coming into being, there is a sustaining concern that it should – which is the core of what we mean by 'creation'. So understood, creation takes us directly to 'man', who is both the source of the question 'Why?' and the realm of its relevance.

This formulation is, perhaps, more abstract than Heschel would approve. But it enshrines his basic theme of divine pathos. We have really reversed Feuerbach and his notion of ideas of the divine as simply the projection of the subjective needs of man, whereby God is the satisfaction of human wishes. Here, utterly contrary, man is objectively the realm of the divine, transitively present in the will to be undertaken.

The Hebrew Scripture, the New Testament and the Qur'an, are at one in this understanding, though the third is averse to the explicit corollary, namely the self-limitation present in this divine creativity. Creation is an act of self-limitation. Christians have always seen in it a *kenosis*, a condescension into the limits of man. The notion of divine concern and care – dominant in Heschel – makes these the form of divine power, the criteria by which omnipotence is understood. Omnipotence is not contradicted by them. For they are its own freely opted sphere. Nor does omnipotence contradict them as if it were mindless of its willed ends. The whole notion of omnipotence has, in fact, to be rightly understood, not as the ability to do anything, however arbitrary, however whimsical, but the ability to be undefeated in its chosen ends – ends turning on the creaturehood that is their sphere.

What is thus the manifestation of God's will cannot be regarded as a violation of His omnipotence. Man's limits have become God's self-limitation. To deny this would truly be to limit God simply by denying His capacity for concern – indeed His liberty to create such as we are as His creatures.

Read historically, this situation spells divine pathos. Heschel sees covenant, election, apostasy, exile, renewal – in Israel – as 'God's experience'. He refuses to read in that conviction any humiliation of God. There is a reading of Psalm 18:35 'When you humble me you make me great,' which sustains his case, if we read, as of God: 'You show me how great You are by Your humbling of Yourself.' Suffering thus has its place in the nature of God. Hosea can read the divine solicitude and pain in his own experience of the anguish of betrayal. The presence of divine pathos is read in the condition of the slaves in Egypt. The Exodus itself is 'the itinerary of God'. 'In all their affliction, He was afflicted,' (Isaiah 63:9) is inscribed across the saga of Israel.

vii

It is the glory and the agony of the prophets that they share – indeed live – this divine pathos. Their response to God so known is costly sympathy.

> To the prophet the pathos is the predominant and staggering aspect in what he encounters...the inner, personal iden-tification of the prophet with the divine pathos is...the central feature of his own life...He is convulsed by it to the depths of his soul. His service to the divine word is not carried out through mental appropriation, but through the harmony of his being with its fundamental intention and emotional content. (pp.307/08).

Heschel's case here may be illustrated by an observation from else-where, asking in relation to Jeremiah, how at many points, one is to know whether it is he or Yahweh speaking. No connectors allow the reader to say for sure. There is a constant mingling of the divine and the prophetic *persona*. God's sorrow and the prophet's suffering are two sides of the same coin. The first and the third pronouns mingle continually.[20]

There is, therefore, something vicarious about prophethood, the state of being-on-behalf-of God. The image of 'the suffering servant' clearly belongs in mysterious ways in this context. It is by his word from God that the prophet shows evil its own image. In his absence evil might not know itself; in his presence it is accused. If popular deafness is prophetic anxiety, popular enmity is prophetic tribulation. Inasmuch as there is never a 'Thus saith the Lord', without a speaking human voice, so there is never a flouting of the Lord which is not a human distress. This is the life-setting of the Biblical prophets, as Heschel reads their significance. In active co-operation with God, 'they intensify the capacity for suffering', both in themselves and in their hearers (p.179). 'No stigma attaches to (such) pathos.' (p.258). On the contrary, it is the very pride of consecra-tion to divine ends.

As such it may well be the theme of the deepest spiritual transaction of mind between the Judaic and the Christian. The significance of Abraham Heschel in this context is to have adumbrated so clearly, if unwittingly, the Christian reading of 'the Word made flesh' in 'the prophet of Nazareth'.

The term 'Incarnation' may be repellent, though Jacob Neusner has freely used it in respect of what he sees, as a loyal Jew, in the human (i.e. 'anthropic') character of the divine Torah.[21] But the logic via prophethood to incarnation has long been central to Christian thinking and Heschel has powerfully seconded it in his presentation in *The Prophets*.

Before attempting to do justice to his veto, it is well to see how almost incarnational much of his language is. History as 'God's experience', Israel as 'an event in the being of God' are phrases well fitted to what Paul called 'God in Christ'. 'Harmony of being with the intention of the divine word' describes the personality in the Gospels as Christians read them – and composed them, 'the pathos of God overwhelming his inner life, his thoughts, feelings, wishes and hopes [in] possession of his heart and mind' (p.308). Or again:

> He is effective, not merely by his word and deed, but also by the force of his attitude which is sensed by his contemporaries to be the manifestation of his inner accord with God. (p.310).

'It is a whole way of being' (p.311); . . . 'being in agreement with the will of God' (p.313); 'His feeling is a fellow-feeling with God' (p.314); 'To feel the divine pathos as one feels one's own state of the soul' (p.319) – all these denote closely what the New Testament portrays as the Son-in-the-Servant in Jesus. Or further:

> . . . interior life . . . formed by the pathos of God . . . is *theomorphic* . . . a divine concern becomes a human passion, is fulfilment of transcendence . . . an identity between the private and the divine. (p.319).

Theomorphic here is precisely what Paul has in Philippians 2:6. 'Prophecy consists,' Heschel writes, 'of a revelation of God and a co-revelation of man' (p.366 and 419).

It must be said here that one needs to be alert to the incarnational mystery implicit in *all* belief in inspiration as well as in revelation, even where there is most resistance to any claim as to the fact of it. If one reads the personality of Jesus – as the New Testament does – as infused with divine ends in compassion and suffering, and those ends realised in the human personality, that, in essentials, *is* incarnation. And it is manifestly akin to the personal surrender into divine employ which Heschel identifies as prophethood. Moreover, in the prophet, who he is becomes, in some sense, crucial to what he conveys. What is he saying? Why does he speak? Where is his warrant? are all questions which tend, inevitably into: 'Who *is* he?' That was how it was with 'the prophet of Nazareth' in the full perspective of coming to terms with him. Perhaps it is important, in our Judaic/Christian relationships, that we escape together from terms which are chronically perverse to either of us, in order to come to grips with what both of us can *mean*. We still have on hand the traditional exclusivity of the Incarnation. But we can most hopefully undertake that task when we have acknowledged how close Heschel is to 'the Word made flesh, dwelling, tabernacled, among us' that we might behold glory. And we have to negotiate also the other exclusivity of peoplehood to God.

viii

How close Heschel is...? How far, surely, he must insist, from any 'Word made flesh'. His reasons are plain. Divine pathos, he explains, is not of the divine essence. It is 'functional' not 'substantial' (p.231).

> God never reveals Himself. He is above and beyond all revelation. He discloses only a word. He never unveils His essence: He communicates only ...Man knows the word of revelation, but not the Self-revelation of God. He experiences no vision of God's essence, only a vision of appearance. A subject of pathos, God himself is not pathos. (pp.435 and 485).

What is Heschel concerned to reserve to God here? Perhaps Christians should defer to his 'negative theology': ('God is not pathos'): it has some currency in Christian quarters also. All worship must allow 'beyond-ness'. But is the 'beyond-ness'(while remaining such) consistent with the pathos? If we can be sure the answer is Yes! then, in effect, we *know* what identifies the ultimate. If the answer is No! then we are engaged in verbal games, perhaps in delusion and the absurd.

There is, here, a fascinating point which explains Heschel's lively interest in Marcion. There has long been an impulse in Semitic theism to do just what Abraham Heschel has done in insisting on this 'otherness' beyond what is 'given' in 'manifestation'. Sometimes it was in the interests of divine sublimity, sometimes of the impassibility of God. For these double reasons gnostics and Christian heretics of the first and subsequent three centuries, sought to distinguish between 'God in Himself' and 'God in Christ', between 'essence' and 'disclosure'. To immunise the divine in Jesus from 'actual' flesh or from 'actual' suffering, he must be thought of either as somehow less than God or as 'God in a charade'. The orthodox Christian faith, through much tribulation, firmly resisted these strains of thought, and affirmed unequivocally the actuality of 'the Word made flesh', as 'very God and very man', in Christ.

Marcion's heretical 'reduction' of Jesus to a sort of 'lesser than God' status was precisely to preserve that divine 'essence' – immune to pathos – which is Heschel's concern. Ironically, it entailed Marcion's relegation of 'the Old Testament God' to a vindictive kind of 'otherness', while Jesus stood for 'divine compassion'. That was a damnable distinction which Heschel's theology, and Judaic loyalty, were bound to repudiate – a repudiation the Church shared (pp.299-305). But can he, or we, truly do so, if we distinguish between 'God in His essence' and 'God in His word[s]' with 'pathos' only 'functional' in the latter?[22] By the logic of his proper repudiation of Marcion, Heschel would seem to have a vital stake in the classical Christian understanding of the Incarnation as veritably 'divine Self-revelation' within history and via human personality. For the concern of that understanding has always been to 'substantiate' the reality of a divine passion, and the final dependability of divine revelation.

But should it, need it, matter that Heschel finds pathos giving us only the 'function' of God and the New Testament has it definitive of the being of God since 'God is love'? Can we not acquiesce in the disparity, in view of the immense territory of faith we share in common? Should 'Incarnation' be a distancing formula? Certain reflections are necessary before we ought to say a firm Yes! to the middle question, a clear No! to the others.

ix

Judaism in general is far from being unanimously with Abraham Heschel and he would himself probably demur on grounds apart from theology. Then there is the exclusivity of *the* Incarnation as Christian faith confesses it. Here because of a certain confusion in *The Prophets* on a relevant point, there is need to take further the interplay of the divine compassion and the human travail within prophetic personality.

We have seen that suffering is entailed wherever there are spokesmen for God who are in no sense mere 'microphones' for God but living, agonising figures in the human scene. What tragically they undergo is because of what vicariously for God they undertake. If the mission is reciprocal – God's and theirs – must not the entail also be? Divine pathos does not become self-exempting when the tragic supervenes in prophetic fidelity to its purposes. It was this conviction which enabled the first Christians to read in the suffering of Jesus the pattern of God's action in the evil of the world. They saw the evil in his being rejected to be representative of 'the sin of the world'. They interpreted his suffering travail as the way God meets it and, in forgiveness, overcomes it. Or, in other language, they took it for Messiahship patterned and Messiahship achieved, and they confessed that 'God was in Christ (this Jesus) reconciling the world to Himself'. Here, essentially, was the divine pathos. As Heschel himself finely says: 'Mystery is not the ultimate. Mystery is surpassed by meaning. Beyond the darkness is righteousness.' (p.214).[23]

However, it is hard to discern whether he truly perceived what the Christian faith holds in this context. For when he adverts to 'passion plays' and *imitatio* he has in mind the mourning for Tammuz, or 'vegetation-resurrection', and disallows divine suffering (pp.320ff.). Oddly, he dismisses mystical *imitatio* as 'remote from history' (p.322), when 'history' – especially via the Eucharist – is its very focus.

The Cross of Jesus, then, at the heart of Incarnation makes concrete, qualitatively, representatively, a translation of divine pathos into the world as realism, most of all prophetic realism, knows it to be. Its being 'once and for all' might be likened (as it was in the Epistles of the New Testament) to the Exodus, as that which forever constitutes identity and holds present and future in its past meaning. As such it is eminently reproducible, in its will to love, to suffer and to forgive, but only so by its being, there and then, what decisively it was.

In a single footnote, Abraham Heschel refers to H. Wheeler Robinson's *Redemption and Revelation*. Had he known the same writer's threefold study: *The Cross of Job* (1916), *The Cross of Jeremiah* (1925), *The Cross of the Servant* (1955), he would have found the titles uncongenial. But he would have been at home in their measure of the inter-penetration of 'God and man as one thought', the core, alike, of his own, and the other's, theology. Robinson wrote:

> Jeremiah feels himself to have been a thought of God, before the divine hands shaped his limbs... The centre of gravity is transferred from his own heart to God's. The moral and spiritual struggle is always between some thought of God concerning us and that rival thought of ourselves

which challenges His. From such a conflict alone is the prize
of high and precious truth wrested...In him we begin to
learn that a *life* is the fullest revelation of truth.[24]

Such kinship of mind does not resolve all problems but it leaves us seeing
each other by a shared criterion which can contain them 'for the time
being'.

X

What, finally, of the fact, earlier noted and deferred, that Abraham
Heschel chooses not to explore the Christian bearings of his characteristic
thinking, that he leaves so much to silence about relationships he might
have been expected to take up? The reasons could not be intellectual. For
nothing could deter his ample intelligence and his eager aptitude for
belonging cordially with experience, as one for whom nothing need be
alien. His doctoral writing cast a wide net within its academic liability, as
the footnotes indicate in *The Prophets*. It is, puzzlingly, the Semitic faiths
outside Judaism that he is least ready to discuss. He exhibits a certain
animus against mysticism, despite his Hasidic bent of mind. His thinking
seems to by-pass the New Testament.

The wise reader will certainly look for a temperamental, not a logical,
reason, for an explanation in the psyche rather than in the mind. It is as
if emotions are too near the surface. The spirit fears to be tempted into
abandonment of deliberate restraint. We have noted his reticence about
the Holocaust, a theme that defies interpreters, imposing silence lest contention fail its measure. There is about him a guardedness – not that of the
Jew who senses threat in every circumstance, but of one who knows the
deep precariousness of Jewishness in being also indestructible. Does this
anxious confidence explain the strange form in which he put the question
to his Christian audience in 1965:

> Is it really the will of God that there be no more Judaism in
> the world? ...Would it really be *ad majorem Dei gloriam*
> to have a world without Jews?[25]

as if any of his listeners would think the answer could be Yes!

What emerges, as in Franz Rosenzweig, is the deep, cherished and
sanctified consciousness of identity which belongs with being Jewish, and
to which the Christian community of faith seems such a threat because in

a twin conviction it finds Messiahship in the travail of Jesus and opens out peoplehood in God to all who will. The Christian calling is not to commit the most culpable anti-Judaism of all by either tacitly or avowedly holding Jewry essentially excluded from the reach of that conviction. But it can only fulfil its proper 'inclusivity' under God in a readiness to rejoice in those present heirs of its own antecedents who, like Abraham Heschel, are 'the rock from whence it was hewn'. Mutual celebration wherever we can is a surer thing than the 'other-ing' of controversy. The 'love of the fathers' which Heschel fervently tells in all his writings is a unifying emotion for all who own them, whether uniquely in the flesh or kindredly in the Spirit.

Chapter 7

ISMA'IL AL-FARUQI
(1921 – 1986)

'Divine Will, Human Faith, and No Place for Paradox'

i

'The Muslim is perpetually mobilised to bring about the actualisation of the absolute on earth.' For the conviction the Muslim holds of the divine unity 'is crushingly compelling by its own evidence that a man must acquiesce in it as to the conclusion of a geometrical theorem.'[1] This robust, confident, programmatic religion – categorically ultimate and politically realisable, given the prerequisites – is a far cry from the mind of the Spanish Christian Miguel de Unamuno, for whom it was 'not rational necessity but vital anguish' that impelled him to belief in God. Yet, in his strong Islamic conviction of a religion, as the Qur'an has it, in which 'there is nothing dubious', either as to content or exercise, Isma'il al-Faruqi is vigorously representative of Islam and highly articulate in being so.

He is, therefore, a very proper subject for the biography of dialogue, in which he engaged in trenchant fashion for some thirty years as a Palestinian exile in the West. His forthrightness made him a very useful foil for the testing and teasing of ideas not only with outsiders to his faith but also within its ranks. There was a certain combativeness about his mind which made him ready for encounter with a relish for its stimulus and its exaggerations. Such a controversialist searches mere mental courtesies and requires rigour of mind as well as long-suffering in the other party. Both are virtues tending to be their best when they are most provoked. It will be fair to say that there are few Muslims in the realm of Muslim, Jewish, Christian dialogue who, from mid- to late twentieth century, have served and stirred it more spiritedly than Isma'il al-Faruqi. The three other

127

Muslim figures to follow here will be in truer perspective if we first take the measure of the lively orthodoxy of which Al-Faruqi was the voice – albeit with idiosyncrasies which both endear and exasperate. His protests against paradox, especially as he thought he saw Christians exploiting it, and his impatience with much in mysticism anywhere, were characteristic features of his thought, as was also his habit of inventing neologisms and using them sometimes in denigration of what he made them signify. Yet all he wrote was sustained by the rational realism, the total adequacy to the human situation, of Islam as he understood it to be. To reckon with him, therefore, is to have the measure of a contemporary, Arab, intellectual presentation of Islam, strong both on theory and programme, and responsive to the perceived issues posed by the relationship with Jews and Christians.

ii

If Isma‘il al-Faruqi felt no need of a theodicy, or a 'justification of God', in his theology, the dimension of tragedy loomed large in his biography. Born of Sunni Muslim parents in January 1921, in the coastal region of Jaffa, Palestine, his youth was clouded by the gathering tensions aroused by the steady build-up of Jewish immigration and the suspicions about ultimate intentions which beset the inter-War period of the British Mandate. The logic of Zionism implied more than 'the national home *in* Palestine', which the Mandatory Power was required to interpret and to implement. However, the intention of statehood only emerged unmistakably as the Second World War concluded. The patrimony of the Faruqi family lay squarely within the area of the partition assigned to be Israel in late 1947 by vote of the UNO. It was completely lost to them in the ensuing conflict as the Jaffa/Ramleh region lay within the new State declared in May 1948. It was never recovered. The loss of ancestral property and security left an abiding scar on the psyche of the young nationalist, then in his twenties. His people became refugees and his education at the American University of Beirut was interrupted through family exigencies.

The trauma of those events needs to be understood in any reckoning with his religious thought. It was as if the need to defy adversity, rather than to interpret it, dominated his thoughts. When he had made his way to the United States, he contrived through some years of business acumen to equip himself financially for a resumed career in academic study, with a penchant for research into the relations of Semitic faiths. In this he was assisted by the lately formed Institute for Islamic Studies within McGill University, Montreal, Canada, inaugurated by Wilfred Cantwell Smith. Here began Al-Faruqi's assessments of Judaism and Christianity in the light of his reading of Islam – studies which took shape in his two early publications: *'Urubah and Religion* and *Christian Ethics.*[2] The ideas developed in these two books were further accented and refined in a vigorous sequence of articles and pieces in the seventies during his academic appointments in the University of Syracuse and Temple University, Philadelphia, when he was active in Muslim/Christian dialogue in several ecumenical conferences and seminars. In 1979 he published *Islam*, an introductory, but significant, manual on the faith for students.[3] But his crowning writing achievement was *The Cultural Atlas of Islam*, in co-operation with his wife, Lois Lamya al-Faruqi, an expert in Islamic Art and Architecture.[4] Its publication almost coincided with their tragic deaths at the hands of an armed intruder in their home in Philadelphia. The pain and shock of that tragedy were deeply felt through the wide circle of their friends and associates who had shared in mental and spiritual exchange through three decades in the Middle East, Europe and America. The sorrow which had encompassed his youth took dire shape in his passing and makes any study of his mind a tribute of soul as well as a quest into perplexity. For the strange vulnerability which marked his life – however much one may be urged to exclude it – must be within the reckoning of a theology which aspires to be faithful to life as well as competent with ideas and concepts.

It would not be disloyal to his memory to surmise that beneath the assurance and verve of his pen there lay a deep concern for the vulnerability of Islam itself. The general reader of his work might not perceive this. For his advocacy of his faith was always trenchant and assured. But in the years before his death be became increasingly involved with the vision of 'an Islamicisation of all knowledge'. He was acutely aware of the degree to which European or western assumptions dominated studies of sociology, psychology and ethics, and how Muslim institutions of higher learning were liable to register lapses from traditional faith within the student body because of the fascination – or the dominance – of 'secular' habits of mind and the attitudes of technology. Rather than engage with the parallel experience of Christian theology and education with their earlier awareness of the incidence of the same problems, Al-Faruqi sought to comprehend the whole issue as requiring, and admitting of, an Islamicisation of the entire educational curriculum, to ensure that the 'innocence' of traditional faith would be preserved from contagion or compromise and initiated into due sophistication only under Islamic auspices. He was instrumental in the founding of the International Institute of Islamic Thought in Washington in the early eighties, with its ambition to serve an exclusively Islamic epistemology to govern all sciences, physical and social, by Islamic norms.

There are crucial issues here to which we will return. For they are in the forefront of any reckoning with Al-Faruqi's part in dialogue. The stance may be readily understood and acknowledged, if seen as a repudiation of the Europeanism or westernism which so often assumes its world-wideness and which non-westerners so understandably resent. If, in Al-Faruqi's case, a 'declaration of independence' sprang from a lively belief in the entire self-sufficiency of Islam, it came also from anxiety and a sense of threat. There may be paradox in that conclusion. But he was by no means the first of thinkers to answer an inner anxiety with an assertive confidence. Since, in his case, the underlying issues were, by their very nature, shared and common, and critical for all faiths, it is the more sad that he did not allow his agile mind and his ardent spirit to search them in tandem with his Christian friends rather than in contention.[5] There are, however, times when we can only relate in terms which the psyche dictates.

iii

Al-Faruqi's Islamic self-sufficiency, nevertheless, expressed and argued itself with spiritedly western patterns of discourse. It could not be otherwise when his whole professional career was spent in western academia. He was apt, for example, to coin his own vocabulary, inventing words like 'peccatism' and 'saviorism' to decry the Christian preoccupation, as he saw it, with 'sin' and 'penitence', and to disavow the notion of 'the redeemer'. He indulged in sharply provocative statements with magisterial assurance, as, for example, the opinion that 'Hebrews as a whole were never converted to the Judaic faith,'[6] meaning that their 'people of God' syndrome had always over-ridden a true monotheism. These features of style were combined with a will to be comprehensive, to structure an entire system as unified as his perception of Islam itself. He had equipped himself in Montreal with the academic skills needed for comparison of the Abrahamic faiths and he was philosophically alert to the obligations they had to metaphysics, epistemology and ethics. He grouped all these under the term 'axiology', or the inherent rationality of truth and value and aimed to give it an Islamic shape.

It is convenient to explore his scheme of faith and religion by studying, in turn, the themes of rationality, Arabism and prophetology. They were closely interconnected in his mind. They were logically followed by his treatment of Islamic polity and the implementation in life and society of the norms and ideals of Islam. In all these areas his thought, for all its Muslim provenance, was in lively rapport with Judaic and Christian comparisons and contrasts. For it was on the anvil of relationships that his steel was forged.

Al-Faruqi derived his confidence in rationality from his understanding of the unity of God, as absolute, evident and all-compelling.

> The first principle of Islamic knowledge is the unity of truth, just as the first principle of human life is the unity of the person, and the first principle of reality is the unity of God. All three unities are aspects of, and inseparable from, one another. Such unity is the ultimate principle.

As such, this divine unity is innately present in the mind as 'certain conviction'.

> It is not an 'act of faith', a 'decision', that man makes when the evidence is not conclusive. Nor is it dependent as it were on him and his assessment of a case from which the apodeictic certainty is ruled out – *not* a wager *à la* Pascal.

The unity of God, the divine reality, is thus 'the hard *datum*' of the human mind, the incontrovertible necessity within human consciousness. Islam, therefore, is utterly rational where it is most dogmatic.

> The doors of natural and humane science and technology are wide open to the most thoroughgoing empiricism possible without the least alienation or separation from the realm of moral and esthetic value.

To be seized by this truth

> ... is to live one's whole life ... under the all-seeing eye of God, under the all-relevant norms of His divine will, under the shadow of impending judgement according to a scale of absolute justice.[7]

Here is religion made axiomatic, so that faith has no necessary engagement with doubt, in a world where there is no occasion for agnosticism,
still less atheism, to arise, whether from pain, or death, or tragedy,
or alienation, or any sense of the absurd. Islam possesses a categorical theology which is entirely rational without the necessity of debate.
'Reason', in man, 'is the godlike organ...the faculty by which like can
know like and man can know God.'[8] We have no need to cry: 'O that I
knew where I might find Him.' (Job 23:3).

In *The Cultural Atlas of Islam*, after presenting Arabia as 'the crucible',
Al-Faruqi writes in the same vein on 'The Essence of Islamic Civilization',
returning to *Tawhid*, or divine unity, as self-evident to human reason
either via study of nature or by divine disclosure in revelation. 'The order
of God' is, on the one hand, entirely disparate from 'the order of man',
Creator from creature. Yet the inaccessible 'otherness' (to man) of God
belongs, ideationally and teleologically, with the human realm. It addresses reason and summons obedience. This obedience, in our case, is
volitional, whereas the rest of nature conforms to God's purpose function-
ally. Apparent contradiction or alleged 'paradox',[9] which Al-Faruqi firmly
disallows, are simply an invitation to look further when solution will be
found. The unity of truth, via the unity of God, is the original fact of all
religion(s). Faiths have, therefore, to co-operate in sifting 'historical
accretions from the original given of revelation.'[10] *Islam* will be their clue,
understood – not by some empirical 'Islam' which may be compromised –
but from the 'essence' of Islam *per se*. *Tawhid* is, at once 'the first
principle of metaphysics, of ethics, of axiology, and of esthetics.'

It is from this 'essence' that *The Cultural Atlas* proceeds to examine
'the Form' and the 'manifestation' which *Tawhid* takes in historical Islam,
with its Scripture, its *Sunnah*, and its institutions of law, society and arts.
The world and man are real and stand in divine purpose consistent with
the complete otherness of the divine Lordship which forbids any and every
concept of shared compassion, or incarnation, or communion. Yet the
otherwise gulf between man and God is bridgeable strictly through
prophetology, through 'messengers' linking the divine will with the human
cognisance and conformity. Any case that human reason, or human
emotion, might be prone to raise against this rubric on experience must be
excluded as incompatible with rationality. The fact of human defiance of it
is not in question. But such defiance has to be dissuaded by prophets,
disallowed by right reason, and deterred by the certainty of judgement. It
will be seen at once how inhospitable this *schema* is to the convictions
about divine Lordship which derive from the Christ-event as New Testa-

ment experience received and expressed it. It is strange that related awareness of 'the greatness of God' could give rise to such divergent perceptions of its meaning and its measure. The things at stake involve some careful notice of what Al-Faruqi understands by the second strand of his *schema*, namely Arabism.

iv

It is perhaps significant that '*Urubah and Religion* was his first published work. For he set great store by the 'Arab vocation', extending 'Arab' to embrace the entire culture and population of the Near East understood as having originated in the Arabian peninsula. Semitic and Arab were, in effect, equivalent with the latter term comprising many other identities as well. This sense of '*Urubah*, 'Arabness', was an ontological reality. It explained the necessarily Arabic language of the final revelation, the Arabic Qur'an. It also warranted Al-Faruqi in seeing as a wilful aberration the Hebraic assumption of a specialness under God unique to them when in truth something akin to it – but not racial or ethnic – belonged by right to '*Urubah*. The Hebraic had to be seen, on this ground, as an aberration because it had monopolised and ethnicised what was a much larger destiny. The 'correction' of it was, in Al-Faruqi's view, a major dimension in the prophethood of Jesus. Abraham, the great progenitor, was for the Qur'an the great iconoclast, the founding exemplar of that *Hanif* quality with which he was 'neither Jew nor Christian'. (Surah 3:67.)[11]

This did not mean that Islam was in any way confined to Arabs. It meant that the Arab genius, in the widest territorial sense, had proved suited to the exemplification of the human response to divine *Tawhid*, not by racial merit but by spiritual reception. Jews and Judaism, from Moses, had – as it were – 'privatised' and so distorted that inclusive Abrahamic faith. They had read a covenant of nature, 'the virtue of happiness and the happiness of virtue', meant for all via *Islam*, into the 'covenant' of Sinai turning unilaterally on themselves. In this way monotheism itself was wrongly annexed to a separate Judaic existence.

Though the Qur'an, in its narratives of Moses, would not align readily with this case, its exponent held it strongly and expounded it not only in '*Urubah and Religion* but in the opening of *The Cultural Atlas*. After reviewing the topography, demography and economy of 'Arabia: The Crucible', he sees the Islamization which followed the Islamic conquest of the Middle East as Arabisation because 'the main principles of Islam were almost identical with those of earlier Semites or emigrants from the Arabian peninsula.'[12]

> Islam sees itself, regarding Judaism and Christianity, as the very same identity but reformed and purged of the accumulated tamperings and changes of their human leaders and scribes. (*Atlas*, p. 10).

Judaism and Christianity, then, are 'moments in Arab consciousness', but impaired, the one by ethnocentrism lending to monolatry, the other by saviourism, tending to polytheism. Authentic religion belongs with true Arab consciousness, understood as an open society, never separatist, and turning on the Qur'an's verdict (3:110) that 'You [Arabs] are the best people brought forth to mankind,' – 'a historical fact that is eternally true.' (*'Urubah*, p.4.)

It is clear that *The Cultural Atlas* is, less romantic, more sober, on this theme than *'Urubah and Religion*, there being almost a quarter century between the two works. We have to decide how this universalising of a particular should be read as an index to Al-Faruqi's mind. Does it emerge from his own biography of suffering via Zionism? Or is it a lyrical gloss on the fact that the final revelation had to be in Arabic? Or does it simply turn on the fact that Arabs, through the Qur'an, were the people who, thanks to the Arab Muhammad, 'enjoin the good and forbid the evil'? Whatever its source, this lyricism does not lead him to approve all that Arabs actually are or that Arab nationalism does. It is, in effect, a will to marry ultimacy with identity – a longing to which all are prone.

V

From this sense of Arabness we are led naturally to prophetology in the Islamic perspective, as seen by Al-Faruqi. In Muhammad, rationality and Arabness coincide in the final revelation, but the final is preceded by the many, and all are a single theme. Prophet may differ from prophet in range of audience or context of time. But all bring essentially the same message and they, with what they bring, are all there is of divine engagement with humanity beyond the occasions of nature and the natural order.

Two issues belong here which Al-Faruqi does not explore. The one is the question whether prophets, historically, can be so readily brought under one rubric of exhortation. The other is whether the prophetic mission in humanity does not point beyond itself to some necessary, and larger, dimensions of divine undertaking in respect of mankind – dimensions which require both the paradox and the reach which Al-Faruqi, on Islamic principles, has necessarily excluded. That second question entails discussion of the measure of human wrong and so, in turn, the divine response which Christology understands.

Can we, for example, comprehend Elijah and Hosea, Muhammad and Jeremiah, on the same errand? 'To enjoin the good and forbid the evil' and to affirm 'the unity of God' is one thing in a context of pluralism and *Jahiliyyah*, or 'ignorance'. It is another, as in Amos, when the setting is not a *Jahiliyyah* of pagans but the connivance with evil of those who have long known the truth. The situation of Ezekiel among weary exiles was not that of Abraham among idol-prone kinsmen. Can the heartache of Jeremiah be comprehended within the same prophethood as the themes of the Qur'an when, in his deepest utterances, Jeremiah is not addressing an audience at all but is wrestling passionately with God? Is the Muslim sense of what prophethood is and means too focused on the sort of arena which obtained in Arabia? And what of the implications explicit in that prophethood in the post-*Hijrah* years? Are these to be equated, as one phenomenon, with the Gethsemane of 'the prophet Jesus'?

These questions merge into larger ones about the human predicament which Al-Faruqi disallowed in his analysis of Christianity and about the Christology which he also rejected. Certainly the two belong together whether in veto, as with him, or in affirmation as with Christian faith.

May not prophethood point beyond itself, precisely because it is so crucial to divine unity and its due realisation by man? It certainly relates God to humanity in terms of claim, obligation, command. It is, on Quranic showing, necessarily repetitious. It entails a long sequence of representatives enjoining and forbidding, directing and guiding, in the midst of a humanity not readily susceptible to injunction, nor heedful of warning. The Qur'an itself is evidence enough of the resistant power of *zulm*, *nifaq*, *dhanb*, *zann*, *istighna'* and *dalal*, the wrong, hypocrisy, transgression, supposition, self-pride and erring, by which unbelievers flout the divine will categorically revealed. To be sure, prophetology has an answer in judgement and dire penalty. It may have its vindication in damnation, as well as via obedience and *Islam*. But vindication it must have. For it is on behalf of God and implements divine unity. There cannot, then, be a final dualism of divine purpose and human contrariety. Clearly, the divine will, however regnant in and with the divine nature, may not relinquish that stake in human response to which prophethood is witness. If we are to believe in prophethood from God we cannot also hold that we are puppets nor fail to realise that there are divine ends turning on human part in them and that this part may be withheld.

Humanity then, in that sense, is a liability for God, if prophethood from God to us is to be significant with the sort of significance which Islam supremely attaches to it – and does so, as it believes, by divine warrant of revelation. The question, therefore, is urgent whether there are, or could be, reaches of divine concern toward mankind, consistent with prophetic sending, but going beyond it into the situation which the rejection of the prophets, or wilful disregard of them, seems to present. For it is precisely at the crucial point of such a rejection undergone by Jesus (whom Islam sees with deep reverence as an exceptional prophet) that Christian Christology arises as disclosing 'a beyond prophethood' in the divine way with humanity. It moves from the seriousness of human wrong, which Islam acknowledges, holds it to be representatively present in the suffering experience of Jesus, and sees him overcoming and redeeming it by the love that accepts to suffer as the condition of such overcoming. Read in that sense (and the New Testament derives from so reading it), the Cross of Jesus may be understood as a dimension of the prophet-sending God who takes a verbal and ethical solicitude for us further into a compassion that meets us in a deed of reconciliation of which suffering love is the indispensable factor.

Such an understanding of what Al-Faruqi dismissively dubs 'saviorism' is in no way disloyal to the role and reality of prophethood. It goes beyond it for its own sake. It does so by its own further logic, namely the realisation of the divine goal in man. It is evidence of a greater resourcefulness and patience in God than law and judgement employ. To think of God as 'Saviour' in no way impugns His unity. On the contrary, it fulfils and expresses it – unless we are thinking of divine unity as a matter of mathematics to be merely asserted, and not as an ultimacy which masters the rivalry of human sin.

It was just such ultimacy which Christian faith identified in the mission of Jesus from 'the bosom of the Father' – as the Fourth Gospel has it (John 1:18); that is, from within the impulse of the divine being and, therefore, consistent with the meaning of creation and with the nature of the divine sovereignty engaging with humanity through the prophets. In the suffering sequel to that mission of Jesus – a sequel utterly relevant to the wayward human reception of the prophets – the first Christians believed they had learned how the oneness of God must be understood. They read the Cross back into the sovereignty from which they perceived it had derived. What was history to them, in time and place, around the presence, the person and the death of Jesus, was index and clue to the mind of the Eternal. 'The Word', they said, had been 'made flesh', and by this 'dwelling among us' had given us to know how the oneness of God should be understood – the God of creation and of the prophets pursuing to the full His enterprise with humanity.

This conviction Al-Faruqi felt it imperative to reject and disallow, albeit on the very grounds on which the New Testament had affirmed it. He appealed – as it did – to the nature of transcendence but with the opposite conclusion. There was for him, by his reading of Islam, an innate veto on the whole Christian reading of divine sovereignty, expressible – and expressed – in the love that comes, the grace that suffers to redeem. It is puzzling to know whether his mind ever really reckoned with thoughts that required a suspension – if only for the time being – of instinctive veto, despite his readiness to argue for a dialogical *epoché*, or abeyance of prejudice, in our mutual relations. If not, he is the more representative of Islam. For there has long been this painful *obstat* in the Islamic mind to condescension as the measure of sovereignty. Yet the theme of the oneness of God which, for Al-Faruqi, argues the veto is precisely what the Christian conviction about 'God in Christ' enshrines and vindicates.[13]

vi

That long impasse between two faiths which Al-Faruqi sharply symbolises turns radically on what may be thought appropriate to God.[14] For him, condescension by the measure of what Christians read in Christology and in the Cross is altogether incompatible with divine greatness. What Al-Faruqi starkly illuminates – though this was not his intention – is that the dictum is a decision humanly taken. The issue is not about divine greatness; it is not even about *Allàhu akbar* as a *confessio fidei*. It is about in what the greatness consists, how the *akbariyyah* is identified. One may, of course, rule out humility, grace, self-expenditure, patience and lowliness, from divine possibility. But that may be no less awry in forbidding dimensions to God than affirming them may be. The issue at least is clarified when it is seen as genuinely obtaining between theologies of the oneness and greatness of God. The criterion of power which wills to negate what gentle pity affirms has no inherent warrant from within the divine unity that is 'most great'. Where verdicts differ they must first realise what they share.

Al-Faruqi's anathema on Christian Christology as flagrantly improper to God turned also on another large theme in his thinking. He believed that what Christians saw as realism about humanity was misguided. In the Christian pattern of faith the divine will to redemption is believed to be responsive to the human predicament of sinfulness and of insubordination to law. The nature of the human wrongness explained the necessary reach of divine compassion, understood within the fidelity of God to creation and to prophethood in divine persistence with the enterprise of man. The fact of the one responded to the need of the other. On what he saw as Islamic ground, Al-Faruqi was moved to deny both. What he read as improper to God he also saw as distorting of man. Notably in his *Christian Ethics*, but also elsewhere, he decried the Christian analysis of human nature as, in the words of Surah 12:53,[15] 'prone to evil'. He accused Christianity of a morbid preoccupation with sin and countered what he called its 'peccatism' with a robust assertion of the inherent rightness and the perfectibility of men and women.

It may be fair to ask whether this spirited reaction against what he saw as the 'pessimism' of the Christian view owed more to his controversial instinct than to constraint from the Qur'an. For it can hardly be said that the Islamic Scripture is not itself realistic about human perversity. The human rejection of the prophets in their long sequence is evidence enough of mankind's obduracy and enmity to truth. Muhammad's own experience in the pre-*Hijrah* years tells the same story. The very sharpness of the issues joined between him and the Quraish and the urgency with which they had to be pursued are eloquent enough of something absolute in the nature of truth and something wilfully resistant to it in the human psyche. On some nine occasions the Qur'an deplores and castigates 'those in whose hearts there is a sickness', in reference to their sinful ways. (Surahs 2:10; 5:52; 8:46; 9:125; 22:53; 24:50; 33:12, 22 and 60; 47:20 and 29; and 74:31.) The sense of *marad*, 'disease', here is of more than acts of wrongdoing. It takes these further into the wrongness within the self, into a wilfulness which is itself reprehensible as a state and not merely for the deeds in which it is embodied.

That sense of things is borne out in the Quranic survey of history, its dark retrospect of the ruin of former tribes and cultures, like the '*Ad* and *Thamud* on whom condign retribution fell and whose desolate ruins impressed Muhammad on his travels. It doubtless also underlay the militancy which Muhammad came to see as indispensable to the victory of God over pagan defiance of the divine unity. The sequence from preaching as *balagh*, or verbal witness,[16] to 'reckoning' in physical combat visibly enshrines the innate seriousness of human evil and argues its

perverse armoury against persuasion. Combat, in turn, necessarily intensifies the necessity for reprobation and 'hardens all within'. Evil becomes
entrenched through the very will to cast it out by force.

That situation is explicit in the Quranic sense of *fitnah*, which initially is
the perversity which persecutes true believers and comes to mean the sedition which resists true believers armed.[17] In both its meanings the term is
index to how complex, subtle and heinous, evil is within the human scene.
There is a tragic sense in which forms of resistance to wrong themselves
succumb to it.

In *Christian Ethics* Al-Faruqi, reassured – as we have seen – by his
reading of the Qur'an's essential 'optimism' about us and a feasible
institutionalising of the good by its precepts and power, found himself
severely critical of what he saw as Christian morbidity and cult of the
tragic. In particular, the doctrine of 'original sin', as he perceived it to be,
kindled in him a lively Muslim hostility. Some Christian interpreters may
perhaps be held responsible for the way he read the doctrine. He took the
theme of 'fallenness' and our being 'in Adam' as an actual physical
inheritance of guilt by which all are necessarily accused and inherently
condemned. The notion of a sinful 'fall' and an arbitrary 'guiltifying' of
man properly offended his sense of the justice and sovereignty of God.
They seemed to him also to cut the nerve of confidence and hope and to
send us back in sloth or panic into the arms of 'the Saviour'. There was
thrust in the legitimate passion with which he made the case, and a sense
that he was fulfilling an Islamic mandate in doing so.

For him, as for many, the word 'original' bedevilled what is here at
issue. That there is a 'bias' in mankind whereby the good is always at odds
with wrong and is never attained in passivity we have already noted – and
noted as Quranic. It is this 'proneness' to wrong which the Qur'an
eloquently tells, that is meant in the Christian term 'original', as something 'there' in the human experience and not attributable merely to
circumstance or to accident or to things unwilled. Nor can it be attributed
only to the body, to 'flesh', and the physical order, where many theories,
gnostic and otherwise, sought to locate it, exonerating the mind and the
will. The 'bias' attends our thoughts, no less than our instincts; it perverts
our logic, making motives masquerade as arguments. It attends our most
religious acts, haunting the soul with pride and self-esteem in the hidden
sins that beset all sanctuaries. It is, therefore, 'original', not in the sense of
being innocently inherited, but in the sense of characterising the personality as such. To express this in the myth of 'the fall' is to say that it is
of the nature of humanity. Birth makes us so, not as an external chance,

but because birth was, and is, our highway into human-ness. We are 'in Adam' by virtue of 'belonging to mankind'. It is the 'bias' of our self-centredness, implicit in personality *per se*, the very characteristic of our predicament as creatures of flesh, of mind and of will, within a divine economy of law to which we are accountable – accountable, not as automata, but as free for an *islam*, an obedience which only the free can bring. It therefore makes for a steady crisis in their freedom.

It may be that what deterred Al-Faruqi from taking the measure of these meanings within what he castigated as 'peccatism' was his opinion that all ideas of man's 'fall' and all yearning for 'the Saviour', were essentially scandalous, a calumny on human worth and dignity, a perversion of the inherent goodness of creation. His suspicions have their place. But they are ill-suited to a true discernment of what is at stake. The seriousness of evil is only the other sense of the sovereignty of the good. The real despair would lie in the 'optimism' that assumes that what is, is all that was meant to be. The invitation to penitence is the surest tribute to our worth. Only in the acknowledgement of wrongness, in realism about how deep-seated, how 'folded inwards' it is, do we truly appreciate our human quality. To be sure, preoccupation with sin and guilt can easily become deplorably self-absorbed. But then a reassuring liberation into forgiveness is the more, not the less, urgent. The subtleties of evil are more truly broached in the Qur'an's concept of *zulm al-nafs*, 'self-wronging',[18] than in the 'peccatism' by which Al-Faruqi interpreted, as he saw it, the New Testament picture of humanity.

vii

The New Testament, of course, is both Gospels and Epistles. It was to the latter that Al-Faruqi attributed most of what he saw as distorted in the Christian perception of the human situation. Though the Gospels extant in the New Testament shared, to a degree, what the Epistles enshrined, suitably aligned with the Quranic Jesus they constituted a realm of exegesis in which Al-Faruqi could develop his estimate of Jesus. Though he subjected the Gospels to strong Quranic pre-suppositions, he sought painstakingly to draw from them what seemed to him the authentic Jesus. Thus he brought an intriguing Muslim element to the long nineteenth and twentieth century 'quest of the historical Jesus', an element to which many looked eagerly during his career at McGill. For, though obviously involved in the scholarly issues around the figure of Jesus, Muslims had all too rarely engaged adequately in the scholarship entailed. Al-Faruqi had the technical equipment but the instincts of mind which he brought to its use largely determined what he found. He did not sufficiently reckon with the way in which the teaching of Jesus headed into suffering at the hands of the society around and with the significance of that fact both for ethics and theology.

He saw the ministry of Jesus as essentially an encounter with Jewish exceptionality. Jesus' vocation as 'prophet from God' in the Judaic context was to retrieve Jewry from their mistaken 'privatisation' of the relation-ship with God through misreading of the meaning of election. That theme had its place in the formulation, in *'Urubah and Religion*, of the thesis of an inclusive 'Arabism' in which Jewry was only a contributory part. How far Al-Faruqi's deep inner reproach of Zionism, as a nascent Jewish nationalism in the twentieth century, belongs with this account of things Judaic, invites reflection. The point here is that it dominated his percep-tion of the role of Jesus as called to turn his Jewish people and time from their exclusivism and summon them into an inclusive monotheism in which no such pride of place and race could properly be theirs.

This perception, of course, fitted broadly into the Quranic scene, where reproach of Jewish 'pretension' over divine 'favouritism' is found. It tallied with the traditional picture of Jesus, as the penultimate prophet, with a mission more limited than that of Muhammad as 'a mercy to the worlds', but nevertheless vital to the Islamic whole. It also served to underwrite the necessity of divine 'rescue' for Jesus, from a resistant constituency provoked by forthrightness and honesty in his address to them. It did not, however, admit of that New Testament dimension of 'long-suffering' from which, in both Gospels and Epistles, the first Christians perceived a redemptive achievement as the action of 'God in Christ'. Al-Faruqi's dismissal of 'saviorism' saw that reading as anathema to God and im-proper for humanity.

There must be serious question whether this theme, characteristic of Al-Faruqi as a lively voice of Islam, does justice to the inner consciousness of Jesus insofar as we can assume to know it.[19] Is Jesus' undoubted critique of contemporary things Judaic only duly understood as within an entire participation in them? Does Al-Faruqi wrestle adequately with the moral sense in which the universalism of Jesus turned on the nature of God as Father and on the openness of grace which, while it duly condemned privilege, could also include those it reproached? What was negated in the ethics of Jesus, namely self-congratulation and collective self-esteem, was within a larger positive which spoke in sublime indifference to race and nation, Jew and Gentile. 'Blessed are they that mourn . . .'; 'blessed are the meek . . .'; 'blessed are they that hunger after righteousness . . .' are benedictions that do not enquire about identity. Likewise in the parables. When 'a certain man' has 'two sons,' or 'goes down from Jerusalem to Jericho', one does not have to ascertain, as priest and Levite must, whether he is Jew or Greek, Roman or barbarian.

It follows that there is a hidden justice in Al-Faruqi's perception of the logic of Jesus' prophethood among Jewish hearers but also a crucial overlooking of its larger relevance in respect of the inclusive grace to which it led and the deeper cost which it exacted of the preacher by virtue of which he could become the Saviour. Yet, if Al-Faruqi's Muslim commitment withheld him from these perceptions, he nevertheless identified the subtle temptation of religion to turn into exclusive privilege – as Islam itself is prone by dint of the final custody of revelation, or the Christian Church, should it make grace its own 'property'. The truth, alleged of revelation, or the meaning understood in grace, belong with their communities only as witness, not as properties of theirs. In pointing so strongly – in the Jewish context – to the equation between faith and peoplehood, between God-confession and God-possession, Al-Faruqi was close to a criterion no less applicable to his own confident Arabism and peoplehood within Islam. He aimed to 'found the universal brotherhood under the moral law'. (*Ethics*, p.35). Yet it is precisely the moral law which, redemption apart, must necessarily discriminate between 'keepers' and 'breakers'.

That theme of 'redemption', which could retrieve the 'breakers' while upholding the integrity of the law that found them such, Al-Faruqi did seek to meet, but in a concept of 'self-transformation' which 'presupposed a will so purified' as to be 'contradictory to assert that it can do evil.' (*Ethics*, p.81) He credited to Jesus such a 'radical transformation of self', as 'a new birth . . . a re-orientation of one's soul to God.' 'Once the soul is properly oriented, it will not fail to bring its decisions and doings into proper relation with God.' (*Ethics*, pp.80-81). Jesus himself attained such a transformation. But he should not be thought a means to it in others. 'The status and worth of his teaching' were 'totally didactic', i.e., hortatory and exemplary. (Ibid. p.82). Jesus was no more than 'an ideational instrument' towards 'radical self-transformation' from which we 'proceed on our own'. That conclusion is index to how far Al-Faruqi had taken the measure of the New Testament thought of 'regeneration', and of how far he repudiated that Scripture's emphasis on the need of redeeming grace in the initiating, the sustaining and the falterings of soul-transformation. It was also, however, a measure of how far he had tried to enter into Christian thought on the mystery of selfhood and the majesty of God.[20]

viii

There is a certain paradox, then, when we turn to Al-Faruqi's firm view of the proper toughness of Islam as a duly political religion in which the role of prophet-power, in post-Hijrah terms, is both necessary and authentic. It is in *Islam* (1979), a textbook in a World-Religions series, that this feature is most marked. Also in *The Islamic Impulse*,[21] a symposium issued after his death, he argues that, the Islamic *Shari'ah* being 'divine and indisputable', state aegis to implement and enforce it is also indispensable. This is the ground of his lively criticism of existing Muslim states as failing in this instrumentality and in a true Islamicity. Inadequately Islamic, non-*Shari'ah*-implementing Muslim states need to be replaced by a true *Ummatism*, i.e., the contemporary structure of *Dar al-Islam* instead of the political separatism which makes Islamic brotherhood a farce. The sacred *Shari'ah* he sees as 'a complete system of desiderata', which the 'action of *Ummatism*' has to encompass in an 'efficacious actualization of the absolute in history'. (Crawford, pp.220-38).

The effect of this characterisation of an ethico-political goal is to obscure the potential of collectives, i.e., states and régimes, to develop the vested interests which are inimical to their true action, and the more so precisely because they claim divine warrant. The miscarriages of 'ideation' of which Al-Faruqi is aware in the personal self are all the more likely in collectives. Yet this arena of corporate wrong and collective selfishness tends not to be registered in the interest Al-Faruqi's thought has in the personal dimension. 'Sins' are the deeds of the individual in the strictly private reckoning characteristic of the Quranic focus on the personal self in final judgement. Though his theory does not call in question the feasibility of the good within the aegis of right political power, his dismayed assessment of existing Muslim régimes would seem to require him to do so. But there is something staunchly Islamic about his confidence that, duly Islamicised, the political order can and will attain divine desiderata for mankind. It is here, perhaps, that the significance – misread by Al-Faruqi – of 'original sin' in its New Testament sense may be seen to be most apposite. States and governments must surely be more than a necessary curb on wrong and sin. But their positive role, in the attainment of justice and the good, will always leave beyond their political achievement the ultimate claims of divine righteousness. That realism, however, in no way absolves them from the utmost duty to an always partial fulfilment. It is the merit of Al-Faruqi's spirited formulation of a theory of Islamic politics that it issues into these areas of debate.

ix

His experience of inter-faith encounter was nothing if not thorough and
existential. He was never other than *agonistes*. As an educationalist he
was keenly alive to the intellectual tensions incurred in the West by
Muslim youth. His resilient Palestinianism, born out of tragedy and
complicated by his American sphere of labour and residence, gave an
urgency and passion to his desire to preserve Islamic identity, to prove its
internationalism and yet to serve its unique destiny. He perceived education to be the critical sphere of this vocation. Hence his long dedication to
academies of learning and the pursuit of dialogue. It was in both,
however, that he sensed the danger of an erosion of youthful faith.
Primary schools and early nurseries could take care of themselves. The
danger came in the sophistication of higher education. There was, to be
sure, the Muslim dictum that it was parents who made children non-
Muslim when they themselves were, whereas Islam was the natural home
of all birthlings. Was there now a sense in which education took over that
malign role and diverted even born Muslims from their true Islam?

The suspicion lay against the social sciences in particular. The natural
sciences were no problem. For Islam had long been at ease with them in a
pioneering way. But the fruits of technology, interpreted within societies
that understood themselves by the light of western sociology and psychology, could be sadly inimical to the absoluteness and integrity of Islam. For
these studies tended to turn all faith and practice into 'phenomena' to be
studied merely as forms of behaviour which forfeited thereby all claim to
be absolute or ultimate. So Muslim minds were weaned away from firm
faith and from 'the Book in which there is nothing dubious' (Surah 2:2).

Furthermore, when those social sciences were 'imaged' in the arts, in
music and drama, in the media, the impact of trivialisation, vulgarisation,
and secularity was intensified. Al-Faruqi believed that it was both necessary and feasible, to seek 'an Islamisation of all knowledge', not only as a
protective device, but as a right implementation of the inclusiveness of
Islam. It was demanded by the sort of theism Islam held, where 'God must
be God', in total acknowledgement and where true religion must teach
and apply the limits of its tolerance. This was no crude obscurantism on
his part. For it proceeded from vigorous intellectual convictions analogous
to those which thinkers in other religions, adamant likewise about their
custody of truth, have enjoined and pursued.

It was this impulse which drew Al-Faruqi into founding and commend-
ing the Washington Institute of Islamic Thought as an international organ

of debate and action. It was a clear protest against, a declaration of independence from, the dominance of western norms in philosophy and society. He sought to begin from epistemology itself, from the grounds of knowledge, to devise and enforce an Islamic sociology, an Islamic psychology and an Islamic ethics. The whole educational system had to be revamped to terminate the long perceived dichotomy between theology, as in Al-Azhar or Deoband, and 'secular' studies as in state universities in the western idiom. Reformers in Islam had merely sought to acquire western knowledge. Now they must realise the extent to which it committed 'a rape of the Islamic soul', and learn 'to recast the whole legacy of human knowledge from the standpoint of Islam.'[22]

Here were deep areas of dialogue, indeed, but precisely where Al-Faruqi wanted, or appeared to want, to be self-sufficient in and with Islam. The questions certainly concerned the meaning of the rule of God and of the *imperium* of man within a technological civilisation. But can those issues of intelligent theism be cornered into one management? *The Cultural Atlas of Islam* was a disciplined presentation of a positive response to that question, offering 'the essence of Islam', as the *Din al-Fitrah* of Surah 30:30, whose nature was that 'for which God had fashioned [lit. 'natured'] mankind',[23] in contrast – he believed – to the ways in which modern western social sciences and politics perceive society. If this is to say that worship must be decisive for the pursuit of knowledge and for the human *imperium* that knowledge bestows, then Al-Faruqi's 'Islamisation' is a shared theism carrying Jews and Christians with him. But its formulation into the specifics of institutional Islam in the temper for which he pleads, leaves many open issues which his Islamic self-sufficiency would foreclose.

When he comes, in *The Cultural Atlas*, to 'the manifestation' of 'the essence', via 'the form', of Islam, he insists that the Muslim's 'life goal'

> ...is that of bringing the whole of human kind to a life in which Islam, the religion of God, with its theology, and *Shari'ah*, its ethics and institutions, is the religion of all humans (p.187).

Yet, despite the evident *à priori* of those clauses, and the distinctions they require even within Islam[24] he finds this 'call of Islam'

> ...a critical process of intellection. It is in its nature never to be dogmatic, never to stand by its contents as if by its own

authority, or that of its own mouthpiece, or that of its
tradition. It keeps itself always open to new evidence, to
new alternatives.... The Islamic caller [i.e. missionary] is
not the ambassador of an authoritarian system, but the
co-thinker who is co-operating with the called in the understanding and appreciation of God's double revelation in
creation and through His prophets.... No healthy mind can
afford to reject the call à priori...' (p.189).

However, 'its claims are naturally directed against the contrary assertions
of other religions'.

Anybody is invited to contend and the Muslim is epis-
temologically bound to prove the truth of Islam's propositions and obtain the consent of the contender. (p.188).

Here, characteristically expressed, is Al-Faruqi's disclaimer of dogma in
dogmatic form, his invitation to the option of submission. Perpetual
openness to new evidence combines with certainty as to its proper context,
and differing religions are not suited to supply it. The call is reasonable
but the reasonable is the Islamic. Truth and advocacy wholly coincide. In
that stout quality, Al-Faruqi is a representative protagonist. But there are
other Muslims to be heard.

Chapter 8

SALMAN RUSHDIE
(born 1947)

'The One it's all about... absent as ever while we suffer in His Name'

i

There are numerous precedents in literary history of authorship leading to incarceration. There is something quite unprecedented about the furore attending *The Satanic Verses*. The aftermath of its publication would seem to be unique in the history of the novel. The range and passion of the issues aroused – not to say their unhappy obfuscation by most parties to them – have been phenomenal.

Need there be apology, then, for its inclusion here in a cluster of studies in the biography of religious dialogue? The book has had a dramatic place in the biography of its author, some would say a tragic one, in that he has become, as it were, a martyr *malgré lui*. The whole resulting encounter with a wounded, yet belligerent, Islam has certainly probed the deep places of the Muslim psyche and touched the nerve of its dogmatic confidence in terms that – for all their crudity – are painfully incisive. It follows that we have in *The Satanic Verses* a *cause célèbre* around which things sublime and squalid engage each other on both sides of the encounter. There is need on our part for the perception which can bear with what is coarse and flippant, or resentful and outraged, for the sake of what is critical and significant within them all.

But can we speak of 'dialogue' in the midst of thunderous confusion? The author's, at points, naive ineptness of judgement in respect of how he would be read, and the predictably passionate hostility rewarding it, would seem together to have precluded hope of real meeting. We are left, it might seem, with 'the adversities of the verses' and with adversarial camps. Is there, on the one hand, any 'inner faith' for 'inter-study'? Is there, on the other, any 'inter-' for which Muslim minds are ready, given the tantalising, fantasising, radical pattern Rushdie sets for it? Is not 'faith' on his part firmly disallowed?

Yes and No. Certain forms of it emphatically Yes. But, with appropriate reservations, decidedly No. Even the reservations have positive implications. There is latent in some forms of anti-religion an implicit search for a religion that could be authentic. The dictum of E.M.Forster: 'I do not believe in belief', Rushdie echoes when he declares: 'I believe in no god', and 'where there is no belief there is no blasphemy.'[1] Only 'our lives teach us who we are' is an ambiguous saying. For it implies there is a 'lesson' somewhere and that experience is capable of teaching it. *The Satanic Verses* studies this tutorial in two contrasted, inter-acting lives, and does so – despite much tedium – in highly effective hints and reasons.

So there is faith here, bemused no doubt, self-taunting, world-interrogating, clichés rejecting and devising, but faith none the less. It will not, then, be incongruous to include him in company with world-historian Arnold Toynbee, or missionary C.F. Andrews, or tenacious expositor of 'faith-ing', Wilfred Cantwell Smith. For Rushdie is busy with the heterogeneity of the world. He is clearly 'missionary' in his satire on Islam, and wistful over 'the One it's all about'. Or, if the reader disagrees, at least Rushdie's presence in this miscellany of minds will be precisely the hotch-potch, the riotous variety, he would find appropriate – the sort of absurdity where 'you can trust an immigrant not to play the game'. (p.365).

Rushdie's world, he tells us, can only be free, dissenting, disputing, debating. Only the eclectic, the random, the hybrid, are right and proper. He is keen for the incongruous. He is ready to concede other people's right to faith on condition of his right to have it in the dock of his irony and contempt. But these are meant to wean them from their absolutes about it. That reads like a pitch for dialogue. There is no possibility of the dissent he admires in the absence of the thing that provokes it. We still need each other even if it is only for mutual repudiation.

It would be wide of the truth to see Rushdie as 'faithless'. 'Where there is no belief' must be taken with a healthy scepticism. He believes. Among his tenets are honourable race-relations for which he worked steadily on Camden Council, on Channel 4 and in his novelist-vocation. He believes in that vocation and accepts with impressive dignity the trauma in which it has involved him. He likes being, with Saladin Chamcha, 'a bystander in his own mind' (p.9), which implies that there is something to take in. That something makes for the legitimacy of fiction and the right to have it 'take off from history'. He believes in the sacred art of writing. He believes in *not* claiming to possess a total explanation. He believes in hybridization, in the adventure of new forms, new images, new perceptions. He believes in the urge to 'say the unsayable'. He believes in the enigma of evil, in the mystery of 'motiveless malignity' (p.424). He is at pains to explore the seductiveness of self, the 'furies' and illusions that haunt the human soul, the fetid springs of prejudice within society, the riddle wherein 'nothing is for ever and no cure... is complete'. (p.540). He only believes in 'no-believing' with urgent limits to it. He cannot complain, then, if the tables are turned and we include him in versions and verifications of faith. There is much faith-evidence that emerges, as we may see autobiographically, in *The Satanic Verses*. Just as the religious believer's faith can be a sustained dialogue with doubt, so Rushdie's 'no-god' unbelieving is a steady engagement in faith. For only so can novels possess and pursue the vocation he holds for them. There is an elusive *teneo et teneor* written across *The Satanic Verses*. The titular incident itself, in Muhammad's career, had to do with integrity beyond temptation. We cannot ponder the satanic and deny that truth matters.

If meaninglessness were all, no sense of it could arise. Absurdity could never suggest itself about particulars if it embraced all. It is only in reference to meaning that the absurd can be identified. We still write of life teaching us who we are, however disconcerting, exhilarating, stagnating or pulsating, life – as the lesson tells it – purports to be. On that score, Salman Rushdie we may say, is full of faith. His forty- some years must tell us why.

ii

Salman Rushdie was turning forty when *The Satanic Verses* was in composition. His book was born in London, out of Bombay.[2] His life belongs with both cities and biographical negotiation between them. 'The distance between cities is always small,' he may declare (p.41). But it is just that 'adjacence' which makes it disorienting for 'translated men' like his Salahuddin/Saladin or fantasising ones like his Gabriel Farishta – characters in whom, we must assume, Rushdie himself is legible. His youthful years began in the restless, shifting theatre of the ambiguous and the indeterminate. His birth was Indian and Muslim. He began life as Ahmad Salman Rushdi. His parents were Anis Ahmad and Negin Butt. Were the holy verses of the Qur'an's opening Surah, *Al-Fatihah*, whispered as piety required in his newborn ears? India, where 'the human population outnumbers the divine by less than three to one', (p.16) inevitably breeds a certain nonchalance (though it can well become fanatical in its own defence). It is a land where film-actors can cheerfully play many divine parts until the confusion seeps into their own unresolvable identity. Chamcha's parents, we are told, had been Muslim in the lackadaisical, light manner of Bombayites (p.48). Religion is conjectural amid 'the anaesthesia of the every-day' (p.302). In the turbulence of adolescence, uncertainty adopts many feints and disguises in 'the bastard child' of cross-cultures.

Schooling at the Cathedral School, Bombay paved the way to Rugby School[3] where Rushdie grew painfully familiar with the racial bias Asians suffer in the British scene and in 'the moral fuzziness of the English, meteorologically induced' (p.354). 'Not all mutants survive' (p.49). But 'exclusions only increase determination' (p.43), and Salman, now dropping the 'Ahmad', learned how to cope with London, 'such a welcoming city' where they 'keep the curtains drawn' (p.208). At seventeen he became a British citizen, marrying in 1976 and studying at King's College, Cambridge. His first ventures were prosaic enough – undergraduate acting and Footlight reviewing, inditing copy for advertisements and attaining to publish an early novel, *Grimus*, in 1975. With *Midnight's Children* in 1981 he was launched on his way, receiving both the James Tait Black Memorial and the Booker McConnell Prizes in that year. *Shame* followed two years later and *The Jaguar Smiles: A Nicaraguan Journey* in 1987. London and its literati had become the other pole of his existence, escaping – by depicting it – that threatening paranoia which, 'for the exile, is a prerequisite of survival' (p.207).

iii

But London could still offer to his ever versatile film-makers the role of a latter day '*Ad* and *Thamud*, those miscreant tribes of the Qur'an's denunciation. It is vital to keep in view the insistent fascination Islam holds for Salman Rushdie, the challenge it presents for him even in repudiation. It is complicated, no doubt, by the Indian milieu *à la* Bombay. Had he come to earth in Lahore or Deoband or Aligarh, his course of life might have been much contrasted.[4] As it was, the *Shahadah* and *Din* were quickly shed, or never comprehended. But the mystery of a religion remained. Rushdie knows reasonably well the verses of the

Qur'an he needs for his inquisition, as well as the traditions that underline his stance.[5] Islam, we may say, is responsible for the content and the violence of his antipathy. It is only by what he sees it to be that he reaches his repudiation of it. As we must explore later he belligerently invites it to respond to some of the most elemental obligations belonging to religious claims – the claim to 'revelation', to mandatory 'rules', to absolutes of truth, to prophetic warrant of authority.

Fiction – especially fiction about 'stars' playing roles of 'archangels' – provides exactly the right elusive, jesting, pillory-ing medium in which to do so. It can be at once scornful and playful, passionate as any crusader and dispassionate as any spectator, in investigating the nature of revelation and the power of faith, the resolute conviction and the desperate deludedness of credulity. Fables can be told in order to make sense of perplexity if only by further confounding it. Fantasy can both hint of incredulity and leave us mystified about believers. All this is grist to Rushdie's mill. But it is important to appreciate that the corn is as real as the millstones. It is particularly through his namesake Salman the Persian – the only non-Arab in Muhammad's entourage and his intimate scribe – that Rushdie makes his indictment of what he sees as the 'convenient' illusions of revelation. His 'dialogue' with Muslims is framed – as we must see – in quite inept, indeed disastrous, terms. But these are no less serious or apposite on that account. It is the very form of his clarity which obfuscates his meaning with it. He is caught in the paradox in which the issues he means to explore are engulfed in the conflict he provokes. His demand for an Islamic *apologia pro fide sua* is countered by a frantic cry of some *pro vita sua*. The fiction which is meant, 'in good faith', to create a certain distance from actuality the better to measure it, comes – in the event – too close altogether to actuality to avail for its interpretation.

Some readers may wonder why the author entitles his wide, panoramic, episodal novel with the title it bears. It is true that 'verses', from hoaxing phone-callers and from 'musicals', punctuate its stories and have 'satanism' in them.[6] It is also true that motives can frame sentences inside minds and upon lips that did not intend, or are moved to disown, them. That is the way that evil works and delusion happens. But to make 'the satanic verses' pivotal to the whole is to concede how central to the author's fascination Islam is so that an incident in the Prophet's experience can focus inclusively the intentions and pitfalls of language, the bond between word and motive, and the conscience in inspiration.

iv

There is nothing conspiratorial about Surah 53:19-25 in Rushdie's context. It is the old Muslim historians themselves who record the tradition of the 'inserted' verses and their later withdrawal by abrogation as satanically occasioned and as loyally disowned. During the hard years of his Meccan preaching of the unity of God and the crime of *Shirk*, or idolatry, Muhammad was offered – so it is alleged – a viable compromise by which the pagan Quraish, the lords of Mecca, would concede the supremacy of *Allah*, thus 'satisfying' Muhammad's mission, while he would, in some sense, certify and concede the tolerable subordinate 'reality' of *Allat, Al-'Uzza* and *Manat*, three female consorts on whose favour Meccans saw their city's prosperity, both in pilgrimage and trade, to be founded. The Prophet would merely allow that they were *gharaniq* whose 'intercession might be hoped for'.[7] It seemed a politic and sensible compromise. But some of Muhammad's followers were deeply puzzled and he himself, returning to the context of Quranic inspiration, became convinced of bad faith on the part of the Quraishi leadership and of misconstruing, on his own part, of the divine will. He loyally retracted the 'concession' and continued on the dangerous path of fidelity to *Allah* alone in unalienated sovereignty. The words about the goddesses had been 'interpolated' by satanic action and were abrogated by the text as it now stands: 'They are nothing but names: you have coined them for yourselves and your fathers, with no warrant from God.'

The incident, real or alleged, involved the whole question of the manner of divine revelation to Muhammad. If words could be in this way interjected to do violation to the true text, how could believers – or the Prophet – be certain that the text elsewhere had been rightly audited or received? For the traditional view of this phenomenon of *Wahy*, or 'inspiration-within-Qur'an',[8] has long been the conviction of an actual 'dictation' of the words, to Muhammad, in Arabic, from God via the mediating 'angel of the Revelation'. This understanding of a syllabic deliverance has long served to reassure Muslims of the infallible nature of the text, as immune from any mental or literary participation in the process on Muhammad's part, he being a totally passive, allegedly illiterate, recipient.

This, as it were mechanical, view of the vital question of the prophetic role, is one that certainly needs to be faced within Islam as being, arguably, disloyal to the Qur'an itself.[9] It was hardly a theme to which justice could be done in a novel, least of all one so provocatively and bewilderingly devised as *The Satanic Verses*. But Rushdie was intent on exploding the whole myth, as he saw it, of such claim to the state of being auditor to the divine speaking and the whole tyranny grounded on the claim. Salman, the sophisticated Persian, is his mouthpiece. Incidents in Muslim tradition in the private affairs of Muhammad could be exploited to accuse him of connivance in the content of the Qur'an.

Did the Prophet lay down the law and the Angel confirm it afterwards? 'I began to get a bad smell in my nose,' Salman says (p.364), about 'revelations of convenience'. He dreamed that he himself changed what he heard uttered to him as the scribe and, subsequently, Muhammad did not notice slight verbal changes, then greater ones. If Muhammad could not notice them, how could the theory of their origin from God in verbal inerrancy be credited? There is much passion in this passage which readers must relate to Salman Rushdie as they will. After reluctant suspicion

> ...it's quite another thing to find out that you were right. Listen, I changed my life for that man. I left my country, crossed the world, settled among people who thought me a slimy, foreign coward...I was sadder than I had ever been. I went out of his tent with tears in my eyes...There is no bitterness like that of a man who finds out that he has been believing in a ghost. I would fall, I knew that, but he would fall with me. (pp.367-68).

Salman senses his mortal peril in Jahilia, the city of Mecca. 'His power is too great for me to unmake him now.' When asked why, he replies: 'It's his Word against mine.' (p.368).

The capital 'W' is significant. Rushdie is inveighing against the dangerous – and endangering – illusion of being God's mouthpiece. Beyond the pretension itself, as he sees it, lies the vacuity of the whole 'God-realm' – 'the Fellow Upstairs' who may just as well be 'the Guy from underneath' (p.318). All is fantasy, as unreal as the roles his character, Gabriel Farishta, plays, as ephemeral as the dreams with which the novel abounds. 'The closer you are to the conjuror, the easier to spot the trick.' (p.363). The result of 'revelation' is a plethora of 'rules, rules, rules', if not Qur'an then Tradition, enjoining on believers a regimen that destroys all liberties, and informs them 'what sexual positions have received divine sanction'.

'I recognise no jurisdiction but my Muse,' swears Baal, the poet of Mecca, the solitary figure in Jahilia condemned to die in Muhammad's victory. Rushdie is likewise minded. There is a coarseness and a vehemence in his denunciation, yet a passion against fear of the truth which rides with a will to liberation from credulity. He would abolish the tyranny of the sacrosanct. He enquires whether religious rules can be immutable for ever. The object of his 'fabulations' is to cajole, tease, worry, provoke believers into seeing their sanctities with the candid eye of honest realism, just as dreams sometimes make vivid what the dreamer loathes but can no longer contrive to escape. For Rushdie there is an inevitability about such liberation unless it is forestalled, excluded by the sort of connivance with illusion which only satire and scorn can dislodge. He is a kind of caricaturist whose work is, at once, recognisable truth and distorted travesty.

V

This quality of *The Satanic Verses* explains the barbed references to a God 'who sounded so much like a businessman' (p.264), and a Prophet in the same idiom, one to whom management decisions are handed down. It underlies the use Rushdie makes of episodes in the Prophet's career. The most notorious – for Muslim readers, or hearsayers – is that of the brothel in Jahilia after Muhammad's only partial (as all things are) victory.[10] He himself is absent in Medina, twenty-five years on (though Muhammad was only eight years away before the conquest and survived the conquest only two years.) Pagan society is reverting to type. The brothel-keeper has the idea that it would amuse the customers if they were allowed the illusion that they were taking their pleasure from 'the Prophet's wives'. So why not jocularly name them so 'A'ishah', 'Hafsah', 'Maimunah', and the rest? The ruse is much enjoyed. But we can easily elide the inverted commas which indicate that it is one. This, of course, is where Muslims were outraged. For the ruse, *per se*, was, at best, flippancy and, at worst, malignity, however strenuously it was protested later that the chastity of the real wives was never in question. Fiction, doubtless, has to insist on its right to fictionality. But if it intends to communicate, rather than to titillate, it is wise to ponder what communicates.

Within that question lies the intriguing problem of why Salman Rushdie has this obsessive preoccupation with Islam and Muslims. There were surely endless possibilities for Sisodia, the film-magnate, to rescue Gabriel Farishta from his 'nervous breakdown' as a fantasiser, in India's *Babel*, rather than bringing a film-star to rebirth by contriving *Gibreel in Jahilia*. Is it that Islam presents the most tormented face of the tyrannies

Rushdie's instinct most fears and hates? Is it the dark shadow of the Ayatollah?[11] Is is that the Quranic notion of 'a satan in the works' gives him a clue with which to probe the indignities and distortions exiles undergo in their adopted lands, sensing 'everywhere the presence of the adversary, *al-shaitan*', 'the satan'? (p.320). This last conjecture has a reassuring hint. For, though he makes Islam the butt and target of his novel, it is much more than Islam which is a field for satanism. Yet it could be the irony of Satan to make it uniquely the thing to hate. One menace in the controversy *The Satanic Verses* has aroused is that of shifting south against Islam the 'defence-at-any-cost' syndrome of hate, now – it would seem – disqualified in its eastern direction against the heirs of Lenin.

Perhaps it was simply Bombay and London in their dual significance which prompted Rushdie to find in Islam, Muhammad and the Qur'an, the arena his art needed both for its imagination and its crusade. Or was it that Islam seemed most aptly chosen for his concerns with the rights and liberties of women? That these are genuine cannot be in doubt, though what may well be is whether his own characterisation of sexuality is consonant with them. There is one notably redeeming comment on this theme in his first characterisation of his Gabriel Farishta:

> In all those years he was the beneficiary of the infinite generosity of women: but he was its victim, too, because their forgiveness made possible the deepest and sweetest corruption of all, namely, the idea that he was doing nothing wrong. (p.26).

That noble sentiment, however, is for the most part ignored in the long sequel when the beneficiary continues to enjoy the benefactions and continues to be victim of illusions of innocence corroborated by indulgent women. Fidelities are not the mode where satanic verses and love's reversals are abroad. Or is all merely fantasy and dream, the hallucination of whisperings of divine authority? How could you make the archangel provide just the right revelation? (p.106).

Yet such very notions prove there must be probity somewhere, however hard to seek or rare to find. In another place, Rushdie ponders whether there are 'things beyond forgiveness'. Saladin Chamcha, before his final 'healing', broods on the guilt of his envy of Gabriel, his cruel seductive enmity against his friend, his callous will to damage what he coveted – and all despite the saving of his life by that same friend. There *are*, it would seem, means of grace and wholeness. They avail, Rushdie explains, in returning to roots and to 'the great verities of love and death'.[12] Chamcha comes to terms with his old father's death when Rushdie's narrative-power, free for the moment from things fantastical and incongruous, is at its ablest. By contrast, Gabriel Farishta, the pseudo-archangel, disoriented by his endless 'parts', haunted and self-deluded, is finally unable to face the logic of his story or wrestle with its questions. He never regains belief, and ends in suicide. Yet it was 'the other fellow' who grew the horrid hair and the horns of a veritable demon.

Elsewhere Rushdie writes of 'the inexorability of an impossible thing that was insisting on its right to become' (p.32), not mere survival through and out of exile, but somehow 'a new birth'. Despite his professed atheism, his carefree disavowal of 'Thou who changest not' and his veto on the plea: 'abide with me'. Rushdie describes these climaxes in the story of his two main heroes as 'opening the heart to God' and asks 'how the loss of God can destroy a man's life'.[13] That doomed character, Gabriel Farishta, figures in an early scene in hospital in Bombay, where it would seem that such loss is inevitable and not, therefore, critical, crisis-making, or ultimately regrettable:

> During his illness he spent every minute of consciousness calling upon God... *Ya Allah* show me some sign... there came a terrible emptiness, an isolation, as he realised he was taking to *thin air*, that there was nobody there at all, and then he felt more foolish than ever in his life, and he began to plead into the emptiness *Ya Allah*, just be there, damn it, just be. But he felt nothing, nothing nothing, and then one day he found that he no longer needed there to be anything to feel. On that day of metamorphosis... his recovery began. (p.30).

Is there, then, a final ambivalence in *The Satanic Verses*? Is man not incorrigibly faithless even in his most insistent self-sufficiency? Is atheism finally a pose, a protest, a gesture? Or is it an option which ultimately disqualifies itself in the very taking? Or do we conclude that Rushdie 'saves' Saladin and 'loses' Gabriel – and both 'religiously' – in order to vindicate the reality of God but has nevertheless to repudiate any such vindication because of what he perceives Islam to do and mean by it? He is – it might seem – at once a vehement and a reluctant iconoclast. If his iconoclasm springs from a perception of Muslims as 'falsifiers' of God, the logic for his atheism, then the sharp irony is that Islam is – and was – in itself an uncompromising iconoclasm, the dethroner of false gods. Before we can explore that irony and its implications, it will be well to take stock of the communication Salman Rushdie intended to achieve. For he insists that there is purpose in his novel. Satan is in earnest where most hilarious. 'Verses' entertain: they also educate. How well does Rushdie do either?

vi

As for entertainment, let notoriety decide. Notoriety will not vouch for education. When Rushdie deliberately chose to identify his Islamic figures and occasions by the names given them in scorn and denigration by their enemies he explains that he did so in order to have them turned, by Muslims, into badges of honour. Others, he notes, have turned the tables in this way. 'The Old Contemptibles' are a fine example. 'Right,' they said, 'you call us that. We'll wear the slandering thing as the very token of our pride. We defy your intended humiliation of us. It will fire and fuel our self-assertion.'

This, of course, is what Rushdie wants all exiles, migrants, minorities, to do in face of dominant and supercilious cultures like the British who feed their ego on the inferiorisation of all others. Mischievous migrant reactors will wilely insert their satanic verses into the mouthings of the self-conceited. So far so good, though it is doubtful whether Rushdie's 'Whig' and 'Tory' have their currency in this tables-turning way, rather than merely adhering as handy epithets.

But can we justify Rushdie's tactic in this fashion? He uses Mahound for Muhammad, adopting the malicious, defamatory term by which medieval Christendom maligned the Prophet of Islam. He dubs the Quraish *Shark* for *shirk*, the term denoting idolatry. It fits perhaps before the surrender of Mecca, but is no term to become ever a badge of pride. He has persecutors call Muhammad's followers 'scum' and 'bums', so that the latter-day ones can transform obloquy into the proper pride of the persecuted. Let them 'turn insults into strengths' and choose 'to wear with pride the names they were given in scorn'. (p.93).

The one snag about this device on Rushdie's part is that the parties involved can only do it for themselves. It cannot be willed *for* them or *on* them, by non-participants in the sense of indignity or by mere imaginers of possibilities. These may perhaps drop hints or muse about examples. But initiatives of this order can only be born of a resilience on which no outsiders can presume. Rushdie, it is clear, *is* an outsider in respect of the impulses that make the believing Muslim. For he has declared himself emancipated from them. The actual response to his invitation to Muslims to emulate Trotsky, who adopted his very gaoler's name, reveals how wide of the mark his anticipations were, if he ever seriously intended them. The heroic way of taking defamation must always be precarious. It never happened with the word 'nigger'. That it could and did with the word 'black' turned on the quality of mind of such as Leopold Senghor, President of Senegal, and Aimé Césaire, poet of the Caribbean, with their notion of *négritude*.[14] But these had a quality of spirit, a capacity for 'two worlds', which could not be reasonably assumed as forthcoming from the normal Muslim readers, or hear-sayers, of *The Satanic Verses*.

Moreover, a responsible 'educator' along these lines needs to appreciate that the 'lesson' can well go the other way. Instead of finding an implied challenge to heroic loftiness of mind, sufferers under what seems like slander may simply conclude that that is what it is. 'Take this and make it your pride' may well be read as: 'Take this, it is the truth about you.' Even in saying the first, does the writer, tongue in cheek, really mean the second? The suspicion may be unworthy. The author has to allow it may be there. He is, after all, writing in Khomeini's world. He may be writing 'in good faith' but that must embrace an honest realism about authorship as having a context as well as presenting a content. It is wisdom to relate these in advance – if education is meant – rather than explain later how well-intentioned he was. A certain writer was asked what he meant by his novel. He wisely replied: 'I do not know what I meant until I hear what the critics say.'

Tested by that rubric there can be little doubt what *The Satanic Verses* has meant. Resentment, anger, calumny, have interpreted it in their own image and it has 'meant' confusion, controversy, passion and transactions of contempt. Before coming, however, to the strife of these 'meanings' it is well to study the central religious question on which Rushdie lays his surgical finger in such scaring fashion, wounding in hope to cure.

vii

It has to do, essentially, with what can be understood by the divine and the human in the partnership – if such we can believe it to be – of 'revelation' and 'inspiration'. There is much that is crude and banal in Rushdie's glib suspicions of cheap collusion between heaven's dicta and a prophet's utterances. But the issue is real and cannot be evaded. Muslims need to dismiss the cheapness and grapple with the mystery. Their difficulty is increased by their instinctive concern to ensure that the source *is* divine and, being such, infallible. The Qur'an is, and must be, 'a book in which there is nothing dubious' (Surah 2:2). This has meant for them the assumption of a total abeyance of the human factor of Muhammad in the recipience of revelation. Hence the belief in his illiteracy and in the Arabic syllables of a celestial dictation in which human thought, will, emotion, have played, and could play, no part. It is this necessity, on the Muslim view, that entails the innuendoes on which Rushdie thrives and for which heaven seems in oddly sustained connivance with Muhammad's situation, precisely because he is *not* perceived as being in any way participant. The cynic roundly concludes that he has to be. For the revelations are, at times at least, so patently 'tailored' for his convenience.

That feature, incidentally, is only 'incidental'. In the deep and crucial areas of the Qur'an's meaning the message could only engage the messenger in hardship, stress and peril. In its entirety the Qur'an was, for Muhammad, no sinecure; there were periods when it was almost a Gethsemane. Wishful thinking has no place in its integrity. What may seem, at minor points, to the contrary has to be gathered into the whole issue of 'inspiration' in its incidence on man and its origin in God and its shape in words.

The problem of eloquence and its sources, of prophetic burdens and their genesis, of divine engagement with human means, is a very ancient one. The Greeks knew much about it in their philosophy.[15] It is central to the Hebraic Scriptures. Wherever it is said: 'Thus saith the Lord', there is a human speaking voice. How are we to relate infinity with personality?

Unhappily, by and large, Islam does so by the principle: 'The more it is divine the less it is human.' In that way Muslims, again by and large, think themselves the more assured, the more guaranteed, the more insistently addressed, in *their* revelation, in their Muhammad. In the actuality of the Qur'an he has to be merely a cypher, a channel, a conduit, so that the source may be wholly God's.

The other way to perceive the matter is by the principle: 'The more it is divine the more it will recruit and activate the human.' That is the Biblical, and most crucially the Christian, principle where, in the latter case, it means incarnation. Here the human is not elided or marginalised but instead, engaged, employed, enhanced and enabled. Truth is then via personality. This does not, and need not, mean that it is less divine, less assured, less mandated. There is, to be sure, a fallibility in all things human. But we need not think of it in terms of the slip-of-the-tongue insertion, by Satan, of the compromising errors, later to be abrogated divinely, as if by an editor's pencil on a script. The fallibility, on another view, is the necessary context of the travail with meaning, as it is with the complainings of the psalmist, the anguish of Job, the 'confessions' of Jeremiah, the composition of the Gospels, or the pleadings of Paul within the churches.

All these, of course, proceed upon a different apprehension of revelation from that of celestial dictation to a wholly passive listener who then becomes a sure spokesman – aside from the occasional aberration from which, as in Surah 53, he is divinely rescued by intervention. Islam and Muslims do urgently need to woo themselves away from a purely passive perception of Muhammad so that his role may be seen in terms of active involvement which, far from undermining the authenticity on which Muslims vitally rely, would perceive it in truer, surer form.

The case against Rushdie and *The Satanic Verses* is that he sets the problem only in its crudest terms and the terms least likely to induce the kind of thought into its implications by which Muslims might respond. The issue needs a far gentler, more patient, perceptive treatment than the vulgar suggestion that Muhammad believed himself somehow privy to God, with a convenient private line to heaven. *The Satanic Verses* has only served to aggravate a religious prejudgement about the Qur'an which Muslims took upon themselves and which has long become a prejudice in which they are imprisoned.

Rushdie may well claim that it was neither his intention nor his obligation to serve any emancipation of them from it. Part of him may well find it only a deplorable index to the reach and misery of credulity – a hardened case beyond redemption. Or he may only have been intending to express a hatred of the tyranny to which religious absolutes must lead, in the suppression of that tentativeness, diversity and flux in which his soul takes pride. But what is worthy in that motive needs the modesty to venture correction more wisely.

The clues to such a venture are not far to seek in the Qur'an itself. Muhammad was emphatically a preacher, a warner, a witness. However, for the moment, we understand his receiving of the content, he had to impart it. The Qur'an is 'recital', not perusal. It was meant to be heard. However far his mind and will may have been in abeyance in the recipience of what he was to utter, once he was its utterer he was in a context, with an audience, at an encounter. As utterer he became, of necessity, a conscious figure, relating, engaging, being contradicted and taking reaction. All those roles were inescapable. The vital fact is that these roles passed into the very fabric of the Qur'an. Controversy with the Quraish duly, and quickly, filters into what Muhammad hears in the celestial imparting of words. 'They are saying' the words report about his detractors. 'Say thou,' they direct, in concerting his responses. The whole Qur'an, once it begins, is situational. It has what Muslims themselves call 'the occasions of revelation' (*asbab al-nuzul*). With his context Muhammad is vitally, even heroically engaged. Can he be less vital, 'real' and 'there' *in* the content of what passes to him from heaven to say? Is he conceivably conscious in one realm and unconscious in the other? Indeed, his *persona* itself becomes central to the whole engagement in Mecca and Medina. What is he saying and by what authority? becomes inevitably also the question: Who is he anyway? There is something like 'truth through personality' inasmuch as the messenger – his warranty, his right, his meaning – become explicitly the message.

Some Muslim thinkers, medieval and modern, have seen this situation for what it is.[16] But on the whole Islam has been reluctant to concede its significance.[17] They have feared – unnecessarily – that to lose a passive mouthpiece is to forfeit a living prophet. Quite the contrary. The Qur'an need not be the less divinely meant for its being more humanly constituted.

We can best illustrate that reassurance in a concluding study of the encounter *The Satanic Verses* provoked between Muslims and seculars, between East and West, between faith as conviction and beliefs as credulity. The immediate point is to argue that when Rushdie satirises 'revelations convenient' to Muhammad's circumstances, 'management decisions' handed down from one 'businessman to another', he superficialises what he suspects. He limits himself to isolated incidents, and ignores the total context. He reads only in a sinister way the event of prophethood and fails to take it in the whole. If personality is indeed recruited into instrumentality on behalf of God the role will certainly be fraught with temptation.[18] Satan may well be afoot with his satanism. The more truly divine the more critically human the cause must be. Aberration may occur, but it can also be transcended and a whole must be seen, not a fraction-part. How well a prophet recognises the subtlety of his inevitable temptations may remain, for posterity, an open question. But the verdict may not ignore what it was all about in its reckoning with incidentals. If Muhammad believed himself divinely made a special case in a matter of divorce or marriage, we have him 'warts and all', and 'revelation' is ill-used. The relation between 'office' and 'person' has always been liable to reproach, whether prophets, writers, novelists, politicians or police. But we do not thereby disown the authentic as literature, politics or society. There is a sense in which Muhammad cannot be incriminated unless he is acknowledged.

It may be objected here that Rushdie's militancy against Islam, the fictional relationship he has with it 'spiralling away into imagination', have to do finally, not with Muhammad's entourage, his wives or his amours, but with the fanaticism, the absolutism, the bigotry, in which it holds its believers. Rushdie could perhaps abide religions, if they could be more modest in their dogma, less adamant in their rituals and their readings of the world. But then, he concludes, modesty is not in their nature. They are purveyors of credulity, suppressors of all freedoms, vigilantes on behalf of One who is never able, or willing, to speak for 'himself', or rid 'himself' of these self-appointed sponsors of 'his' mystery. The episode in Chapter viii of the pilgrimage through the Arabian Sea to Mecca is a grim satire on credulity, on self-hypnosis, perhaps reminiscent of mass suicides elsewhere. We can read the wistfulness within Rushdie's anger. He quotes with approval from Henry James:

> Life is no farce...it fructifies...out of the profoundest
> tragic depths of the essential dearth in which its subjects'
> roots are plunged. The natural inheritance of everyone who
> is capable of spiritual life is an unsubdued forest where the
> wolf howls and the obscene bird of night chatters. (p.397).

There has been much howling and chattering since *The Satanic Verses* renewed that 'forest' image. What of 'the natural inheritance' of spiritual capacity it has revealed?

viii

The answer cannot be reassuring unless we read it faithfully. The format of Rushdie's novel has embroiled rather than enlightened the adversaries. We have seen the worst of both worlds – an irate Islam in hue and cry against a writer, a liberal establishment in urgent self-exoneration of any liability for it. We have witnessed the thesis of an untrammelled autonomy of the imagination pitted against the urgent claims of religious absolutism bolstered by psychic fears and social insecurities. Writers have asked why their proper liberties, vital to integrity of mind not to say the sanity of society, should be subject to the direct, or indirect, veto of benighted bigots. A whole bottle of *genii* has been uncorked.

The twin issues are, perhaps, the nature of blasphemy and the meaning of liberty. Can blasphemy exist in a secular society – not, here, the question of whether it can obtain for *this* religion and not *that* – which is a matter of equal justice – but whether blasphemy is feasibly indictable or identifiable in the contemporary scene. The best route to any answer is to move into the parallel question of freedom. For it is assumed – by those so minded – that liberty has a sanctity, an ultimacy, which may not be impugned. Such liberty is the bedrock of a free society and the *sine qua non* of literature.

On that view there can be no constraints on the imagination. Novel-writing has to be a completely autonomous pursuit. The principle, as with all science, has to be: 'If we will we may.' Otherwise writers become the slaves of some ideology, some tyranny, some régime, that subdues them to its will. We must stand for the autonomy of the imagination if we are to escape the menace of censorship, overt or covert.

Here, however, we come upon the ancient question: *Quis custodit ipsos custodes?* 'Who will guard the guardians?' and find ourselves caught in a paradox. For there are no *custodes* if autonomy is complete. So there is no question of their needing to be, or being, in fee to anything. We arrive at total irresponsibility, unless, of course, we can conceive some kind of self-responsibility, self-censorship, which takes account of things outside the self and its intentions. But then we are no longer autonomous. We are cognisant of some constraint.

Or are we? Is there no way in which the constraint can be taken into the autonomy, perhaps even enhance and ensure it? The Highway Code is a gross violation of my liberty to drive as I will. But observance of it, in curbing my motion, serves my mobility. On the 'society' of the roads, it cannot be otherwise. The analogy is too easy for the complexities of society, of publishing and writing, of circulating in print into the public highways. But must it not in some degree obtain? Poisons carry labels to warn; libels are by law indictable; damages are assessably real. Can it be otherwise with beings 'capable of spiritual life' in a subduable forest? As Salman Rushdie himself concedes in *Is Nothing Sacred*, something has to be if only that we may learn where liberties are forfeit.[19]

By the same token, we are back in some sense with 'blasphemy', with that which cannot be, if other things are what they are. Unlimited tolerance refutes itself, since it destroys the discernment by which alone it is practised. 'We do not need,' Rushdie writes, 'to call [this reservation] sacred, but we do need to remember that it is necessary.'[20] One can appreciate the motives behind the choice of word, given the monstrosities committed in the name of 'the sacred'. Yet 'the sacred' has always been the sublime form of 'the necessary', its heart-sanction, its mind-condition. For the necessarily sacred is only so in the abiding sanctuary of awe and wonder, of humility and worship.

These, to be sure, can be turned into the perquisites of perversion and become creatures of an absolutism which betrays them. Some would perceive such a perversion in some expressions of Islam and on that ground heartily deny them. The remedy then is not to seek some illusory escape from their necessity but to let their inherent sacredness restore the sanctuary no perversion can destroy.

In its own terms, and in its full significance, Islam was – and is – just such a witness to the ever-necessary sacred. The irony is that *The Satanic Verses* missed the meaning of what is being affirmed in its preoccupation with what is being perverted. The Islamic cry: *Allahu akbar* often seems and sounds like *Islamu akbar*. It is then a cry of communal self-assertion, of the pride of a religion. Yet Islam is, in intention, on behalf of God. *Allahu akbar*, 'God is greater',[21] means the due and necessary subordination of all things under God, God being the only right 'absolute', the absolute which alone properly makes all else relative. When made duly 'relative' all other 'absolute' claimants – nation, party, commerce, power, art, science, technology – may become beneficent because they are no longer supreme but in a right hierarchy. Otherwise they might well become damnable. The iconoclasm of Islam is against all such idolatries usurping what is due to God alone. In this demand to 'Let God be God', it enshrines the meaning of its Scripture and understands the role of its Prophet.

It follows that there is a sense in which God has 'to be let be'. A sovereignty essentially existent has, at the same time, to be humanly acknowledged. That is the nature of the 'sacred' in the meaning of the 'human', not compulsive but waiting on consent, real but also to-be-realised by man, a Lordship whose service is perfect freedom.

Prophethood had to do with the crisis implicit in a divine sovereignty turning on human awareness. In the confusion of his dreams and his film-roles, Gabriel Farishta demands to know: 'Should God be proud or humble, majestic or simple, yielding or un-? What kind of idea is he? What kind am I?' (p.111). The answers inter-depend. The puzzle of the world, the human riddle, the enigma of evil, have to be seen within an intention of meaning, a purpose of art, of which God is the ground of will, and we are the deputed servants in making the intention, the meaning and the art our own, since not otherwise can they be fulfilled. This is the Qur'an's definition of 'man under God', the bearer of the *khilafah*, or 'dominion-status', in which he is at once free to serve and serving only in freedom. According to the Qur'an, it is in letting God be God that we let the human truly be. The secular assumes an autonomy; the sacred accepts it only as an obligation. All things may be subject to us only because we ourselves are subject to God.

It is wiser to receive *The Satanic Verses* as within that understanding of magnanimous Lordship, rather than in umbrage or retaliation. The ineptness of some of its strategy, the vagaries of its imagination, the frivolities in its earnestness, may be held within the mercy of 'the compassionate, the merciful'. It has a vibrancy that lives with the tumults, the illusions, the amours and futilities of a cinematic world. It struggles to disentangle the real from the phoney, the vistas from the visions, the worthy from the meritricious, using fiction to identify fictions. It summons faith and religion to a proper loyalty, in castigating their pretensions and their cruelty. In all these ways it may be said to be, however clumsily, on behalf of God. Even if we went to see it as a satanic insertion into our truth-possession it will be the manner in which we rescind it and restore the sound version which will test and try the integrity we claim. And the last word will be with God.

Chapter 9

SALAH 'ABD AL-SABUR (1931 – 1981)

'The Blood He Draws from the Veins'

i

It would be wrong for missionaries, guardians of faiths, and academics, to suppose that significant religious exchange was confined to their auspices and assumptions. There is a form of spiritual converse between poets and dramatists, situated within faith-systems and encountering each other with no other constraints than those of quest, of conscience and of sympathy with the human scene as the endlessly fertile realm of their imagination and their perplexity. It often happens that their perceptions are more incisive, less preconditioned, than pundits and custodians can allow themselves to be.

One intriguing feature of mid- and late twentieth century Arabic poetry and drama has been the impact upon its writers of the Christian author of *The Wasteland, The Four Quartets* and *Murder in the Cathedral*, T.S. Eliot. There is a discernible 'biography of dialogue' between his themes and theirs, not in the literal sense of actual discourse, but in the shape of a vision shared, an interpretation of experience, and a tribute of creative imitation. Eliot's drama-study of the murder of Archbishop Thomas Becket, commissioned for Canterbury Cathedral in 1935, has a remarkable counterpart in the verse play of Salah 'Abd al-Sabur, of Cairo, exploring the strange martyrdom of the Muslim mystic, Al-Hallaj, in Baghdad in 922 CE.

The two historical events signified profound issues, the one in Christianity, the other in Islam – issues of authority, power, truth and martyrdom apt to be brought together despite the cultural disparity. The two literary events brought Canterbury and Cairo into imaginative partnership in giving those issues dramatic expression. In both cases the form of drama required verdict – or, if not verdict, participation – on the part of an audience. Art, in that sense, is the most dialogical form of all. In much theology, and certainly in polemic, sides are already taken, positions are 'establishments' of loyalty liable to disallow overmuch interrogation. Some dialogue may only camouflage this situation. Drama breaks it open by making the stakes visible, articulate and indeterminate and, in so doing, arousing the sympathies and the honesties crucial to decision. In this capacity – and in present context – drama in the hands of T.S. Eliot and Salah 'Abd al-Sabur was liberated for its theological function by their choice of pivotal figures in their respective traditions, an Archbishop and a Sufi saint, incarnating, we may say, that most searching of religious tests – the equation between truth and the person, between self and office, between knowing and being. To have done so with such telling effect, the one in salute to the other, makes 'Abd al-Sabur with T.S. Eliot most proper for inclusion here. We would be mistaking what literature is were we to exclude it from the transactions of faith.

ii

'My Life in Poetry'[1] is, significantly, the title of Salah 'Abd al-Sabur's one documentation of himself. The rest is in his verse, and it was verse for which he lived. Born in 1931, he spent his youth in the final years of the British occupation of Egypt and the fluctuating fortunes of the war years, 1939-45. He was twenty when the Revolution intervened, at the outset of his student days in the University of Cairo. It would seem that he would have us take the retrospect of his formative years from the mirror of his own poetry. His instinct is to invite his reader to a sort of human anonymity in which the personal is no more than an index to all mortal state.

> I was born like the thousands who are born
>> in the thousands of days
> Because a poor man one night went into the embrace
>> of a poor woman.
> I grew up like the thousands who grew up
>> feeding on the bread of the sun
> And drinking the waters of the rain,

Like the thousands whom you meet on sorrowful roads,
And you wonder how they survived
    and how they became strong,
Despite the deprivation of their lives.[2]

He became literary Editor of the celebrated Cairo daily *Al-Ahram* and of the influential literary journal *Al-Katib*. Literary criticism and literature became his dominant concerns but he pursued them with a lively sense of social injustice which involved him in socialist ideology and a study of the social sciences. He was an admirer of 'Abbas al-'Aqqad[3] – a prolific writer in Egypt at mid-century, and an interpreter of the role of Islam in its contemporary issues. The Algerian revolution may also be seen as a factor in Al-Sabur's mental experience. Far more decisive was the issue of Palestine and the struggle for the survival of the Palestinian homeland after 1948 and 1967.

As with many younger Arab poets, whether or not Palestinian by birth, the trauma of that tragedy became a focus of the anguish and the enigma of human experience itself. Salah 'Abd al-Sabur was arguably among all Egyptian writers the most urgently preoccupied, at the deepest level, with that common Arab crisis of soul. The titles of his early published poetry belong with that preoccupation and its distress: *Al-Nas fi Biladi* (1957) -- 'People in My Country'; *Aqulu Lakum* (1961) – 'I Say to You', with its echo of the words of Jesus and its cover jacket showing a thorn-crowned head.

It is clear that he saw poetry and literary criticism as the appropriate sphere of his response rather than political commitment. That sense of destiny owed something to the example of Taha Husain, the blind doyen of Egyptian letters, to whom Al-Sabur referred in *Madha Yabqa minhum li-Tarikh?* as one 'who arose after a millenium to present us again with our Arab heritage'.[4] He sees 1920-1950 as Taha Husain's era, admiring both his social conscience evident, for example, in his *Al-Mu'adhdhabun fi-l-Ard*,[5] and his leadership as a literary critic and renewer of Arabic prose style and historiography.[6] A still later generation has tended to break away from the aura of Taha Husain, and the tradition of liberal scholarship he represented has lacked successors of his prestige and calibre.

'Abd al-Sabur moves in a less extensive field but his interest in European authors belongs with that 'Mediterranean' sense of Egypt which Husain did much to foster by the western direction of his mind in balance with the eastern, Arab version of Egyptianism.[7] There were, however, in

'Abd al-Sabur's authorship influences drawn from medieval Muslim writing, notably Al-Mutanabbi and Abu-l-'Ala al-Ma'ari, to whom he paid tribute in an article in 1971 as significant mentors.[8] From both he drew the stimulus of a rugged independence of mind and a healthy scepticism over the pretensions of power, both political and religious, as well as a lively exemplification of the role of poet and thinker in Arab culture.

Orthodox Islam scarcely figures in his autobiography and his verse, nor, explicitly, does debate between religious faiths. His dialogue is much more with the inner search in what he calls 'the time of lost truth',[9] and the bearing upon it of mainly western literature. He sees prophets, philosophers and poets as together the mentors of humanity. There is no mistaking his sense of urgent vocation in the task of the writer. He stresses repeatedly the seriousness of the burden and has nothing but scorn and reproach for dilettante pen-pushers who care only for trivialities of style and content.

He records his arousal to the problems of life and death, of good and evil, through 'metaphysical poets', and his own growing awareness of youthful distress – dreams and sex, meaning and tradition, 'things permitted and things forbidden', as the Qur'an has it, eternal bliss and eternal fire. He cites Kierkegaard's dictum that human existence is essentially religious anguish.[10]

Some people, he notes, respond to perplexity by clinging to their inherited faith. Others adopt a superficial atheism. To him both these attitudes are naive. Thought about death is for him the starting point of thought about God. 'In my early youth,' he explains

> I was deeply immersed in religion, so much so that I remember one occasion when I actually prayed through a whole night long in the desire to attain the station that some perfected saints tell of, when their hearts are empty of all things save the remembrance of God...I stammered through the verses and then sought to rid my soul of every thought other than the thought of God. I continued praying constantly until I sank down exhausted. Weariness and concentration brought me to such a pitch of consciousness that I persuaded myself there and then that I had seen God.

A bright radiance seemed to engulf him in a halo of light. At that very moment he was reciting the passage from the Qur'an (Surah 7:143): 'And

Moses collapsed in a swoon.'[11] He was fourteen at the time and caused some consternation among his family.

The experience brought him no inner peace. Rather it deepened his sense of unease. How to explain it? For some months he tried without avail to repeat the experiment. It was followed, in much confusion, by a complete denial of God, perhaps impetuously begotten of Darwinian thinking mediated by the secular Copt, Salamah Musa,[12] and corroborated by Nietzsche's disclosure of 'the death of God'. 'Abd al-Sabur became, for a while, an ardent prosecutor of the theists. The position seemed coherent and unitary. It tallied with his sense of religious tyranny described in 1955 in his *Diwan*: 'People in My Country', where he deplores the wretchedness of a village community cowed and intimidated by 'the fear of God' via mosque preaching oblivious of the curse of poverty, and where finally a youth raises a challenging fist to heaven.[13]

It was an awakened sense of the misery of the poor which weaned him from self-indulgent literati and drew him to the idea of literature as the seed-bed of a social conscience. He came back to faith in God, via a train of conviction that moved through 'society' as an ideal, to 'man' as the arbiter and custodian of nature and the world and, in this 'humanism', the necessity of worship, i.e., of the referability of all things to God as the ultimate security of truth, justice, freedom and compassion.

'Accordingly, I became a sufferer' he writes, 'and that has continued to be my existential position – the position I have chosen.'[14] Such faith entails perpetual struggle to realise the spiritual in the fabric of the material. 'I have now come to be at peace with God. I believe that all that adds to the experience of *humanitas*, to human awareness and sensitivity, is a step towards perfection, a step towards God.'[15] Man has to shape and purify existence at the same time, as a witness at the end to the worth of his life on earth. The venture and the struggle are where art and religion meet. It is the theme which must infuse the worlds of politics and of technology yet cannot be attained by these, but only by the integrity of the personal self committed to the human meaning of the whole.

'Abd al-Sabur's, it might be said, is a humanism in which traditional Islam plays no obvious part and may even be seen as inimical. Yet in its own idiom, and without Quranic citation, his *Hayati fi-l-Shi'r* certainly echoes two crucial Islamic thoughts: the 'return' of all things to God, and the demand for integrity within the self to which the Qur'an's reproach of *zulm al-nafs*, or 'self-wronging', is vital.[16] We shall see later how the second belongs squarely with the study he makes, via the tragedies of Thomas Becket, Archbishop, and of Al-Hallaj, cordwainer and mystic, of the nature of martyrdom. We must turn here to how his poetry, located now in the story of his mind, enshrines his faith.

iii

The twin ideas in his poetry are the plight of humanity and the invitation it presents to the artist first to convey its measure and then to hearten the vocation of courage and compassion. 'In my poem *The Shadow and the Cross*,' he explains, 'my concern was to speak of types of humanity who are incapable of realising themselves and fear the need to try, dying before they have known death. I have spoken of the death of the living in their cowardice and boredom and mindlessness.'

> This is the age of boredom,
> Puffing at hubble-bubbles is boredom...
> I returned from the ocean of thought without thought
> Thought encountered me but I came back thoughtless...
> I am he who lives life with no dimension
> Who lives life without time, with no dimension
> ...without glory, without a cross...
> This is the age of lost truth.

There are echoes here of Eliot's *The Wasteland* and 'I had not thought death had undone so many.' The poem depicts a lostness which persists despite calling on God in *Salat*, performing the pilgrimage, killing the pilgrim sacrifice and paying the *Zakat*.[17]

The themes are bitterly renewed in *Ta'ammulat fi Zamanin Jarih*, 'Meditations in a Wounded Time', where the poet has a grim nightmare in which he is shot and hung in a museum. He imagines he is visiting a similar fate on passers-by. The futility of things is captured in the echoes of the poem *Dhikriyyat*:

> As dark as a subterranean vault that evening.
> His troubled face peering through a chink in the wall,
> He looked out. The wind was reverberating round the cottage,
> The thunder, like a rumbling echo, blasting the city,
> Lightning lit up the sky in vivid flashes,
> The horizon a dense thicket of glowering plants.
> He found for himself no way to salvation

And he died in his prison in his wretched hovel.
After a year – so it is said – life crept
Back into his soul and body.
He began to long for rescue.
His face peered through a chink in the wall:
'Welcome!' He closed his eyes, shoved open the door,
And turned. The sky was a rippling pool,
Compassion for its waves, sun and moon – in the vastness
A boat. He drew himself up, a broken old figure,
Wrapped his old clothes and gathered his old belongings.
Hungry and thirsty, bedraggled, in all that existed
He knew in his heart he had none who loved him,
When, suddenly, a princess appeared before him.
Clad in an izar, white as pearl, sweetly she stretched out
To him her silvery arms endearingly and from her
Radiant lips she threw to him a flow of loving kisses.
But he turned round to her, apprehensive of mistake,
As if – so it is said – it was some giant
That went by.
He died, dear princess beautiful, the death of a martyr.
He never returned to life. The martyr never returns.
And you ask me: 'Why in the evening have you told me
His story? Why did you not send it into the oblivion
Of dead remembrances?' Dear princess, when I made
A pledge to him he was dying. Lady, Did you not know
That I am silent? He peers out through a chink in the wall,
His face troubled, every dark evening like a subterranean
  vault[18]

Such is the martyrdom of the commonplace, a fate the more pathetic for
being unrelieved by great issues.

In *Ahlam al-Faris al-Qadim*, 'Dreams of the Ancient Knight', 'Abd
al-Sabur addresses one he calls his 'enchantress', who both beguiled and
betrayed him. 'If only' runs through its lines. Would he were 'two waves
on the shore, grasped by one current', and drawn up by the sea in the tide;
or 'two wings of a seagull . . . hovering over the ship's wake.' Instead, he
goes on:

I am a crippled experimenter
On the edge of a world heaving with confusion and decay,

A world devoid of beauty
Which granted me darkness and gloom ...
I was once, in byegone days ... a heroic knight ...
I would wish, on hearing the laments
Of the wretched and the weak,
That I could nourish them from my grieving heart ...
What befell the heroic knight?
His heart was plucked out.[19]

His past years, he regrets, have been lived in vain. With no roof to cover him he can only share the futility he registers and refuse to seek immunity in unconcern. For it is the task of the poet to belong inexorably with the human condition and to give voice to its meaning.

The affinity of this poetry with western writers like Albert Camus, Franz Kafka, Samuel Beckett, and Eugene Ionesco, is clear. But unlike the view that 'one can deal with modern man only by derision',[20] 'Abd al-Sabur feels with anxiety and hope. His hope, however, owes little to orthodox religion. Another of his poems describes an uncle Mustafa, who loves another Mustafa, i.e., Muhammad, and who spends the evening holding spellbound a group of men with stories that only 'stir the anguish of nothingness in the soul'. The poet reflects on the word *kun*, 'be', the command at creation and its mysterious relation to the word *kana*, 'and so it was'. There is a sense of the harshness of God, whose 'face' is the burning sun and the moon's crescent a part of his 'forehead'.[21] Azra'il, the angel of death, comes to take away the soul, and the end is a futility striving to be defiant.

It is the Palestine tribulation which kindles 'Abd al-Sabur's verse into more explicit defiance of events. His poem on 'The Tartars attacking' borrows from medieval history to symbolise Israeli enmity and occupation, with refugees fleeing along choked roads, dust filling the landscape, and darkness shrouding camps crowded with resisters, and 'eyes tearful in defeat'. Though the village is reduced to rubble the vow of return hardens the will. Weeping will not be in vain, when 'we shall build what the Tartars destroyed.'[22] Yet

In this world I own nothing but the word: Peace!
Upon the heart of the weak what can the weak bestow?
To the naked what can the naked give
Save the word?[23]

In 'A Song to God', in *Ahlam al-Faris al-Qadim*, 'Abd al-Sabur concludes:

> O our mighty Lord, O my tormentor,
> Weaver of dreams in my eyes,
> Implanting certainty and doubt,
> Sender of pain, gladness and woes...
> Am I not saved yet
> Or have you forgotten me?
> Woe is me! You have forgotten me.[24]

In the poetic context of quest and frustration we turn to study at some
length, the poet's finest poetic drama, *Murder in Baghdad*, for its skilful
handling of a profound religious theme and its studied 'dialogue' – in form
and substance – with Eliot's Christian treatment of a partially parallel
tragedy. The two dramas together present a crucial religious issue which it
will be proper to study in some detail as embodying the possibility of
fascinating mediation between Islam and Christianity.

iv

It has to do with problem of the self, but not the self as thus far
portrayed and pondered in the personality of this one Egyptian poet.
Rather it is the problem of the self in the anticipation and the circumstance of martyrdom. The possibility that the very immolation of the
self, by the self, in readiness for – even in the yearning after – martyrdom
could still be self-serving and self-loving, measures how insistently inescapable is our egocentrism. In his private devotions, later published as
Markings, Dag Hammarskjöld asked:

> Would the Crucifixion have had any sublimity or meaning if
> Jesus had seen Himself crowned with the halo of martyr-
> dom? What we have added later was not there for Him.
> And we must forget all about it if we are to hear His
> commands.[25]

Let us leave till later that issue in the case of Jesus and his Gethsemane. Hammarskjöld himself, as Secretary-General of the United
Nations through turbulent years (1953-1961), was keenly aware of how
vulnerable he was in the perils of peace-making and peace-keeping. When

he was killed, mysteriously, in a plane crash in the Congo his fears were fulfilled. The precedent of his own envoy, Count Bernadotte, murdered by Israeli terrorists in 1948, was never far from his mind.[26] 'Death,' he had written in 1952, 'is to be your ultimate gift to life.'[27] In his integrity he was keenly aware of the temptation implicit in his very dedication to the cause of peace and his readiness for death in its pursuit – the imagined halo around the real obedience.

This is the theme explicit in the verse-dramas of T.S. Eliot and Salah 'Abd al-Sabur. Archbishop Thomas Becket, in the former, knows the brooding menace around him when he defies King Henry II and returns to Canterbury after eight years of exile. We need not stay over the issue of 'criminous clerks' and much else between himself and the King. The amenability of clergy to the royal courts involved the large issue of the priority of 'the things of God' over 'the things of Caesar'. That Church/State tension inevitably took on the passionate 'interests' of personality. These, on Becket's side, were accentuated by the suspicion that, after being the boon companion of the King and owing his high office to the assumption of his congenial co-operation, he had perversely transformed himself into the uncompromising champion of church dignity to cloke his own overweening pride and ambition. The more he denied the charge the more he wrestled inwardly with the fear it might be true. In any event, it was impossible to separate champion and cause. The issue had become Becket's honour in the name of the Church's cause. The two were inseparable in fact, but properly separable in ethics.

This inescapable ambivalence between *officium* and *persona* is the central study of Eliot's *Murder in the Cathedral*. Whatever the status of the individual the theme is present in every religious existence. Believers cannot neutralise themselves in the act of belief. An indifferent devotee is a contradiction in terms. The self is inalienably present in every conviction about the self – sin, guilt, repentance, salvation, destiny, bliss – all have to do with the 'me-ness' at stake in them. Whatever, though inclusive of all mankind, is *about* 'me', is also 'mine' possessively. Self-knowing, self-defining, self-reckoning, even self-denying and self-reproaching, are all 'self-seeking', not merely as a search for who we are, but as a conscious will to have it. The self in being is always the self in becoming and both mean motivation, the one essentially the other operationally. Such is our egocentric situation. The Archbishop cannot isolate himself from his office. Nor more can any one, however lowly the 'office', status, relationship, may be.

Theravada Buddhism has long been aware of this situation and concluded that, since the self is inherently incapable of escaping it, and existence is inherently 'sinful', the only answer is an ultimate evaporation of the self, interpreted as an illusion, and the attainment, by long discipline, of the state of non-self in the undifferentiated unity of non-being.[28] In the view of Judaism, Christianity and Islam, that conclusion does violence to the significance of personality and denies the possibility of an unselfish selfhood. It only solves the problem of self-centredness by eliding it. Yet the relevance of Theravada Buddhism abides, if only in insisting that real selflessness within real selves is no sanguine expectation. Egocentrism as our natural situation is the very text of life. Ego non-centrism as a moral and spiritual salvation is the ever precarious work of grace.

It follows that in exploring Eliot's portrayal of Archbishop Thomas Becket's temptation to the paradoxical 'sin' of martyrdom – if such he allows it to be – we are close to the heart of selfhood as the core of all religion in the subtle art of man as an 'I'. Not even a martyr 'I' is exempt. Religions have made martyrs and in turn made much of them. For, death being the final mystery of the self, the inviting of it for faith's sake is, *de facto*, the ultimate self-surrender. To be sure death is 'the last enemy', the inevitable. But to let it come prematurely as the accommodated 'friend', for a faith's sake, is to maximise our self-forfeiture. Yet, for that very reason, the self will visualise beyond it. What reproach (of others) will the martyr perpetuate? What reward will he inherit? What vindication will his blood enjoy? What is posthumous may well compensate for what is suffered, even though he does not survive to see it.

There is, of course, a very large cult of martyrdom in Islam. Its soldiers have resolutely died in battle in immediate expectation of ensured Paradise. The very word *shahid* (as also in Greek) means both 'martyr' and 'witness'. The desirability of martyrdom *fi sabil-l-Illah*, 'in the path of God', and in *Jihad*, from the days of Khalid ibn Walid to the Ayatollah Khomeini, means that the maximum self-denying can earn the maximum self-deserving at the bar of God. The issue of integrity is, therefore, also at a maximum, with temptation critically real.

Denigrators of Islam, as we have seen in study of Salman Rushdie, have detected elements of the same issue in what he called 'revelations of convenience' in the career of Muhammad himself. We noted there that the issue needs a deeper cast of mind than Rushdie was equipped, or willing, to bring to it. But to identify malice or satire in its treatment in a novel is not to resolve the issue where genuine reverence must pursue it. Explicitly in the Qur'an itself the status of Muhammad becomes a salient question for his hearers or deriders. From: 'What is he saying and by what warrant?' they pass instinctively to: 'Who is he, anyhow?' The nature of the message entails the self of the messenger. All the chroniclers and historians tell of Muhammad's initial misgivings about his own genuine call, his legitimacy with it, even his sanity. Was he deluded in its reception? deceived in its content? abandoned in its delays? In full flow, *its* vindication was bound also to be *his*. So, triumphantly, it proved when Mecca capitulated. When 'religion was wholly God's' (Surah 8:39), its realisation was uniquely Muhammad's. His very singularity as the only recipient of the Qur'an made him the subject of the solitary relationship to God enshrined in the Islamic *Shahadah*: 'There is no god but God: Muhammad is the apostle of God.'

If it is proper to look into the inner meaning of that status within its bearer, we find ourselves pondering a supreme occasion – actual or potential – of the temptations of selfhood. Thought on them had better await our study of 'Abd al-Sabur's portrayal of those that belonged with the mystic Al-Hallaj, with whom Al-Sabur chose to relate a Muslim study of the self in the crisis of coveted martyrdom. Having Eliot and Al-Sabur together in this way can well serve as a prelude to venturing further into the hallowed territory of two founder-figures. It will be our duty, *en route*, to clarify where the two dramas of Canterbury and Baghdad differ and where they correspond.

V

In the first of the two acts of *Murder in the Cathedral*, Eliot builds up the sense of foreboding that hangs over the city and the cathedral, as interpreted by the Chorus of 'the women of Canterbury'. The quarrel with the King has passed the point of no return. Ambitious knights are set on ridding the Crown of 'this turbulent priest'. Impending evil stalks the scene and Becket prepares his people and himself for 'the doom on the house'. It is mid-winter and 'he comes in pride and sorrow, affirming his claims'. There is 'a final fear that none understands', except – perhaps – the Archbishop himself. He is beyond the temptation to worldly pleasure, beyond the lust for political power, above the snare of outright rebellion against the King. Rejection of all these narrows the situation into the option of suffering. Temptations refused are escape avenues closed.

But there is the fourth temptation – to face martyrdom with a subtle expectation of a martyr's humiliation of the King, to 'indulge the pleasure of his higher vices', to do 'the right things for the wrong reason'. Such a tempter 'always precedes expectation'. As 'saint and martyr, rule from the tomb,' he insinuates, 'I offer you what you desire.' Thomas is acutely aware of the dilemma. Suffer he will, but 'can he neither act nor suffer without perdition?' The menace of self-seeking dogs his self-oblation.

The only answer is to will to embrace the necessity to suffer but to do so willing thereby a 'purity of heart' that knows and means not to allow what would pervert it.

> For they who serve the greater cause may make the cause
> serve them, still doing right . . .[29]

In the Sermon which Eliot sets between the Acts, Thomas muses on martyrdom and affirms the 'good faith' of his will to suffer, as a will that identifies and resists its possible inauthenticity. The true martyrdom is never coveted but always a readiness.

> A Christian martyrdom . . . is never the effect of a man's will
> to become a saint . . . A martyrdom is always the design of
> God . . . It is never the design of man: for the true martyr is
> he who has become the instrument of God, who has lost his
> will in the will of God and who no longer desires anything
> for himself, not even the glory of being a martyr.[30]

The reiteration indicates how pervasive the fear of insincerity may be. In the second act the murder takes place, Thomas is hallowed in self-surrender into death. In a deliberately contrived anticlimax, Eliot has the three knights who kill him justify their action, as if in a contemporary public meeting, which requires the audience to reach their own conclusion about the motives and merits of the central victim. The near bathos of this scene is meant to 'secularise' the whole issue as if its religious intensity could be reduced to a calculus of vulgar *pro* and *con*. The Chorus, however, is in no doubt that a fearful sacrilege has been perpetrated against a true holiness. 'Clear the air! clean the sky! wash the wind!' 'The sin of the world' claims the blood of martyrs, who 'forever renew the earth.'

Within this central theme of *Murder in the Cathedral* there are several Islamic accents, unconscious, no doubt, but no less significant on that account. *Mukhlisun lahu al-din*, 'religiously sincere before Him' is a frequent refrain in the Qur'an: 'the law of God above the law of man'; the danger of having God's cause as our own; and how 'ambition fortifies the

will of man to become ruler over other men', unless such ambition is
resisted – if resisted it should be; all these have obvious bearing on
Muhammad's people.

vi

Ma'sat al-Hallaj has, likewise, two acts, with – in all – five scenes. 'Abd
al-Sabur uses bystanders as Eliot uses his Chorus to elucidate scene and
motive, and he inserts prose passages – in Qur'an style – after the manner
of the Christmas sermon in the cathedral. But the murder is not impending, as in Eliot; it is already committed when the action opens, with the
corpse of Ah-Hallaj suspended from a tree, done to death by a Muslim
form of 'crucifixion'. The action is, therefore, retrospective, tracing the
factors in what had transpired and, as in Eliot, leaving a verdict in
suspense for the audience to decide.

The antecedents of the two martyrdoms are, of course, quite contrasted, unified, however, by the common theme of the will to suffer, the
mysterium fascinans of a martyr's mind. What was it that carried the
'cordwainer' of Baghdad to such costly immolation?

Abdu -l-Mughith al-Husain ibn Mansur, named Al-Hallaj by his trade,
was born in 858 and reared in Persia as a devout Shi'ah Muslim. In early
youth he joined a Sufi monastic brotherhood but left the Order when he
was around thirty for reasons which may have had to do with a desire for
a greater relevance to social poverty. In his drama 'Abd al-Sabur lays emphasis on this break and attributes it to social compassion. One of the perpetual issues within all mysticisms is that of whether the will to mystical
ecstasy forsakes the world or whether it returns to it in kindled liability for
its redemption from ignorance and evil.

Al-Hallaj became a celebrated preacher, travelled to India, Asia and
Mecca and came to enjoy, in Baghdad, a wide reputation as saint and
teacher. At the age of sixty-four he was arrested, slain, mutilated and
burned. There is much that is obscure about his story. Miracles which are
told of him may be ascribed to occult powers,to hypnosis, and the form of
Shi'ah Islam which he led. The actual charge against him at his trial,
according to the surviving record of the clerk of the court, was that he
taught that the *Hajj*, the mandatory pilgrimage to Mecca, could be
performed without travelling there.[31] But tradition surrounds the event
with other themes. Did he, or did he not, say the Sufi formula: *Ana-l-
Haqq*, 'I am the real', or: 'I am the true', using one of the names of God.
These, according to his son, he allowed others to use in letters sent to him,

such as 'O Nourisher', and 'O Bestower'. Or it may be that what he really said was: *Ana ara,* 'I see.'

In either case he would be broadly in the usage of his Sufi contemporaries, Al-Tustari (d.896) and Al-Junayd (d.910), in claim to the unitive state of absorption into God in the ecstacy of *fana*', or the passing away of the empirical self so that: 'I am He whom I love and He whom I love is I.' In that event the issue of his trial would have been the view of his accusers that he was literally blaspheming, claiming divinity for himself *qua* person – clearly a fatal heresy. It may be that for Al-Hallaj to disabuse them of that utter misconception and to interpret to them the real meaning would have been precluded by the nature of Sufi experience itself, as that which cannot belong within explanation, speech, or rational discourse. To think that it could would be to betray its utter inwardness and to disavow the insight by which it had been known. A mystery beyond articulation to a court, even under pain of death, would be sealed in the victim's readiness to die.

Whether or not this gives us the true reading of his 'murder in Baghdad', or whether other – political and theological – issues were involved, it is this will to suffer and to die which fascinates 'Abd al-Sabur and draws him to its dramatic portrayal. In the opening scene of *Ma'sat al-Hallaj*, a merchant, a peasant and a mosque preacher stroll in the public square discussing the swinging corpse. They talk laconically, the preacher sensing a moral to use in his Friday sermon. 'Words' killed him, a crowd leader says – the cry of 'Heretic!' Sufis merely 'let him die', ambivalent about his significance and preferring a mystery not explained. They are only sure of his will to die believing in the fertility in 'the blood he draws from the veins'. (p.7). Shibli, a Sufi companion of the dead saint, laments the death and hints that Al-Hallaj should have remained a pure Sufi free of the world's cares. Was it worthy of his sacrifice? Perplexity broods over all.

It is only partially dispelled in the next scene, in which Al-Hallaj and Shibli are discoursing on the central dilemma of the mystic: Is the quest an end in itself or for the sake of the world? Movingly, 'Abd al-Sabur has the saint urging upon himself the plight of mankind.

> The poverty of the poor, the hunger of the hungry:
> In such eyes as theirs I see a glow which means
>   something . . .
> Tell me, Shibli, how can I close my eyes to the world
> And not wrong my own heart? (pp.12-13)

Injustice, oppression, disease, pain, racial stigma, defilement – these cannot be ignored. But Shibli argues that 'evil is old in the world' and 'each man must find the road to his own salvation.' (p.15). Another mystic breaks into their conversation with word that Al-Hallaj is under suspicion by the authorities. He had better be discreet. They talk of the dupes of the hopes that wait on power and how they should react to fear and intimidation – by silence, by flight, by exile, by trust in the protest of words, by waiting on miracle? Al-Hallaj rejects the thought of pilgrimage which might offset suspicion and tells Shibli why he abandons the robes of the Sufi Order the more truly to be absorbed in love to God in compassion towards man.

In the next scene, we overhear the conversation between a lame man, a leper and a hunchback, commiserating over dubious cures. Three Sufis enter and deepen the earlier theme of Sufi withdrawal and engagement. Should 'the Vestment' mean immunity or ministry to need? To discard it is to be like the rest of men; to wear it as a spiritual élite is to ignore the world. Al-Hallaj appears inviting the poor and needy to his arms while merchant, peasant and preacher trivialise exchanges. Quoting from the Qur'an's account of the creation and dignity of man, Al-Hallaj bewails the evils that plague the human story and warns that ritual acts, prayer, Qur'an recital, pilgrimage and fast are only 'steps taken by the feet'.

> But the Lord seeks the heart,
> And only love, which is of the heart, pleases Him . . . (p.29)

He is interrupted by law officers who interrogate him about his doctrine. Al-Hallaj quotes Surah 24:35: 'God's light is the lamp', but adds, suspiciously: 'My thinking is the opening of the niche . . .'[33] – the closest 'Abd al-Sabur comes to the celebrated phrase alleged of Al-Hallaj, as his supreme 'heresy'. The saint refuses to enlighten them further: 'Do you not know that love is a secret between two lovers?' (p.30). But the mystic secret that cannot be divulged sets the trap of condemnation. At once Al-Hallaj senses an unworthy pride in his appalling risk-taking. Yet how could he 'leave these words unspoken'? Bystanders and Sufis protest: 'he is delirious', 'he is old and deranged'. Al-Hallaj, looking towards heaven, yearns to be punished in what is mingled fidelity and presumption.

Act 2, Scene 1, finds Al-Hallaj in prison. Like Joseph of old he encounters two prisoners, who alternately mock him, find him incomprehensible, deride him, respect and love him. The author brings together vulgarity and sanctity, the raw world and the holy fool. When the prisoners fight, a guard mistakes Al-Hallaj for the culprit and beats him cruelly, only to be melted by Al-Hallaj's reaction of accepted humiliation as proof of God's favour. Prison conversation is resumed. The second prisoner, telling his story of privation and frustrated hope, talks of retaliation and escape. Al-Hallaj pleads the utter complexity of evil in realms no avenging sword can reach and gropes for assurance in his own struggle.

The final scene brings the drama into Baghdad High Court. The prisoner faces his three judges, who – prior to his entry – have debated his case after some initial banter in which their characters are revealed. The first strand of the charge – political miscreance – is finally refuted by the appearance of a messenger who reports that the Sultan has cleared Al-Hallaj completely of any involvement in incitement to rebellion. This aborts the long discussion about sedition and the rights of power over the subject's life. But in the view of two judges it does not exonerate. The implications of 'wild words', suspicious behaviour, religious eccentricity, extravagant piety, all remain. Only one named Ibn Surayj reads Al-Hallaj as a man of pure intention and protests against 'the temerity that questions a man's faith'. He resigns from the court, urging that only God has that right. The other two proceed to sentence after questioning Shibli who answers evasively about Al-Hallaj's version of active Sufism, and pleads to keep his secret. He is dismissed and Al-Hallaj is condemned to die, his 'words about poverty' merely 'a veil for his heresy'. The judges lay the onus on the clamouring crowd.

The drama of the court-room scene leaves the issues open. The sentencing judges hide behind the mob. They are not themselves ex-ecutioners but officials of the State. For Ibn Surayj 'justice is an ever recurring question', not a mere creature of power. (p.62). The others cite the Qur'an on 'the punishment of those who spread sedition in the land', (p.59, c.f. Surah 8:73). In his long *confessio*, disclaiming mere 'defence', Al-Hallaj describes his painful search for truth, his gnawing fear that in the forms of religion and the sensual vision of Paradise he was 'selling his prayers to God', worshipping his self-love. He found a loved teacher and learned to lose himself in love to God. He came to belong with the wretchedness of the poor yet could not look for their liberation to corrupt power. Poverty has to abjure hate and bow to love. (pp.63-70).

The dramatist makes few allusions to the Qur'an – only the familiar: 'He is our Creator and to Him we return,'(p.72) and an echo of the question in Surah 47:24, in Al-Hallaj's: 'Can a word open hearts that are sealed with locks of gold?' (p.69). There are, however, several references to the passion of Jesus. It might be said that there are closer parallels to the cross in Jerusalem than to the murder at Canterbury. 'His blood be on us,' is said by the mob and the two judges (pp.5, 75) and Al-Hallaj counts as his 'friends' the verses and letters of the Qur'an and 'the words of him who was sad and forsaken on the Mount of Olives.' (p.19). The second prisoner in the gaol quotes to him 'the words of his model, Jesus'. (p.45).

Allusions apart, central to the whole is the theme of the self in the turmoil of anticipating death as the final, the only, context of fidelity to truth. There *is* vicarious meaning. It is 'as though the burdens of the world were upon his shoulders,' mutters the strolling preacher (p.3). 'True love is the death of the lover', (p.21) who invites his beloved 'to eat together the bread of our Lord and Master.' It is an invitation to surrender. Yet its exemplar, Al-Hallaj, is beset with misgiving, lest in his coveting of death into transcendent love he is still a self seeking its own. 'Can he', as with Thomas, 'neither act nor suffer without perdition?' Perhaps, as with all such 'guilt', the sense that it might be so is the one proof that it is not. Integrity, either way, is all. Al-Hallaj's last word in *Ma'sat* is 'God is our Creator and to Him we return.'

vii

Both Eliot and 'Abd al-Sabur people their verse with the raw, vulgar, obscene, confused, fickle, oppressed humanity of the real world – a world where power is corrupted and common folk suffer, grope and die. Both plead for a faith that belongs with them, for exemplars of truth who see through the shams, identify the temptations and reach for purity of heart, but who only attain that quality by a willingness to die. There the inner testing of the soul arrives, in that such willingness – being the zenith of love – leaves them no escape from the fear that the self they yield may still be the self they deceive, that self-sacrifice must know itself as self-regard.

The two dramas are a far cry from *The Satanic Verses* in the quality of their art and the discipline of their themes. But their study of the religious self-in-crisis returns us to the 'self- issue' – if we may so phrase it – in the Muhammad of the Qur'an and the Jesus of the Gospel. 'The true greatness [of the prophet],'wrote Abraham Heschel, 'is his ability to hold God and man in a single thought.'[33] He means that revelation is not a passive receptivity as if the prophet were merely a microphone for God, but rather that inspiration co-operates with the active mind and emotion humanly immersed in all that the message signifies and with the necessity why it must be uttered. The messenger then is only rightly a mouthpiece in being truly a person.

We have seen elsewhere that the traditional Muslim view of the role of Muhammad is to think him a mouthpiece only, dissociated, in mind and emotion, from both the content and the expression of what he tells. Personality, of course, is vitally present in the Qur'an when he faces the consequences and the controversies to which his message leads – a fact which is very evident from the text and the sequence of the Scripture. But orthodoxy requires to believe that the personality so engaged evacuates again into Quranic receptivity in order that the deliverance of the words may be wholly God's. There is thus a kind of oscillation between an impersonal passivity that receives and an active personality that avails once the words are uttered.

This account is far from suiting the actualities of the Quranic situation. It would seem that it is rigorously held, nevertheless, as part of the religious demand for that which is 'guaranteed' and 'infallible' – being so obviously from outside the Prophet's will and, therefore, the more incontestably 'the Word of the Lord'. Yet it would seem, on the contrary, that the passive theory of 'revelation' plays into the hands of sceptics who want, maliciously or otherwise, to suspect that Muhammad, at least in later stages, could 'induce' the deliverances at will and in his own interest. Sceptics may think what they will and anathemas can suffice for them. Believers may dismiss them with contempt for them and anger at their blasphemy.

Yet, with proper reverence, the issue persists. It would be more intelligently studied if we were allowed to ponder the self of Muhammad, in the shape of the text, in no way non-entitled, but as fully engaged – not, thereby, to scout its authenticity but to establish it. To think of 'God and man in a single thought' would actually locate the integrity of the Word more deeply, more vitally, than celestial dictation ever could. The more integral the partnership the more existential the prophethood. Then the final security would be that 'sincerity' (*ikhlas*) for which the Qur'an pleads, and without which the achievement of Muhammad could never have come to pass.

In Surah 80 there is a revealing rebuke to Muhammad who is called to task for disdaining a blind recruit on whom 'he frowned' (the title of the Surah). Was it not in inwardness that the rebuke was registered, perhaps even anticipated on reflection? Perhaps, similarly, we can leave within Muhammad's human conscience those passages detractors delight to allege as self-serving, as capable of being understood within a rubric of sincerity, provided we acknowledge the genuinely human factor (and not otherwise) that can register the flush of success, succumb to impulse – as at the battle of Uhud – and zealously read revelation as coinciding with desire, and yet – over all – be absolved of any pervasive insincerity.

Any study of the self in Muhammad in association with the cause of God goes deeper far than these passages of 'convenient revelation' which critics interrogate into the arena of warfare in 'the path of God'. Here there was the risk of martyrdom by death in battle. The self was certainly in radical expenditure. But fight requires the willing self to lay aside the scruple of self-doubt, the suspicion of self-seeking. Its very vicissitudes come into the Scriptured revelation. Jeopardy already stands in the logic of legitimacy. The cause has already absolved its pursuit when that pursuit is martial. If in battle for faith the fallen are martyrs, they have exacted from fallen enemies the same role, and is it well to martyrise evil? Or, as Al-Hallaj asks the belligerent prisoner: 'Who will give you a seeing sword?' (p.50) – a sword whose using does not blind. For

> They die not well that die in a battle when blood is their argument.

The point takes us far from the immediacies of *Murder in the Cathedral* and *Ma'sat al-Hallaj*, where martyrs have only to search the conscience that suffers, in the bearer, not the doer, of death. Yet it belongs squarely with the reverse situation when the prophet suffering becomes the prophet armed. When 'the greater cause' is served by force, its servants may the more palpably 'make the cause serve them'. For such is the nature of combat.

viii

Returning to our cue from Dag Hammarskjöld, what of the passion of Jesus which so evidently underlies the work of Eliot and Salah 'Abd al-Sabur? There have been Muslims who wondered whether Jesus' prospect of 'resurrection' did not somehow make inauthentic the experience of Gethsemane. Assured of such a sequel, could not anything be bearable? Was Jesus in truth tempted, like the Archbishop, by vistas of posthumous glory? Hammarskjöld's reverence disallowed the thought: 'What we have added later was not there for Him.' But have we 'added' it? Do we not identify in Jesus 'God and man in one thought' and that – not merely in the capacity for revelation – but in the actuality of Messiah, 'God in Christ reconciling'?

The Gospels depict a Jesus who shrank desperately from impending agony and death. He was no ardent would-be martyr. But he recognised the gathering crisis of rejection and saw that he could not evade it by smooth words, by eluding its centre in Jerusalem, by abating to be who and how he was. He read the crisis as 'the cup my Father has given me'. The prospect and the reality of suffering were implicit in the entire situation to which, in the given world of Jewry and Rome, his ministry had brought him. He did not possess or desire the option followed by Muhammad who, around 619 and before the chink of hope out of Yathrib, had entered a Gethsemane of his own.[34] The Gospels see the self of Jesus as inwardly minded into the mind of God. If we choose to attribute this delineation to the disciples later, it seems incredible to think they could have been its authors and he not.

Gethsemane and its sequel, therefore, stand for Christians as the paradigm of how we should relate the sovereignty of God to the evil of the world, namely, in the love that suffers to redeem, but only so because 'God and man – one thought' – the eternal wisdom and the human travail. Then resurrection does not obtain as a happy ending superimposed on a sad tragedy, nor as a compensating eventuation making travail inauthentic as its prelude. On the contrary, it obtains as the evidence, the quality, of what was always there, 'the victory that overcomes the world'. As such it qualifies to ensure and undergird the victory of all other sufferers who can traverse the labyrinths of the self, in wretchedness and hope, by the same criterion of love and the available resources of grace.

The verse dramas of Eliot and 'Abd al-Sabur can well stand in their own right as poetry and art. Theology should not annex them. Yet there is about their quest into selfhood and suffering, into evil around and tragedy within, into the temptations of religious pride and the subtleties of sin, a reckoning between faiths that formal dialogue might never attain. Theirs is certainly the context into which we can best place the burdens of the human condition as we find them in the poems of 'Abd al-Sabur earlier reviewed. For it was a kind of dumb martyrdom which he there portrayed, the anxieties of the common self. In translation, the writer's name means: 'The probity, the rightness, of the servant of the patient Lord.' There seems a fitness there.[35]

Chapter 10

ASAF 'ALI ASGHAR FYZEE
(1899 – 1981)

'The Plight of this Arabian Faith'

i

'Abandon it altogether?... an attitude to which I am entirely opposed.'[1]
What could be meant by a 'plight' to stay with, seen to be such by one of
the most prominent exponents of Islamic Law this century?[2] Is there a hint
of tension when a committed Indian Muslim refers to 'this Arabian faith'?
Isma'il al-Faruqi could not complain for, as we have seen in Chapter 7, he
readily identified Islam as the quintessence of Arabism,[3] conceding as he
did so that Islam has greatly exceeded its Arab denominators of place and
speech and culture through its fourteen centuries. Nevertheless, across all
its wide, ethnic and territorial dispersion, Islam has remained 'an Arabian
faith', by virtue of its inalienably Arabic Scripture and its final, un-
repeatable Arab Prophet. That dominant circumstance has always been an
issue where the Qur'an and Muhammad have travelled beyond the
peninsula of the Arabs. The reasons why for A.A.A. Fyzee are not far to
seek.

Before exploring them we have to ask why 'plight' should be the word
he chooses, writing in 1962. It has, of course, good associations, as in
'plighting troth'. But he is not intending it in archaic terms. The word has
to do with what is 'bound up' with a situation, as 'complexion' (with which
it is associated) is what belongs on a face or can be given to a situation.
'Plight' in Fyzee's context has to do with a predicament, seen as critical,
possibly dangerous, and certainly urgent. It means for him that all is not
well but can be rectified and needs to be addressed. We may assume that
the reference to 'Arabia' hints that he will be responding in, and from, the

Indian milieu. He accepts the trans-cultural, universal community of Islam but requires that Bombay be heard as well as Mecca or Damascus or the Azhar in Cairo. That Bombay has an angle on all things Muslim we have learned in Salman Rushdie, but from a very different ethos in the same Bombay.

We had better come to biography here by first appreciating the setting. A.A.A. Fyzee's mature years were spent in the trauma of the partition of the sub-continent and the creation of Pakistan. The controversies which led up to it, and the aftermath which followed, sharply divided Islamic India. The will to have a 'Pakistan' or 'country of the pure', where a Muslim population was in the majority goes down in history as an eloquent witness to the self-understanding of Islam. But it was not unanimous. There were those, like Asaf Fyzee and his great mentor Maulana Azad, who believed profoundly in the other option of all-India unity. They anticipated the enormous cost in life and limb, in human misery and exile, that partition must entail, and wanted to spare a common homeland that tragedy. They believed in Islam's destiny as a religion and without benefit of majority statehood. This they read as a true vocation. There was a deep logic in their position, at least in Indian terms, despite the age-long tradition of the power dimension in Arab, Ottoman, Mamluk and other Islam, including much of their own Indian retrospect.

But the popular fear of the vulnerability of Muslims in an undivided India, liable to the vagaries of majority Hindu attitudes, prevailed. The Muslim League, from the time of the Lahore Resolution of 1940, made partition an adamant demand, insisting that the Muslim League alone could speak for all Muslims. Under the astute leadership of Muhammad Ali Jinnah, who was, privately, a very secular Muslim, that demand was fulfilled. The closer India came to independence, the more absolute became the doctrine that Muslims (in their majority areas) were 'a nation' and not merely 'a community'. Thus Pakistan, East and West, came into being as a separate independent State, created to realise the only true and secure Islamic existence.

The clear illogicality of that decision lay in the fact that it condemned Muslims remaining in separate India to a condition in which Islam was for ever to lack the one prerequisite of survival, namely its own statehood. There could not be further Pakistans. Those Muslim millions would have to accept the very vulnerability which the case for Pakistan declared to be entirely unacceptable. Indeed, there were those in Pakistan logical enough to anticipate that Islam in India would wither away.

Survive it did, but only by virtue of a confidence in its survival power as a faith and an ideology, which Pakistan saw as misplaced. It could be argued that, in one sense, Pakistan could somehow assist by its existence those it had to leave outside its borders and its panacea of statehood. But Pakistan also deepened the problematics of Indian Muslims. For, through at least a decade after the partition, suspicion was cast over the Indian loyalty of Muslims precisely because of the new, independent neighbour. Were they simply delaying a departure to it? Were they lingering with no good purpose? Could their loyalty be trusted? How would they vindicate their Islamic and their Indian identity as one integrity, despite the ever-present symbol in Pakistan of these being incompatible?[4] Would their Hindu compatriots in separate India be tempted into reading *their* statehood – though with a secular constitution – in terms like those of Pakistan but on behalf of Hinduism? How, in short, would Indian Islam take its new and permanent vulnerability?

No study of the inner faith of Asaf Fyzee would be right if it failed to appreciate the reality of this situation as faced by thinking Muslims pre- and post-partition. In the wake of a tragic upheaval and chronic mutual occasion of bitterness, they had to work out the logic of their opposition to partition and apply themselves to existence in co-operation and 'just as a religion', making good an urgent co-citizenship in truly Muslim terms. There were few precedents to guide them. Some in the Muslim masses might reconcile to exclusion from the Pakistani solution in a stolid sort of communalism, securing faith and psyche in the solace of dogma and tradition. Indian Islam since 1947 has not lacked emulators of extremists elsewhere. But the new situation called for creative deployment of the spiritual resources in the Qur'an and the *Shari'ah*. The loss of exclusive Muslim control of prestigious educational institutions like Aligarh and Osmania Universities, and many political factors, demanded a leadership of vision and energy, such as Asaf Fyzee, in his specialist field of jurisprudence and *fiqh*, was equipped to bring.

ii

The intellectual and spiritual resilience of Indian Islam was amply proved by such contemporaries of Fyzee as Dr Zakir Husain who became President of India in 1967[5]. His tenure of the highest office of state was a remarkable symbol of the intentions of state-secularism at a time when the constitutional self-definition of Pakistan was still indeterminate.[6] Though less highly placed, there is point in taking Asaf Fyzee as an articulate

representative of Indian dimensions of Islam for two reasons. The one is
that we can readily gather around him – as we mean to do – other voices to
counter any suspicion of an isolated mind. The second is that Islamic Law,
not politics, was his field. As the author of *Outlines of Muhammadan
Law*,[7] a well established text, his angle on the issues was always perceptive
and practical. He carried the specifics of society, as law handles them, into
his more philosophical reflections on the nature of Islam.

Law, it has often been remarked, is more central to Islam than is
theology. To be sure, its doctrine of the Qur'an and of Muhammad's
prophethood provides it with rigorously theological ethics and it understands the norms of society as God-ordained. It follows that it is more
concerned with 'doing' than with 'being' and 'knowing', as the task of
faith. Lawyers, therefore, are often more central to Islamic responses than
theologians. The cutting edge of change is more immediately in their field,
especially where new patterns of circumstance are continually emerging
and, as in India, the situation lacks the reassuring sanction of statehood
and dominance.

Yet, if the legal front is where concrete decisions obtain, the logic of
them has to be sought within, and even behind, the religious authority on
which hitherto the science of *fiqh*, or jurisprudence, has relied. In that
way, law and theology have always been mutually engaged in Islam, but
with practice according to the former, rather than speculation in the latter,
the predominant concern. Indeed, speculation in doctrine for its own
sake, or divorced from concrete situations, has often been decried or
avoided in Islam. A lively lawyer, then, can prove a surer guide than an
abstract theologian, the more so if he is also an educationalist familiar
with public administration, and has first class qualifications in the classical
languages of Islam – Arabic, Persian and Urdu.

Asaf Fyzee was all these. His early education at St. Xavier's College,
Bombay, took him to the Oriental Languages Tripos at St. John's College,
Cambridge where he was a Foundation Scholar. He studied law at the
Middle Temple, London, where he was called to the Bar in 1924. He
began practice in the Bombay High Court the following year and continued there until he became Principal of the Government Law College
and its Professor of Jurisprudence in 1938. There he spent the testing years
of pre-partition debate and controversy, culminating in 1947 when, in the
very throes of partition, he took up membership of the Bombay Public
Service Commission for two troubled years. Like many academics in
newly independent states, he was recruited for diplomatic service – in his
case suitably as Ambassador in Cairo, returning to India in 1951 to join

the Union Public Service Commission in New Delhi. From 1957 to 1960 he was Vice-Chancellor of the University of Jammu and Kashmir. During that tenure he visited McGill University, Montreal, as a Professor in the newly founded Institute of Islamic Studies, headed at that time by Wilfred Cantwell Smith.

In 1962 he returned to Cambridge, to St. John's College, as a Commonwealth Fellow, renewing association with Professor A.J. Arberry in Oriental Studies. He had then finally retired from Government Service and was engaged on a translation of the Fatimid (Shi'ah) Textbook of Muslim Law, *Da'a'im al-Islam*, 'The Pillars of Islam', of Al-Nu'man, the eminent Qadi in tenth century Cairo.[8] His sojourn in Cambridge also gave him opportunity of reflection on Christian Scriptures, notably the Gospel according to John.[9] Coincidentally, he had published at the time of his return to Cambridge his four essays on *A Modern Approach to Islam* which are a terse summary of the shape of his mind. Ten years later he had the satisfaction of election as an Honorary Member of the *Deutsche Morgenlandische Gesellschaft* of Marburg, the oldest Oriental Society in Europe, restricted to twenty members.

iii

The central place of Al-Nu'man's *Da'a'im* in Fyzee's academic concerns derives from his allegiance to the Isma'ili expression of Shi'ah Islam. It is always well in religious studies to hear from minorities. They are an index to the tensions implicit in majority positions and they represent the will to diversity that must somehow assert itself even in the most monolithic systems. The broad distinctions between Sunni and Shi'ah in Islam are well known and do not call for exposition here. Minority verdicts, no doubt, are capable of extreme fanaticism and the Shi'ah are no exception. They are liable to much fragmentation inasmuch as the separatist principle by which they came into being has a habit of repeating itself. Luther defying Rome may be himself defied by the same plea that 'One can do no other.' So it has proved within Shi'ah Islam with its division into the Seveners and the Twelvers and other groups like the Ibadis and, more distantly still, the Druzes.

Yet, given the temper of mind that Fyzee possessed, the very fact of minority identity generates a capacity for detachment and tolerance. The Isma'ili knows he cannot dominate. His very status may make him minded to translate his need of comprehension into a ready practice of it. Where there is a genuine piety the sectarian may well be a most useful mentor precisely by being not the major representative within the whole. Asaf Fyzee qualifies well in this sense. His intellectualism ensured that his attitudes were always perceptive and urbane, and vigorously aware of the dangers of stagnation attending Indian Islam in the aftermath of grievous partition. It also made him receptive to the long Indian tradition of Mughal eclecticism, symbolised by the Emperor Akbar and sharply reversed by the militant, and ultimately disastrous, policy of the arch-Sunni, the Emperor Aurangzib.

As an Isma'ili, Fyzee valued religious pluralism as the context of his own particularity, with a lawyer's pragmatic sense of the necessity of mutuality between the segments of Islamic faith. He could happily set alongside each other the 'Instructions' of the Sunni Caliph 'Umar and the *Da'a'im* of 'Ali, Caliph and Imam, and paragon of all the Shi'ah. There was, for him, no need to obtrude what had been bitterly at stake between the emotional heirs of either figure in reaching what most concerned him, namely, the articulation of an intelligent Islam in the world as it was and as it could only be in what lay immediately ahead. His preoccupations with jurisprudence meant that Fyzee did not explicitly extend that instinct to inter-faith debate in detailed terms. His Islam was orientated, within itself, to coexistence beyond itself as the only feasible frame of reference for its own meaning. 'Approach to Islam' – or, indeed, 'approach' anywhere as a turn of phrase – is a curious usage. For it can only happen outside its quarry. It offers an image of how we might 'come at' something, be it a time bomb or an interview, whereas it is a 'coming with' that is in point. However, the usage persists and Fyzee must not be reproached for employing it. In studying his *A Modern Approach* we find ourselves moving from and with Islam. Neither he nor his critics would be writing if they were not already there, *in* Islam. Every faith *is* an inter-faith, non-participants apart. It is his side of such a dialogue with which we are concerned in Fyzee.

iv

As a jurisprudent, Asaf Fyzee might have been expected to read vocation in terms of a juristic view of the Islamic *Shari'ah*, of what could be proved to be 'correct' by reference to its texts and organs. Instead he saw law within a more inclusive concept of *Din*, or 'religion', embodying the ideal life of Islam in which more than one law-system might find its due place by reading of the Islamic mind. Here exposition must resort to

Maulana Abu-l-Kalam Azad to whose quality of thought and leadership Fyzee was deeply indebted. With impeccable Muslim antecedents, actually born in Mecca, and nurtured in Arabic and Sufi culture, a lively journalist and, in due time, a close colleague of Mahatma Gandhi in leadership of the Congress Party, Azad (1888-1958) became, both in politics and character, the epitome of the Islamic logic for a united India. It was, perhaps, in his example in the face of sustained vilification that he best represented the necessary art of vulnerability that must always be the test of true religion in the secular and plural world – an art traditionally uncongenial to the original mind-shape of Islam. Fear and avoidance of it had, of course, lain behind the separatism of the Muslim League – the body which from the late thirties demanded to be the sole mouth-piece of Indian Muslims and so sharply resisted Azad's distinguished contrary voice, 'In *India Wins Freedom'*, [10] wrote Muhammad Mujeeb (of Maulana Azad's narrative of its winning):

> ...there is not even a passing reference to the invective, the abuse and the gross insults heaped upon him by his Muslim opponents...He could eliminate irrelevant religious considerations when thinking of, or discussing, purely political issues. This detachment was possible because of the sincerity and strength of his religious belief. [11]

Fyzee turned admiringly to Azad's inspiration and set the Azad Commentary, *Tarjuman al-Qur'an*[12], in the forefront of his own 'approach' (MAI,pp.1-24), as expressing 'the essence of Islam', and as a ground for the legitimation of the secular state as compatible with it. To be sure, the sovereignty of a parliament in which Muslims would always be a minority would be arguably regulating Muslim affairs in ways which, traditionally, non-Muslims could have no writ or right to enjoy. Yet moral tests could still confer Islamic legitimacy on that situation, given its significance for nationhood and within agreed prescripts based on mutual co-operation. Institutions acquired such legitimacy, even as secular, to the extent in which they enshrined 'the essence of Islam', within what Azad called 'the law of universal goodwill'. Virtue and merit were to be greeted and trusted wherever found. Had not Muhammad in Medina concerted one *ummah*, or 'body-politic' with non-Muslim tribes around the city?[13]

In a sense, once partition had happened, Muslim 'tolerance' of the secular state was the only option. But for Fyzee, as for Azad, this was not the ultimate ground of the position. Together they made evident its roots – as they saw them – in the Qur'an, via the concepts of *Rububiyyah*, or 'divine Lordship', ordaining *taqdir*, understood as the role each had to play, and enjoining on man that dignity within *Din* that made him custodian of the good earth on behalf of God as *Al-Rabb*. The concept of *Dar al-Islam* had to be understood as obtaining without separate statehood by virtue of the occasion – within Hindu/Muslim/Sikh/other 'Indianization' – for the active achievement of the ultimate Islamic *Jihad* which had to do with the faithful struggle for the good whatever the odds and whatever the cost.[14]

On this view, acceptance of the finality of Muhammad meant also that the true Muslim accepted all the prophets in the conviction of the essential unity of their messages. This was, of course, easier in respect of the monotheisms. The idolatrous nature apparent in Hinduism presented acute problems. Azad's strong Islamic monotheism firmly resisted what he saw as 'definition by negation' in the Upanishads. For this denied to mankind the possibility of positive belief. Hindu non-duality, *advaita*, could not be reconciled with the *Allah/'abd*, Creator/creature, Lord/servant, relatedness as the Qur'an knew it. Nevertheless, could the moral teachings in Hinduism, as far as they went, and as cultural philosophy rather than 'revelation', still be comprehended within an Islamic rubric of value? 'Indianization' seemed to require so.

v

In pursuit of these impulses as truly Muslim, Fyzee takes pains to expound Azad's exegesis of the opening Surah, *Surat al-Fatihah*, as the clue to the whole Qur'an. He lists its verses as enjoining a right awareness of the divine attributes, the law of just returns attending good and evil actions, judgement after death, and the path of rectitude and right conduct. *Hamd*, 'praise', must undergird all living. For the world is the arena of God's provident mercy and sustaining, nourishing Lordship. Equity in benefaction characterises the divine ordaining or *taqdir*, which has implication in the laws of science and the moral order.

Such 'destinating' is not, however, arbitrary but wise and imbued with *hidayah*, or 'guidance', in which the senses and the rational faculty in man are recruited. In this way the Qur'an itself must be seen as rational in its appeal to mind and spirit, inviting the self to reverent apprehension of nature and meaning. Its concept of divine *Rahmah*, 'mercy', embraces evolutionary development and is manifested in order and beauty and justice. It is active in the gift to the world of successive prophethoods,

united in a common summons to men, and warning against evil. The result
is a discrimination which discerns the right from the wrong.

Fyzee, following Azad, is alert to a difference between the ethics of
Jesus and the greater realism of Muhammad. He sees the 'hard sayings' of
Jesus about 'turning the other cheek', 'loving enemies', and 'not resisting
evil', as broadly impracticable for ordinary folk but as hyperbolically
phrased for Jesus' immediate context of Jewish strife. Muhammad's more
attainable ethic has a universal relevance in being both feasible and realist,
restraining but not ignoring human nature. Fyzee underlines the call to
compassion 'even in the most . . . intractable worldly or political or personal affairs.' (MAI, p.15).

Divine justice ensures that every action has due reward or requital,
following logically, not arbitrarily, from God's rule. This is the *kasb*, 'the
earning' of men's deeds, not to be confused with Jewish particularism or
Christian ideas of 'original sin', devolving on each generation. Fyzee,
however, attempts no deep study of what these themes might mean, being
content with a brief dismissive notice.

He adopts an interesting distinction Azad makes between three ascend-
ing meanings of Muslim experience. The first, *islam*, is the familiar
believing and belonging with performance of the Five Pillars. The second,
iman, is a stage of more developed faith and spiritual awareness. It leads,
thirdly, to *ihsan*, 'well-being', in a mystical perception of the divine
reality. A religiousness, transcending the 'normal' claims and beliefs
of Islam, suggests a clear potential emancipation from formalism and
rigorism and serves well to accommodate such Muslims to a discerning
pluralism, as in the case both of Azad and Fyzee.[15]

Religious diversity is in mind where Fyzee distinguishes between *Din*,
'religion' *per se*, seen as one, and 'legal, or ritual, form', *shar'* which may
be various. Diversities in the latter are seen as a test of goodwill, intended
so by God Himself to necessitate tolerance consistently with firm faith.
This attitude, taught by Quranic verses, prevents religions from being
necessarily adversarial, since *all* are in essence true as a common gift from
God, while customs and rituals, and – in part – laws, differ and should not
be thought to possess determinative control over salvation. However, in
line with the last verse of *Al-Fatihah*, there *is* an astrayness about some
religious forms and attitudes on which divine 'anger rests'. Fyzee sees
these as attaching to the annexation of religious faith or practice to the
vested interest of a race, or class, or sect, or other form of *privilegio*
arrogated to these and contravening the inclusive revelation finalised in
the Qur'an.

Asaf Fyzee depends heavily on his great contemporary and concludes his exposition of Maulana Azad's Quranic theology by observing:

> Such a simple and logical concept of the basis of Islam seems to be singularly appropriate at a time when humanity is grappling with the forces of fear, jealousy, greed and hatred all over the world. It is a message of everlasting Beauty, Truth and Justice. (MAI, p.24).

If theologians must feel that it leaves many open ends and is innocent of questions beneath it, it none the less represents a bold dialogue within Islam and it suffices a lawyer for other conclusions to which we now pass.

vi

It is as a lawyer that he shrewdly both affirms and eludes the familiar Islamic understanding that 'law is not distinct from religion' (MAI, p.85) and that Islam fills the whole of life. But he then distinguishes between *Shari'ah* and *Fiqh*, seeing the former, not in the traditional sense of explicit directive, but as the all-embracing idealism of Islam, while *Fiqh* is the power of reasoning by which God would have us deduce and formulate the detailed structure of law. 'The path of *Shari'ah* is laid down by God and His Prophet: the edifice of *Fiqh* is erected by human endeavour.' (MAI, p.85). This gives to *Fiqh* and to the role of jurisprudence a much wider, fuller, freer task than they can properly enjoy when *Shari'ah* is understood as itself having already foreclosed, in revelation, the prescripts of Islamic life, leaving to men of law only the much narrower role of limited adaptation to social change. Traditionalists must necessarily regard such spiritualising of *Shari'ah* as dangerously innovative. In effect, 'the divinely ordained path of rectitude', which *Shari'ah* is, passes rationally into the trust of 'law as a science'.

Fyzee proceeds to locate the science of law firmly within the aegis of the democratic state where laws have to apply equally and impersonally to all citizens. The corollary is that religion has to do with personal inwardness where the *Shari'ah*, as spiritual ideology, has its 'inner core of belief'. Ritual rules and what he calls 'trappings' may be communal property, but *qua* the state, all religions must be equal. Courts of law cannot determine the truth(s) within beliefs nor enforce obedience to them. 'How,' he asks, 'can a matter of faith be a matter of enforcement?' (MAI, p.86).

> The cognition of God is a mystery and man is forever
> pursuing it. In this pursuit all men of faith, regardless of
> their particular religion, are equal ... Laws are like metals in
> the crucible of time and circumstance: they melt; they
> gradually solidify into different shapes; they re-melt and
> assume diverse forms ... But the mind and conscience of
> man is free. (MAI, p.87).

In this liability of *Fiqh* to responsible change in the hands of lawyers and within the state, Fyzee is ready to draw freely on the resources of other systems, English, Dutch and French, and, so doing, fulfilling loyalty to the *Shari'ah* in the exercise such borrowing indicates of care for reason and conscience as a God-given duty. It was a most radical and explicit way of rewriting the Islamic precept that religion and law are one and indivisible. In effect he has redefined both, inasmuch as religion becomes revelation to, for and in conscience, while law becomes the conscience in rational obedience and discrimination under the rule of God.

Fyzee holds that this understanding of Islam is salutary for belief itself, for theology and doctrine. It admits of a range of attitudes, of a partial agnosticism, a certain flexibility in evaluating personal Islam. It allows us to discern between what may be meticulous in ritual duty but poor in faith or character. It recognises a *de facto* diversity in how far Muslims measure up to their credal and ritual obligations. In this context Fyzee writes with disarming frankness. He concedes that he does not accept 'that Islam, *as interpreted by the Imams of authority* [his italics] ... is beneficial and true.'

> However, I am not a non-believer ... I would like to redefine
> my faith ... In this quest and in this adventure, I firmly
> believe that Islam, as I understand it, has much to offer to
> the human spirit in the 20th century. I cannot, however,
> accept its definition as laid down by the generally accepted
> Sunnite Imams or by any of the Shi'ah schools. (MAI,
> p.91).

The crux of his redefining lies in the necessity, as Fyzee sees it, to appreciate the seventh century context of Islamic origins and not to 'go back' to the Qur'an then, but to 'go forward' with it now, and proceed upon its vision of the sublime unity of God in terms of our own time and our own India.

> I wish *to understand* the Qur'an as it was understood by the
> Arabs of the time of the Prophet only to *re-interpret* it and
> apply it to my conditions of life, and to believe in it as far as
> it appeals to me as a 20th century man. (MAI, p.94)

What India does to 'this Arabian religion' is to invite its participants into
the eclecticism and catholicity to which the Indian ethos of diversity and
mysticism must surely point all its citizens.

Fyzee commends 'comparative religion' and European pursuit of its
study to Muslim theologians, without himself developing its implications.
He is alert to hybridization evident in Islamic sects and stresses the need
among Muslims for a more informed perception of Judaism and Christianity, including – he notes – a comparative philology along the lines of
Arthur Jeffery's illuminating study of Quranic words.[16] Here he is advocat-
ing just the awareness that rigorists fear and reject, namely the intrusion
of 'comparison' and, with it, of external criteria, into the citadels of the
sacrosanct and the authoritarian. He finds such a theological register of
otherness vital to the separation of religion and law, of worship and the
state, to which he is committed. 'The living Word of God' cannot be
imprisoned in a Book, nor can tradition be made an infallible source, nor
law books fill the role conscience should enjoy.

In this context a sense of cosmology, old and new, serves to rein-
force the distinction, necessary in responding to the Qur'an, between
literal, and poetic, truth. Surah 3:7 makes a vital distinction between the
'categorical' and the 'allegorical',[17] which must be fully invoked to allow
reason to over-rule credulity and equity to rewrite prescripts wherever
Quranic legal dicta from the Qur'an run counter, e.g., to the rights of
women, or the liberties of conscience. The 'gate' of *Ijtihad* must be
re-opened and never closed.[18] It must be recognised that there *are* radical
diversities of definition of what constitutes the 'true' Islam and what
identifies the 'right' Muslim. He notes, perhaps with a certain Indian
satisfaction, the dilemma of Pakistan itself in this respect, during the
Inquiry into the Punjab Disturbances of 1953,[19] when '*ulama*' characterised other '*ulama*' as 'unbelievers'.

The logic of the impossibility of a rigorous identification of Islam and
the Muslim must be that

> . . . no matter what the '*ulama*' say, he who sincerely affirms
> that he is a Muslim, is a Muslim: no one has the right to

question his beliefs and no one has the right to excommuni-
cate him. That dread weapon, the *fatwa* of *takfir*[20] is a
ridiculous anachronism. (MAI, p.107).

Fyzee sustains his advocacy of a freely defined Islam by appeal to such
fellow Muslims as Humayun Kabir[21] and to Jewish and Christian writers
emancipating themselves from Rabbinic rigorism or crippling dogmatism.
He is not deterred if some of these have seen Islam as the locale *par
excellence* of the 'closedness' which some Jews and Christians – with less
revelatory warrant – have allegedly imitated. Even if it were so – which
Fyzee denies – all the more reason for re-reading its genius now.

All the more, inasmuch as 'Islam has ceased,' he avers 'to be
dynamic...ceased to lead people in right direction.' (MAI, p.107) He
judges that many Muslims no longer belong deeply within the motions of
ritual, that reactionaries are too many, and that yearnings after theocracy
have misread and ill-served the present needs. He turns to what is
explicitly a Jesus-parallel, an almost nostalgic characterisation of the
Arabian Prophet, as poor, lowly, gentle, kind and truthful, to whom the
call came, in fasting and musing, to undertake 'the Word of God'. Fyzee's
section on 'The Re-Interpretation of Islam' in *A Modern Approach* ends
in a devout *confessio* which warrants Aziz Ahmad's tribute to him as
'emotionally and spiritually involved', in marked contrast to those Muslim
'secularists primarily concerned with the establishment of cultural identity
between Islam and Hinduism in India.'[22] It is a verdict well deserved.

> My faith is my own, a faith fashioned by my own outlook on
> life, by my own philosophy, my own experience, my own
> intuition. I give to every Muslim, indeed to every man, the
> right to fashion his own faith...I believe that the Qur'an is
> a message from God. It is the voice of God heard by
> Muhammad. Muhammad gave it to us in the words of
> Muhammad, in the very speech of Muhammad, the Arabic
> language. I believe that in every age those words must be
> interpreted afresh and understood anew. I believe it is the
> duty of every Muslim to understand this message for himself.
> I do revere the great interpreters of Islam...I cannot agree
> that they are the keepers of my conscience. (MAI, p.110).

The distance of that *confessio* from the formal orthodoxy of Muslims is
evident enough. But it was authentic for him in the love Fyzee declared for

the three languages of his career, Arabic, Persian and Turkish, together with the Urdu of his home. He rejoiced in the wealth of art and architecture, of craftsmanship and poetry, in the Islamic tradition. He insisted that 'few civilizations... served literature, science and philosophy as Islam had' – a claim which made him all the more distressed by what he saw as supervening centuries of intellectual atrophy and decline, traced to fanaticism and bigotry. Whatever assessment of this 'Islam' other Muslims might have by other, and cautionary, lights, there can be no doubting that Asaf Fyzee kept his inner faith in honest debate with itself. How did it effectively translate into a philosophy and sociology of law?

vii

It meant that the divine sanction of conduct operated through the human conscience and not otherwise. It followed, further, that equity, not rigidity, should guide the application of law in its incidence as reason must in its roots. It followed, again, that there was no mandate whereby any structure like the Islamic *Shari'ah* could wisely abjure the comparative studies that opened it to the wisdom of jurisprudence in any and every culture. For there were common features of human existence *per se* which obtained for all, however diverse these might be by factors of time and place. Certainly the flux of time which all suffered, most of all in the twentieth century, imposed comparable burdens of thought and suggested some concert to undertake them.

These *desiderata* could only be achieved if Muslims knew rightly what they meant by *Allahu akbar*.

> The theory that law is God-made is, in the language of the
> law a legal fiction, the main object of which is to create a
> moral sanction of the highest efficacy for what in effect is
> nothing more than a legal norm. (MAI, p.33).

Fyzee does not stay to ask here whether this sophistication about a divine that serves a function can, in fact, operate once it is seen for the fiction it is said to be. That, no doubt, is the ultimate question set by secularity. Yet it is one that Islam must allow. For the emphasis in Islam has long, and traditionally, been that God is 'functional', in that His Word, the Qur'an, intends to command rather than, in any theological sense, to reveal (except insofar as directive discloses divine nature).[23] The Scripture is meant for the mediation to mankind of the divine will with a view to *Islam* within it. Fyzee, for all his 'liberalism' is, therefore, right in seeing 'revelation' as sanctioning what is right and condemning what is wrong. Substituting, on his part, conscience for Qur'an in this way makes the equation more crucial than it would be if Scripture – as in the Christian sphere – purported to disclose something of the very nature of God to which, then, conscience would have to be responsive, but responsive in terms of imitating a quality, not of substituting a role. This is not, however, a reflection that occurs to Fyzee. He is content to see in God the ordaining of conformity – but in his own idiom of the religious conscience.

By that idiom he readily recruits what he sees as the pure monotheism of Descartes, of a world that is morally governed by 'a supreme *Numen*', self-existent, just, infinite, omnipotent and free, requiting evil, and properly to be worshipped. Islam, he says, shares this essentially and only adds certain ritual and legal principles, apart from which it is fundamentally at one with the same tradition in Judaism and Christianity. Fyzee's case is made with quotations from the Qur'an on God as 'the owner of sovereignty' and 'master of the universe'. As contrasted, for example, with the thought of Raimundo Panikkar for whose 'theandrism' man is as 'necessary' to God as God is to man, he is fully Islamic in his sense of the divine Lordship and otherness and, in that way, is avoiding any conscious dealings with 'the Vedic experience' and the *advaita* of Hinduism. Inter-faith in his Bombay context is the much more pragmatic exercise in communal compatibility. He is negotiating in mind much more with the modern West than with the holy men of Varanasi. He is, after all, essentially a lawyer.

There is an interesting sense in which Fyzee's view of the relation of religion to law requires no great significance in respect of the distinction between Sunni and Shi'ah. For either system mediates in its own way the claim of the sovereignty of God upon the society of Islam. That single feature in measure neutralises the otherwise divisive criteria the two systems hold for how the mediation truly happens. Fyzee's academic focus on the *Da'a'im* of Al-Nu'man does not require him to be partisan. Beyond the overall authority of the Qur'an, Sunni and Shi'ah differ in nearly all else. The Shi'ah restrict the legitimacy of *Hadith*, or tradition, to relation by the Imams. The canonical collections, therefore, differ significantly. The pattern of consensus via *Ijtihad*, on which the Sunni community relies for valid development not repugnant to the Qur'an and beyond the attainment of strict *Qiyas*, or analogy, is no consensus at all for the Shi'ah. Only the *Mujtahids*, as mouthpieces of the Hidden Imam, can achieve

Ijtihad or law-definition. They alone have the correct key both to the Qur'an in exegesis, and to the *Shari'ah* in interpretation. *Mujtahids*, in that sense, do not belong in Sunni Islam. There is perhaps a further sense in which Fyzee's association of divine law with reason and conscience fosters compatibility between structures of faith not only as between Sunni and Shi'ah but between Islam and outsiders also.

Our concerns do not involve us in discussion of the careful, scrupulous treatment of legal history, the corpus of Muslim law, and law reform which Asaf Fyzee achieved professionally in his *Outlines of Muhammadan Law* and other works. His inner faith-scrutiny had essentially to do with that profession of law. For that reason, the reader misses dimensions of faith-interrogation such as one would better expect from poets and true theologians – dimensions of the tragic and the *angst* which must belong with the mystery of God as they do not belong with a lawyer's concern for His 'governance', especially in those terms Fyzee made his own. But it is right that he, and his kind, should be represented here if only to indicate the versatility of Islam in due self-realisation in situations that search its identity and in personal perceptions that respond.

Chapter 11

RAIMUNDO PANIKKAR
(born 1918)

'The Saffron and the Rose'

i

'It is the reader who redeems the writer... This compilation is only a timid invitation to what it wants to say.' The modesty is disarming but the timidity, though doubtless honest, is not readily apparent in a work of some 600 pages on *Myth, Faith and Hermeneutics: Cross Cultural Studies* – a major contribution to inter-faith debate that makes strenuous demands on the reader.[1] Some will find themselves hard-pressed to understand where, or how, they might 'redeem' the writer. For the content is far-reaching and ambitious, and the style – as in all the author's numerous books and essays – subtle and exacting.

On count of both style and content, Raimundo Panikkar is a very personal writer, his writing, as he puts it, 'being co-author of his life'. Semitic and Asian faiths come together in his mind and spirit with a lived intensity that has made him a unique and eminent figure in the encounter of religions this century.

After a cluster of studies involving Christian, Jewish and Muslim writers in reckoning with each other and with themselves, we pass to three wider-ranging personalities more comprehensive in their issues, though not necessarily, for that reason, more searching in their quest. Panikkar, Toynbee and Smith have in common a will for the oecumene of mankind, an ambition to grapple with the entire predicament that makes religions plural. They each write out of the education an intellectual life-commitment has given to their scholarship and there are intriguing similarities in their perceptions. However, Raimundo Panikkar is

distinctive among all our *dramatis personae* here in possessing two
'bloodstreams' of faith within his own birth and nurture. His thinking, as
he notes self-deprecatingly, often takes place in four languages. He hints
that it would be simpler if he had only one mother tongue, since 'a man of
many original languages has no [one?]word of his own.'[2] Some readers
might well echo the wish when Panikkar's facility in expression enables
him to weave apparent incompatibles into a persuasive harmony. This
feature of him, to which we will return, may be taken to symbolise the
very core of the religious problem. Maybe a spiritual sense of what need
not divide has to be inborn in one's physical genesis, just as the sense of
what must divide often belongs insistently with the irreducible identities of
birth, nurture and family. Yet such a conclusion would only leave the
essential problematics of diversity unresolved – unless we are to conclude
that inter-marriage is the crucial factor in their resolution. This, in
turn, would be to assign acute spiritual and intellectual vocation to the
mechanics of heredity – plainly an impossible proceeding. If hope cannot
properly lie that way, gratitude may register when it happens.

ii

Raimundo Panikkar was the child of Ramuni and Carme, his father an
Indian Hindu and his mother a Spanish Catholic Christian. Barcelona,
the city of his birth and first student years, was the heart of Catalan
Catholicism and from 1936 to 1939 – crucial years in his maturing – the
stronghold of Republican Spain, its fall in January 1939, to the Franco
forces, being the signal, two months later, of the collapse of all resistance
and the final surrender of the Republicans. Panikkar's youthful studies
were continued in Madrid, Bonn and the Lateran in Rome, but also in the
Indian centres of Mysore and Varanasi. His doctorates were triple – in
Chemical Science, in Philosophy and in Divinity. He was ordained priest
in Varanasi in 1954 after a five year stint (1946-1951) as Professor of
Indian Culture and Comparative Cultures in the Theological Seminary,
Madrid, and three further years in Chairs of Religious Sociology and the
Philosophy of History. Following pastoral duties in India, he became
Professor of Religious Sociology in Rome and from 1964 to 1971 com-
muted regularly between Varanasi, Rome and Harvard, USA in Visiting
Professorships and academic activity of increasing range and fluency. In
1971 he became Professor of the Comparative Philosophy of Religion in
the University of California, at Santa Barbara, a post he held until 1986.
His versatility and depth of religious insight and experience of world

cultures brought him numerous honours, and occasion to test and develop his thought in converse, both professional and ecclesiastical, with a rich diversity of people, priests and monks, sahdus and gurus, monists and trinitarians, east and west.

There is a warm fervour about much of his writing, despite the often elusive shape of his argument and the complexity of his terms. His own biography is manifest throughout. For his thinking is forever exploring the meaning of his own being. What might be, to some, issues of cerebral discourse, of abstract logic or mere phenomenology are, for Panikkar, a reckoning with his own selfhood as heir to two worlds. Writing in 1978 in *The Inter-Religious Dialogue*, he declared of one juncture in his mental travels: 'I "left" as a Christian, I "found" myself a Hindu and I "return" as a Buddhist.'[3] The discerning reader knows from within that the three verbs are inter-changeable in the three clauses. For what is distinctive about him is his capacity to hold together both the personalism of the Semitic religions and the advaita, non-duality, experience of Asian faiths in a way that necessarily forces discussion back into the criteria by which such congruence of seeming incompatibles might, or might not, be justified. To this we will return.

Biography is evident not only in the instinct to affirm 'both-and' against 'either-or'. It is there clearly in the progression within his writing sequence. In the first edition of his influential *The Unknown Christ of Hinduism* he had seemed to hold that in the historical Jesus the fullness of revelation had occurred, that there was decisive normativity in Jesus and Christianity. In the revised edition seventeen years later he abandoned this sense of Christhood in favour of the wider concept of 'the Christic', of which 'the Christ event' in the New Testament was only one 'identification' of an 'identity' or transcendent mystery known in all religious experience. Thus no faith had final normativity for all the others.[4]

The search for what he called 'symbiosis', or fusion of faiths beyond the level of doctrine, needs to be carefully reviewed below. The immediate point is its pursuit as a life-concern, as the *motif* of his own Indian/Spanish birth, the passion of his Hindu/Christian nurture. The oecumene of faiths was somehow within his ethos, the extension of the will to unify within Christianity urgently taken into wider fields by a radical reckoning with what purported to divide and why it might not do so. Many others had seen the logic of such extension of the will to relate from the inter-Christian to the inter-religious and had realised how vastly more exacting were the issues it incurred.[5] But none felt the urge more strongly than Panikkar and few were so well equipped to undertake the philosophy, and the soul-travail, it required. 'Inter-faith' had to become, for him 'intra-faith', seeing that what concerned external relationships belonged inwardly within each and all and required them to realise and discover what they had all alike, and all along, possessed, namely 'the Real', diversely 'apparent' to them. For Raimundo Panikkar, now a septuagenarian, the vocation abides.

Looking back in the Preface to the revised edition of *The Unknown Christ of Hinduism* over half a century of his 'intellectual and spiritual wonderments', he makes enigmatic reference to Hindu/Christian fusion under the familiar imagery of the walk to Emmaus.

> There has been a fellow-traveller in my journeys to the different lands of Man...I thought I knew who that companion was...There came, however, a critical moment when I reached my ancestral dwelling-place at the peak period of my life: my companion disappeared...The settlement I had now reached was my own village. And so, instead of retracing my steps to a City of Peace, to look for, and perhaps find, my partner again, I proceeded alone to a battlefield ravaged by fratricidal warfare. Shocked and pained...I remained a conscientious objector...[6]

The associations with Luke 24 are evident enough and the Hindu *Bhagavad Gita* opens with a muser on a battlefield refusing (at first) to be a participant. Here the reader has somehow to retrieve the meaning, wondering how the 'ancestral' shaped the 'critical', how the ever-latent Christ could possibly 'disappear' or forsake, and why 'shock and pain' did not yearn after reunion with him. But teasing enigma is the way of Panikkar. Such is the companionship of his mind.

iii

Exposition is a complex task, if an expositor is not to be forever scrutinising by canons he is not meant to bring or misreading even as he reads. It is useful, by way of preface, to illustrate the reading problem by noting what Panikkar does with Biblical citation. Quotations on fly-leaves can well be left to suggest as they may but is that facility unlimited? Panikkar cites Kena Up. ii.3 and blends it into Paul's use of Isaiah 65:1, in Romans 10:20: 'I have been found of those who did not seek me: I have shown myself to those who did not ask for me.' In the Upanishad the 'I' has become 'It'; the Jew/Gentile contrast is ignored and we have: 'It is not understood by those who understand it: it is understood by those who do not understand it.' The only kinship between opened covenant and philosophic enigma is the common feature of paradox, which can hardly admit of the plain disparity. (UCH, p.31).

Elsewhere Luke's phrase that 'the kingdom of God comes not with observation', i.e., by being placarded: 'Here, here, there, there,' (Luke 17:20) becomes: 'One is He whom sages call by many names,' i.e., the Christ may be hidden anywhere. There is a similar ambivalence in the use of John 1:26: 'There stands one among you (in-between you) whom you do not know' with: 'The Spirit whom all the gods worship is seated in the middle.' (UCH, p.vii). Was the Baptist affirming 'the radical relativity' where the *madhyamaka*, the 'mediator,' moves to unify?

Matthew 18:20: 'Where two or three are gathered together in my Name there am I . . .' may well be recruited to mean that wherever there is real suffering, Christ is there to receive our ministry. That is true enough. But does what the Gospel writes intend to mean that where there is real love between persons Christ is there? And what of 'real' in this context?[7] The New Testament passages about 'rain on the just and on the unjust', and 'tares among the wheat' (Matt. 5:45 & 13:25ff.) are made to yield the dictum that 'faith, as it were, believes in the non-faith of others', i.e., 'trusts the non-believers' in the will 'to be as tolerant as God Himself.' (RCN-CS, pp.152-53). The alignment here is ingenious but leaves the reader wondering whether ingenuity makes right exegesis. Panikkar, however, relishes what he calls the 'polyvalence' of words and happily extends it to the sense of texts. The underlying question of hermeneutics can usefully come after seeing the pattern of his mind in the sequel to his Emmaus walk.

iv

It is a pattern which is glad to begin at Emmaus and equally glad to leave behind the specifics of the conversation, the quoted Scriptures, the Messianic theme and the breaking of the bread. Panikkar begins from 'Christ' because – as he concedes – it is where Christians start, where his Spanish mother's land belongs. But a Hindu polyvalence has to take over the word and comprehend it in a form which leaves behind the immediacies of the Messianic, rooted as these were in the anticipations of Judaic faith and in the radical fulfilment Christians believed that Jesus had given to them. Those immediacies involved faith in covenant, in the significance of history, in a certain exclusivity of providence via Sinai and the prophets. The Church saw this providentiality achieved – and re-covenantalised for all humanity – in the strange particularity of Jesus in whose Cross and passion divine love had engaged with 'the sin of the world' and suffered for its forgiveness. In consequence incipient faith had called this Jesus 'Lord'.

All this had its sharp characterisation. Like the inscription placed on the Cross, it stood in 'letters of Hebrew, Greek and Latin', and from these its universal expression began. The specifics were sharp and crucial. But Panikkar sees them in a feasible dissociation from their history – this being only a manifestation of a reality capable of being otherwise known and diversely identified. What the Christhood of Jesus signifies is not confined there but belongs – even without its Jesus-nexus of the Beatitudes and Gethsemane and the Eucharist – in a reality known there but not only there. How this reality participates in 'the Christ' as 'other' than the historic 'Jesus-Christ' is, in the end, ineffable mystery. That mystery simply disallows the word 'other', as one that begs the question by merely presupposing distinction. Distinction is what the alternative view disallows.

Panikkar explains: 'The sacredness of everything dawned upon me. Thus I am at the confluence (*sangam*) of the four rivers – the Hindu, Christian, Buddhist and secular traditions.' (UCH p.1x).[8] He insists, therefore, that, while we may truly say: 'Jesus is the Christ', we may not say: 'The Christ is Jesus'. Similarly, it is true that 'Jesus is Lord'; it is not true that 'The Lord is Jesus'. The second in each of these pairs where the predicate of the first has become the subject of the second would only be true if *not* meant restrictively. 'The Lord is not Jesus' if we intend to mean 'Jesus alone'. For 'Lord' has a much wider reach. 'Jesus', truly is 'the Christ' but since – for Panikkar – there are more 'Christs', to say, restrictively, that 'the Christ is Jesus' becomes untrue. 'Christ' and 'Lord' are titles, not names and, as such, belong to many names. In Jesus we make a Christian identification of an identity wider, larger, than the location, in Jesus, that Christians give to it. If other religions are minded to query why *their* 'reality' should carry the Christian term, Panikkar's reply is that *he* is starting from a Christian premise.

The nub of the matter, of course, is here. It might even be thought pretentious, or imperialist, to will one's own denominator on all – though Panikkar is no ally of the 'anonymous Christians' thesis of Karl Rahner.[9] But the more the connotation is believed to fit, the more it diversifies away from the connotation of its origin. Panikkar, as it were, wills to resolve particularity into universality by simple extension – a process in which it is at once forfeit and fulfilled. 'The corn of wheat dies' and 'bears much fruit' (John 12:24) but not, surely, in the sense the passage intends. For Jesus' reference was to a death, impending there and then, which his reproductions do not die. Panikkar is looking for Christs who do not learn their meaning in Gethsemane. He is justified in doing so only if what is definitive in the Christhood of Jesus is not restrictively definitive. His belief that it is not poses the open question of all dialogue: in what terms of reference does faith move and how far does faith control them?

We have noted in C.F. Andrews a yearning, in response to India, to extend 'The Christ...beyond the sunny hills of Galilee' and the sharpness of Gethsemane. But in Andrews this was a warm motion of the heart. In Panikkar it is a much more sophisticated intellectualism. 'We cannot,' he declares, 'limit Christ to a historical figure.' For to do so would imply denying his divinity.[10] Not a historical person, he is the divine person who assumes in himself all history. He cannot be confined to a descent of God at a given moment for a particular, or universal, purpose. (RCNC, pp.163-64). There is in history a mediatorship of Christ which is total and unique, irrespective of creed, place or time.

> Christian faith enters in, not indirectly denying anything in the religions of the world but, in affirming that the Christ, which all religions in one way or another acknowledge (Isvara, Tathagata, Lord), finds his full, or at least central, epiphany in Jesus, the Son of Mary. We mean to say that this ontic mediatorship of Christ is independent of the religion an individual may profess and from the place and time of his existence on earth, whether inside or outside Christianity, or within or without the historical existence of the visible Church. (RCNC, p.164).

Panikkar allows that there is a 'risk' in speaking throughout of 'Christ' as a synonym for 'the transcendent divine reality...whatever degree of reality we may be disposed to grant it.' How our 'disposition' can well be 'grantor' here is perplexing. But he is clear that

> ...it is an incontrovertible fact that the Christ in whom Christians believe cannot be simply equated with the Isvara of Vedanta...If we start with the historicity of Christ, essential though it may be, we are liable to be gravely misunderstood...To admit the Christian idea of history,

indispensable though it may be for an understanding of the
historical Christ, is to pre-suppose the Christian concept of
Christ. (UCH,pp.163-65).

There has to be an ontic Christ, he urges, before there can be any historical Christ, this being – for him – how the Logos precedes 'the flesh'. Yet it
was the Logos that 'was made flesh'. How the Logos may be other than,
more than, 'the flesh was made' to be, is a 'debate' that 'cannot', he concludes, 'be within the compass of this essay.' Yet he sees 'the Christian
kerygma as 'the *mirabilia* of God, of which the Mystery of Christ hidden
in God is the *alpha* and the *omega.*'
    The issue here is one we will encounter in Wilfred Cantwell Smith in
Chapter 13, namely how far does the historical suffice the ontic? If not
fully, then discrepancy haunts the meaning and in speaking of 'the Christ'
we play a language game. If fully, then 'the reality we are disposed to
grant the transcendent' must turn conclusively on that history. Panikkar
feels that this alternative – thus posited – offends against a Hindu attitude
to history. Therefore, let the Hindu seek otherwise, and elsewhere,
'anything endowed with the richness of that reality for which Christians
have no other name than Christ' (UCH, p.5), and let Christians, by the
same token, relinquish the 'monopoly' that ensues (falsely) from their
view of historicity. 'The Logos made flesh' can be decisive for them so
long as it does not have to be determinative outside them. Yet 'the to
whom? of all human search' can still be named 'the Christ'.
    The evident 'polyvalence' here around that crucial term certainly
reaches out to the instincts of Hinduism but does it not also deprive the
term of its originating definition? Will the formula: 'Christ is not the only
Christ' really stand if 'Christhood' has no necessary identity? If it does
not, then both the term and the statement are vacuous. Panikkar laudably
wants to deny Christians a monopoly as if 'Christhood' was a prerogative
reserved for them alone, believing correctly that 'a Christ-symbol valid
only for them would cease to be a living symbol for them also.' This is true
enough as a confession of that availability for all which characterises the
New Testament faith about the Gospel, about 'the sin of the world' and
about an inclusive divine forgiveness. But must we not distinguish
between non-monopoly as to the intent of truth and relinquishment –
potential or actual – of its content? What deserves to be universal in its
human range must surely be comprehensive in its human meaning. Would
not a diversified Christ imply the contrary?
    If Raimundo Panikkar's handling of history and reality within a

Christian/Hindu Christology leaves these open questions, might they be more satisfactorily explored through the concept of God rather than of 'the Christ'? That would locate them in less explicitly Christian ground and allay the suspicion of others as to being unduly 'Christianised' by the point of departure. Christology, of course, will always be central to a theology which is Christian. That centrality may be more wisely discerned by not requiring it to be first assumed as, thus far in Panikkar, has been the case. What, then, if we pass to his 'cosmo-theandrism', as he is minded to describe it, his theology of God in man and man in God?

V

We might well begin with Panikkar's intriguing dictum: 'Trust the God who trusts men' (RCN-CS, p.153.), which is important, later, for his attitude to secularisation. In present context, it reads like a strongly theistic view for which Creator and creature, God and man, are in objective relation, Giver and receiver. That is the familiar Semitic view of the transcendent Lord and the human subject. This theological 'personalism' Panikkar acknowledges and shares, but only on condition of its being fused with a fully Asian view of complete non-duality in which God, man and the world constitute a single unity of undifferentiated being. He wants the both/and of Christian and Hindu religion by which he can both hold and surmount the familiar distinction between transcendence and immanence. His thought here, confident enough to him, reads elusively to others and is involved in the meanings he attaches to myth, *logos* and spirit. Being, as cosmos, is theandric being wherein man is as necessary to God as God is to man. In *The Trinity and the Religious Experience of Man*, he writes:

> The Upanisads point to a religious attitude that is not founded upon faith in a God-Thou, or a God-will-sovereignty, but in the supra-rational experience of a 'Reality' which in some way 'inhales' us into himself. The God of the Upanisads does not speak: he is not Word. He 'inspires', he is 'spirit'.
>
> In the personalist schema God ... is Someone, he is a Person who calls to himself another person, is met, so to speak, face to face and is capable of either responding by love to another's love, or refusing to do so. In the schema of the Upanisads the main place is not given to call/response nor to

acceptance/refusal. The basic categories here are knowledge
and ignorance. The Absolute is discovered in its own realisation, i.e. in the experience in which it is attained.[11]

This is no longer 'meeting' but 'union'. The contrast is familiar enough
and fairly stated but it is obviously straining language. For we are still in
need of pronouns: 'he' 'himself'. And what are we to make of 'the main
place' if no partial one remains?

Panikkar seems to fear that understanding God as 'beyond', 'exterior',
'other', in relation to man is to have only the *Deus ex machina* idea of
sheer arbitrariness and intrusion. But the clue of mutual love would
eliminate this ('God trusting man') and allow us that reconciliation of
'transcendent' and 'immanent' which is ensured by 'Incarnation' and
realised in 'the Holy Spirit'. To have only that theism, however, would
arouse Panikkar's misgivings about historical particularity as well as failing
his will to be at one with Hindu *advaita*, or non-duality.

In *Myth, Faith and Hermeneutics*, he addresses his mind to the question
how the *advaitin*, the self in undifferentiated union with the Absolute, can
also be in *bhakti* devotion to the Lord, in the mutual 'belovedness' which
means Thou/I duality. Yet to speak here of 'mind' 'addressing a question',
is somehow inappropriate. For no rational answer can be given; nor can
the issue truly be a 'question'. Interrogation can only happen where there
is objectivity. Otherwise, all is all. For the *advaitin* to apply personality to
the Absolute is idolatrous. Yet the question must persist if any legitimacy
is to remain in Hindu *bhakti* itself. Can love be another name for
experience of the Absolute? Can *advaitin* be lover? Or, more intriguingly,
'may friendship find a place in heaven?' Panikkar, as Christian/Hindu,
dearly wants to insist that *advaita* is not monism. Perhaps there is, he
thinks, a clue in the fact that 'if the structure of the ultimate is love' then
bhakti devotion is 'love loving love' and 'love of love is like an eye that
sees itself, or a will that loves itself.' (MFH, p.281). Yet, if love is all there
is, what has happened to *them*, the lovers? Are we not back at monism?
All has happened within the inner life of the Absolute – a view which
seems to be confirmed when Panikkar adds: 'An *advaitin* has realised the
absolute non-duality of Being.' Yet who, then, *is* he? The one who is
aware is necessary to the awareness. There is no place for dualism, but,
being there *he* restores it.

The only escape here is to think that reason is not all. But this, in turn,
is yet another logic. Panikkar concludes that 'the Thou' in love to the
Absolute is 'the consciousness that the 'I' not only *has* but *is*.' The

advaitin loves as the Absolute does. In effect here, if one speaks of 'the love of God', Panikkar means that we merge the genitives: the 'of' is *both* subjective and objective. The *advaitin*, he says, 'is full of personality but devoid of individuality.' (p.286). Yet is not individuality where personality has being?[12]

vi

That seemingly we have arrived at a quandary need not be disconcerting. We are beginning to understand that enigmatic smile of the Buddha. Panikkar is adroit in recruiting for this quandary of love within Being that has somehow to disavow our personal empirical 'being-in-self', a Hebraic concept, namely, that of 'taking God's Name in vain' in the Decalogue. He argues that objectifying God is failing to recognise that God's name can only be used in the vocative. He cannot be 'called', He can only be 'called upon'.[13] Every denoting name must be a false one. To want such 'names' is to enclose God within our categories. In them we make false images in our imagination. For, since no names 'attain to God', God has no 'name, cannot be situated, is not, indeed, a 'he' at all. Only silence does not fall into contradiction. 'The true awareness of the Absolute is to have none.' Here we are squarely within an exposition of Buddhism. We seem to have come a long way from 'the God who trusts man', and trusts man with words. Yet Panikkar's sympathy with Buddhism inspires the subtlety of his exposition:

> For the Buddha eliminating the name of God is the supreme religious undertaking... The Buddha does not answer by silence: he does not answer. What the Buddha does is to silence the question. He puts the question in question. His hope is the elimination of any future.

Yet this does not make the Buddha 'an agnostic'. It shows him 'the Enlightened One', who has discovered that he has nothing to ask. For to 'question' ultimate Reality can have no meaning. Everything is reduced, not to the absurd, but to the sublime. It is disconcerting, however, to find Panikkar linking this Buddhist theme with Jesus 'giving Pilate no answer' in the Passion story, on the ground that 'questioning', in either case, had not 'grasped its proper limits'. (MFH, pp.258-70). It is fair to ask how it might all relate to the anguish of Job, where questioning is, in no sense, a 'desire to find a crutch outside Reality', but, instead, a search for an integrity that has reckoned with reality. It is significant how readily the mind of Panikkar escapes from the trauma of evil because of fascination with the Absolute. The formula of 'love within love' has much explaining to undertake if it is not to make 'unquestioning' quite incompatible with love's meaning. Could 'love' remain 'love' if hidden, silent, callous, in enigma?

That issue brings theology round again to Christology where Christian faith finds the resolution of divine love and human tragedy in the long-suffering of 'God in Christ'. But this Panikkar reads as paradigmatic, as enshrining the God/man, the theandrism which he affirms as meaning

> ... the infinitude of man, for he is tending towards God, the infinite, and the finitude of God, for He is the end (*finis*) of man... Man and God are neither two nor one... An integral anthropology implies a humanist theology... A purely transcendent God is an abstraction of the same sort as a purely independent man. There are not two realities: God *and* man (or the world): but neither is there one: God *or* man (or the world), as outright atheists and outright theists are dialectically driven to maintain. Reality itself is theandric. (TREM, pp.74-75).

The Christian form of this theandrism is the mystical Body of Christ, or rather what Christians so name. For therein 'God, man and the world are engaged in a unique adventure and this engagement constitutes true reality.' But the same would be true of what Buddhists call *dharmakaya*, the taking of the Eightfold Path. Either way, man has 'this tremendous experience of being a theandric being.'[14] Myth, *logos* and *pneuma* (or spirit) pertain, in differing ways, to this experience, so that it may be described as 'trinitarian'. But 'theandric' is Panikkar's preferred word.

He would have us beware, however, of 'objectifying' God outside the manwardness in which, for Panikkar, His reality consists. This is what misguided theists do. Nor should we 'subjectify' man outside his Godwardness which is the way of atheists. Yet, as we exclude these non-theandric ways, we should not think of our having a knowledge of God which is cognitive in the traditional sense. There has to be here what he calls a 'fasting from thought'. Faith is this inner acceptance of our theandric being, with which 'believing' is in fact synonymous. So 'belief' is not a formulation, but the experience itself.

> To say: 'I believe in God' is cognitive only in the sense of the
> act of believing: it is not cognitive as to its content. For the
> belief is only real that does not know *what* God is [i.e. does
> not externalise Him as a 'fact']...The question about God
> [e.g. do you believe in God?] either destroys itself because it
> does not know what it is asking for, or dissolves the God we
> are asking about into something that is no longer God but a
> sheer idol. The God of belief is a symbol but not a concept.
> In a way we believe only [what we believe to be] the unques-
> tionable. (MFH, pp.5-6).

Panikkar's theandrism makes the divine a corollary of the human and the
human a corollary of the divine. Faith is an intuitive awareness of our
human nature. We will find a comparable view in Wilfred Cantwell
Smith.

Profound issues are at stake here about Christian theology and about
the implications for inter-faith. It is right not to reduce 'knowledge of
God' to the level of empirical knowledge and the rationality this under-
girds. We do not know God like the formula: H_2O is water. But should an
intuitive theandrism be oblivious of the sense-and-mind context in which
human-ness exists and via which, sacramentally, experience of Godwardness is discovered in beauty, wonder, pain and being mortal? Will not
historicalness, as the sphere of such experience, have some part to play in
the disclosure of its actual import? How, then, can we say that 'the
believed is not the known'? Given the endless diversity of the myths that
have purported to house this theandric experience, are there no criteria by
which they might be sifted, sorted and scrutinised?

Theandrism is profoundly right in refusing to think of God or man other
than in a mutuality to deny which would be to deny both. But within the
mutuality there must surely be room for that about God which is more
than, though not alien to, the human relation, and room, too, for that
about man capable of ignoring and disowning the mutuality which, in the
human case, makes it only definitive in freedom and, in the divine case,
only realised in grace. On that condition alone can we find in the
theandric what is requisite if there is truly to be 'love within love'. For only
in grace is love truly divine as a critical initiative; only in freedom is it truly
human as a willed response. For love accepts to be wanted and awaited.
That risk must be central to any theandrism that has understood the world
and belongs within it. But these are Christian bearings on a theology that
has cherished the ambition to remain Christian yet Hinduise itself. It is

time to turn to the implications of Raimundo Panikkar's thinking for
inter-faith relations explicitly and, through these, its significance for
secular irreligion.

vii

His starting-point is necessarily Christian. For it is Christianity which,
for Christians, poses sharply the relational issues by virtue of its own
premises regarding Jesus as 'the way, the truth and the life'. His desire is
to affirm the centrality of Christ and of the Church, yet also to locate both
Christ and Church, essentially and sacramentally, within the life of the
religions everywhere. If his theandrism holds, there is already in humanity
everywhere what he calls 'the cosmic covenant', by which man is related to
God in mercy and providence. To that covenant, the *kenosis* of the Lord
Christ into the lives of Christians, brings ultimate interpretation. He
would prefer not to allow the usage 'non-Christian', since it obscures how
Christ and his sacrifice are – he believes – already present, if concealed, in
the quest of the other faiths. He is admonished, like Peter in Acts 10:28,
not to 'call anything profane or unclean', 'Even admitting,' he writes
rather cryptically, 'that the fullness of revelation is to be found in
Christianity, most of the Christian truths are to be found in other
religions.' (RCN-CS, p. 146).

All created existence is a Christophany, since the living God 'includes
Himself in the whole of His creation'. Therefore it is open to all mankind,
by having the genus as 'creature', to fulfil the 'Christic' vocation by
sharing in the 'divinization of the world'. Such 'ontological union with
Christ' co-works with him to the building up of 'the body of Christ'.
Meanwhile the Christian community remains the custodian of where this
inclusive Christophany may be read, as it were, in the original. 'All that
exists is a crystallization of the divine act of love.' To participate in this
recognition is not to 'have faith', as if faith were a possession; it is the act
of 'just believing'. Panikkar believes that this can be contagious, just as a
'holy' person brings an aura of holiness. And it may also be vicarious,
pending the non-believer's own discovery. Panikkar is thus hostile to
'conversion' as something to strive to bring about from outside the other
man's theandric truth. 'Trust the un-believers,' he argues, without – on
this showing – identifying what 'unbelief' might be. Indeed, 'the Christian
believes for them in such a way that they do not need to believe.' 'I can
assume even the non-faith of the unbeliever.' (RCN-CS, p.147-153).

It is only when 'belief' is rationalised that plurality of beliefs becomes a puzzle or a scandal. 'If faith is what it claims to be' it can be 'as tolerant of God Himself'. As Smith has it, (see below), to be in 'faith' is to realise that there are no 'others'. God is God of all and for all and not only the 'our God' of those who believe. As Panikkar sees it, there is an inclusive relevance in Christ's sacrifice in which non-believers share. But they do so in terms of their readiness to collaborate in the work of co-redeeming both themselves and that part of the cosmos in which they are immersed. This is done 'by means of continuing and applying, collectively and personally, the redemption of Christ'. Meanwhile the sacramental action of the Christian community of 'explicit' believers shapes 'the Eucharistic economy' in which this assimilation to Christ takes place for its 'implicit' collaborators. (RCN-CS, pp.170-78).

While it is certainly true that human activity may have redemptive value without a clear awareness of the Christ-event, and that the Church has no monopoly over its own secret, it is surely inconsistent with those two truths to suppose that Christian faith need not, and should not, strive for recruitment into the explicitness, into discipleship to the Christ-event. If one is to trust non-believers, even as God entrusts them with freedom within a divine patience, must one not trust them in the integrity of their doubts, the sincerity of their alienation from the Church? There seems to be no place for a crisis of repentance, for the perversity of the 'trusted', for 'death and resurrection' as the moral 'revolution' in the soul,[15] in Panikkar's schema.

viii

Writing some twenty years later than the source just reviewed, in *The Myth of Christian Uniqueness*,[16] Panikkar reverts to his loved imagery of rivers: 'The Jordan, the Tiber and the Ganges.' He sees in them 'three kairological moments of Christic Self-Consciousness'. He invites his readers to understand what he calls 'the Christic principle' as neither a particular event, nor a universal religion, but 'the center of reality as seen by the Christian tradition.' After pausing over 'witness, conversion, crusade, mission and dialogue' as five 'periods' in Christian posture among the faiths, he uses the Jordan, the Tiber and the Ganges to symbolise – in sequence, the historical Messiah and exclusivism; the Tiber the imperial will to a Christian inclusivism; and the Ganges the necessary pluralism. With the three rivers, in broad terms, he associates what he distinguishes as 'Christianity', 'Christendom' and 'Christianness'. Only the third can belong with the present *kairos*, or age, of post-imperial pluralism. The third holds more loosely to credal and ecclesiastical tradition; accepts as being such, those aspects of the religions that are irreconcilable; renounces monotheistic assumptions of a totally intelligible Being; allows myth as 'the horizon that makes thinking possible'; and obeys a principle of tolerance that lives by confidence, not by adjudication as to truth.

We have to note that Panikkar does not mean, by the Ganges, some 'Jordan of Hinduism', but an inclusive river as symbol of the wide world. Every religion should be seen as expressing, concretely, some form of humanness. 'No single notion can comprehend the reality of Christ'; 'Christianness', distinguished from both Christendom and Christianity, will be inwardly plural. It must allow for the radical change in the world view obtaining when there was Christendom.

> Christianness stands for experience of the life of Christ within ourselves, insight into a communion without confusion with all reality, an experience that I and the Father are One', that labels do not matter, that security is of no importance. (MCU, p.113).

Such is Panikkar's 'interpretation of Christ in a theanthropocosmic vision'. As if in hesitant, yet bold, debate with himself (and even more with his Catholic priesthood), he characterises 'the Christic principle' as 'the word that is in every authentic word'; 'the crossroads of reality where all realms meet'; 'everywhere and elusively present wherever there is reality'; 'that about which one should not believe that it is here or there'. This, 'through our own synergy, is what I believe to be the Christ.'

These are eloquent words. Anticipating Christian demur, he goes on: 'I insist that with such a view of Christ I am not escaping the scandal of the incarnation and the process of redemption. I am not ignoring these historical facts. It is simply that I do not worship history . . . Every being is a *christophany*.' To be sure, we do not 'worship history'. But do we not worship what history contains, with wonder that it should have done so? Where else might 'the Lord God omnipotent reign' if not *there*, in the wounds of Jesus, crowned with thorns? How, and why, can we use the word 'Christ' to comprise all that Panikkar has listed when it could equally well be 'x'[17] or 'y' or 'mystery' or 'the un-named'? How do we identify 'authentic' in 'the word' or 'the reality' that has 'the crossroads'? And why, in this inclusiveness, should *the* (sic) incarnation constitute a 'scandal'? Panikkar's 'Christic principle' need cause no Jew to stumble, no

Greek to cry 'Folly'. The paradox implicit here is evident when he notes – in respect of *The Unknown Christ of Hinduism* – that by the title he meant not 'a Christ known to Christians but unknown to Hindus': He meant the Christ unknown to Hinduism and *a fortiori* unknown to Christians also.[18] It is right to observe that the Christ, who was known to the first Christians, only so became known to history at all. Only on the ground of what he occasioned them to become to him, as disciples, witnesses, writers, apostles, was he ever available to become later, supposedly, 'unknown'. They apart, oblivion would be all. History, then, must remain central to his definition and to his identity – urgently so if he is to be loved as the surrogate for 'the authentic word', the clue at 'the crossroads of reality'. The Ganges of pluralism has somehow to find a confluence with the waters of the Jordan, the more so if 'the scandal' of the Incarnation is to be neither eluded nor revoked.

Among the points of his agenda in this *confessio* Panikkar declares: 'We should not be satisfied with merely exegetical approaches. We should allow for a possibly new Christian awareness. (MCU, p.111). Noting the alignment of 'possible', 'new', and 'Christian', here, it is time to turn to how he sees Scriptures and hermeneutics in the context of his 'Christianness'. For clearly the issue of history and faith hinges on the meaning of language and the interpretation of documents of faith.

ix

Panikkar's approach to the text of the New Testament may be gauged from a distinction central to his thought:

> Either we identify the Christian fact with historically existing
> Christianity and then we have one religion among others,
> with no more rights than any one of them, or we believe that
> the Christian mystery bears a universal message capable,
> first of all, of being understood and then followed by any
> man regardless of his colour, culture and religion.

But in what does the 'mystery' consist? Can its 'rights' be dissociated from those of the 'fact'? Is not 'historically existing Christianity' itself index to the universal comprehensibility of the 'message'? Panikkar's intention, clearly, is to de-historicize, even 'de-kerugmatize' the content of the New Testament, to disavow its capacity to determine, and patiently to discipline – as need may be – the identity of Christianity. His ground is the radical differentiation he makes of myth from Logos and Logos from *pneuma*. Only the third, 'Spirit', is capable of being universal. Myths are many and though they energise the imagination they do not absolutize truth. *Logos* presupposes the rationality which mystery must transcend.

It follows that the authority of any and every Scripture within the several religions has to be subject to 'the Spirit'. Theology passes consciously from myth to Logos, while worship lives by both, but must finally reach beyond them into the pure awareness in the Spirit where all is one. Hermeneutics, then, the right apprehension of the sacred text, is more than mere 'exegesis', or the 'drawing out' of theme, the study of sources, the savouring of metaphor, the discerning of context and the perception of rational meaning. Hermeneutics must get beyond both text and context to find the universal realm to which their partiality relates them.

There are 'horizons' to which Scriptures belong in which their meaning expands through time. 'Context' is not merely what situates the immediate passage. It has to be the ever-changing experience through which the reader passes. There was long ago the 'context' of the tribe, the 'context' of 'the chosen', the 'context' of the 'historic faith'. If these were not superseded the meaning would be like a 'deposit of faith', like a frozen river whose very being is contradicted by its immobility. New insights emerge and Scripture has to be 're-heard' accordingly.

We have seen elsewhere in Chapters 1, 5, 7, 8 and 10 how crucial the place and the problematics of Scriptures have been in the biographies that variously wrestled with them. Panikkar's 'solution' is at once too trite and too total, a *tour de force* almost and, at the same time, a *non sequitur*. It seems to ignore the actual role which Scriptures have played – some would say, must play – in the structures of belief and the rites of worship. Authority cannot be de-contextualised in this way. It cannot exist in dissociation from the wisdom in which it is believed to be rooted, as in the *Dharmapada*, nor from the status it bears, as in the Qur'an. The river – to borrow Panikkar's favoured metaphor – has cut its own banks and only through them does it flow. The current is reciprocal to what contains it, be it the Jordan or the Ganges.

This is not to deny that Scriptural rivers flow through new territories and under different clouds. It may even be agreed that 'waters' are common to them all – yearnings, pleadings, findings, questionings, aspirings. But these have cut differing streams and been fed from uncommon watersheds and snows. We may have hope to bring custodians of Scriptures together by dint of the same terrestrial ground they must now irrigate. Panikkar's typology of rivers is intriguing. But there are cities, citadels and temples, on their banks, which are there because the rivers are. Scriptures are a more formidable commodity than a de-historicizing 'Spirit' will suffice. Perhaps Scriptures would have us think that a de-historicizing Spirit is a contradiction in terms, unless we are to say, with Shakespeare's Richard: 'Now mark me, how I will undo myself.' To 're-hear' must be wisely to hear again.

X

If we may pass from rivers to plants and colours, 'the saffron and the rose' seem fitting emblems of the twofoldness of Raimundo Panikkar's life and thought. Saffron has become the property of the Asian monk, while 'the mystic rose' is a figure of Jesus' Incarnation, as by 'stem and flower'.[20] Panikkar's pursuit of dialogue, with his unique equipment of mental landscape and dual heredity, leaves many loose ends and these demand better justice than this chapter has accorded them. But the gist is here, the co-habitation of 'the saffron and the rose'. It may be fitting to conclude with words of Mahatma Gandhi, much relished by Panikkar and more than once invoked:

> The rose transmits its own scent without a movement. You must copy the rose: the rose irresistibly draws people to it-self and the scent remains with them.[21]

If, however, this fragrant metaphor is well discerned it must argue not only the futility of religious propaganda but also the pointlessness of dialogue itself. And is there not a discipline of propagation within the silence of the scent?

Chapter 12

ARNOLD J. TOYNBEE
(1889-1975)

'Seeking an Explanation in which we Find Ourselves'

i

He felt he had to aim for the truth that excluded nothing,[1] yet had to conclude that he could only do so by way of paradox and silence. There have been few historians more ambitious to comprehend a whole, to repudiate all isolations in a panorama of erudite comparisons and to trace relationships across the entire 'oecumene' of mankind set in a universe of endless space and immemorial time. Toynbee's vision was eager to take in the future with the duties it demanded of the present. If some of his anticipations made, for the most part, at mid-century read curiously in its final decade, a mind for prospect out of retrospect is at least adventurous. His breadth of historian's ambition was served by an instinct to detect intriguing parallels in the vast diversity of human annals, of empires, creeds, cultures and value-systems. Was the loved device of capitalising crucial words a way of somehow giving solidity and stature to the entities they denoted, as though actors in a drama personally addressing the imagination? They abound everywhere – Human Nature, Non-Human Nature, Western Man, Original Sin, Western Civilization, Civilised Society, Late Modern Western Man, Wars of Religion, Technology, Reality as Pity, and scores of others, all within the secret – could we know it – of a Spiritual Universe.

Lecturing in 1956 to Christian seminarians, Toynbee observed that he had never been a missionary, that he was not a theologian and that he had 'no direct personal experience of the field of contact between Christianity and any of the other great living faiths.'[2] That modest disclaimer might be

222

thought admirable qualification given that he was widely travelled, expertly versed in international affairs, and steadfastly preoccupied with a vocation to spiritual and intellectual integrity. The evidence of all three is copiously documented in the edition of his rich exchange of letters with Columba Cary-Elwes, a Monk of Ampleforth, friend and mentor sustained through four decades.[3] To its significance we will return.

'Religion,' he declared in 1948, 'is the serious business of the human race,'[4] and through seven decades his tireless imagination was dedicated to exploring in what the seriousness consisted and in how it might be served. The exploration was on a vast scale but in its deepest reaches it was inward and personal. The inner faith which sustained him did not engage with other faiths in formal dialogue as if such encounters could begin to satisfy what obtained between them. His synthetic mind could only take them in, situated within the panorama of the whole human story. Moreover, his own religious understanding had steadily to reckon with negative conclusions such as honesty demanded and which alternative religious interpretations of the world could not evade. If there is any propriety in including him in our present concern of trouble for truth it can only be as the story of a mind lifting the specifics of religions into great world denominators mere comparativists would ignore. The disciplines informing his historical ambition and the gifts of intellect and industry which he brought to them were precisely what true penetration into religious diversity needs. Toynbee is the more significant for our purposes of faith-relation in being a superb practitioner of human enquiry and reflection for their own sake. Faith, for him, was always passionately self-conscious, yet also self-deprecatory and self-interrogating. All issues were first joined within himself.

ii

It is necessary first to have the measure of his inner Christianity. Despite his disclaimer about 'being Christian' it was undoubtedly the faith with which 'he had a lover's quarrel'. His perspectives came to referent in the crucifixion of Jesus understood as the credential of divine love in self-giving for mankind and, as such, the pattern of moral human emulation as being the clue to human meaning. That reading of Christianity, however, found itself unable to accommodate the traditional Christian orthodoxy of the Creeds. There were times, even so, when he was able to yield his soul to the mystery of Christian worship, and the caveats of his reason were temporarily laid aside.[5] It seems right to think that he was closer to Christianity than his disavowals of dogma suggested, the more so in that some of these are readily taken into a more perceptive sense of what such dogma intends. Certainly it was the credential of God as love in the Cross of Jesus which dominated his esteeming of other faiths and which, at some strain, he sought to will for them or to read into them in his synthetic studies of their history and culture.

Before considering what this Christian frame of reference meant to Toynbee and how he applied it, it is wise to review the lively biography that shaped his mind. He was the son of Harry Valpy Toynbee and Sarah Edith Marshall. Born in 1889, his early formative years belonged in the heyday of Victorian confidence and power. His mother gave him a ready sense of history – she was an active historian – and his father, and the uncle after whom he was named, were social workers who alerted him to a conscience about social injustice. His home was gently Christian though without the sharp accents which, however, a great-uncle, strove hard to make good by drilling Arnold Joseph in Biblical recitation. To this factor we must attribute the free and frequent Biblical quotation or allusion occurring throughout Toynbee's writing. There is, in marked contrast, a paucity of reference to the Islamic Qur'an or to the Scriptures of Asia.[6] Even when most ill at ease there, Toynbee's mind was steeped in the Bible.

At Winchester and at Balliol College, Oxford, he received the other crucial dimension of intellectual prowess, namely a rigorous training in the literatures and history of Greece and Rome, in which he excelled and which became his stock-in-trade, enriched by the travels he made on foot in 1911-12 in Greece and Italy, where both archaeological and political interests were quickened and deployed. One vital consequence of that journey was the acute dysentery which was judged in 1914-15 to make him unfit for military service in the First World War. He was forever aware of the implications of that reprieve, writing in 1969: 'Ever since 1915 I have been surprised at being still alive.' (*Experiences*, p.105). With half of his Oxford and school contemporaries killed in the War, he never ceased to feel bound over to purposeful living. During the war years, at the Peace Conference where he was a delegate, and in the inauguration of what became the Royal Institute of International Affairs (Chatham House), he devoted himself to careful documentation of peace issues, writing his annual Surveys in the twenties as deliberative means to identifying minutely the things at stake. The conscience he brought to this activity sprang directly from the grief of war. He read diplomacy, like Dag

Hammarskjöld, as constraining the soul, in the art, not merely of the possible, but of the true. Forthright in his indictment of Turkish atrocities against the Armenians, he was no less so in sustaining Turkey's case when Greece and Western allies overran the Smyrna region in the twenties – an integrity which cost him the Chair in Byzantine Studies he had briefly taken up in London University, which had been funded by Greek sympathisers who expected a partisan professor.

Resuming his work at Chatham House the incentive to make sense of international relations began to fuse with the classical heritage of his Oxford studies. The fruit of that fusion was to be the (ultimately 12-volume) work: *A Study of History*.[7] He had already been struck by the discernible parallel within the strife of Sparta and Athens and, long centuries later, the wretched, wasteful slaughter between the Allies and the Central Powers in 1914-18. He began to ponder the idea of 'the historical contemporary', the near identity between separated ages of human politics, the recurrence of patterns, the inherent kinship of causes and effects. If these were seen against the vast prehistory of the earth, the feel of being contemporaries astride the centuries became even keener.

In pursuing this clue to meaning in time, of recurrence in history, it is important to remember for our perspective here that Toynbee was impelled by two profound religious impulses, with a third stemming from the second. We need not enquire about the precise chronology of their interaction through the long years in which *A Study of History* came to fruition. Its title stated its intention with simple directness. But it was also 'a study of man' and 'a quest for religion'. His Hebraic/Graeco-Roman/Christian disciplines of mind shaped his ambition to interpret but the arena was 'civilisations' wherever they had appeared, to be searched and assessed in their own right and by their own lights. For civilisations were the legible clues to the nature and meaning of man. If religion, in the final sense, is returning the part to the whole, relating to 'the beyond which is akin', then there is no more thoroughly religious enterprise than such as *A Study of History* undertook. For it posited what is humanly 'akin' in history, aimed to identify the kinships and to search for the connections that related them, each to other and each to all. Toynbee's enterprise was eminently reverent precisely in being eminently inquisitive.

iii

The two crucial elements in Toynbee's thinking were the reality of suffering and the actuality of sin. Was it from his ardently evangelical great-uncle that he always referred to the second as 'Original Sin', in capital letters? If so, he gave to it a range and a subtlety of which many evangelicals would be strangely unaware, meanings which could well indict them in its accusation. To this we will come. It was, however, reflection on suffering which required reference back to itself as vital to any honest perception of the world.

The War which had decimated his generation and shadowed his maturing years was – as we have seen – a tragic factor. But there were others in his story. The mental incapacitation of his father at a relatively early age had evoked from the son a compensating sense of liability for time, the consecration of effort and the urgency of opportunity. As an undergraduate and a don at Balliol he had given his rare endowments of mind and spirit a pattern of diligence which was his response to family pain. But there were other accents to tragedy in his later career. He had indulged intelligent hopes in his writing of Surveys only to find himself documenting repetitive follies in the thirties. He found in a post-World War II Conference maturer pain than had been the case in 1919. Was the 'wheel' of a linear progress of history belied by the 'shuttle' of a back and forth tapestry of hesitant design?

There was also the breakdown of his first marriage to Rosalind Murray and the suicide, in 1939, of his eldest son. Separation and divorce spelled deep tribulation – evident in the correspondence with Toynbee's Roman Catholic friend at Ampleforth to whom he confided the trauma of indecision and the perplexity of the factors which turned, in part, on his wife's conversion to Roman Catholic faith. That later he found solace and peace in marriage to his colleague, Veronica Boulter, at Chatham House did not entirely terminate the inquisition of doubt and perplexity in which, with rare and frank persistence, he probed his motives and brooded on unanswered things.

His intelligence was too positive to fall back, as absurdists do, on the futility of the meaningless as an escape from learning meaning. But both the panoramic world of the historian and the private world of the man had for their common theme the mystery of suffering. It was this which drew him sympathetically to Buddhism and made him insistently hostile to Semitic convictions about divine omnipotence (at least as he read them).

But it was not the *dukkha* of the Buddhist scheme which he had in mind by 'suffering.' That had to do with the human condition read as implicitly frustrated, caught in the futility of 'desire', and needing to be delivered from the illusion of selfhood by gradual, and ultimate, extinction of the will to be. That philosophy could find no place in the search for relevance and meaning that lay at the heart of all Toynbee's endeavour to explore, to clarify, to interpret and to possess history. Suffering, for him, was precisely within, and because of, the reality of meaning, the authenticity of the self, the implication of time. Frustration might well attend our experience; it was not the clue to it. It was an active, committed, living suffering Toynbee required himself to understand.

The Mahayana tradition in Buddhism drew admiration for its capacity in compassion and there were times when he felt able to align it with the compassionateness of Christianity. But the bleaker Hinayana, or Theravada, tradition of Buddhism he deprecated, not only as lacking the compassion of the later School, but as sadly misreading the nature of humanity and evil. It represented for him only another instance – and that a despairing one – of 'mankind's impatient eagerness to have its ambiguous situation clarified.' (*Experiences*, p.139).

He had, however, a similar verdict for what he saw as the Judeo/Christian/Muslim assurance about both the goodness and the power of God. Toynbee insisted he could not have both and that he must opt for compassionate goodness by denying any compatibility with it of omnipotent power. 'Let God be love', he would say, echoing ardently the words of the First Epistle of John (4:16) without – apparently – realising that so to confess was also to confess the truth of divine power, in that love is its very shape.

This, however, is to anticipate. Toynbee linked suffering inexorably with 'original sin'. There was, he argued, a manifest flaw in the universe, and there was a flaw in humanity. A principle of evil was present in all things, which Zorastrianism, for example, had frankly conceded. Zoroaster's was a faith he could well have espoused, had he been differently nurtured or differently timed. As it was, Toynbee must 'reconcile' divine love with the human scene, not impossibly in terms of omnipotent power, but via a divine surrender into suffering and evil as interpreting where human explication lay – namely in suffering love – and as construing how human conduct must learn its pattern. Such divine surrender Christianity had affirmed in the Cross of Jesus. But this, as he put it, must not be 'capped by resurrection'. For 'resurrection' is a triumphalism which will not admit that 'love cannot save life from death'. It can only fulfil life's purpose. (*Experiences*, p.163). Love has to be an end in itself. Only as it is so, as in no way unlocking ultimate mystery, can it be consistent with the real obduracy of the way life is. Only so can it be loyal to its own *raison d'être*.[8]

iv

When Toynbee thought and wrote of 'original sin', his great-uncle's theology may have been in the hinterland of his mind. But the mainland was his own awareness of history. He did not mean some crude idea of an inherited taint, whereby guilt was natally transmitted arbitrarily to the human embryo. That notion would be at worst a total travesty, at best no more than a symbol of the truth that personality was by nature prone to self-centredness. It is well here to keep in clear view a vital distinction which Toynbee did not always recognise.[9] There is the egocentric *situation* in the physical, metaphysical sense that all human experience transacts itself in selves, breathing, sensing, belonging, aspiring, dying as in-alienable, irreplaceable, separate identities, as private as their individual digestions and their individual minds, albeit only so within society. This individuation is one thing, neither reprehensible nor escapable. It is the universal predicament of man, the very predicate of life itself. Self-serving management of individuality is quite another.

Moral egocentricity is a selfish exercise of individuality and not in-evitable within the situation in which we are egocentrically existent. Hinayana Buddhism, however, holds the belief that an unselfish selfhood is impossible. We are inherently self-aggrandising merely in being self-existent. For this barren philosophy Toynbee had no sympathy. Selfhood needed to be transmuted into a love-idiom which presupposed desire. But, as with Francis of Assisi, the self had to be magnificently *there* in order to be love's vehicle and ground.

'Original sin', then, did not mean some essential futility, some cosmic fraud in our being. On the contrary, it meant that there was a crisis at the heart of selfhood – the real crisis which Hinayana Buddhism obliterated but which Christian, Biblical faith knew only too well. For it perceived the contrary equation – if we may so speak – between the 'ought' and the 'deed' within the human will. Toynbee was fond of Ovid's *Video meliora proboque, deteriora sequor*, in Book vii of *Metamorphoses*: 'I see and approve the better, I follow the worse.' Paul had told the Romans much the same in his Epistle: 'The good that I would I do not; the evil that I would not, that I do.' (7:15-21). An ultimate explanation of this enigma was far to seek and perhaps unattainable. What mattered was a policy, not a theory. The policy consisted in knowing it for what it was, the rejection of facile illusions concerning it, and a resolute conformity to the counter-patterns of divine love exemplified in 'the story' of the divine Lover who had undertaken to share the entail of the situation and demonstrate its due correction. In that correction, however, there was no cosmic clue, but only a pattern and a saving grace. 'Let this mind be in you which was also in Christ Jesus.' (Philippians 2:5).

We defer some implications of Toynbee's Christianity here in order first to reckon with his clue of 'original sin' in the sphere of human history. It lay, he thought, in what might crudely be described as man's inability to dispense with institutions. For institutions simply 'writ large' the innate self-centredness of man. Indeed, they gave it legitimation and passionate incentive. Human collectives undertook and – literally – established corporate egos, and these had far more warrant, as collective nosism, or 'we-ness', demanded, than the private urges they enlisted and enlarged. Nations, tribes, states, empires, systems, creeds, religions, cultures could all alike engage in self-aggrandisement and self-blindness. History, without cynicism or illusion, could be read as the saga of 'original sin'.[10]

Toynbee's bent for historical parallels, his feel for 'contemporary' time as measured by content rather than era, and his quest for patterns in the weaving 'shuttle', led him to elaborations about which more discrete historians, secure within their specialisms, have demurred. His schema of challenge and response, ascendancy, growth, decline, rout-and-rally, and decay, his notions of withdrawal and return, schism and palingenesis, do not directly concern our study here nor – with some later exceptions – do the arguments they generated. What is presently relevant is an appreciation of how Toynbee's perspective changed, particularly after Volume vi of *A Study of History*, in the direction of a greater centrality of religion and of the religious factor.

Earlier he had thought of religions as the chrysalis out of which a civilisation came. The civilisation was the historian's primary concern. Later he reversed the order and thought of religion as having priority over culture, the political organism and régimes of power. The change was in part due to the logic of observed behaviour – given the clue of collective egocentrism, the political mechanisms of 'original sin'. 'Oecumenical empires' as he liked to call them, allowed the cult of power to over-reach either its range or its wisdom, unlearning due humility in the lust of possession or the pride of being. National states, for their part, breaking free of imperial control, manifested the same chronic tendency to see the autonomy within as combat without, to locate security in aggression. The value-systems which may have informed their rise and prosperity were forfeit to their pretensions or eroded in their ambition. Nemesis overtook them when response failed the misread challenge of time itself.

For Toynbee the vocation of religion was to be keenly alert to the in-

corrigibilitiy of sin and, therefore, acutely aware of its own pitfalls in collective institutionalising of its own participation. For faiths, like any other
'establishment' in history, have necessarily to function through structures
of doctrine, symbol, ritual and authority, which expose them to the issue,
if not the bane, of vested interests. These may desperately impede or quite
contradict their real task as custodians of that by which all other custodies
are judged or served.

V

Postponing Toynbee's controversial inclusion of twentieth century
Zionism in his diagnosis of errant nationalisms, it is well at this point to
assess his vision of Islam. His long engagement with Middle Eastern
politics, his interest in the Turkish secularisation of Islam, and his
admiration for the Syrian dimension in the Mediterranean world, did not
prevent him from a critical cast of mind about things Islamic. He was well
aware that Islam did not share – apart from its exceptional moralists[11] – his
understanding of the 'flaw' innate in mankind. He was alert to its basic
idea of the amenability of man to divine law, once ignorance, or
Jahiliyyah, had been overcome by final revelation through the Prophet.
But this often disproven optimism apart,[12] there was also – and surely akin
to it – Islam's emphasis on the sheer omnipotence of God which
necessarily excluded that dimension of divine self-expending in love which
Toynbee set at the heart of his thought and which he correctly recognised
as made explicit in the Christian doctrine of the Trinity. Despite the rich
implication of the *Bismillah* (In the Name of God, the merciful Lord of
mercy, *Al-Rahman al-Rahim*) the unitary emphasis of Muslim theology
precludes the self-emptying theme which Toynbee so cherished in his
reckoning with Christianity.

In that sense Islam quite failed to meet his criterion of 'believable'
divinity, though he was ready to associate it 'as a higher religion' – a
category he often used – with divine love. He wrote, for example, in *An
Historian's Approach to Religion*, that Islam was 'a version of the new
vision of God that had been attained by Judaism and Christianity'.[13] This
perhaps was so in the sense of that monotheism which, elsewhere, he
described as 'Islam's creative gift to mankind . . . We surely dare not throw
this gift away.' (ConT, p.87). It was not so in the sense of the perception
of 'the suffering servant' as the clue to God on which the New Testament
faith had turned but which could in no way be posited of Muhammad after
the *Hijrah*.

That event Toynbee saw as 'the counter-transfiguration of a prophet...into the successful president, by invitation, of a rival oasis-state.' (HAR, p.110). All his instincts required him to disavow, as ever religiously appropriate, the appeal to force on which post-*Hijrah* Islam relied both under Muhammad and under the Caliphs. However, it seems fair to ask whether Toynbee truly assessed the inner Arabian situation in which Islam arose. He tended to see it as a 'Syrian' response to the challenge of Graeco-Roman civilisation, which may well be true of its developed, sophisticated culture but in no way tallies with the Arab interiority of Islam as nourished in Muhammad's own Hijaz.

On many counts, then, Toynbee 'could not pass Islam's tests either' (*Experiences*, p.136). He recognised what he called the 'Herodian' and 'Zealot' patterns of response within Islam to modern issues – the malleable accommodations and the rigorous rejections. He thought that perhaps the two greatest points of Islamic relevance to humanity lay in its capacity for human community across the divides of race and in its antialcoholism. In the second he had in mind the devastation inflicted on Pacific Islands and elsewhere by Western alcoholism. In the former he was reckoning appreciatively with the significance of the Pilgrimage in Islam and its symbolisation of the equal status of all races. (ConT, p.205).

It seems strange that Toynbee should have missed the deep significance of Islam for his own cherished theme of non-idolisation. For it was at the heart of the meaning of *Allahu akbar*. One could rightly say that the great burden of the Qur'an is the evil of pluralism, of tribal deities aiding and abetting the feuding of their local protégés. To be sure, the gods of the Meccans were literal idols, like those which Abraham, in the Qur'an, could demolish with an axe and hammer. But as such, they symbolised passions, vested interests, social intangibles and it was with these that Muhammad was essentially engaged. Hence the *Hijrah* to Medina the better to subdue them. That militancy may well be reprobated. But demur about the means does not reprove the end. Rather, it is in being about the purpose that the method must be censured – as it would differently be if it were mere free-booting, or brigandage, in the interests of fighting for its own sake. Muhammad could claim to be belligerent to end belligerence in the only way, *in situ*, he could do so, preaching having failed. Rightly to dispute that is not to deny that idolatry lay at the heart of the tribalism and that what was being unified in heaven by 'the word' was being unified in the Arabian world by 'the raid'.

We may say that what mattered ultimately was a successful iconoclasm, the end of idolatry. The divine unity, as Islam has it, necessarily relativises

all other potential or actual worships. Indeed, God is the only absolute that can rightly do so. The idols of Abraham's and Muhammad's
iconoclasm may have been crudely pagan. But they represent those other
deifications – of power, class, technology, statehood, commerce, culture –
which humanity erects, all in evidence of their incorrigible pseudo-
worshipping. Many of these dimensions or structures have the possibility of beneficence, even of validity – provided they are relative to the
sovereignty of God. Otherwise they are demonic and ultimately dam-
natory. Toynbee saw that chronic self-idolisation of human institutions as
the central blight of history. It is strange that he did not recognise the
crucial relevance to its incrimination and correction of the central witness
of Islam that 'only God is God', and that 'to let God be God' is the only
sure way of 'letting man be truly man'. Such is the meaning of reiterating:
Allahu akbar – whatever you may be thinking, desiring, enthroning, admiring, remember: 'God is greater.'

The Qur'an is also closer than Toynbee apparently realised to an
awareness of what he delighted to call 'Non-Human Nature' and its claim
to sacramental use. He tended, as many others do, to decry the Semitic
faiths as exploitative of nature and improperly arrogant about humanity's
'dominion status'. The complaint about the latter hardly rides with what
Toynbee had to say about the centrality of 'individuation', and the
precious meaning of personality. But the crux here turns on realising that
'dominion' – *khilafah* in Islam (identical meaning) – is not sovereignty, but
entrustment. It is a human empire *over* things only in being a human
amanah, or stewardship, *under* God. This meaning emerges very clearly
in the Qur'an by its doctrine of the *ayat*, the 'signs' of God in the natural
order – signs which human knowledge registers and exploits *qua* science
and which human wonder acknowledges *qua* gratitude, a gratitude which
issues into worship – *not* of the phenomena or the techniques, but of the
Lordship whence they come. In those convictions Islam may be squarely
aligned with Toynbee's own sophisticated iconoclasm, and his passionate
environmentalism. In that sense he could have 'passed its tests'.

He would doubtless concede so. For he had decisive honesty of mind
but the same honesty would also properly restrain his concession. For –
these agreed concepts apart – is not Islam, precisely because of its ardent
stand against pseudo-gods, inveigled into self-idolatry? That would be his
charge. *Allahu akbar* becomes *Islamu akbar*. Religions are the worst
offenders, for interior reasons, in the original sin of self-deification, of
chronic self-centredness. They are unwilling to call in question their
unique necessity to God. For the most part, by being what they are, they

lack the very capacity to think or act outside what they can never relinquish – their *magisterium*.

Toynbee thought perhaps he had found in Christianity, potentially, the one exception, the faith that might have in the self-expending God the clue to its own self-expending vocation. However that may be, he was sure that by the shape of its genesis it was not so with Islam. Its forcible-ness and its finality debarred it from the necessary humility of self-questioning, self-abnegating, except in the hearts of those mystics whose aberrations or excesses of devotion its custodians disowned. It was not for him surprising that religions should be 'betrayed by what is false within', as George Meredith had phrased it in *Modern Love*, xliii. They were for ever 'oriented towards a centre that lies in themselves'. (HAR, p.10). The idea that there could be, in now-past history, 'the seal of prophethood', the terminus of divine revelation, was to deny the openendedness both of truth and of response to truth. It was the will for security characteristic of the religious mind wistful for the guaranteed. Whether one sees prophethood as 'scientific' or as 'poetic' truth, finality could only be in the patience that freely discerned it. To claim it otherwise was simply to give revelatory form to an inviolate self-sufficiency.

vi

It is ironic that the faith whose ritual conceived the scapegoat should itself have been so often, and so tragically, cast in that role. Arnold Toynbee's inner debate with Judaism can be readily guessed from his basic criteria about human nature, non-arbitrary divinity, cultural egocentricity and collective forms of self-image. Perhaps it was here that his dictum that 'tolerance does not become perfect until it has been transfigured into love' (HAR, p.256), was hardest for him to apply. For Zionists and anti-Anti-Semitists he became, sadly, a sharply controversial figure.[14] *A Study of History* found little favour in Jewish quarters. If, like all his writing, it was 'intellectual work from the saddle' (HAR, p. 270), for these 'his mount was prejudice'.

In this, no doubt, Toynbee was caught, as many others, in the situation for which all attitudes to things Judaic are Anti-Semitic if they are not approbatory. The tangled problematics of the State of Israel have only intensified that liability. Yet there are points at which readers find failing him that gentleness to which all his logic led and of which he was so impressively capable in a conscience passionate for integrity. It is sad that his writings betray no awareness, for example, of Abraham Heschel, his

close contemporary, who possessed *within* Judaism just that criterion of
monotheism which Toynbee held with equal emphasis.

But, despite the deep Judaic roots of his conviction about suffering as
the clue to God, and despite his Biblical instincts, he was scandalised
by the theme of 'the jealous God', and he read in 'chosen people'
status a subtle expression of corporate identity, a divinely sanctioned
egocentricity. Like the Islamic concept of Muhammad's finality enjoyed
by an Arabic revelation, it needed to undo itself and inclusify mankind
within its deeper prophetic insight into the compassion of God. Jewish
opinion was naturally outraged when he discerned affinities between an
ethnic distinctiveness of destiny and the *folk* doctrines of Aryan vintage
and the concept of 'holy Russia', or when he associated Jewish/Christian
Messianism with Communist dialectic and eschatology.

Was it another version of the misreading of monotheism that he had
made in respect of Islam, namely, the argument that the One God's
hatred of 'gods' only served to sustain His devotees' exaltation of themselves as necessary, either credally or racially, to that solitary divine
eminence? It is true that there are hints in the Bible that 'alien' equals
'heathen', and that the ethnic separateness of Israel corresponds with the
one true worship. 'In Jewry is God known . . . ' (Psalm 76:1).[15] Toynbee's
sense of the capacity for self-deception implicit in 'original sin' prevented
him from conceding that there might be integrity in Judaic conviction as to
Jewish status, just as there might be also in Muslim assurance about their
being possessed of God's last word. But in his scepticism here, despite its
controversial consequences, he was close to a central dilemma of all
religious belief. We might call it the 'pride of truth'. Doubtless there exists
the same situation in Christian faith, except that it is differently located in
a community that does not require any race for its indispensable locale
and no indispensable language for its Scripture.[16] Such 'pride of truth' for
Toynbee only concealed, did not justify, itself in the familiar insistence
that there was nothing meritorious about Judaic privilege. It existed, the
protests ran – like the Church but in a different way – for the sake of those
outside it. Such warrant, while plausible, indeed admirable, was still a
self-deception.

It is well to reflect that there is no escape from this situation in the
'modesty' – if it may be so named – of the pluralism of which Hinduism at
times is capable. Plural worships may well readily accommodate each
other, since none need to be exclusive. But they, too, must be adamant
about their 'modesty' and as firmly rejectionist of 'singulars' as these are
of them. There seems no escape from this logic except in the humility that

co-exists honestly but, so doing, continues to point to what it believes must be decisive, faithfully identifies what it is and why it finds it so.

Arnold Toynbee did this resolutely in pointing to the centrality of the personal self and in affirming the transcendent clue of self-expending love in God. Those with other 'decisives' were free to do the same but their doing so would not lessen either the warrant or the insistence of his own. He seems to have found that humility of conviction-in-tolerance hardest to sustain in his engagements with 'the chosen people'. This was particularly so when that 'chosen-ness' chose to fulfil itself in Zionism – in Zionism not simply as an agricultural cherishing of soil and habitat by a religious love, but in competent and necessarily combative statehood which left un-resolved the question whether its meaning was religious or political and, if both, how they could justly be combined.[17] He saw such politicization of Judaic religion as tragically disruptive of Middle Eastern history, as it has more and more proved to be in the tragedies of Lebanon and the West Bank since his death.

All historical events, it might be argued, are intrusive upon some *status quo*. What for Toynbee was still more important was that the Judaic 'already-there-ness'[18] in truth and faith, by virtue of right descent, was contrary to the personalism which, for him, was fundamental to faith. 'Every soul,' he wrote, 'has a right to commune with God in God's own way,' and no other soul had the right to intervene. 'There is no such thing as a belief that is not held voluntarily through a genuine, spontaneous inner conviction.' (HAR, p.250). Jews might well claim that, at least in their case, birth was 'God's own way'. We might also add that 'spon-taneity' is hardly feasible *in vacuo* or, as with the fabled *Hayy Ibn Yaqzan*, by parentless intuition.[19] But Toynbee, even so, saw the Judaic 'generation to generation' sequence of *de jure* legitimacy as a formula of faith which, while it might well admit of the most exacting personalism, in no way necessitated it. So deep did Toynbee's guiding principles run that he could disregard what might be urged against them, whether in encounter with other historians over his lively schema, or with Zionists over their reading of the writ for the repossession of Palestine. But in neither arena could he be accused of being either imperceptive or ill-informed.

vii

Toynbee's esteem of the Buddha and his response to the Mahayana Buddhist tradition may be best studied in the context of his Christianity. He firmly distanced himself from the Theravada strain of Buddhism as

violating totally his commitment to the preciousness of individual personality and for its utter pessimism about authentic selfhood. He felt that
the Mahayana tradition modified this negativism by its role for *bodhisattvas* and by its emphasis on the Buddha's withholding from the ultimate
bliss of *Nirvana* for the sake of enlightenment of the still deluded. In *An
Historian's Approach*, he sought to hold, at one and the same time, the
Judaic/Christian/Islamic theism with Hindu *Brahma* and Buddhist *Nirvana*. 'We cannot think of Reality as being either *Brahma-Nirvana*, or
God, exclusively.' (p.17). When he 'dropped into Judaic/Christian usage
the reader . . . [had to] . . . construe the language as shorthand script referring to Reality as *both* personal God *and* impersonal *Brahma*.'

There was much, of course, at stake in this merger of seeming incompatibles. The latent contradiction is carried further where Toynbee associates the Buddha's self-yielding postponement of entry into bliss, with
the crucial passage in Paul's Letter to the Philippians (2:5ff.) on the
Christ's self-giving, or *kenosis*, into humiliation, suffering and death.[20]

> It will be clear that the Mahayana and Christianity have two
> intentions in common. Instead of kicking against the pricks
> of Suffering, they both accept suffering as an opportunity for
> acting on the promptings of true Love and Pity . . . The trail
> has been blazed for man by a Supreme Being who has
> demonstrated his own devotion to the ideal by subjecting
> himself to the suffering that is the necessary price of acting
> upon it. (HAR, p.86)

What is confused here is whether the 'suffering' in question is veritably
and historically encountered in the active context of qualitative and
original sin, or whether it is conceptually incurred by one who, being on
the very brink of bliss, is hardly enduring it. Involved there, also,
is whether the 'suffering' is inherently that of human *dukkha*,
'impermanence-in-futility,' or whether it is redemptive in that evil is
vicariously forgiven at the point where it is suffered.

The contrast is, of course, vital to a Christian theology. Does history
matter? It is surprising that so eminent a historian as Toynbee, one so
versatile in time's interrogation, should have failed to reckon with the
actuality of Jesus' Cross or with its comprehension in the New Testament
as engagement with 'the sin of the world'. As we have seen elsewhere
in these biographies, the point is vital. The New Testament sees the
crucifixion as the indictment of humanity, not merely of Jews and Romans

who happened to be around. It takes the fact of *this* 'end to the Beatitudes' and all else about Jesus as index to what human wrong is and does and means. To see it so is the well-spring of repentance – the repentance which knows itself included in: 'Father, forgive them...' Here, in blood and wounds and death, is something other than foregoing, for the time being, an assured *Nirvana*. There is a sense between them in which love may be participant, but no sense in which the loves can be identical.

It is, perhaps, this neglect of the Gethsemane within the Philippians passage which explains Toynbee's reference elsewhere to 'the vision of a self-sacrificing figure'[21] or 'the story' of a transcendent being exemplifying divine capacity for sacrifice. Had the historical Cross been in a more theological reckoning consonant with what learned it in the first place, Toynbee would have been saved from those frequent comparisons he made between Gethsemane and the stories of 'vegetarian gods', of Tammuz, Adonis and Osiris,[22] in which, as he oddly alleges, 'the passion of Christ was foreshadowed... the culminating and crowning experience of the suffering of human souls.' (ConT, p.234). To link, as he does, the Christian Eucharist with such 'rites of spring' and vegetative renewal is to obscure its rigorously redemptive quality in grim, not natural, history. What, in this context, are we to make of his observation that

> An historian can trace back the hallowing of a particular
> spot to historical events that *have nothing to do* with the
> essence of the religion (HAR, p.278). (my italics)

In respect of the Cross the place and time had everything to do with the essence of Christianity.

Yet, in a very revealing passage, he comprehensively expresses a profound Christian perspective and gives implicit reasons why – as he puts it elsewhere – 'I have never repudiated my membership in the Church of England.' (*Experiences*, p.143).

> The creation itself is a supreme act of self-restraint, self-
> abnegation and patience.... I believe God acts in the world
> always unobtrusively and humbly, and this is one reason for
> the irony in human affairs, the confounding of the powerful
> and wise by the lowly and the simple. God always incarnates
> Himself in a form in which no one expects Him and in which
> few human beings ever recognise Him. So we have to

beware of taking it upon ourselves to act for Him with a self-assertiveness that would never be shown by God Himself. (HC, p.294).

There is much of Paul's 'wisdom of God to the lowly' and of 'the God of patience and hope' in the New Testament in that *confessio*, though Toynbee's Catholic correspondent felt obliged to reply that 'God *is* assertive-Truth. In the matter of truth, there cannot be anything but assertion.' There, to be sure, was 'dialogue' even if the comment, somehow, terminates it.

viii

Yet that moving sense of the 'diffidence of God', the divine *kenosis* implicit in creation itself, need not require, as it does for Toynbee, the option for goodness *against* power, the conclusion that a good omnipotence is refuted, seeing that the good can only *demonstrate* a will that lacks the competence. Throughout, Toynbee insists on this agnosticism. Self-expending divine love is, indeed, the ultimate for our responsive motivation; it is not ultimate in ontological power. Zoroaster has it right. We must concede an irreducible dualism. Yet, doing so, we can still hold and follow a religious finality, rooted not in inassailable knowledge as to doctrine, but in unmistakeable vocation as to conduct.

This is the religion we can trust without compromise and without the negative scepticism which must associate with all else. At points, Toynbee seems to hope or imagine that all 'higher religions', especially Hinduism and Buddhism, will finally converge towards such a consensus since – as he thinks, perhaps in sanguine mood – 'All philosophies and religions would agree that a human being ought to strive to extinguish his self-centredness. (*Experiences*, p.154). With elements of all 'grafted in', Christianity may be left as 'the spiritual heir of all the other higher religions' – with one world-wide civilisation playing a part. From this perspective, 'the greatest event in the history of mankind...will still be the crucifixion and its spiritual consequences.' (ConT, pp.237-40).

But this conviction does not make Toynbee a classical Christian. On the contrary, he would be one (though not explicitly with many Jews), in disallowing 'the Resurrection'. Love neither seeks, nor can it have, that kind of vindication as if there was an ontological omnipotence after all. It can only assert itself for love's own sake and be for ever uncorroborated by more than its own vocation. It is not merely, as – for example – with

Heschel and Wiesel that Hallelujahs are premature; it is that they are inappropriate. 'The Lord God omnipotent does not reign.' We are all too eager to give our consent to Easter and that should warn us to restrain the urge since it asks for the unverified and the unverifiable.

> Ultimate Reality is other than Alpha and Omega . . . Love at all costs is an end in itself and needs no resurrection . . . In capping the Crucifixion with the Resurrection and the Ascension, the Christian Creed has given Jesus' self-sacrificing death an anticlimax and has tampered with his humanity in a way that diminishes his spiritual stature rather than enhancing it. (*Experiences*, p.163 & 178).

The conclusion, however, for classic Christianity in no way follows if the exaltation of Jesus – Resurrection and Ascension as one whole in the New Testament – is understood as precisely the form and symbol of that love-ultimacy in which Toynbee believes. For 'resurrection' is not, then, some vegetative renewal, nor yet a contrived happy ending to a tragedy, but – on the contrary – the meaning of Gethsemane read from its own text. It is Toynbee's ultimacy of divine love actually generating conviction about itself in the experience of men. What it 'verifies' is not from without fortuitously or surreptitiously, but from within essentially and truly, not some *deus ex machina* but *Deus in amore*. It is where Toynbee is invited to be sceptical about his own scepticism as to how ultimate love can be in the self-definition of God. It will be right to see the great Crucifix, as he dreamed himself doing at a time of acute anxiety, in the Chapel, of Ampleforth Abbey, and know himself clasping it as the words came: *Amplexus expecta*, 'Cling and Wait'.[23] But only Resurrection tells us why we wait.

ix

All the foregoing was, for Toynbee, 'the explanation in which we find ourselves'. The message of religions about transcendent Reality had to belong with its significance for the inward self of personal man. That self, too, could only rightly have itself by the principle of self-giving in love. We had 'to lose to find'. Such 'loving because He first loved us' (1 John 4:19) was the heart of all ethics, the nerve of that social action which his family auspices embodied.

It was this genuinely unselfish selfhood, as a possibility of grace, which

alerted him to the hidden paradox of Buddhism and tempered his enthusiasm for all he found admirable in the Mahayana tradition. For there
had to be a 'desire' even for the abatement of 'desire'. The self was
ineluctable, as martyrs knew in their immolation of it, and mystics in its
only suppositious abeyance in trance and ecstacy. Clearly the self must be
involved in any suspension of its 'self-interests'. Writing in *Civilisation on
Trial* on 'The Meaning of History in the Soul', he wrote that 'Individuality
is a pearl of great moral price...of absolute value to God' (p.255,259),
and elsewhere that 'Self-fulfilment only comes when it is unsought.'
(HAR, p.87). What was admirable in the Buddha's practice, i.e., defer-
ment of *Nirvana* in the interests of 'the lost in illusion', was 'clearly nobly
inconsistent with what he preached'. (*Experiences*, p.137).[24]

But was this principle of self-giving as the way to authentic self-being a
clue for religions themselves? Their self-centredness in exclusivism, arrogance, 'us-only true', spiritual and political 'nosism', was plain for all to
see. It demonstrated the egocentricism of great collectives. Was there a
way, then, for these also to abnegate themselves? Toynbee in effect asked
this of Christianity, on the strength of the verse in John 12:24 about 'the
corn of wheat' only fructifying by 'death' in the ground. Yet, dialogue
might say to him: 'That principle identified the Cross itself and with the
loss of the perspective of that Cross the principle itself would no longer be
known, identified and enshrined. Therefore, for its very sake, the principle must not forfeit the faith of the Cross.'

No doubt, with different accents, Judaism could equally invoke its utter
necessity as witness, or Islam its doctrine of Muhammad's finality and,
alike, plead non-arrogance in so doing. The cases are not the same, but
the logic might be. Must we not conclude that a proper humility in
religions is not to be equated with indecisiveness. Rather it consists in
identifying and holding the decisive dimension for the sake of which it
must understand and fulfil its selfhood. Let it do so, however, with a
genuine will to curb the 'vested interests' of that selfhood, where not
warranted by the decisive thing. These 'interests' – doctrinal, institutional,
collective, psychic, traditional – will only be subdued by vigilant resolve
and a posture of maximum openness and humility of mind.

Toynbee was fond of citing his hero Quintus Aurelius Symmachus: 'The
heart of so great a mystery cannot be reached by following one road only.'
(HAR, pp.251,285, CARW, p.111.) But he was no syncretist, for all his
synoptic vision of history. He named Alexander Severus, whose chapel
had statues of various deities including Christ.[25] 'The revelation of the One
True God...to be accessible to all men...has to be diffracted.'[26] But

'when it comes to suffering, I am a Christian and not a Buddhist.' (HC, p.??) He might ask, perversely: 'How can the presence of a hypothetically infinite and eternal God be supposed to make itself felt more palpably in Palestine than in Alberta?'[27] But always...

> This God of many epiphanies but only one Passion... As we stand and gaze with our eyes fixed upon the further shore, a single figure rises from the flood and straightway fills the whole horizon. There is the Saviour...[28]

Toynbee's rich span of years was resolutely filled with omniverous research and copious writing. In old age and long retrospect of travel and report he was often occupied with the mystery of death. 'The further shore' came more palpably into view as he feared, not about demise itself but about the circumstances which might attend it. In the event he did have to experience almost total incapacitation from thought and speech for some weary final months. For all its inner pain, it was perhaps a fitting completion to an unrelenting dialogue which shirked no province of historical imagination, no realm of human suffering. He was, we may say, the more honest in being, at once, inconclusively a questioner and conclusively decisive. Faith, with interrogation, was his mind's adventure and his heart's rest. He only sought – and surely found – 'an authority that deserved to be believed'.

Chapter 13

WILFRED CANTWELL SMITH
(born 1916)

'All Inner Faith is Inter-Faith'

i

We must begin by realising that 'faith' is never properly a plural noun. It is accumulated traditions, doctrines, symbols, usages and images which diversify the singular thing they enshrine, articulate and nourish. If these are what engage attention in what is commonly meant by 'inter-faith dialogue', participants will do well to see them as belonging, albeit by mutually disconcerting ways, in a shared response to the transcendent where they are essentially one. 'Religion', rightly understood, is not 'beliefs'; it is 'a humane science', a human sense of totality as mystery, as meaning and as responsibility. Faith is, indeed, 'inner', but we will not use that adjective as if, by virtue of differing forms, the 'inward' truly differed and so needed adjudication as to its peculiar 'truth'. The pluralism we are often found sifting with a view to unilateral or distinctive 'truths' is already singular in its inner capacity as faith. Any 'dialogue' is first about that unity before it can rightly be about diversity. 'Inner' and 'inter-' – we might say – are simply interchangeable. When we speak about *our* faith – unless we err – it can only be the inclusive, not the restrictive, pronoun we intend.

Such is the radical thesis of the Canadian scholar Wilfred Cantwell Smith. It belongs with a significant biography of dialogue, an impressive sequence of influential writing and a variety of important institutions where his ideas have found recognition and following. It is well fitted to round out the several issues we have encountered in the personalities reviewed in previous chapters. It has within it just that quality of penetrating sympathy and astringent cast of mind appropriate both to appreciate and to interrogate all the foregoing. A concluding chapter – among other things – will aim to do the same with Smith himself. His story yields several clues to his thought.

The Christian background of Wilfred Cantwell Smith's career is very evident in his sustained concern with Christian missionary thinking and action. Unlike some academics he has never dismissed or ignored the problematics of a believing will to be articulate and to recruit in and from the world. His concern has been critical but perceptive, not only of the issues which evangelism and ministry entail, but of the implications of their repudiation for sincerity in other forms of relationship. One would surmise also a deeply Christian factor, and perhaps also a Platonic one, in his robust confidence in a universal human awareness of the divine and its claim. It is there, too, in his firm repudiation of secularity, i.e., 'god'-lessness, as incompatible with a truly human self-awareness.

He gladly acknowledges the Christian character of his home, his parents and his early nurture in his loved Toronto. After Upper Canada College, he studied also in the Universities of Grenoble and Madrid with later research in Cairo, Cambridge (England) and Princeton, USA following nine formative years in Lahore, Pakistan. Posted there in 1940 at the age of twenty-four, he was lecturer in Indian and Islamic History at Forman Christian College and representative among Muslims of the Canadian Overseas Missionary Council, departing in 1949 to become Professor of Comparative Religion at McGill University, Montreal, in which context he inaugurated the pioneer Institute of Islamic Studies to bring together to mutual profit scholars both Muslim and Christian.

In his Lahore days there was a strong Marxist element in his thinking about religion in society which he found confirmed in his studies of the passions and pleas involved in Muslim separatism in the build-up of Islamic self-definition in the sub-continent prior to the creation of Pakistan.[1] Those studies within his post-graduate research[2] emerged in *Modern Islam in India*, his first published book.[3] Their bias for economic factors as always primary he later deplored as a youthful gesture of enthusiasm eclipsing a more rounded picture. His firm, later confidence in the priority of the 'religious' factor – understood in the terms still to be explored – may be seen as something of a conversion. What he later believed to be his maturer mind was admirably documented and distilled in *Islam in Modern History* which appeared during his time at McGill.[4] Writing later in 1963 he dropped an intriguing hint that his sense of the primacy of ideas might be suspect to some precisely because it was a second enthusiasm on the part of one who had earlier seen ideas as merely 'episodic' amid economic forces. He wrote:

> It may be that my current tendency to see much of man's history as a history of religion is a trifle overdone.[5]

It is a 'may be' to which we will have ample occasion to return.

Through four decades from his arrival at McGill, Wilfred Cantwell Smith established a formidable reputation for incisive thinking in the history of religions across Canada and the United States by his tenure of a sequence of eminent posts. In 1964 he became Professor of World Religions at Harvard University and in that capacity succeeded Dr Robert Slater as Director of the Center for the Study of World Religions. From 1973 to 1978 he was Professor of Religion at Dalhousie University, Halifax, Nova Scotia, before returning to Harvard as Professor of the Comparative History of Religion and Chair: 'The Study of Religion', becoming Distinguished Professor on retirement in 1984. Visiting professorships have been held at the Universities of London, Princeton, Toronto, and Washington. A long, well sustained sequence of published articles, lectures, and wide travels, with the major publications we must explore, have shaped for him a unique place in the elucidation of the meaning of religious faith and in the investigation of its continuity, past and future.

ii

There are two distinguishing features of Smith's writing. The one is a careful, insistent definition of basic terms. The other is the almost total absence of the poetic. It is rare to find any quotation from poetry, art or drama which might kindle and illuminate the imagination or suggest an affinity of meaning emotionally shared and sublimely registered. To turn to Smith after the aphorisms and sometimes near lyricism of Abraham Heschel is to be in different world. There are many cross-references in his prose and footnotes to his own other works – a feature indicative of the strong intellectualism on which he relies. The warmth of sincerity lies below the surface of the case-making. This austerity of presentation is always salutary and nowhere is its discipline more necessary than in the realm of religion. Yet meeting sometimes happens in the indefinable and Smith is, for clarity's sake, intent on definition.

His motive in this characteristic is not simply the laudable one of spelling out terms, the instinct which begins all discussion by reaching for the dictionary. It is, rather, the will to put his case across by a radical re-reading of crucial terms, like 'faith', 'belief', and 'truth', so that his point is actually argued in the form of precision with a term. He is ready to sustain his case by close etymological examination of words – if need be in several languages – so that the dictionary itself is put to rights. His precision, if sustained, requires the abandonment of received meanings as misleading. He intends a re-writing of terminology itself as the soundest way to compel attention to what are, for him, misconceptions and thus to sharpen the obligation on his readers to rethink what familiar assumptions, verbally entrenched, have misread. The strategy is a lively one, though traditional usages have a way of reasserting themselves and refusing to submit to what he requires of them – a fact which has significance. Usages which will not consent to lapse may well be persisting by more than sheer stolidity in undissuaded users. But Smith's readers are at least aroused to think they may have been mistaken – at which none may well complain.

'Faith' is the first and most vital of Smith's definitions. The word, never properly plural, should be thought of as an adjective, attaching always to 'persons', and not be confused with 'beliefs'. But, as a descriptive of what belongs to persons, faith can be understood as a verb, comparable to 'hope'. We can arrive, by that comparison, at 'faith-ing' by which is meant the exercise of an innate capacity for the transcendent, a responding to ultimacy, the moral and spiritual faculty by which we make sense of the world, a personal openness to reality. As such, faith is a quality of human nature, 'a humane science', the axis of meaning which gives unity to the content of living. It could almost be described as the human potentiality for being human. It is our strange dynamic towards becoming our true selves and becoming divine.[6]

This 'capacity for authenticity' has many different specific formulations-in-association, via doctrines, rites, symbols and institutions. It can readily be thus diversified, since these formulations all belong as the particularities of those who within them have faith. Smith is insistent that the equation between 'faiths' and 'beliefs' is a modern usage, much to be deplored. He maintains that 'believing' properly means 'trusting', and that its current usage – 'holding a dogma' – distorts the meaning. But if we take 'beliefs' in his sense as only 'items of credence' then it is perverse and false to call these 'faith' or 'faiths'. They are only the intellectual and institutional expression of acts of faith. They are the deliberate 'housing' in concept and action of what faith means to 'faith-ing ones' in their context of time and culture. Smith prefers to speak of 'cumulative tradition' rather than systems of doctrine, as the context in which faith is diversely expressed, communicated and bequeathed. No such single tradition can impose its own norms on the reality of faith. As grammars are to language, we might say, doctrines are to faith. Language is one; it is diversified by the grammars in which it is fashioned. Theology, then, if we can stretch the term to include non-theisms, is like the relation of art criticism to art. It ponders and assesses what is inherently *there* as 'faithful faith-ing'.

Beliefs, then, are answerable to faith in the transcendent. Unless they can be rescued from the modern idea that they are the central element in religion, matters of mere credence – which Smith doubts – they should be understood as only vehicles of the act of having faith. As such, their plural diversity need not be thought of as requiring mutual belligerence, or rejection, or antagonism. They are not the criteria of true faith but legitimate forms of true faith-ing.

This stance, on Smith's part, works two ways. It obviates controversy inasmuch as it leads minds back from the aberration which preoccupied them with the truth-question *about* the items of belief, to the truth-finding *through* them. But, precisely by that emancipation from truth-debating over the items, it calls men into preoccupation with the integrity of their own truth-loving. They become aware of truth-diversity in that they find their own beliefs queried by outsiders, yet have to realise that those outsiders are proceeding on convictions through which faith is active. Plurality dispels the naïveté which thinks that only our own presuppositions should obtain. For truth is finally only *in* persons not in propositions. The latter are clues to the faith of persons, not referential to reality itself except as enshrining the integrity of the faithful who make them.

iii

This position on Smith's part has deep implications for the theory of knowledge. It affirms a fundamental human capacity for recognition of, and response to, the divine. It would have to see the sense of meaninglessness, so prevalent in current western thinking, as a kind of paralysis of the spirit. There is no logic by which rationality can arrive at its own absurdity. Truth-perception is a concomitant of human being *per se* and, as such, a necessary orientation towards the divine. We need to beware of the sociology which sees all believing as socially conditioned or constructed as if the diversity of social context – though manifestly pluralising its forms – thereby disqualified any veritable reference to reality.

We have also to beware of the empiricism which restricts the range of verifiable knowledge to the mathematical, the geometric and the sense-perceived. The verification principle which obtains in those areas is not appropriate to the religious awareness which has its own form of cognition of truth as a constituent of human personhood. To be sure, religious affirmations relate to the divine only indirectly, but the indirection derives from the nature of human finitude within which it does not falsify the knowledge of the divine. To think that it did would be to stultify ourselves.

Smith's view of religious knowing means that truth is not limited to objective fact where the true/false alternative avails. To apply that religiously is too simplistic. He sees in secularism a kind of militant either/or which is often 'missionary' in its impulse to demand acceptance of itself by all and sundry. It wants to limit truth to its own limited range of cognisance of meaning, whereas religious truth opens out human awareness to realms of perception, response and liability which rational positivism could never realise. Ignorance is a more proper antonym of truth than falsity can be, if what we are aware of in human personhood is truly comprehensive.

Smith wants to insist that statements are true according to the meaning their authors intend. 'Meaning *of*' cannot be isolated from 'meaning *for*'. When we fail to appreciate this, controversy *about* meanings will cease to talk *to* participants; it will only talk *past* them. What, on one count, we may wish to deny, on another count may be true. It is false to hold that the earth is flat, but its curvature is such that a builder may still rightly use a spirit-level. Could we, he suggests, substitute 'witness-bearing' for 'truth-claiming'? If we do, it will be right and necessary always to have the insider's verdict on the meaning of a *confessio*, or a rite, or a symbol. Only so do we really personalise meaning – which is what we must do since faith is an activity of persons and – persons apart – is not resident in propositions or systems. But it is denied that this leads to entire subjectivism since *ex hypothesi* persons, in their capacity for the transcendent, are cognisers of reality by being such. Religion *is* 'the humane science'. Its findings are historically diverse and essentially congenial. No one interpretation, therefore need impose itself on another. They may well assist each other to mutual enlargement.[7]

iv

It is just such a movement *Towards a World Theology* which Wilfred Cantwell Smith proposes in his book of that title which is the climax of his writing.[8] 'Theology' needs to be understood here, not as weighting the enterprise towards a Semitic, western frame of reference, but as standing in for the transcendent in any and every faith-system. He believes that the history of religions can be written 'in the singular'. There is a coherence in their enormous and bewildering diversity. He would like 'someday to construct a scholarly presentation of the religious history of humankind as a global continuum' (p.18). The time is ripe. For it is evident how far science, technology, speed, politics, economic pressures, all compel the peoples into mutual existence and interaction of mind. This mutuality has now to become avowed, deliberate and progressive, abjuring self-sufficient privacy. Religions can be helped to this by realising how their 'reification' as '- isms' is a modern phenomenon which has hardened them into identities, whereas they are in constant flux and process within and between themselves. Only by insisting on the personal equation, this Hindu, that Buddhist, these Jews, those Muslims, can we expect, or deserve, to know the faith-having which animates and transacts what abstractions like Hinduism, Buddhism, Judaism, Islam purport to denote.[9] This emphasis makes bold with the paradox that 'there is no such thing as Hinduism: there are only Hindus', or: 'Islam is what Muslims say it is.' If the circularity here is obvious – and makes its point absurdly – it is worth heeding as a corrective to the blandness which talks undiscerningly about 'Hinduism teaching . . . ' or 'the Bible saying . . . '

Towards a World Theology has an interesting note of autobiography at this point. Smith records his twenty-five year quest to understand Islam – 'Islam' as the religion Muslims own. Through Muslim friends, mainly intellectuals, he realised that they too were in search of it and for what, to themselves, it might mean to hold it. This dynamism inherent in the personal factor brought him to a lively perception of Islam in its being and becoming. His Muslim friends, he claims, 'were not captured within any forms.' Islam-for-them could not be apprehended in the abstractions purveyed by outsiders as what Islam was, or had been (p.30). We can well take the point of this personalism without conceding the parallel fact that numerous Muslims belong with an Islam that is not in search at all but is insistently identified with a dogma they are bound to defend. In arguing from 'friends' one must only make the right ones, or ignore those who see all overtures as inimical. Nevertheless the explicit hope of community in quest is right and Muslims themselves have approved it. In *Le Personnalisme Musulman*, Muhammad Lahbabi argues that the *Hijrah* itself in the very origins of Islam demonstrated a personal obedience of faith countermanding tribal loyalties and city ties.[10] But a right testing of religions by adherents must be inclusive of the whole range of these and of the ways in which they may disqualify each other.

'I am proposing,' Smith continues, 'the conceptualisation of historical process as the context of religious life and participation as its mode.... I am not willing intellectually to let anyone define being Christian in a way that reduces the role of the Bible in my parents' faith; just as I am not willing to let anyone define it in a way that would exaggerate it in mine.' (p.36). Faith as it is, has been, and yet will be, within the personal discovery and expression of it, must always be the index to what the faith is. Perhaps we should only guardedly speak of 'the faith' at all, if we mean a static orthodoxy. For the latter never exists outside persons and by that necessity is never finally static.

Smith finds his thesis heartened by the realisation at this point that even from 'mission' and controversy the process of being Muslim within Islam or of being Hindu within Hinduism (using all entity terms as meaning 'cumulative traditions') and the rest, has been stimulated and assisted. Thus, for example, the great Jewish writer, Martin Buber, despite his bizarre characterisation of Christian faith as merely 'believing *that*...' in contrast to the unique Judaic 'trusting in...' has, nevertheless, deeply alerted Christian theology to the meaning of his I/Thou 'dialogue' in Semitic theism.[11] Comparably the Hindu thinking of Radhakrishnan was deeply affected by his studies at Madras Christian College.[12] Theodore Herzl, Smith argues, has been 'a significant thinker in Islamic history' (p.42), by virtue of what Zionism has entailed on Arab Muslims. Similarly Western technology and the assumptions it brings powerfully bear on Indian mentality. For 'to build a dam in India is to take part in the religious history of Hindus' (p.42).

Smith looks forward to such inter-involvement becoming a conscious, deliberative, joyful process in which what he calls 'corporate critical self-consciousness' may develop so that each individual or identity participates in the religious history of mankind. This will enable a global sphere of reference for theology in which none will be exclusivist and none will insist on trying to interpret others by categories alien to them. For these, he believes, will inevitably misrepresent (p.109).[13] Since truly faith is not an 'it' but an 'us' and a 'me', a true universalism can only mean a diversity in unity – the unity consisting in the 'faith-nature' of the respective identities. Each theology is legitimate, in that sense, in its own right and in its own light (p.110). No outsider can theologise about another's faith, since faiths are not objectified when they are possessed. 'Insiders', he seems to suggest, will always, and necessarily, be 'outsiders' to each other. Nevertheless, we are somehow one in exercising the faith which only our 'cumulative traditions' diversify.

In this conviction Smith is close both to Schleiermacher and to Feuerbach. He resembles the former in seeing Christianity as simply one kind of faith, a version of a much wider religiousness. He is akin to the latter in deriving the content of faith from the subjective experience of man, though, in Smith's case this is held to correspond, in an indirect way, with the *real* divine. 'Faith is one's existential engagement with what one *knows* to be true, good and obligatory.' (p.119).

The stance can be illustrated from an article contributed by Smith in 1980 to the *International Journal of Middle Eastern Studies* with the weighty title: 'The True Meaning of Scripture: An Empirical Historian's Non-Reductionist Interpretation of the Qur'an'. Claiming that meaning exists only inside the consciousness of living persons, he declares:

> The Qur'an has meant whatever it has meant to those who have used or heard it or appropriated it to themselves... The Qur'an as Scripture has meant whatever it has meant to those Muslims for whom it has been scripture... We leave out nothing that Muslims have seen in it... The meaning of the Qur'an is the history of its meanings... [It] lies not in the text, but in the minds and hearts of Muslims.[14]

That 'meanings' have been personal and, therefore, idiosyncratic, is true enough. But do we not end in atomism or solipsism unless we concede that there is, necessarily, about the text of a Scripture that which must delimit, if not control, what can be read in, or into, it? And will not such limit bear on the 'Muslim' identity that readers may claim as their warrant to read what they will? Indeed, were there any 'Muslims' at all when the Qur'an began to be heard? And does it now exclusify its meanings to 'insiders'? And has it no relevance to what can be described as 'insiderness'? Muslims go on suspecting or denying that status in one another. Is the text in no sense a referee between them when they do?

However, let us defer a critique while we take the measure of Smith's 'one faith – different men' account of what is between them.

V

Assuming in this way the presence of the transcendent in all religions,

Towards a World Theology aims to foster a self-consciousness within the many forms of religion, an openness to the single denominator of 'faith' to which they all give their particular expression. This means 'a theology of the religious life of mankind', a human faith-history, for which contemporary global awareness has paved the way. The 'world' as known to faith can now more readily belong with the 'world' as known to travel and a single history. A sense of 'the earth of us all' has to coincide with an understanding of religions as holding within their diversity the single denominator of faith, so that its forms of expression learn to repudiate exclusiveness and see their shape as no longer competitive but simply multiform.

The history of religion must supply the data for this world-theology. This must obviously include 'revelation' and Scriptures. But these which, at least among the Semitic expressions of faith, have been definitive in partially exclusive ways, will now be possessed in terms, not of authority to monopolise what faith means, but to witness to historical data concerning it. The actual or potential divisiveness of Scriptures will be neutralised by receiving them, at the hands of their 'insiders', as repositories of the ongoing history of faith 'in accordance with them.'[15] Scriptures, via their custodian-receivers who, as we have seen, alone 'know' them, are 'witness-bearing' not 'truth-refereeing'. The familiar impasse of rival authority is avoided, or should we say, voided, by transferring the significance from the letter of a text to the perception of a meaning. This will be in every case strictly an internal liberty – though it is hard to see how there can be mutuality in the meaning witnessed and not in the exegesis which discerned it.

This seems to mean that if faith is really singular Scriptures can be somehow orchestrated compatibly with it as the main bearers and guardians of the history of the data of this one faith's sub-communities. This clearly demands vital new attitudes in exegesis and new concepts of loyalty. For guardianship of Scriptures has long been crucial to the perpetuation of religious identity both documentary and psychic. New concepts of the very nature of custody and continuity are involved.

It is very right, then, for Smith to turn to enquiry as to how the major 'cumulative traditions', with their Scriptures, symbols, rites, memories and saints, would respond to the perception of themselves required in *Towards a World Theology*. From one angle he can only conjecture. For only insiders can decide. Yet it is consistent with the idea of a single nature to faith that he should venture to answer for them, despite his outsider condition. The venture disclaims all prophecy, and intends, of course, no im-position. But without the venture the whole thesis would, as it were, disown itself by neglecting what is a clear corollary of its own confidence.

Readers of *Towards a World Theology* are not unanimous that its author succeeds. But his conjectures are consistent with his theory. One nagging problem is, of course, whom to ask. For there are so many differing insiders. Indeed, if we give due weight to the emphatic personalism of Smith's conception, it must follow that there is no voice of consensus which could give the answer as dependably that of the cumulative tradition existing, only variously, in them as persons and not in texts or creeds or forms as such.

That is only one perplexity. Another has to do with the interior logics of the religions against this theory of their essential unity, this relativising within it of their specific forms. Both points can be seen in a brief review of the responses Smith, and others, can envisage. To begin with the senior cumulative tradition – Hinduism, or – more Smith-wise – that of Hindus. Here there is a degree of *déjà vu*. They value this tolerance, as wiser than western sophistication, arrogance or cavalier scholarship. For they have long ago affirmed the relativity of forms, the plurality of worships, within a broad monism. In any event, they are not troubled by pluralism nor have they newly – or ever – sensed it as a problem. To accommodate Semitic-style theism would be difficult for many among Hindus. They would rather settle for a freedom to differ without a theory of also comprehending. And there are urgent practical issues, like caste, that must have precedence over abstract dialogue.

What of Buddhists? Those at least of the Theravada school would find theism impossible to admit within their scheme of things and would substitute a Dharmalogy for theology. Moreover, the central role of the self which Smith assumes in his sense of the personal in faith runs counter to the illusoriness of personality in the Buddhist concept of *anatta*, or non-self. It might be said that the meditative techniques of the Buddhist search for escape from the illusion of selfhood could align, in some sense, with response to transcendence. But is there not a crucial disparity between a theistic and a Buddhist understanding of what transcends? Most Buddhists would prefer to speak of 'a humane discipline' rather than of 'a humane science', if the latter term indicates – as it does in Smith – some genuinely cognitive status in faith. If we speak of a 'corporate critical self-consciousness', Buddhists would surely wish to take the 'critical' element much further, beyond the relativising of religious doctrines as in Smith, to an ultimate scepticism about either the knowability of truth or the significance of persons in time.

Asian faiths would certainly welcome the Canadian's will to humility in preference to the often supercilious attitudes of Western scholarship towards them. Smith tells how 'in [his] particular case ... an awareness of the pain and resentment on the part of Asians, before the aggression' of much of that scholarship, inspired his will to foreswear its ways.(p.78).[16] But in saluting his will to 'world theology' their reservations remain over its Judeo-Graeco-Roman humanism. Their report might well be: 'a welcome gesture, and a right direction, but further yet to go.'

vi

What of the response of the 'Abrahamic faiths', the Judaic, the Islamic and the Christian? Even when we have decided from which representatives – if such exist – it would be most hopeful and prudent to enquire, formidable hurdles will persist. Jews, no doubt, will resist whatever equalises variant expression of faith understood as truly common across religion. For this calls into radical question Judaic exceptionality. Jewish existence may be a paradigm of what is somehow meant to characterise all humanity – as we have seen in Abraham Heschel – but that can only be so as the exceptional Judaic existence under God is strenuously maintained. When that maintaining takes the political form of Zionism in Israeli nationalism, seen as the true image of the Judaic worldwide, the Judaic separatism would need to plead exemption from 'a world theology', precisely for the sake of sharing in it. That paradox is inseparable from Jewish self-understanding within any wider understanding of humanity. The other side of the paradox is that *Towards a World Theology* must seem to Jews a very slender protective against Anti-Semitism, preoccupation with which, as we have seen in Elie Wiesel, its passionate spokesman, is perpetual in Jewry. For many within the Judaic tradition, Smith's 'corporate, critical self-consciousness', hopefully embracing all, has not appreciated how far being 'critical' has to exempt one from being 'corporate'.

The bearings of Wilfred Cantwell Smith's thought on things Islamic is the liveliest of all. For it was there that his major investments of scholarship lay prior to his wider concerns with the history of religions. His *Islam in Modern History* is rightly held a seminal work in the exploration of contemporary Muslim experience, its chapters on Pakistan and Turkey being particularly perceptive.[17] *Towards a World Theology* is asking radical things of Muslims in its will to locate in them, not in the text of the Qur'an, the being and definition of Islam. Muslims, to be sure, could readily accept an inclusive thesis about "faith' as 'religion' fulfilling the meaning of man, but only so long as it is identified by, and in, Islam. Islam, as *Din al-Fitrah*, is what 'religion' was always meant to be and always has been when it has been uncorrupted by *dalal*, or error and misguidedness.[18] One recent writer has the point clearly but echoes a chorus of Muslim voices. There is a unity of all revelations, corroborating both the divine unity and the unity of mankind. It is Islam universal and universal Islam.

> This teaching provides *the venue of appeal* for the religions of the world to cast off the shells of later accretions, perversions and distortions brought into existence by human ignorance, ingenuity or vested interests, and to return to the original message in the light of reason and with the assistance of the Quranic revelation, finally bringing about the unification of religions in the divine Truth and paving the way for the unity of mankind.[19]

In that sense Islam ante-dated the quest for 'a world theology' by fourteen centuries. It was not, however, a quest but an attainment, unfortunately frustrated by wilful or deliberate astrayness from it.

This, of course, is a very different 'venue of appeal' from the one Smith explores. It does not begin to concede that what, above, are described as 'accretions, perversions and distortions' might conceivably be genuine responses to mystery, to suffering, to guilt, to tragedy, as honesty requires and love dictates. The thesis that all 'faith' is Islamic when it is properly articulated is patently false to the diversity of the arguments and the motives from which diversity of faiths derives. By the same token, it is a falsity which Muslims, by virtue of their own identity, can hardly be minded to acknowledge. Yet such acknowledgement is what Smith is asking of them.

Perhaps there is an implicit recognition of this fact in his emphasis on 'Islam being what Muslims say it is', if he can find Muslims 'to say' that alleged 'distortions and accretions' might yet be allowed their authenticity within a genuinely 'world theology'. If that is his aspiration it would seem to have but slender ground. Moreover, traditional Islam has not readily taken to 'any Muslim' having the right to have the Qur'an 'mean' what he/she takes it to 'mean'. Quite the contrary: reading of the Qur'an's intent and import has always been carefully tied to *Ijma'* (consensus) turning on *Ijtihad* (scholarly initiative) with the latter – in Sunni Islam – carefully circumscribed by qualifications which make it far from being a free-for-all. Shi'ah Islam has even more daunting criteria for the valid possession of the Qur'an.[20]

While a minority of Muslim humanists may find themselves able to respond to *Towards a World Theology* in its own terms all others will see themselves essentially at odds with its will to enlarge the parameters of legitimate faith beyond those finally and infallibly set by Quranic revelation and its derivative *Shari'ah*. The masses apart, the pundits and custodians would find it uncongenial to allow that 'all revelation is fuller potentially than it is actually'. (p.175). The finality of the Prophet means finality and signals the one criterion of all else. 'Truth', to be sure, 'is a humane concept', Islamically apprehended. But to continue, 'not an objective concept', as Smith does (p.190), is to exclude the Muslim understanding of the Qur'an as communicating what is objectively *there* in the unity of God and the details of His will. 'The truth that transcends' has been Islamically defined and with it the response it requires from the humanity it unifies.

Smith, then, would seem to be asking of *Dar al-Islam*, in the words of Shakespeare's Richard II: 'Now mark me how I will undo myself.' It proposes world community in its own idiom. Isma'il al-Faruqi insists that the ecumenicity of Islam gives *dhimmah*, or minority, status with religious rights to other faiths, but only on condition that Muslims themselves do not accommodate the religious notions of those minorities in their own 'tolerance'. For to do so, in compromise of the given content of Islam, would be equivalent to treason, inasmuch as the Muslim participates in the wholeness of Islam not simply as a believer but as a subject of the Islamic State. On that reckoning only Muslims who exiled themselves, or who by force of circumstance lived outside such statehood, could respond theologically or intellectually to the kind of relationship to diversity which Smith envisages.[21] The instinctive political dimensions of Islam as *Din wa Dawlah*, 'religion and state', would, for most Muslims, preclude even tentative, let alone final, hospitality to the kind of inter-participation in 'faith' that Smith desires. The traditional political sanctions require that minorities privatise their rites and doctrines, and that Muslims conform to theirs as those who are politically, as well as spiritually, 'believers'. The fact that the association between the two aspects of 'believerhood' may vary widely from Muslim to Muslim, and from State to State, does not really diminish the self-sufficiency of Islam. Much greater hope for interest 'toward a world theology' must be had from places, like post-partition

India, where Muslims live in vast numbers outside Islamic statehood and without both its benefits and its constraints.

vii

Towards a World Theology makes disconcerting demands on any Christian 'cumulative tradition'. Indeed, it proposes a fundamental quarrel with the New Testament. Smith modestly disclaims any specialist scholarship in the New Testament field, but nevertheless takes up a position which might be thought to require it. For he repudiates the belief that something decisive and definitive happened there and, with it, the sense of an inclusive relevance belonging there. Faith in Jesus, Messiah crucified, is simply the Christian shape of faith as the humane science to which Christians belong. Its efficacy, or validity, for them does not constitute it a clue or a crux to meaning for all. Mission with it, at best, can only be an invitation and not an urgent *kerygma*. The kerygmatic Christianity of the New Testament differs only in form, and not in kind, from any human faith open to transcendence.

Thus he disapproves of the Christian conviction which looks back to a single, pivotal event by which all else is understood. To talk of 'the Christ-event' is to hold what, in a phrase unhappily inconsistent with his faith-respectfulness, he dubs 'the big-bang theory of Christian origins' (p.155). That there are historical issues around Christian origins is not in question, and it is right for orthodoxy to be ready to explore them and to keep in mind the 'silences' of those from whom we do not hear, in case what avails is only the verdict of those who won out over, for example, Jewish Christians of other mind. But, recognising that necessity, there is sober ground for holding that the understanding of Jesus as the Christ via the Cross, which the Church came into being by learning, was authentic and that He was its real author and not they, his disciples.

The sense, however, in which that Christ-event may be held to be inclusive and decisive needs to be carefully understood. It is not arbitrarily asserted or imposed on a reality in the human world on which it does not fit. It is seen as definitive of what obtains between men and God because it enshrines the actualities of love and sin, representatively and qualitatively. That evil is only truly mastered in and through the love that suffers is what we find explicit and actualised in the Cross. But the principle we identify as operative there is everywhere reproducible in the will to forgive and the more reproducible because it has been once for all identified – and identified in that which becomes a history, enacts a sacrament and perpetuates a living community. 'Let this mind be in you which was also in Christ Jesus...' (Phil.2:5). The analogue for the first apostles was the place of the Exodus in the self-awareness of Jewry. *What* they had to be in every generation was identified in *where* they had once been. In the Christian case, the Cross can

> Enforce attention like deep harmony...
> For they breathe truth that breathe their words in pain.
> He that no more must say is listen'd more...
> Writ in remembrance...

It is this sense of things Christian which must deplore Wilfred Cantwell Smith's insistence that no faith's Scripture can be quarried, still less possessed, by those outside. Only those 'to the manner born' can understand. This may be salutary as a warning against spiritual 'imperialism' and the foisting of 'readings' where they cannot fit. Every Scripture must be referred respectfully to its own custodians. But that right principle is far from excluding reverent attention, even patient comprehension, from outsiders. To hope so is surely congruent with Smith's own confidence that faith is everywhere something common within its various shapes. If it is 'a humane science' then nothing human can be alien. We must somehow inter-penetrate in Scriptures as well as in life and refuse to privatise our sources, containing – as they must – issues which *mutatis mutandis* cannot belong inside them without obtaining between them. The broad issue, for example, of opposition to prophethood, its painfulness, how borne, how diagnosed, how surmounted, is present in both the Qur'an and the New Testament. Muhammad is in a sort of Gethsemane before the *Hijrah*. It is better to seek the interpretative clues by which we can speak to one another than to suppose they do not exist.

'Irenics' not polemics is surely a right formula. But is it not best fulfilled in bringing to each other what we diversely hold, rather than subsuming it in a sharing of 'faith' for which issues within forms are not for investigation but only for recognition? The matter might be put in terms of a distinction of which Smith is fond. He invites us to note the difference if, and when, we use the words Muslim, Hindu, Buddhist, Christian and the rest as adjectives and when we use them as nouns. 'Hasan is a Muslim', says one thing; 'Hasan has Muslim qualities' is another 'Am I a Christian?' and 'Was that a Christian deed?' are different questions. Plainly the adjectival usage is generally looser, even interchangeable. Christian/Muslim generosity may be more readily shared than the noun attached to either person. To be 'a Buddhist' is not to be 'a Christian', despite a certain mutual Buddhist/Christian quality of, say, meditative silence.[22]

But is this welcome point in Smith consistent with his accent on 'insiders' and 'outsiders' (both are nouns), restricting 'faith-content' to their own communities while wanting us all to be adjectival in some single sense? Any 'corporate critical self-consciousness' is bound to have us in the capacity of 'adjectives' by something nounal, and this will incorporate us. Can it ever attain to describe something we no longer are as 'nouns'? There is, of course, here the puzzling question of how 'nounal' and 'adjectival' can drift, or be read, apart. But, that aside, the Christian 'cumulative tradition' will see the wiser course to be in gentle, open, critical interpretation of its content by scrupulous, hopeful search for whatever criteria for its meanings can be seen in, and drawn from, the credentials of other faiths. It will do so within the open future that *Towards a World Theology* assumes and with the urgency of its sense both of the human scene and its own conviction. It will see no call to forego the central event of its identifying history nor find that Christ-event other than potentially inclusive of the human future, not as an arbitrary 'truth-claim' but as a 'truth-presentation', a 'witness-bearing' that has nowhere else to go.

viii

That Christian conclusion about *Towards a World Theology* may be reinforced by certain more general considerations that critics have drawn who would prefer to see themselves as neutral. Is there not – it has been asked – an intellectualist élitism about his version of the future between faiths? And in falling back on the plural ('faiths') in that question – a usage Smith rejects – are we not implying, in effect, his seeming lack of realism? The two spheres of doubt belong together and can be developed here in one.

We noted earlier the possibility that, in turning away from his strong, youthful Marxism in *Modern Islam in India*, Smith had become over-sanguine of the role of religion in society. Has he ignored the enormous capacity of religions for apathy, corruption, fanaticism, and connivance with social evil, their propensity 'to enjoin the evil and to forbid the good' in consequence if not in precept? 'Corporate, critical self-consciousness' would seem a far cry from the mutual anathemas that entrench isolation of minds, and from the auto-persuasion which ousts everything critical by fortifying prejudice and enthroning the infallible.

Hopelessness, to be sure, should never thwart or decry the springs of hope. Hope has always 'to create the thing it contemplates'. Dialogue anyway has always been a minority pursuit. But that circumstance has to discipline what it can effectively pursue. While the case for world community is as urgent as Smith argues, and as exciting, what is viable about it might suggest concentration less on a world theology as on a world economy, a common market of moral endeavour rather than a negotiation of minds about what transcends. So realists have argued, though perhaps in Smith's favour there is a larger realism which concerns what must underlie a less ambitious one. One cannot handle the world without convictions about it.

We have seen how Smith's own friendships in Pakistan and elsewhere were academic and scholarly, with Muslims whose 'ideal of Islam has been an evolving human vision' (p.30). But what of those for whom there is no 'evolving vision' at all in the struggle for survival, in privation, misery, illiteracy and a sordid world? And what of the negative 'evolution' towards bigotry and the demonism of collective self-interest, expressed in religious fervour feeding on hostility? Can spiritual 'inwardness' of the part of some – maybe a very few – do duty for the relevance of religion as a whole? The question obtains, seriously, if not equally, for all religious establishments. And, as we have learned from Arnold Toynbee, religions can never escape the bane and the necessity of institutions. The fact is surely germane to hopes of their 'evolution'. It is well to believe that 'Islamic truth must necessarily transcend Islamic actuality' (p.30) as must truth and actuality in all traditions. But actuality must always be in the reckoning as to truth.

Towards a World Theology has been queried on another, related, ground. Given its accent on present and future, has humanity, perhaps, arrived at a stage in which there is no longer 'a humane science' of faith – a time and a mentality from which the transcendent is effectively elided? Smith has dealt trenchantly with the follies of logical positivism. But the apparent loss of transcendence goes much deeper than talk of any 'verification principle'. If he is proceeding on 'an organising principle by which one is open to the infinite' (p.110) what of those who apparently are not so open and forebear to be 'organised'?

The question, of course, will beset all other accounts of what religious faith is. Smith's 'world-theology' is peculiarly liable to it. He would doubtless reply with Muhammad Kamil Husain: 'Atheism is a failure to understand what human nature is',[23] and see, in his own words, how the sense of the transcendent, within and without, is 'virtually ubiquitous'. (p.55). One can point to 'the wound of absence' and to the bizarre forms by which secularity afflicts itself when ultimate mystery is denied or discounted. But at least faith, whether posture or tenet, orientation or doctrine, needs to reckon with uncompulsiveness and with the paradox of the evident negligibility of God. It must also take that reckoning into its account of itself.

Here, afresh, we come upon Smith's strange unwillingness to allow any inter-penetration of theologies in order that they may only meet in 'corporate consciousness', as an 'internationalism' without 'nations'. 'Faith,' he insists, 'can only be theologised from inside. One community's faith is, on principle, precluded from being the object of another community's theology.' (p.111). It is hard to see the sense of this demand. Does not the pressure of secularity – if nothing else – require them to bring together their respective 'theologising' about the faith which, *ex hypothesi* in Smith, they share as common? If their own 'inwardness' has to formulate itself in their internal theologies, can these not associate them even when formulating separately what they allegedly have as common? Is dialogue simply a state of consciousness and not also a transaction between what is 'cumulative' in each 'tradition'?

The point has added weight when we consider how inwardness itself depends upon traditions. In emphasising how religious awareness is always inward, does he sufficiently allow for the degree to which it is receptively so – receptively, that is, in relation to givens which it did not originate and can only receive? Doubtless the Hindu Temple is what it means to the worshipper but could it mean if it were not there? And would it be there by the worshipper's mandate, or leave, or option, and not, of necessity, as a 'given' that addresses him? The face of the Buddha signifies, the crucifix signifies; but only in a context to which devotion is responding. Must not all this symbolic 'associationism' central to religion be the realm of gentle, patient, inter-conversation – certainly within the conscious mutuality Smith commends but also in an open encounter of scrutiny, discerning, probing, questioning and, hopefully, comprehending how and why they belong with the transcendent?

It is, for example, true to say that *all* human history is *Heilsgeschichte*, 'sacred story'. (p.172). But will that dictum – for all its truth – distinguish how Moses at Sinai, or Muhammad on Mount Hira' or Jesus in Gethsemane are? Will it not matter to explore how, and will that exploring be irrelevant to 'corporate self-consciousness'? Or do we conclude answers are either unattainable or incommensurate? If they are, from what will corporate consciousness be built? We can, and must, assume the presence of transcendence in all religions. But is there a theology of universal religious experience that we can hope to reach?

Wilfred Cantwell Smith has aptly summarised the message in his incisive writings and lively intellectual leadership: 'Recognise,' he says, 'the faith of other men and then realise that there are no other men: there is only "all of us..."' (p.103). But what if the recognising has us realising still that there are 'many of us'? The question persists, from his and from twelve other biographies of dialogue. How do we conclude?

Chapter 14

A LANTERN ON THE STERN

i

Is the wake what we most need to illuminate? What of light on the prow? Important, no doubt; but biography is necessarily retrospect and can only illuminate what has been travelled. Light astern is all that can be had for those who come behind. Samuel Taylor Coleridge's phrase fits our conclusions well. His philosophy was modestly entailed 'Aids to Reflection'. Such is what we intended in these thirteen biographies of dialogue. What light do they cast on the journeys undertaken?

One of the immediate effects of light is to make us more aware of the nature of darkness precisely by undertaking to dispel it. The lantern's success against the darkness depends on its penetration. As St. John has it in his Prologue, 'the darkness does not overcome it', yet it remains in contention at the penumbra. Thus perplexity may well remain the first lesson of inter-faith encounter. It is well it should be so. For if we are traversing a wide sea there is no point in imagining it to be a pond. Some of our foregoing biographees knew this well and their sense of perplexity, as in Henry Martyn, was by no means inconsistent with their sense of truth and mission. In fact, it was conviction which made them alert to how disconcerting the actual world could be. Others, by contrast, leave the impression of having too readily laid the spectre of diversity or accommodated it in a manner too facile for its implications. Our choice has deliberately preferred the agonisers to those who, in John Bunyan's phrase, are 'strangers to much combat...'[1] within themselves. Appearances in this regard, may be deceptive and we must beware of supposing that those who, like Raimundo Panikkar, contrive a ready treaty between the smile of the Buddha and the Cross of Jesus, do so without inner travail.

A lively perplexity has many sanctions. Plurality has a way of dispossessing us of familiar assurance. We have believed that man is properly a questioning creature, only to be told that questioning has to call itself into question. Not that silence constitutes an answer, but that unquestioning *per se* is our only proper stance. Yet, bewilderingly, the claim puts itself in words and pleads a logic, the logic, namely, that there is no principle of sufficient reason by which truth can be identified. As for revelatory authority, is not this diversified into institutionalised options sanctioned by long prestige and tenacious assumption to which multitudes of adherents remain necessarily wedded in the pressures of living and through the psychic patterns of vital identity? Perplexity, then, may be fraught with fear and fear is rarely a wise counsellor. The threat of an incipient distrust enters into realms where only trust properly belongs. Yet it is just the warrant of trust that is most exposed to necessary interrogation of the doctrines, the usages, the instincts, on which inevitably it relies.

If there is no escape from a wise perplexity, the obvious further lesson of the light is a right humility. Confession in that sense comes from almost all our practitioners of dialogue. The point can be trite enough. But genuine humility is an elusive thing, if only because the very search for it is liable to forfeit it. It has itself a built-in temptation to pride. For it is obviously superior to arrogance. Moreover, there are those who would be truly humble of and for themselves who argue themselves out of the virtue by the claim of what they represent. As Arnold Toynbee saw, and taught so insistently, assertion can be beguiled into aggrandisement simply by being on behalf of causes and collectives where private interest only finds itself by corporate proxy. It is difficult for propaganda not to be conceited. Humility, then, has to be vigilant with itself if it is to concert and consort with conviction. Witness may have improper, as well as proper, motives. Dialogue has to sift our intentions if it is to be truly authentic as an inner disposition and rightly communicative as an inter-venture.

But a due perplexity and partnering humility are requisite only because there is engagement. Issues and personalities are face to face. We are not saying, in the words of the poet Philip Larkin, about Hull where he lived: 'I like it because it's so far from anywhere else.' We are renouncing isolation. We have conceded the plural world. We intend to co-inhabit and we are exploring spiritual, and other, co-habitation. Yet we are habitués of familiars which others do not share. Tolerance, as Panikkar observes, is the social form of patience. But tolerance cannot be neutral or it would cease to discern, and patience is pointless that does not know what it is awaiting. What does 'a lantern on the stern' serve to illuminate so that we know, in Henry Martyn's words, 'what we seek after'? What light is there for us on where we are?

ii

Perhaps we can well begin with the issue of 'conversion'. For it besets the path of dialogue as an awkward fellow-traveller. It will be noted that none in our portrait gallery are 'converts', though most have undergone much change within their souls in remaining what they are. Is dialogue a venture in dissuasion leading to alternative persuasion? Certainly there has to be dialogue about the question, so that – in that sense – the answer cannot be crudely negative. But nor can it be crudely positive. Sincerity is liable to be untested or unwanted in what is mere exchanging of ideas. Truth asks more of us than mutual politeness.

There are those, like Mahatma Gandhi, and many in the Judeo-Christian context, who insist that inter-conversion is no part of authentic inter-faith. For these, a *sine qua non* is a secure and secured identity. There can be no anticipation of movement of allegiance or revision of belief. The questions that revolve in dialogue must always do so in eccentric circles, so that common territory between them always retains its own centre and its own radii.

The position can readily be understood as responding to the claims of loyalty and as a condition of the good faith of dialogue itself – if the good faith can go no deeper. Yet will it not leave out what cannot well be excluded if we are truly in search of one another? For we can only finally be found where we essentially are, and hospitality can hardly be exempted from relationships. To be sure – though there may be some common market of ideas – we agree that we are not pursuing salesmanship. There may be numbers in our communities who are practising such arts and believe them to be appropriate to witness. Over these we have no direct control and must disown them, without thereby suggesting that we have nothing to commend. C.F. Andrews, as we have seen, underwent a conversion of the hope of conversion and we may well 'walk in that light'. But will we not stultify meaning if we see it calling for no response and disturbing no complacence and no apathy? All the practical things we propose to do together are in suspense without the diagnoses that take us squarely into faith as clue to their achievement.

Must we not say that dialogue, in fact, fails – or, rather, has not really occurred – if it merely entrenches identity? Perhaps, in the case of some, that is what we want it to do. We may be merely seeking allies in ulterior designs, or looking for confirmation of what we have always thought. But should not dialogue, in fact, cause us at least some disquiet – not as though we were compromised by it, but because it does indeed undo our equanimity? 'People,' Robert Louis Stevenson observed, 'are generally cast for the leading parts in their own imagination.'[2] Encounter ought to revise our judgement about who we truly are and why. This is the more necessary since we come to it, for the most part, as custodians, sponsoring, and being sponsored by, the faiths we bring. We are professors, clergy, rabbis, imams, with a certain status, if not stature, and prudence is desirable to retain it. Prudence, too, clothes itself in propriety and loyalty. Moreover, embarrassment would certainly ensue if dialogue proved, in fact, to be occasion of outward changes in identity. Yet can loyalties for ever exclude discoveries?

This is not to argue that relations between faiths should – or indeed could – become fluid and volatile.[3] But it is to register how subtly mere formalism or artificiality, even hypocrisy, may overtake them unless some conversion, some openness to new becoming, informs them. Faiths will, no doubt, differ in their instincts here. Some Hindus will find it quite congenial, seeing themselves as innkeepers at home with guests and transients; Semitic believers far less so, but on differing grounds. The Judaic is explicitly bound by covenant and election, the Islamic by final revelation and 'the seal of prophethood', the Christian by the centrality of Christ. Yet each of these 'exclusives' has interpretative potential awaiting what only cross-examination can evoke.

In the end only each faith can resolve the question of its will to re-persuasion and determine where its frontiers of finality lie and what, enclosing, they must also exclude. Christians will certainly not be true to their charter if they are manoeuvred into the implication that only they themselves are intended in the Gospel.[4] It is a Gospel for which 'whosoever will may come' is mandatory, a Gospel where there can be no exclusions, explicit or implicit. For exclusions, whether of Jews or 'Gentiles', would violate the very grounds by which the excluders could themselves belong, namely the openness of grace. Accessibility is vital in 'whosoever will...' but so, in the same phrase, are freedom and utter spontaneity. Openness is one thing, solicitation is another.

We conclude that experience in genuine encounter one with the other conduces not only to felt perplexity and necessary humility but also to a new self-awareness. It must surely be that thanks to one another – the Muslim among us must discover that, however crudely posed by Rushdie, there belongs a deep issue over the Qur'an. A right perception of the mediation between the divine and the human requires to be understood. The Christian among us is made to know what Jewry sees as the desperate 'overloaded-ness' of the conviction about the Cross of Jesus and its 'bearing' of 'the sin of the world'. We must undertake to align what we believe to be the inclusiveness of redemption with the Jewish protest about the evident, tragic, unredeemedness of the world. The Buddhist among us has to appreciate that the thesis about the self as incorrigibly self-centred leaves no significant personhood for which the intended liberation could avail.

Inasmuch as outsiders see our interior tensions more readily than we who are within them, the reading, or mis-reading, of them – whichever it be – is plainly the liability of our convictions. So also is the issue of how our appeal to criteria relates to theirs. That quandary may, at times, have the effect of distancing us further from each other. When, for example, a Hindu sees all exclusivity as spiritual immaturity, he speaks out of the – to him – emancipated inclusivity of Vedanta where 'essence' is One whatever the 'manifestation'. Though he purports to unify, the principle on which he does so is no less intractable than the contrary stance of the monotheist which he condemns. There is obviously no inclusivism which can embrace all on terms acceptable to all. On that showing there are no real inclusivists. We are all equally, if differently, at odds with each other. There is no search for a world theology which does not have to disavow on the way to it things vital to those it would unite.

If, in this way, diversity enters into the very grounds by which we might resolve it, it is clear that witnesses are what we must remain, the one to the others – witnesses, however, in a temper schooled by lively understanding of this situation. We realise ourselves to be on behalf of that which we can only commend and not impose, a reverent pro-existence within an open co-existence. This necessity will hardly please the absolutists. But not consenting to it will dissociate our witness from the bearings it must find if its meanings are to carry.

A faith to commend, within an acknowledged pluralism, argues a readiness for fellow-commenders. We do well then to see the whole issue of conversion – and, with it, of human convertibility[5] – within the worth of the faith which proposes it and of what it intends by it. Whether people are to be recruited to it surely turns, effectively, on what is seeking them and what it may have in hand for them and achieve through them. There is something rather facile about the dictum that talks of making 'x' a 'better x' – be he Muslim, Jew, Sikh, Christian or Brahmin – without reference to the ultimates in 'x' as human and to the means and ends of the 'bettering'. Acknowledged diversity cannot mean that these are all identical or that there is no need to sift their credentials and their policies. Intentions for the human have to be rooted in interpretation of its nature. When Jesus was asked by intrigued observers what they must do 'to work the works of God', he recommended that they 'believe on him whom God has sent'. (John 6:28). For faith would be the crux of the work of God within them and so, in turn, of any work of God through them. By the same token it must be the content of faith which warrants its witness and the same content which must make the disciples it anticipates.

So all questions concerning a faith's quest for allegiance must be allowed to turn on a faith's trust of meaning. Truth must surely be set to multiply its representatives, but always after its own image. For so long faiths have been seen as proprietary, holding exclusive rights and exercising unilateral custody. This has meant the 'nosism' Toynbee so much deplored. It has obscured the incidence of common truth in all and sometimes exaggerated the disparity of answers and disregarded the parity of questions. We have too often heard trumpeted: 'The Bible says...'; 'the Church says...'; 'the Qur'an says...'; 'the Dharma is...', as if they were not addressing the same world or were not beset by the same mystery. Only when we fully undertake to be mutual can we be rightly representative of what is distinctively our own, commend it and properly recruit to it. This posture will be neither some feeble *bonhomie*, nor a belligerent arrogance but, instead, a reverent yearning with truth and aspiration for fellowship because of it. The degree to which faiths can conceive themselves and discipline themselves in this way will turn on what their content is and how truly it structures their relationships. What it means by the making of disciples will hinge on what disciples are made to be. All questions of 'converting' must return to what 'conversion' is about.

iii

Thus we come round again to the duty of every faith to discover what it is that makes it distinctive and requires it to remain so, a duty pursued in the utmost readiness to repudiate what is arbitrary or could be perverse, in the decision and to maximise, loyally, what – along with that decision – remains significantly in common. The decision is not one which any faith can make for another, except insofar as the readiness may prove contagious.

This active self-definition will be deferential to heritage and tradition but not imprisoned by them. There is a sense in which all our biographees are pioneers. They are frontier folk. Their instincts have been to engage with what is at stake, however disruptive of their peace of mind. For them – at least at times – peace of mind has itself been a delusion or a compromise. They have conceded the necessary disquiet in the situation they have entered. India and Islam have disturbed their sense of perspective; the Holocaust has desperately threatened their covenanted identity. Only Isma'il al-Faruqi is unique among them in seeming spurred rather than sobered by encounter. Even Rushdie, assured in the escapism of fantasy, conceded to being taken aback by what ensued. In varying degrees issues are registered without concealment and, therefore, without the self-indulgence which falls back on bare assertion.

This means that there has to be a realism which staunch orthodoxy might not allow to be the case, in its anxiety to affirm and preserve. Dialogue requires us to forego dogma to the extent that we survey its content with other eyes, present without our normal defences of apologetic in a will to relate meaning here to meaning there, undertaking the adverse reckoning that others bring. This is the opposite of the old catechesis in which truth was inculcated by the device of posing its own questions and supplying its own answers. As an educational method for the illiterate within the fold catechisms had their point, but the range of question and of answer was self-enclosed. Faith presided over its own interrogatives and gave them its own answers. Dialogue, not being tutelage, brings both into open forum. Faiths, in that way, forego their securities in order to transact their meanings.

In this realism there lies an intriguing problem which, in some measure, was known to all our venturers, though it sat lightly on some of them. As biography, what we have studied is essentially personal. What of the bearing of private initiative, or movement of awareness, on obligation to community and allegiance, without which persons would not be, in their privacy, who and what they are? The matter may be peripheral for academics who may be assumed to be free-ranging, responsible only to the canons of their discipline. But what of those officially entrusted with the care of faith, whether in mosque, or church, or gurdwara, or synagogue, or shrine? The form of such 'offices' with differentials between 'laity' and 'clergy' will vary widely; the fact of them obtains throughout religion. Dialogue can hardly be conceivable without pulling at the tether which ties its participants to their 'official' loyalties, their necessary heritage. Inter-faith necessarily tugs at inner faith, seeing that practitioners are involved who neither are, nor can be, unilateralists. In converse, they are not in negotiation. They move in that context which Islam, for purposes of jurisprudence rather than theology, calls *ijtihad*, or the personal initiatives of the duly qualified venturing what may anticipate, and eventually enjoy, general consensus. On the way to this aspiration, however, there may be many heart-aches and inner anxieties. If these are the burden of the 'moving spirits', it must be in the genius of their respective faith-systems to sustain them in assuming it. That faiths currently differ radically in that capacity to allow and uphold their inter-faith respondents is painfully evident – a fact which becomes part of the fabric of dialogue itself.

iv

There is, however, in all this a larger lesson in realism on which we have 'light from the stern'. It has to do with the subtlety of evil in religion itself. There are times when readers of Raimundo Panikkar or Wilfred Cantwell Smith – though certainly not Toynbee – might think themselves in an erudite, orderly, reasonable world of spirituality splendidly innocent of the coarse, the trivial, the banal, the corrupt or the licentious. Faith is posited on its best behaviour – rational, instinctive, amenable to mystery, in potential or actual rapport with the transcendent. Things squalid or mundane, contentious or bigoted, do not figure in the reckoning. If we are proposing, in some sense, to make 'religious' a common denominator in a feasible oecumene of meaning, we had better be aware of *all* that it denominates. If, in truth, it is a 'humane science', it is also a human travesty of the humane. We need not approve the philosopher David Hume's wild dictum that to know someone for 'religious' is to know him for 'a rascal'.[6] But rascality abounds in the guise of obscurantism, hypocrisy, self-deception, perversity both moral and spiritual. There are so many ways of 'taking the Name in vain', of recruiting allegedly transcendent mandate as sanction for envy, place-seeking, contention, obduracy, lovelessness and callousness. A right theology has sterner tasks within the psyche than with the mind. 'Truth in the inward parts', as the psalmist sought it, is more exacting than the logic of a credo, the niceties of a ritual or the benchmarks of a discipline.

Realism about religion is a vital element in our discovery of each other. For our inner compromises, our private and collective sins in the practice of religion, have a spiritual kinship which no honesty can mistake. It is here, for example, that the Buddhist sense of our incorrigibility in selfhood, the pitfalls of the egocentric situation, reflect the intimacies of every sanctuary, whether personal or corporate. Self-interest shadows all

our walking in our several lights. Our mortification exalts us, our abnegation indulges us, our humility commends us, our orthodoxy approves us,
our penitence satisfies us and our lawfulness distinguishes us. We can take
the point of the penitent publican in the parable and give thanks that we
are not 'as this Pharisee'. Religion is as adept as politics in the art of
self-justification. How right the Buddha was in focus on the self as the
crucial point. Alerting to it is one thing, its salvation is another. For
Buddhist-style will to dissolution has to be 'desired', and therefore offers
no rescue from its own dilemma. The will to detachment continues to
'attach'. Our only escape from the self is in possessing it rightly in a
penitence that has no logic of pride – thanks to the meaning of grace.
Humour also helps here as a sense of what is fitting brought on by the
incongruous.

This theme of religious penitence deserves to be focal in contemporary
dialogue, responding to an honest realism about us all. Such penitence has
also to be vicarious, making – as it were – 'apology' to God, to what
transcends, to 'sovereign good'[7] (phrase it how you will) for what must be
deplored, condemned, disowned, repudiated. It is only by a due register
of evil that truth is acknowledged, not in the abstractions of argument but
in the worth of integrity and of the will to it. Here is the ultimate
inter-religious vocation, uniting us in the common need of it, and duly
distinguishing among us the 'salvation' we hold concerning it – law, discipline, grace, Torah, Qur'an, Dharma, *bodhisattvas* or the Christ. At
least our apology for 'religion' will do well to stay close to that about us all
which most desperately needs it.

Is it in this context that we should set the meaning of the Holocaust?
The presence of Elie Wiesel in our exemplars is eloquent reminder of its
grim exceptionality as a deliberate, calculated, virulent, enormity of evil.
Jewish minds deeply need that sense of things and strenuously resist, as
somehow conspiracies of extenuation, any implication to see and tell it
otherwise. That posture is legitimate and demands respect. Yet there is
nothing in history which is essentially dissociate from the human whole.
Evil may be exceptionalised in its quantity, its incidence, its immediacy of
time and place and story. Its quality everywhere, every-when, evidences
all humanity. No victim has more than one self to forfeit, one personhood
for prey and pain. The entail of evil is collective, cumulative, its perversity
manifold and long in incidence and origin. If religion is truly returning the
part to the whole, it must be brought back thereby to 'the sin of the
world', to the realism which allows itself no illusion about the patterns of
history and shares the penetration Shakespeare or Dostoevsky had into

the wrongness of mankind. It is here that Arnold Toynbee has so necessary a place, despite the prejudice he at times indulged, in the self-awareness of religions. However, we only encounter evil duly if, at the same time, we know that our honesty is no surrender to despair, nor a morbidity that merely mourns. For the seriousness of evil is only the corollary of a transcendence which has it figuratively and redemptively overcome in the love that undertakes its cost.

But if realism, undeceived about the world, is the lesson of dialogue and the best tutor of hope, faith must remain honest with itself. That need is well intimated by the study of Salah 'Abd al-Sabur as truly inter-religious both in origin and theme. The will to martyrdom has long been the ultimate test of fidelity. It is, therefore, the ultimate religious measure seeing that life itself is bartered for truth's – or love's – sake. By the same token, it is also the realm of the supreme temptation, as we have seen in the reflections of T.S. Eliot and 'Abd al-Sabur on Thomas of Canterbury and Al-Hallaj of Baghdad. Even here there is no escape from the spectre of the false self, from the inauthenticity possible even in self-abnegation. Paul had seen as much in celebrating love in his Letter to Corinthian Christians. The utmost in religious ultimacy has still to search itself lest it be deceived.

The lesson abides in all the lesser, lower reaches of religious being and does so on every side of dialogue. Encounter that may be properly doctrinal, mutually intellectual and truly open, needs to be also a recipro-cal search for pure intention. Whatever role there may be for dialogue in the elucidation of meanings or the nurture of mental awareness of the other's rites and symbols, its central core must surely be an inner reckoning with ourselves, with the worth of what we identify as truth and the integrity we bring to it. That integrity will depend, in turn, on what our beliefs require of us in gentleness with them, in the readiness to be proved mistaken, in the capacity for penitence, for forgiving and being forgiven. Recent decades have seen some progress in meetings of the mind, in the practicalities of relationships. Spirituality – despite the popular usage of the word – is harder to come by and no less hard to define. In a very different context we are still where Henry Martyn was in 'longing to know what we seek after'. 'Dialogue', 'theology' even hy-phened with 'a world', are discursive – as the terms by derivation show. Through them and beyond them is the need, not only to be with each other *about* meaning, but somehow also so *within* it. We must have the aspiration even where it is unattainable.

V

Such aspiration can then attempt the practice of compassion – compassion in the real world fulfilling the logic of the light that discloses perplexity, humility, realism, penitence and aspiration. By their differing impulses all faiths in some sense enjoin compassion. 'Thou shalt love thy neighbour who is as you are' defines the human situation as *de facto* shared and so *de jure* bonded.

> I was born of woman and drew milk,
> As sweet as charity from human breast.
> I think, articulate, I laugh and weep,
> And exercise all functions of man.
> How then should I or any man that lives
> Be strangers to each other?[8]

Faiths have often militated against that common humanity by their convictions of 'electedness' or their perception of identity as combative by divine sanction. To have compassion in every sphere of reference as the ruling principle of relationship would draw the sting from the incidence of inevitable diversity in belief and culture while subduing these to the discipline of a perceived humanity. It would mean requiring diversity not to divide in the actualities of communal existence and social context. The will to have it so would be the surest education into perceptions which might, in turn, refine the abstractions of dogma by which attitudes and traditions have been shaped. The closer dialogue can come to the onus of compassion in ethics, environment, social justice, and economic structures, the more telling will be counsels about 'world theology'. Sinking a well, draining a swamp, or fighting spoliation, may conduce better to the testing of religious adequacy in response to the human scene than consultations on theology. For it is deeds which have the salutary perspectives on the world, as orphanage, as hospital, as prison, as precariousness and tribulation, as hurt and competition, as market-force, and mortal foreboding. Compassionate alertness to all these will better sift theologies, interrogate religious symbols and haunt our rituals, than endless disquisitions withdrawn from them.

A familiar tradition of Muhammad is in point here. It concerns 'evil situations' and how a right Muslim should respond. 'Let him change them with his hand' is the first directive – action, initiative, succour, resourceful intervention. If such is not possible, 'let him change them with his tongue' – protest, repudiation, exposure, identifying the evil for the evil it is lest it present itself as 'good'. Let conscience speak. If, however, neither can avail, 'let him change the evil in his heart'. Take the awareness inward, cherish contradiction of the wrong, do not be daunted into acquiescence, continue to hold out against it in the inner self. 'This,' the tradition continues, 'is the weakest of the three.' That verdict some would quite reverse. For bearing evil in the heart, in refusing to yield to it, can over-master it and, by bearing, redeem it. That is the principle of the Cross.

However interpreted, the rubric of compassion serves both to invite religions to a common agenda and, thereby, to make their mutual relations significant beyond mere discourse or comparison. It must immerse them all, comparably, if not equally, in the global urgencies of the time – urgencies which make their former privacies and enmities both irrelevant and culpable. With all the practical arenas of vocation to life as it is – and must become – there are innumerable, less tangible, realms where old controversies could give way to the search for contemporary wisdom and guidance. This would bring the content of faiths into close engagement with the liabilities of the sciences and the perceptions of the arts.

Here, among the themes that are, or ought to be, religious, must be the sacramental trust of the natural order, the meaning and fulfilment of human sexuality, the moral issues of developing technology and the significance of the secularity that finds religion either readily dispensable or inherently futile. All these require inner faith to explore, with the arts, the consciousness of contemporary man – a task which, in itself, creates an inter-faith situation. For what is at stake belongs, essentially, with all faiths and with each in cultural or traditional distinctiveness. If compassion, as contrasted with self-preservation, is to be the monitor of faiths, then they must relate with attentive sympathy to the bewilderments, the yearnings, the tangles which current literature discloses, to all that 'beckons and baffles'[10] in the human predicament. Only by going out of their securities will they properly do so – a condition which must mean a livelier perception of each other.

The hope in many cases may be far to seek, given the degree to which precisely this vocation evokes the fear, the stress, the introversion, which refuse or scout it. In so far as this obtains, so much the greater is the urgency. We are brought back, in conclusion, to the point earlier anticipated, namely the need for every faith to identify what is the heart of its *raison d'être* among all the others as irreducibly distinctive and as the crux of its relationships. We might say that faith knows itself inwardly in how it would outwardly be known.

vi

'As we are known' must seem to the cynical a poor formula for a right perception of Christianity. For it has been 'known' in so many confusing guises and surmises even to despair of any final definition. We do well to be aware of what the poet W. B. Yeats had in mind in writing of those who 'swept the sawdust from the floor of that working carpenter',[11] but had 'a working carpenter' been all, history would not recall him.

We can perhaps agree to begin with the loved New Testament phrase which has passed into Christian Liturgy: 'Our Lord Jesus Christ.' Embryonic creed is there, as well as personal and corporate devotion. The pronoun 'Our' must have its weight, not only describing a circle round a centre, but also because the possession explains the possessed. The Christian event as personal in Jesus belongs within the Christian event as personal also in his people. Neither dimension in the one event belongs to history or faith without the other. Only second to what Jesus was to his disciples was what he occasioned them to be to him. His personality, ministry, suffering, death and resurrection, had their meaning in making those disciples into apostles through awareness of it.

From that event came the New Testament, at one and the same time its text and context. No one can escape the fact that Christ, in original Christianity, was a mediated meaning, in what *they* became by virtue of all that *he* had been. At the heart of both was the forgiving compassion of the Cross as the index to 'the sin of the world' and to how Messianic hope would translate into Messianic fact in answer to it. So 'the love of the crucified Christ' – his in the deed and theirs in the perceiving – became 'the way, the truth and the life'.

But because it took place within the divine pledge of Messianic action, it became also the index to the nature of God. For God, in Hebraic tradition, is no more essentially discerned than in that wherein Messiah is identified. For Messiah is, by definition, that by which the creator-God may be seen and known to be self-consistent in responsibility to human history. It is how divine reality comes through where it most needs to, in response to the destiny and tragedy of mankind. That God had been true to Himself in Jesus as the clue to that self-consistency, or – in old language – as 'the place of the Name of the Lord', was the conviction that shaped the

Christian faith and community. The nature of God is a love that cares and comes, suffers and redeems.

The matter is there, in inclusive brevity, in John 14:1: 'You believe in God: believe also in me,' – Jesus speaking to his disciples, according to John. Both verbs can be either affirmative or imperative, statement or plea, and they are interchangeable. We come to God on the ground of Jesus, but only because we believe we have in Jesus God's expressive ground. There is a necessary circularity here but an experimentally true one. Wherever one enters a circle one is brought round to where one started. Come to God because of Jesus; come to Jesus as being where God comes. This is Christian faith. Humanity is invited to recognise in Jesus as the Christ the sufficient evidence of God by God's own warrant – sufficient, that is, for faith to comprehend, to answer and henceforward to commend.

Such faith cannot claim to be demonstrable, as by a Euclid in his theorems or the chemist in his laboratory. Were it to think that way it would cease to mean at all. But Christian terms of humanity as being 'risked' – as love does – by a sublime anticipation which could prove infinitely resourceful in the odds it took, seems not at all incongruous when we ponder the world. There *is* a manifest entrustment in our being what we are, and contemporary experience makes it ever more amazing. There *is* a strange ambiguity about omnipotence if we consider that very negligibility of God which informs current secularity. If we are to believe in a supreme goodness which intended the world we must concede it to be undergoing what old writers in Christianity called a continual *kenosis*, a will to be hedged around, like a patient educator, by limitations incurred in what is undertaken and implicit in the nature of it. If we are to reconcile divine love and omnipotence (and neither has meaning if we do not do so), it must be in long-suffering. If God, in R.S. Thomas' dubious phrase, is 'the code to be cracked', then long-suffering must be the key.[12] Love of Christ resolves our doubts and forecloses our other options by its gentle, inescapable constraint. It invites us to register our life in the world, the world which is our life, as neither a fraud nor a cheat, neither a delusion nor an enigma, but rather an enterprise of compassion launched by creation, corroborated in personhood, and interpreted in Christ as the theme of the long-suffering of God.

That God has defined Himself for us in Jesus and the Cross of Jesus is the founding conviction of Christianity. The perception of it was the inauguration of the Church. It remains the distinctive witness which requires the Christian to belong loyally within the vast enquiry that

breathes in the religions of mankind. It is reassuringly consistent with
what in bewildering inconclusiveness all religions seem to indicate, namely
the elusive presence which, alike, they seek. Clearly nothing can purport
to be the answer except it be commensurate with the yearning it must
satisfy and belong within the idiom of what yearns.

It is our being here that we interrogate. The will to explain it, to fulfil it,
to acknowledge it for gift and treasure, trust and wonder, is there like a
pulse within it. Where, then, its whence and whither? The mystery points
beyond itself. We sense our indebtedness beyond ourselves. So doing, we
imply a giving, a risking, reciprocal to our indebtedness, awaiting its
recognition. The transcendent concerns us being itself concerned and we,
humanity, are that concern.

How then does this divine solicitude encounter us? Clearly not in
stridency or coercion. Stridency would not woo us as we are being wooed.
Had coercion been the chosen option it could have been so *ab initio*. We
do not experience arbitrary force – witness the very diversity of the
interpreters. Might we not even wonder about the diffidence of God, the
strange patience of what 'has let us be', in both senses – creation and
hope – of that eloquent phrase? We can feel with the urgent plea of the
psalmist (74:22): 'Rise, O God, say something on your own behalf', and
not only, as there, because 'brutal men taunt you all the day', but because
there are so many puzzling, even raucous, voices 'saying for Him'.

What, then, should He say that rides with the need to hear it? What will
be the self-disclosures, the disclaimers, of this transcendent who has
suffered us to be, whose sufferance we constitute? What do we hear from
this God we ignore, this God we annex, this God we banish, this God we
malign, this God we evade, this God we grieve, this God we misconstrue –
and all within a patience that will not let us go? What might appropriately
vindicate this elusive presence, this evident *kenosis* of compassion, this
infinite heart-ache that bears with the world and never forfeits the love by
which the entire risk proceeds? For the paradox of the question is our only
comfort. To register that divine patience is the only way to measure the
divine sovereignty – if we are not to dissolve all in negation and despair.

The Christian faith is that this elusive presence, this infinite tolerance of
the being of mankind, this competent sufferance of the world, has
dramatised itself in the passion of Jesus as the Christ, has played its hand
in that inclusive symbol of how elusive presence is revealed, how it is
fulfilled in the mystery of evil via the love that suffers. The Cross enables
us to identify what omnipotence means and bears in pursuing the enterprise of man. It leaves us ever realist about how frail, how devious, how

perverse, how fraught with destiny, is the human scene. It makes us ever persuaded of the loving competence of God.

From the beginning of the New Testament faith, hope in God, about God, because of God, was seen to be cruciform, as was also the clue to the predicament of man. The shape of the Cross – present in the mortal frame of our physique – is the pattern at once of being vulnerable and being in embrace. One cannot be crucified with the clenched fist of hatred. The bond within compassion is to suffer and be suffered for – and this is what we comprehend to be obtaining between God and ourselves. 'Christ crucified is the power and the wisdom of God.' The elusive presence confirms itself in where, and how, it seeks and finds us, as the ever decisive presence – 'God in Christ reconciling the world.'

If here we have God speaking on His own behalf, God on His own terms, those who find Him so must be within what they know definitive and serve its definition. For it is of such a sort as gently to recruit them into its patience, into the unremitting enterprise of its commendation. Commendation is all that divine patience allows itself, having so conclusively interpreted the world. We learn to ally ourselves with what God has been doing all the time.[13]

NOTES AND REFERENCES

Introduction

1 Hinduism, for example, is characteristically tolerant of diversity. Yet in actual terms it is no less resistant to conversion out of it than faiths it would accuse of truth-monopoly. Gandhi held 'conversion' to be false in any direction, a treason against birth. All faiths seem equally tenacious of adherents, retentive of their own in respect of people, even if apparently loose about their tenets.

2 William Shakespeare, *Timon of Athens*, IV. iii. II; 176-178.

3 In: *The Pen and the Faith: Eight Modern Muslim Writers and the Qur'an* (London, 1985).

4 Robert Frost, *Complete Poems* (New York, 1949), p.48: 'Mending Wall'.

5 F. Wayte, *China and Foreign Powers* (London, 1927), App., quoted by Arnold J. Toynbee, *Civilization on Trial* (London, 1948), p.72.

6 The words 'barbarous' and 'barbarian' derive from the sound non-Greek words made on Greeks, i.e. 'bar-bar-bar'. There is a similar connotation to the Arabic word *'ajami*, 'Persian', or simply, 'non-Arab' and therefore 'uncouth'.

7 See Chapter 11 below and his: *The Trinity and the Religious Experience of Man* (London, 1973).

8 See Chapter 7. Notable among his neologisms was 'peccatism', decrying the Christian doctrine of human sin, and a related depreciation of 'saviourism'. A useful handbook of the vocabulary of the faiths is: Peter D. Bishop: *Words in World Religions* (London, 1979).

9 See Chapter 13 below. The principle is attractive but becomes circular if we continue: 'Muslims are what Islam requires them to be', and the definition of either is also circular.

10 Surah 56:79: 'Let none touch it except the purified', has sometimes been interpreted as restricting the handling of the Qur'an to Muslims only. But its probable sense is a proper cleanliness. The Qur'an was initially preached to non-Muslims and is manifestly meant for all.

11 A possible analogy here – used by William Temple – is of the streams of water from the hills descending towards the basin of the tidal river which receives and fulfils them but to which they contribute. So reason and intuition feel their tentative way towards that which 'revelation' offers to them as their vindication and fulfilment, making them party to its fullness.

12 It may be that some 'revelations' purport to enclose, or finalise, all that other, previous 'revelation' has affirmed. This is the case with the Qur'an. But this claim about a 'unity' of all 'revelation' contained in one's own faith, turns on the corollary that all others, insofar as they differ, are to that extent deviant or corrupted. It therefore comes to mean an exclusive legitimacy for the one faith that has this alleged unitary 'revelation' rightly. We are back with revelatory pluralism.

Chapter 1

1 The Cape Territory had been Dutch from 1652. The British took it in 1794-95 after the French armies had entered Holland, but restored it to the Batavian Republic by the Treaty of Amiens in 1803. After the outbreak of hostilities after the collapse of that Treaty Britain recovered it and in 1815 the Congress of Vienna perpetuated British control.

2 He realised, of course, that the proposal was currently impracticable. See S. Wilberforce (ed.), *Journals and Letters of Henry Martyn* (London, 1837), Vol.1, p.466.

3 *Journals*, Vol.2, p.56. 3 May 1807. He thought that a similar establishment of British power in Persia would be the best circumstance for evangelism there.

4 So much for the alleged collusion of mission and commerce. The East India Company, under pressure from the evangelicals, did re-define its attitude, but its personnel, by and large, and 'on location', were instinctively hostile to chaplains consorting with 'worthless Indians'.

5 *Journals*, Vol.2, pp.14-15. 1 February 1807.

6 George Smith, *Henry Martyn: Saint and Scholar* (London, 1892), pp.128-9.

7 Constance E. Padwick, *Henry Martyn: Confessor of the Faith* (London, 1922), p.84.

8 Echoing the phrase of Edwin C. Hoskyns: *Cambridge Sermons*, ed. Charles Smyth (1938).

9 See R.C. Zaehner, *Concordant Discord: The Inter-Dependence of Faiths* (Oxford, 1970), p.198.

10 *Journals*, Vol.2, p.252 and see: John Sargent, *Memoir of Henry Martyn* (London, 1816), p.107.

11 *Journals*, Vol.2, p.252. 30 August 1809.

12 *Journals*, Vol.2, p.173. 28 March 1808.

13 *Journals*, Vol.2, pp.34-35, 23 March 1897.

14 *Sermons*, 1st Edit. (Calcutta, 1822), p.271, No.xiv.

15 *Journals*, Vol.2, pp.91-92, 20 July 1807.

16 *Journals*, Vol.2, p.31, 14 March 1807.

17 *Sermons*, p.274, No.xiv.

18 Sargent, p.127.

19 Ibid. p.127.

20 *Journals*, Vol.2, p.55, 28 April 1807.

21 *Journals*, Vol.2, p.15, 4 February 1807.

22 He thought, for example, that the Qur'an would 'sink into contempt' once readers could 'discover' the contents of the New Testament. *Journals*, Vol.1, p.466.

23 Sargent, p.179.

24 On the reaction of Carey to the disastrous fire, see George Smith, *The Life of William Carey* (London, 1922), pp.197-98. The Serampore printing of Martyn's work came only after the European, Sir Gore Ouseley, having nursed Martyn in Tabriz, made good his pledge to him by personally delivering the Persian New Testament to a press in St. Petersburg and proof-reading it for publication in 1815.

25 Padwick, p. 144.

26 As, for example, when he was told in Shiraz that when a certain Muslim, 'Abbas Mirza, had contrived to kill so many Russian Christians, Jesus in the fourth heaven had clutched Muhammad's skirt and implored him to restrain the killer. 'I was cut to the soul at this blasphemy,' wrote Martyn, 'I could not endure existence if Jesus was not glorified.' *Journals*, Vol.2, p.373, 8 September 1811, and p.389, 24 January 1812.

27 Most poignant among them his farewell to Lydia Grenfell, whom he had long yearned to make his wife, a Truro girl on whom his whole love was lavished but never decisively returned – a circumstance which only sharpened the pain of Martyn's own misgivings, not of affection, but of vocation. Chaplains' wives could come to India, but what of his own life-expectancy and Christ's expectancy of him? These intimate struggles, however, are part of a different reckoning.

28 Samuel Lee, *Controversial Tracts on Christianity and Mohammadanism* (Cambridge 1824). Those by Martyn himself figure on pp.80-101, 102-123, 139-160.

   At the beginning of the First Tract, Martyn insists that he writes 'not for mere purpose of dispute'. He discusses the nature and credibility of attesting 'miracle', and treats of the *'ijaz*, or miraculous quality of the Qur'an's Arabic, adding that this 'evidence' is only within the judgement of Arabs. It is contrasted with the compassion-miracles of Jesus. He deplores that Muhammad resorted to force.

   The Second Tract moves from 'no good reason for faith in Muhammad' to the 'positive' case against faith in him. He has no prophetic foretelling, was initially 'pagan', used violence and made many marriages. He made salvation depend on good works and repentance alone.

   The Third Tract decries the Sufi system as seeking truth by abstraction from humble sense-experience where all thought must begin. He aims to explain 'why God has not shown mercy without the obedience of Christ'.

29 *Journals*, Vol.2, p.35, 23 March 1807. '...afraid' may mean apprehensive that educated youth would be less tractable, more freedom-loving and therefore more likely to resent and resist the Company's interests; or it may mean a fear of Hindu-Muslim disquiet – though in retrospect Indian religions have been singularly indulgent about Christian education of their offspring.

30 'The sufficiency of the Scriptures' is the famous principle of Article Six of the Book of Common Prayer. It differs from 'infallibility' and relates to all things 'necessary to salvation'. Like the Canon of Scripture it is designed to have a restrictive effect in excluding outside sources which might affect, or distort 'the balance of truth'. 'Sufficiency' cannot have an inclusive effect, given that the

geographical range is so limited and the historical setting so particular. For geography and history are so much responsible for the 'feel' of culture. All Scriptures in all religions suffer inadequacy in this sense, but some more than others. It is only by a wise sense of precedent discernible in apostles in their *sphere* that Christians in a different *milieu* of place and time can avail to be loyal. Martyn's problem was to read such precedents aright, or perhaps to find them at all.

31 *Journals*, Vol.2, p.250, 31 July 1809.

Chapter 2

1 *What I Owe to Christ* (London, 1932), pp.12, 21.
2 The issues of New Testament criticism impinged on the Christology of the time and required reappraisal of how the human circumstance of Jesus related to the divine self-disclosure. The growth of agnosticism – wistful or aggressive – posed the problem of integrity in a new way for believers. 'Agnosticism' in one sense was a misnomer, for 'agnostics' at least believed that they did not *know* and doubt is no less a dialogue with faith than faith is with doubt. It is a dialogue in which 'organs of truth' are vitally at stake – reason, Scripture, experience, intuition and the rest. Andrews came increasingly to let the primacy of 'experience' have priority.
3 In practical terms, he helped to ensure that the Principalship of St. Stephen's passed to Susil Rudra, the first Indian to hold it, rather than to the still fledging C.F.A.
4 Rabindranath Tagore (1864-1941) was a Bengali poet, Nobel prize-winner and mystic philosopher, son of Devendranath Tagore of Calcutta, a notable reformer of Hinduism. *Gitanjala* or 'Offering of Song', was published in 1916 and, with others of Tagore's numerous works, attracted wide admiration in the West for its commendation of Indian mystical themes.
5 Leslie Brown, *Three Worlds, One Word*, (London, 1981), p.39, recalls one such occasion in Ootacamund when C.F.A. was refused welcome at a hill station by a senior missionary whom Brown, as a novice, had no power to override.
6 *Christ in India*, Paper, 1910, quoted in Benarsidas Chaturvedi and Marjorie Sykes, *Charles Freer Andrews: A Narrative* (London, 1949), p.64.
7 *India in Transition*, Paper, 1910.
8 In a Preface to the *Collected Writings of Swami Rama Tirtha*, cited in Chaturvedi, p.65.
9 Ibid. p.61.
10 Thomas Hill Green (1836-1882), of Balliol College, Oxford, was a leader of Oxford philosophy and an active citizen with a lively sense of social responsibility. A metaphysician and moralist with a deep belief in the implications of the Incarnation, he nevertheless felt unable to 'subscribe' to the prerequisites of Ordination, on which he engaged in spirited debate with his pupils who, within the Church, took stock of his fertile, sifting mind in their own theology. Hence *Lux Mundi*.

11 *The Renaissance in India* (London, 1910), p.247. He anticipated what he called 'the naturalization of the Christian message amidst Indian conditions of life and thought, via art, music and poetry'. p.220: The 'evils' to which he referred were the caste system and the Muslim will for 'separatism'.

12 Ibid. p.144.

13 See: *Zaka Ullah of Delhi* (Cambridge, 1929), p.xix.

14 *Christ in the Silence* (London, 1933), p.120.

15 *Zaka Ullah*, Intro. and p.104.

16 It was after a sermon in Simla that Andrews became closely acquainted with Lord and Lady Hardinge to whom he also ministered in a pastoral way. Hardinge was almost fatally wounded in a bomb attack in Delhi. He forbade reprisals and accepted Andrews' counsel that birthday parties should be held for children in hospitals and orphanages in June 1913 in celebration of his escape. On other occasions he was instrumental in shaping Government thinking by dint of introductions to Indian leaders.

17 Robert Frost, *Complete Poems* (New York, 1949), p.476, 'The Lesson for Today'.

18 See J.N. Farquahar, *The Crown of Hinduism* (London, 1913).

19 In a Letter to Tagore, quoted in Chaturvedi, p.102.

20 *What I Owe to Christ* (London, 1932), pp.97-99.

21 Ibid, pp.218-220.

22 In a Letter to Tagore, quoted in Chaturvedi, p.111.

23 Ibid. p.164. One may recall all the sinister implications of 'whiteness' – leprosy, death, frost, pallor, fear – in Herman Melville, *Moby Dick* (New York, 1851), Chap. 42.

24 *Christ and Prayer* (London, 1937), p.131.

25 Albert Schweitzer, *The Quest of the Historical Jesus*, trans. W. Montgomery (London, 1910), pp.399-401.

26 *The Inner Life* (London, 1938), p.31.

27 *Christ and Prayer* (London, 1937), p.116.

28 From a Pamphlet: 'Why I am a Christian', originally written for a newspaper in Japan.

29 The incident is quoted from Andrews' narrative in Chaturvedi. p.224.

30 Ibid., p.310.

31 See note 5 above.

32 Cremation being the Hindu mode of disposal of the dead. The Codicil ran: 'I desire...to be buried in the Christian faith as a Christian, near St. Paul's Cathedral, Calcutta, if possible, with the blessing of the Metropolitan whom I have deeply longed to serve as my bishop, as a priest of the Christian Church and a minister of the Christian faith which I hold with all my heart.'

Chapter 3

1 C.E. Padwick, *Temple Gairdner of Cairo* (London, 1929). See also: *W.H.T.G. to His Friends, (Some Letters and Informal Writings)* (London, 1930), edited by Margaret Gairdner.

2 *The Master of the Impossible*: *Lilias Trotter of Algiers* (London, 1938), and *Call to Istanbul*, (London, 1958).

3 On Louis Massignon see: *L'Herne*: *Cahier Massignon, Textes et Inedits*, ed. Jean-Francois Six (Paris, 1962); Youakim Mubarak, *L'Oeuvre de Louis Massignon* (Beirut, 1973); and Guilio Basetti-Sani, *Louis Massignon, Christian Ecumenist*, trans. A.H. Cutler (Chicago, 1974).

4 In *International Review of Missions*, Vol.xxviii, No.2, (1939), pp.205-16. See also: 'North African Reverie', Vol. xxvii, No.3, (1938). pp.341-54.

5 R.S. Thomas: 'The Chapel', *Laboratories of the Spirit* (London, 1975), p.19.

6 In a letter to the writer, 12 February, 1967.

7 Quoted in her *Call to Istanbul*, p.vii.

8 The Beirut Arabic Bible, published in 1866, was the fruit of the labours of Eli Smith and Cornelius Van Dyck with Butrus al-Bustani and Nasif al-Yazigi, their Syrian colleagues. All were able scholars but they were liable to retain Hebraisms and Graecisms in their Arabic and it was not their intention to have the Qur'an for a 'referent' in resolving stylistic questions. The quite contrasted character of the Qur'an would, in any event, have made such a policy difficult, except in the area of separate terms and idioms. It was to explore these for what they might convey of shared spirituality that Padwick's study of Muslim Prayer Manuals was meant.

9 The meaning of the Greek *entos* is 'in your midst' or 'between your ranks'. The context makes it clear that the sense is not about some private inwardness; it has to do with the actuality of the Gospel in the immediacy of present history. There is no need to be gazing around with this or that 'alarum' ('Lo, here! lo, there!') exciting you. You are encountering the kingdom all the time.

10 *Islamic Culture*, Hyderabad, Vol.xl. No.1, (1966), pp.49f. Though critical he wrote with characteristic courtesy and praised the careful scholarship.

11 This is not to say, with Wilfred Cantwell Smith, that 'meaning' belongs universally only in terms of 'faith' as 'a humane science', which is itself 'singular' and cannot be plural. There are no 'faiths'; there is only 'faith' with which people are variously 'faith-ing'. (His term to suggest a parallel between 'hope' as unitary and 'hoping' diversely). See note 17 below and Chapter 13.

12 On Sufism and the Sufi Orders, see J.S. Trimingham (a book with that title), (Oxford, 1971), and also A.J. Arberry, *Sufism* (London, 1950) with R.A. Nicholson, *The Mystics of Islam* (London, 1914), and Anne-Marie Schimmel: *Mystical Dimensions of Islam* (Chapel Hill, 1975).

13 *Muslim Devotions*, p.xiii.

14 There have also been modern views on the term *Rabb*, such as those of the Indo-Pakistani poet-philosopher, Muhammad Iqbal, which emphasise a connection with the verbal root 'to rear', or 'to nourish', so that the meaning can be associated with 'evolution' and 'education'. But the primary Semitic sense of lordship must be paramount.

15 *Taharat al-Qulub* (Cairo, n.d.) p.177.

16 The Name '*Al-Samad*', used of God only in Surah 112, means one who has all resources in himself. The word is in apposition to the phrase: 'Unbegetting, unbegotten', which is so often cited as a supposed disavowal of Christian theology. It certainly reads as a comment on *al-Samad*, i.e. One whose Being is eternally Self-subsisting, underiving and underived.

17 As Wilfred Cantwell Smith in *Towards a World Theology* (London, 1981), and *Questions of Religious Truth* (New York, 1967). See Chapter 13 below. Smith writes with a strong confidence in human 'religious awareness', despite the prevalence of the secular temper, and sees it within all the diversity which gives 'structure' to it.

18 It is wise to insist on *this* 'associationism' between God and man, explicit as it is in creation, revelation, *Tasliyah*, and Incarnation, inasmuch as 'dissociation' is often used to identify what is meant in Islam by *Shirk*, the cardinal sin of alienating 'divinity' from God Himself to idols and pseudo-gods.

19 *Muslim Devotions*, pp.123-24.

20 Ibid. pp.165-66.

21 Ibid. p.170.

22 Ibid. p.204.

23 *Taharat al-Qulub*, p.177.

24 See several examples in *Hirz al-Jawshan* (Cairo, n.d.) an extremely popular manual. Also my: *Alive to God* (London, 1970), pp.88 and 108.

25 *Muslim Devotions*, pp.217-18.

26 Ibid. p.45.

27 Ibid. p.219, and appended note on the possible sources of the prayer.

28 Henry Martyn, for example, in his *Persian Tracts*, argued that penitence did not suffice except in association with atonement.

Chapter 4

1 *Legends of Our Time* (New York, 1968), p.233.

2 *Recalling Swallowed Worlds*, p.610. He adds: '...where Christians have scarcely any access.'

3 *Legends*, op. cit. p.73.

4 *Night*, trans. by M.E. Wiesel (New York, 1960).

5 *One Generation After* (New York, 1971), p.73.

6 Ibid, pp.46 and 51.

7 See the questionnaire and survey of Holocaust survivors in their reactions to Judaism and to faith in: R.R. Brenner, *Faith and Doubt of Holocaust Victims* (New York, 1980). Brenner found that some survivors felt they had to repudiate Judaic faith altogether, as something thoroughly betrayed by God. Others saw such a conclusion as a 'victory' for Hitler and resolved to become more assertive, more insistent in their Torah piety.

8 *The Jews of Silence* (New York, 1966), p.82.

9 The quotation from the Talmud comes in *One Generation After*, p.44. See also: *The Gates of the Forest* (New York, 1964), p.192.

10 *Legends*, loc. cit., p.26.

11 Quoted from Paul, Romans 8:24, in his own context of Christian anticipation of that which is 'not yet', but 'shall be' on the basis of what 'has already been'. Judaic hope, as for example, in Martin Buber, Franz Rosenzweig, Gershom Scholem and many others is still essentially future and is only 'hope'

because nothing has yet claimed or availed to realise it. Waiting in such openness is the nature, and genius, of Judaic fidelity.

12 *The Oath* (New York, 1973), p.73.

13 Ibid., p.88.

14 '...against man...' here in the sense that the brutality, the calculated degradation, which the Nazis inflicted on their victims, outraged humanity *per se*. The appeal against them could only be to what they had flouted and defied.

15 *The Oath*, p.76.

16 'Love of neighbour as yourself' does not mean that self-love is a model or a measure of neighbour love. The command arises from the fact that 'he is as you are', i.e., a common humanity dictates as duty the compassion one would will to receive. The human situation is an experience of things reciprocal.

17 It is evident that the elements of Hebraic self-consciousness are shared by all human identities. The Kikuyu, for example, live 'facing Mount Kenya', understood as the gift of their God via their ancestors, making tenancy of the land not merely economic but sacral. Parallels abound. What is different in the Hebraic is the intensity of the awareness and its moral guilt-forgiveness imprint via the prophets.

18 *The Letters of a Post-Impressionist: the Familiar Correspondence of Vincent Van Gogh*, trans. A.M. Ludovici (London, 1917), p.65.

19 *The Complete Writings of William Blake*, ed. Geoffrey Keynes (Oxford, 1966), 'The Marriage of Heaven and Hell,' p.153.

20 *Days of Remembrance*, p.16.

21 Perhaps the best commentary on Versailles (though Wiesel would not think so) is G.A. Studdert-Kennedy's poem: 'Dead and Buried,'
    Then they wrapped my mangled body
    In fine linen of fair words
    With the perfume of a sweetly scented lie,
    And they laid it in the tomb
    Of the golden-mirrored room
    'Mid the many fountained garden of Versailles.
    Jesus and 'the peace'!

22 See Jacob B. Agus, *The Meaning of Jewish Identity*, (London, 1963), Vol.2, p.449. Christopher Ricks observes in: *T.S. Eliot and Prejudice* (London, 1988), p.76: 'The fact that there could appallingly be no doubt in the case of Hitler and the Jews should not be allowed to petrify or putrefy our entire world into one in which *all* prejudice is indubitable in being entirely dissociated from any antecedent causes, provocation or evidence.'

23 See, for example: Rosemary Reuther, *Faith & Fratricide, Theological Roots of Anti-Semitism* (New York, 1974); Jules Isaac, *The Teaching of Contempt* (New York, 1964); Alan Ecclestone, *The Night Sky of the Lord* (London, 1980); also my: *This Year in Jerusalem* (London, 1982).

24 *A Jew Today* (New York, 1978), pp.5 & 17.

25 *The Oath*, pp.56 & 79.

26 *Conversations* p.48.

27 *The Oath*, pp.63, 56 & 79.

28 *Gates of the Forest* (New York, 1966), p.223.

29 *One Generation After*, p.189.

30 *The Testament* (New York, 1981), p.20 He writes to advise the young and to have them remember: 'You can die in Auschwitz after Auschwitz.'

31 Robert McAfee Brown, *Elie Wiesel: Messenger to all Humanity* (St. Louis, 1983). There are times when this study allows its zeal to endanger its perceptions.

32 *One Generation After*, p.128.

33 Ibid., pp.129-132.

34 Ibid. pp.151-55.

35 *Souls on Fire* (New York, 1972), p.143.

36 *A Beggar in Jerusalem* (New York), pp.244-45. In this work the past in Europe and the present in Israel are woven together.

37 *One Generation After*, p.131.

38 Ibid., p.129. It is significant that he writes here: 'Palestine'. The name was long current for, e.g.; the Palestinian Talmud, and to denote 'Palestinian Jews' before and during the mandate period. It was, of course, used in the Balfour Declaration. It is since the occupation that 'Judea and Samaria' have been insistently used. Menachem Begin declared that if the land really was 'Palestine' Zionists were 'invaders'. There had to be, for him, a territorial, historical, demographic 'de-construction' of 'Palestine'. But that is where 'the Messianic adventure' is, and 'Palestine' is the ultimate test of its 'Messianic' quality.

Chapter 5

1 'The Christian Scriptures' is used here to avoid the implications, for Jews, of the usage 'the New Testament' which we will abjure completely in this Chapter. We do not wish to imply the relegation of 'the Old'. Indeed, 'the Old Testament' should be included in the phrase 'the Christian Scriptures', if we are thinking Christianly. Yet that imperialist adoption of 'the Hebrew Scriptures' as properly possessed by Christians also offends much Jewish feeling. 'The Christian Scriptures' here means Matthew to Revelation, leaving open the question of 'two testaments' and of 'the unity of the Bible'.

2 Among them Reinhold Niebuhr, Peter Schneider, Paul Van Buren, Roy Eckhardt and numerous others.

3 Political Zionism was very much a minority movement in its early decades and strenuously disavowed by most Jews on grounds of ideology as well as practicality. It was seen to endanger the 'good faith' of Jewish participation in nationhood in the Diaspora. It was Nazi brutality from 1933 and still more after 1940 which tragically vindicated the Zionist logic. Some still disapproving Diaspora Jews were not won over until the seemingly miraculous events of 1967. What Israel has needed to become, by dint of statehood, in terms of violence and repression, leave in painful suspense still basic questions about the identity of Judaism. James Parkes had seen war service in 1914-18 and been gassed at Ypres. His brother and sister were killed in that War. He had, therefore, a lively sympathy with Israeli embattlement before and after the establishment of the State, but not an impartial view of its significance.

4 *Good God* (London, 1940). Revised and reprinted in 1962.

5 Ibid. p.45. Italics mine.

6 Ibid. p.44.

7 The book was enlivened by recollections like the following: 'As a child I used to speculate on how the golden crowns [c.f.Revelation 4:4,10] got back on their heads for further casting. I thought perhaps cherubs ran to pick them up and put them on again. I had a fearful and wonderful idea that perhaps new crowns continuously grew.' Ibid. pp.81-82.

8 He also noted that the Palestinians were present in the maximum numbers that could sustain a livelihood: *Voyage of Discoveries* (London, 1969), p.236f. Arguments about sustainable levels of population were often exchanged by officialdom also and repeatedly disproved by events. Are there ethnic factors in land capacity?

9 Ibid., p.236. This was to overlook how essentially European (Russian, Polish, Austrian, German) the Zionist leadership was and would remain. The 'oriental' Jewish elements in Israeli society only came even partially to challenge this dominance of late.

10 The Balfour Declaration of November 1917, implied this even in apparent reassurance. In saying that the establishment of 'a national home for the Jewish people *in* Palestine' was not to be to the detriment of 'the civil and religious rights of the existing population' it could be read as meaning there would be no 'political rights', since – given these – civil and religious rights would not need safeguarding. The Jewish Agency so argued. The phrase 'the existing population' may have seemed reassuring but it refrained from using their name: Palestinians. Were they really anonymous? Arabs always resented that implication, the more so as the land in question was designated 'Palestine'.

11 See below.

12 *Foundations of Judaism and Christianity* (London, 1960), pp.200f.

13 The expression, of course, invites debate as to how 'original' is identified, on which more below. But there can be no doubt that Jewish initiative had a major part.

14 *Foundations*, p.153.

15 Ibid. p.187.

16 Walter Eichrodt, *Man in the Old Testament*, tr. R. Gregor Smith (London, 1951), pp.10; 23f.

17 In much contemporary Jewish thinking there is a marked tendency to locate essential Jewishness in the moral and the spiritual rather than in the ethnic. 'Seed' and 'birth' remain vital concepts, though by some discounted altogether. Being 'chosen' might then be an ethical option for all peoples. See, for example, Jacob B. Agus, *Jewish Identity in an Age of Ideologies* (New York. 1976), p.280, rebutting F. Rosenzweig's 'racial mystique'. Clearly, goodness cannot be genetically ensured.

18 Without being simplistic about 'Christ in all the Scriptures'.

19 It is interesting to note a Muslim angle on Christian universality. A Christian Coptic writer, Nazmi Luqa, raised much opposition by his book: *Muhammad: Al-Risalah wa-l-Rasul*, 'Muhammad, the Message and the Messenger' (Cairo, n.d.), arguing – on behalf of Islam – that Christianity was too lofty to serve a universal role. It was an ethic suited only to exceptional people and had to be

replaced – by Islam – if mankind in general were to have a feasible religion. The Jewish view had been that Christianity was too 'risky', i.e., too accommodating of 'Gentile' 'evil', to achieve right living among the nations at large.

20   That Messiah never comes in order that Messiah may always be awaited was central to the thought of Martin Buber. Another eminent scholar of Judaica, Gershom Scholem emphasises this necessary futurity. True hope has always to be on ahead. See: *The Messianic Ideal in Israel*, tr. W.F. Stinespring (London, 1956).

21   *Foundations*, p.202.

22   Ibid., p.206.

23   Ibid., pp.207-08.

24   There is a strange, and surely perverse, way of putting the case for the exclusion of the Jews from the Gospel and the Gospel's reach to Gentiles only. It consists of reading *ethnoi*, 'nations', in Matthew 28: 19 (the 'commission' of the Church) as *goyim* ('outsiders') in the restrictive sense. One can then argue that the very mandate of Christianity has explicit confinement at its heart. See *Ends and Odds*, of the Centre for the Study of Judaism and Jewish/Christian Relations, Selly Oak, Birmingham, No.40 (January, 1990). But the Gospel was written in Greek and to read the verse as *goyim* in the rejecting sense is to defy the steady world-reach of the obedience to the command and the emphasis: '...came into the world...'; '...for the sins of the world...'; '...so loved the world...' Are we to assume that all non-*goyim* have gone out of the world?

25   Among them the Judeo-Christian obligation to the secular world and the western decay of religious faith. Writing in *The Times*, on 27 June 1970, Parkes saw 'scientific humanism' as 'a third channel of action of the Spirit of God in secular political life', i.e., 'man's calling to understand and master the material world.' Judaism, he held, had been the prime tutor in this humanism. Both faiths could be its mentors.

Chapter 6

1   The quotation in the heading comes from: *The Prophets* (New York, 1962), p.179. Subsequent references are bracketed in the text. For disavowals of Heschel's 'divine pathos' as uncongenial to Judaism see: M.Vogel, *The Death of Dialogue and Beyond* (New York, 1969), pp.173f. Eliezer Berkowits and Leon Roth are well known demurrers.

2   *A Passion for Truth* (New York, 1973).

3   In an Address to American Reform Rabbis, 1952.

4   *Union Theological Seminary Journal*, New York, Vol.xxi, No.2, Part 1 (Jan. 1966), pp.117-134.

5   Ed. Samuel H. Dresner, *Abraham J. Heschel, The Circle of the Baal Shem Tov* (Chicago, 1985), p.xxv.

6   *A Passion for Truth*, p.301. Two references to the Holocaust in *The Prophets*, p.185 asks: 'Is it easy to keep the horror of wickedness from turning into a

hatred of the wicked?'; p.285 says: 'To a generation afflicted by the fury of cruel men, by the outrage of abandoning God, no condemnation is too harrowing.' In the UTS Lecture Heschel includes Christianity with Jewry in the victimisation:

> Realising that it was Christianity that implanted attachment to the God of Abraham and involvement with the Hebrew Bible in the hearts of Western man, Nazism resolved that it must both exterminate the Jews and eliminate Christianity, and bring about instead a revival of Teutonic paganism. (p.118.)

7 UTS Lecture, p.124. It is necessary here to query his view of a 'de-Judaization' of Christianity. Was it not, rather, a Judaic self-exemption from it in the traumatic aftermath of the Fall of Jerusalem in AD 70 – exemption from a faith of thoroughly Judaic roots and origins, which took on the Hebrew Bible, rejected Marcion, had a deeply Hebraic vocabulary of faith and salvation, and remained unmistakably Palestinian in its most 'Hellenised' writing, i.e. the Fourth Gospel? There are many imponderables in Christian origins but 'de-Judaization' is much too simplistic a term to apply to them. In being 'for Gentiles' the faith was not essentially 'against Jews'.

8 Ibid., pp.124-133.

9 Loc. cit., pp.249 and 255.

10 Ibid., p.265.

11 Numbers 23:19, quoted in UTS Lecture, p.119.

12 This sentence (*The Prophets*, p.266) is quintessential Heschel.

13 It is clear that they ought to be. For, within creation and being human, the factors which – in the Judaic view of 'election' – belong with it are, manifestly, universal factors. They are tribe, land and history, people, territory and memory, the who, where and whence of *all* human experience in human collectives of identity. Moreover a sacral, or sacred, sense of the 'given-ness' of all these, attaches to them in some form in all cultures. Do not all identities, just by being such, in measure 'elect themselves', i.e., interpret themselves as legitimated in ancestry, habitat and tradition? If so, does not Jewry belong with all mankind seeing that all identities are distinctive as inwardly known?

14 *Conservative Judaism*, Vol.25 (Fall, 1970), 'On Prayer,' p.5.

15 *God in Search of Man: A Philosophy of Judaism* (New York, 1955), p.39.

16 *Israel: An Echo of Eternity* (New York, 1968), pp.32,115,138,145,159,209,223.

17 Ibid., p.17.

18 *A Passion for Truth*, p.87.

19 Footnote references indicate dates after 1933.

20 Ed. Robert Alter & Frank Kermode, *The Literary Guide to the Bible* (London, 1987); Joel Rosenberg, 'Jeremiah and Ezekiel', p.186.

21 Jacob Neusner, *The Incarnation of God, The Character of Divinity in Formative Judaism* (Philadelphia, 1988). He sees 'the incarnation of God' in the portrait of God as moved by human emotions and as the converse of 'man in the image of God'.

22 There is a parallel in the Islamic insistence of, e.g., Fazlur Rahman that the Quranic revelation is strictly 'functional' and brings no knowledge of God. *Major Themes of the Qur'an* (Minneapolis, 1980), p.1.

23 Here, is he not going beyond 'function'?
24 H.Wheeler Robinson, *The Cross in the Old Testament* (London, 1955), pp.156 and 165f.
25 UTS Lecture, p.129.

Chapter 7

1 Ed. S.C.Crawford, *World Religions and Global Ethics* (New York, 1989), Isma'il al-Faruqi, Chap. 8, 'Islamic Ethics', p.212.
2 '*Urubah and Religion: On Arabism* (Amsterdam, 1962). *Christian Ethics; A Historical and Systematic Analysis of Its Dominant Ideas* (Montreal, 1967).
3 *Islam* (Niles, Illinois, 1979).
4 *The Cultural Atlas of Islam* (New York, 1986).
5 An Islamic resentment at the assumptions of western pride in enjoying all necessary contemporary wisdom and, thereby, assigning the world's religions to a necessary tutelage in accommodation to an inevitable secularity, may be appreciated by reference, for example, to Arend Van Leeuwen, *Christianity in World History*, trans. from the Dutch by H.H.Hoskins (London, 1964). Van Leeuwen asserted that 'religions' would be obsolete within a quarter century and needed to be reconciled to their demise – a task in which Christianity might serve them by dint of its longer experience of the factors tending to an allegedly inevitable secularity. There was a certain arrogance in this analysis. Even supposing the expectation to be right (time has disproved it) faiths must be left to their own resources in responding to destiny. But Van Leeuwen's stance demonstrated an aspect of the situation in the sixties to which Al-Faruqi was reacting. See his remark in *The Cultural Atlas*, p.xiii: 'The Orientalists have never proved themselves capable of *epoche* (laying aside of pre-judgement) in interpreting the religion and culture of Islam.' See also, Ibid, p.60: '... Muslim dissatisfaction with western interpretations of Islam.'
6 '*Urubah*, p.16.
7 S.C.Crawford, op. cit. pp.212-13. 'Apodeictic', here, means what is incontrovertible and demonstrable.
8 Ibid., p.217. 'Like knowing like' is an interesting formula here in respect of a theological knowledge absolutely feasible to man, since the 'unlikeness' of God is so insistently stressed in the Qur'an and in Islamic doctrine. 'None is like unto Him,' Surah 112: 4., et al.
9 Al-Faruqi's resistance to paradox runs through his whole theology and underlies his rejection of the need for any 'theodicy', or for an appreciation of the issue implicit in the concept of divine omnipotence and human freedom in wrong. For him, 'internal coherence precludes the recourse to paradox as theological principle.' *Christian Ethics*, p.11.) It is one thing, however, to resort to paradox too readily, quite another to suppress its presence out of a dogmatic endearment to rational solutions. For it is a wise rationality itself which experiences paradox and, not least, in the tasks and themes of theology. The classical Muslim

theologians had to wrestle with it in 'reconciling' the nameability of God with His entire transcendence.

10 *Cultural Atlas*, p.79.

11 The *Hanif* (pl. *Hunafa'*) in the Qur'an connotes one who stands outside Arab paganism by holding a form of monotheism which is, nevertheless, distinguishable from the theisms deriving from Moses and from Jesus and antecedent to Sinai and the Torah. For Al-Faruqi's account, see *Cultural Atlas*, p.61.

12 Ibid., p.19.

13 If we think of the 'unity' of God, not as a mere mathematical number but as an 'unrivalledness', or 'ultimacy', 'sovereignty' that has no 'elsewhere also', then – on the Christian view – it must signify redemptive 'ultimacy' whereby evil, as counter to that sovereignty, is overcome in an undivided 'rule' of God. Hence the faith in divine initiative to accomplish that 'unity'. In a revealing exchange in conversation at Chambèsy, Switzerland, Al-Faruqi discounted any such initiative but did so by failing to take the point in a *reductio ad absurdum* which substituted a pointless conjecture for an intelligible conviction. If 'and was made man' was to be affirmed as part of a theology of divine unity, why not: 'and was made brick'? See: *International Review of Missions* (Geneva), Vol.lxv, No.260, (October 1976), pp.400-409.

14 To write of 'what may be thought appropriate to God', may seem to imply that we humans have some role as jury here. How would such an attitude, or presumption, square with the concept of revelation which gives us to know what *God* wills to disclose, and over which we have no writ or right of question? Yet though Scriptures – Islamic or Christian in different ways – are 'given', the *datum*, they cannot be merely an 'it is so' and relate to us, mankind, as addressees, with minds to bring, imaginations to respond and wills to yield. Must not revelation, to a degree, involve an enabling of comprehension, a negotiation with thought and a rendezvous with hope and fear, desire and satisfaction?

15 The phrase occurs in the story of Joseph when, resisting the blandishments of Potiphar's wife, Joseph is aware of 'the bias towards evil' which belongs with *al-nafs al'ammarah bi-l-Su'*. It is the nearest the Qur'an comes to a sense of an inner liability to sin, present in the human psyche. The 'soul prone to evil' is linked with the 'soul self-reproachful' (*al-nafs al-lawwamah*, (Surah 75:2) and the 'soul at peace'. (*al-nafs al-mutma'innah* (Surah 89:27).

16 *Al-balagh*, the speaking of the message communicating truth to hearers, is stressed in the pre-Hijrah Qur'an as Muhammad's sole duty. It is contrasted with *al-hisab*, 'the reckoning', which belongs only to God. (For example: 3:20; 5:99; 13:40; 16:35; 24:54; and 29:18. The distinction bears strongly on the meaning of the Hijrah as a passage beyond *balagh* alone.

17 This development in meaning of a keyword in the Qur'an marks the sequence in Muhammad's career. The continuing factor is enmity and resistance to his message; when the latter passes into what Al-Faruqi calls 'battlefields' (*Cultural Atlas*, p.298) and issues are militarily joined, unbelief becomes also conspiracy.

18 'Self-wronging' or our degrading of our own selfhood, is a significant Quranic term, in the phrase about unbelievers: 'It was their own selves they wronged.' (e.g. 2:57: 7:160; and numerous other passages). See further my *The Mind of the Qur'an* (London, 1973), p.99.

19 This, of course, is a large theme. See, among others, J.N. Sanders, *Jesus and Judaism* (London, 1985); John Riches, *Jesus and the Transformation of Judaism* (London, 1980); and James H. Charlesworth, *Jesus within Judaism* (New York, 1988).

20 Is there a parallel in the issue within Buddhism, between the Theravada and the Mahayana as to the 'left alone-ness' of the individual self in respect of 'salvation', and the availability of 'grace' from outside the self?

21 *The Islamic Impulse*, ed. B.F.Stowasser (London, 1987), pp.226-243, where Al-Faruqi writes on: 'The Islamic Critique of the Status Quo in Muslim Society'.

22 Isma'il al-Faruqi, *Islamisation of Knowledge: General Principles and Workplan* (Washington, 1982), p.14.

23 Surah 30:30 uses both verb and noun: *fatara* and *fitrah*, to denote God's action in the genesis of man *and* the human nature which that action created and willed. Islam, as the 'pure religion' (*hanif*), exactly fits and fulfils that nature and the divine design within it. The verse might almost be rendered: 'the religion for which God made man religious'.

24 Muslims are not, of course, unanimous in their comprehension of the elements within Islam which Al-Faruqi lists here. One example would be the rich vein of Sufism, or Islamic mysticism, for which he has little enthusiasm. See, for example, *The Cultural Atlas*, pp.295-304, a mere ten pages.

Chapter 8

1 From 'In Good Faith', *The Sunday Independent* 4 February 1990.

2 It is useful to compare Rushdie's 'parables' from 'the city' of heterogeneity and bonhomie, with 'the city' in Albert Camus for whom the concentric circles of the canals of Amsterdam symbolise the subtleties of guilt and hypocrisy, or, again 'the city' in Charles Dickens as witness to the indestructibility of human goodness despite the labyrinths of circumstance and crime. Dickens was capable of infinite satire, fantasy and human perception, but always with healing intent.

3 Rushdie's experience at Rugby School no doubt 'interprets' the incident of the schoolboys and the kippers in *The Satanic Verses*, pp.44f. Page references are inserted, for convenience, where their use occurs.

4 Lahore – the Punjab's intellectual and religious capital; Aligarh – the seat of the Islamic University which grew out of Sayyid Ahmad Khan's 'Aligarh College', meant to nurture a modern, 'liberal' education to lead Indian Islam out of the stagnation following the tragedy of 1857; Deoband – the seat of the movement to purify and renew Islam which sprang from the legacy of Shah Waliyullah (1703-1762) and his son, Shah 'Abd al-'Aziz (1746-1843). Deoband and Aligarh stood for contrasted responses to Islamic destiny but there was no doubt about their virility. To do Bombay justice, mention may be made of A.A.A. Fyzee (1899-1981) whose *A Modern Approach to Islam* (Bombay, 1963), (had their paths crossed) could have served Rushdie's adolescence well. Professor Fayzee was a distinguished jurist, Cambridge Fellow, Ambassador of India in Cairo, and (earlier) Principal of the Law College, Bombay. See below, Chapter 10.

5 He quotes from N.J. Dawood's English translation and that of Muhammad Ali, of the Lahore Ahmadiyyah Movement. Apart from the Surah 53 passage, he cites only Surah 2:30f on the dignity of Adam and the angels' demur at his being entrusted with the world, and Surah 18.50 (p.353). These are very scant allusions considering the centrality of the Qur'an to his concerns. He does not reckon with those dimensions of the Qur'an which could have served to give him pause in his strictures. But he is clearly conversant with the broad picture as found in Ibn Hisham and the early chroniclers. He takes liberty to return Muhammad to Mecca fifteen years after his death, (i.e. twenty-five years from 622 CE. (Muhammad died in 632.)

6 Notably in Chap.vii, 'The Angel Azraeel', where Saladin Chamcha works out his 'motiveless malignity' (S.T.Coleridge's phrase) on Gabriel Farishta, after which he compels himself to ponder how far forgiveness can go in absolving guilt.

7 See W.Montgomery Watt: *Muhammad at Mecca* (Oxford, 1953), pp.101-09 for a discussion of the technical points involved in the whole episode. *Gharaniq*, 'swans'? or 'exalted birds'? may denote 'intercessory beings' in 'recognition' of whom Muhammad would not be forsaking the Lordship of *Allah* as One, but only conceding intermediaries. Rushdie is interested in the fact that the deities the Quraish wanted to retain were 'female', sex-bias thus intruding into the issues of pluralism and unity.

8 On this pivotal term, reference may be had to the discussion in my: *The Event of the Qur'an* (London, 1970) pp.25-39 and: *Muhammad and the Christian* (London, 1984), pp.81-99.

9 See below for the evident personal engagement of Muhammad in the discharge of the message, whatever may have been the case about its initial reception in his mind and speech. The Qur'an is believed in Islam to be the direct verbal 'speech of God', of which Muhammad is, as it were, the human echo. Yet Surah 2:97 says: 'We have sent it down upon your heart', 'the heart' being the seat of the emotions and the motive of the will. See, further: *The Christ and the Faiths* (London, 1986), 'Capacities in Revelation', pp.52-73. It will be clear from the chapter on Isma'il al-Faruqi how insistent the 'passive' view is, though it is disputed strongly by Fazlur Rahman, *Islam and Modernity* (Chicago, 1982), and *Islam* (London, 1966).

10 The Egyptian novelist, Najib Mahfuz (born 1912), with whom Rushdie has been compared by some, describes in *Awlad Haratina* (Beirut, 1967), trans. into English by Philip Stewart, as *Children of Gebalawi* (London, 1981), how the situation always deteriorates after a prophet's demise, when his followers quarrel and evils return to erstwhile haunts. This Mahfuz perceives to be the case with Moses, Jesus and Muhammad, whom he denotes with thinly disguised pseudonyms. Mahfuz is no less radical than Rushdie but there is a keener tone, a more incisive quality, to his narrative.

11 As. for example, when Farishta is transported in a parody of the Prophet's 'night Journey' to Jerusalem and finds himself looking down on densely packed throngs of chanting people – manifestly Teheran. (p.216ff. 'After the Revolution there will be no more birthdays. We shall all be born again.')

12 *The Sunday Independent*, 4 February 1990.

13 Ibid.

14 *Négritude* was first used, in 1947, by Aimé Césaire, whose poem: 'Hurrah! for those who never invented anything', exactly fits Rushdie's counsel that the best thing to do with scoffing is to wear its labels (libels) proudly. Similarly, Leopold Senghor, first and long-time President of Senegal, demonstrated that 'Black is beautiful', both by his splendid French poetry and his political leadership. As earlier a French Senator, he contrived to adorn 'blackness', not by a repudiation of all things 'white', but by a shared humanity. *O si sic omnes.*

15 See, for example, *The Dialogues of Plato*, where Timaeus, 71, considers that prophetic inspiration does not 'ride' with normal mental self-possession but somehow overrides it. In Ion, 534, Plato reasons that divine inspiration takes over from mental awareness when true 'poetry' occurs. But at least the *afflatus* has its seat within the self. The Qur'an, of course, is proceeding on a very different, and Semitic, idea of how God 'inspires'.

16 See, more fully, the study here of A.A.A. Fyzee.

17 One example of the 'reluctance', indeed total disavowal, occasioned by *The Satanic Verses* is: Shabbir Akhtar, *Be Careful with Muhammad: The Salman Rushdie Affair*, (London, 1989). He stands firmly by the view of the 'infallible dictation of Scripture' and requires that this cover all contents however uncongenial they may be to our 'taste', and adds: 'Muslims quite rightly interpret the Koran to be an error-free corpus undiluted by human factors external to its incidence.' Faith in it is an all-or-nothing affair. (pp.97-98). But were there no 'human factors' *internal* 'to its incidence'? The phrase would seem to mean that all human factors were external to its incidence, i.e., it happened, Muhammad being entirely passive.

18 This theme is best studied below in the chapter on Salah 'Abd al-Sabur.

19 In the Herbert Read Memorial Lecture, 6 February 1990, *Granta* (Cambridge, 1990), pp.7f.

20 Ibid. p.16. What I have called here 'this reservation' he sees as 'the privileged arena' in which writers can 'hear voices talking about everything in every possible way'. But he adds that this does not mean 'that writers want an absolute freedom to say and do whatever they please'.

21 The form *akbar* is comparative without any comparison worthy to be stated. It is not superlative: 'the greatest'. Whatever it be, in your mind or experience, say: 'greater is God.' This dethrones all pseudo-claimants to power, trust, authority, and worth/worship. So doing, it legitimates what is duly subordinate and has its proper worth in being so. This has to be so (indeed the more so) if the 'whatever' is 'Islam' itself.

Chapter 9

1 *Hayati fi-l-Shi'r*, 'My Life in Poetry (Cairo, 1981).

2 *Ma'sat al-Hallaj*, ('The Tragedy of Al-Hallaj) (Cairo, 1965), Eng. trans. Khalil I. Semaan: *Murder in Baghdad* (Leiden, 1972), p.63.

3 In *Al-Hilal* 7 April 1967, p.74, *Sha'iriyyat al-'Aqqad*, He criticised him, however, for a poetry that was over-philosophical, at the expense of sensuous feeling.

4 ('What Remains of them in History?') (Cairo, 1961), p.32. Taha Husain, blind from infancy, achieved a Doctorate at the Sorbonne and became the literary leader of his generation in Egypt. He was Dean of Arts at the (new) Cairo University and briefly Minister of Education. His studies on Pre-Islamic Poetry aroused strong conservative opposition for their implications in respect of the Qur'an. He pursued a critical scholarship in hope of nurturing a more perceptive religious allegiance.

5 ('The Oppressed in the Earth') (Cairo, 1949), in which, in a series of pen-portraits, he depicts the privations and sorrows of the poor, the disabled, the discarded people.

6 Notably in his *'Ala Hamish al-Sirah* (Cairo, 1933), 3 vols., in which he discussed the background and content of the traditions of the *Sirah*, or 'life-course', of Muhammad, writing – particularly for the new generation – in its 'Margins'.

7 There has long between a duality, in Egypt's sense of itself, by virtue of its 'presence' at Alexandria in the Mediterranean and – thanks to the Islamic invasion in the seventh century – its ties with the Arab East. Taha Husain in *Mustaqbal al-Thaqafah fi Misr*, 'The Future of Culture in Egypt' (Cairo, 1938) was eager to claim the former as the right direction for its consciousness – much to the disapproval of the advocates of a pure 'Islamicity' bound into Arabia.

8 Abu-l-Tayyib Ahmad al-Mutanabbi (915-965), of Yemeni birth, achieved great reputation as a poet, claiming almost a prophetic mission in its pursuit (Hence his name: 'pretender to prophethood'). He played a large role in the courts of rulers in Aleppo and Cairo, and has enjoyed a lasting reputation as a superb Arabic stylist, despite (or perhaps because of?) his disillusion with religion. Superstition and credulity he satirised vigorously. Abu-l-'Ala al-Ma'ari (995-1058) was an existentialist with a deep sense of the absurd long before the twentieth century exemplars of the position. Blind from infancy through smallpox, he wrote deep, poetic (and prose) portrayals of the human condition and musings on mortality. He became a famous recluse in his native village, Al-Ma'ara near Aleppo.

9 *Hayati*, p.123.

10 Ibid. pp.111-112.

11 Ibid. pp.113-114.

12 Salamah Musa (1887-1958), a prolific writer and journalist, modelled an autobiography: *Tarbiyah Salamah Musa* ('The Education of Salamah Musa') on that of Henry Adams of the same title. He popularised evolutionary theory and was widely read by Egyptian youth of his time.

13 *Hayati*, p.115 where he quotes from *Al-Nas Fi Biladi* (Beirut, 1965 ed.) p.35.

14 Ibid. p.120.

15 Ibid. p.121. He continues: 'I believe that the goal of existence is the overcoming of evil by good through long and bitter struggle, in returning to original purity – not a purity which is blind and anonymous, as it was when it emanated from God, but a purity that has passed through testing and emerged from it, like gold coming from the fire, pure and moulded. The responsibility of man is to shape existence and purify it at the same time.'

16 He does not use the Qur'an's word *raja'*, but *'ada*, Yet the theme is the same – our destiny beyond death. *Zulm* in the Qur'an is the act of 'wronging' in which true relationship to God, or others, or the self, are distorted, perverted or abused.

17 *Hayati*. p.123. *Al-Zul wa-l-Salib*, in *Aqulu Lakum* ('I Say to You') (Beirut, 3rd ed. 1969), pp.60-71.

18 *Al-Nas fi Biladi*, pp.73-76.

19 *Ahlam al-Faris al-Qadim*, ('Dreams of the Ancient Knight') (Cairo, 1961), trans. by M.M. Badawi in *Journal of Arabic Literature*, Vol.1,1970, pp.117-119. The sentiment is reminiscent of C.H. Sorley: *Marlborough Poems* (Cambridge, 1919), in which the poet broods on his own impotence in contrast to the living thrust of a flowing river and yearns 'to be a part of one great strength that moves and cannot die.' pp.51-53.

20 Will Sypher: *The Loss of the Self in Modern Literature and Art* (New York, 1962), p.93.

21 *Al-Nas fi Biladi*, pp.35-37.

22 Ibid.

23 trans. by M.M. Badawi in *Journal of Arabic Literature*, Vol.2 (1971), pp.101-103.

24 *Ahlam*, 'A Song to God'.

25 Dag Hammarskjöld: *Markings*, trans. by L.Sjöberg & W.H.Auden, (New York, 1964), p.151.

26 The Swedish envoy of the UNO murdered by Israeli terrorists in September 1948, to thwart a finalisation of partition via an agreed peace plan for Palestine. The assassins were never brought to justice.

27 *Markings*, p.xv.

28 Often called 'the oceanic feeling' in which personal identity is merged in totality. It is not properly understood as 'annihilation' (for there is no 'entity' to 'annihilate'. A 'drop' *is* in the ocean but no longer as 'drop'. Mahayana Buddhism mitigates the severity of the Theravada tradition.

29 T.S. Eliot: *Murder in the Cathedral* (London, 1968 Ed.) p.41-48.

30 Ibid. p.53.

31 The Sufi was liable to say: 'If you are far from God now, you will remain so in Mecca. If you are near to Him now, there is no need to travel.' Or a 'saint' himself could be as good a *qutb*, or 'axis' as any *Ka'bah*. Such notions were, of course, anathema to the custodians of pilgrim rites and obligation.

32 The verse was much beloved of Sufis. For 'the light' in 'the lamp' in 'the niche' could admit of many mystical meanings. Here the spirit of the devotee enshrines the divine light.

33 Abraham J. Heschel: *The Prophets* (New York, 1952), p.21.

34 After the deaths of Khadijah, his wife, and Abu Talib, his uncle and protector, and with the unyielding obduracy of the Quraish, Muhammad's situation was dark and dangerous. Enquiring pilgrims to Mecca from Yathrib (the city which became Al-Madinah) paved the way for the *Hijrah* and with it the prelude to ultimate triumph.

35 *Sabur* (from the root S B R-'patience') is one of the Names of God, and *'abd* is the human 'servant'. The root, S B R, verb and noun, is very frequent in the Qur'an, though Al-Sabur itself does not occur there. It is listed in Edwin Arnold's *Pearls of Faith*, as the ninety-ninth Name: 'O loving-kind, long-suffering Lord, once more we praise Thee, magnifying Al-Sabur.'

Chapter 10

1   A.A.A. Fyzee: *A Modern Approach to Islam* (Bombay, 1963), p.vii. (later: MAI)

2   In his *Outlines of Muhammadan Law* (Oxford, 1949), New edition 1964.

3   In: '*Urubah and Religion* (Montreal, 1962) See Chapter 7, above.

4   What partition entailed on the millions of Muslims remaining within political India, and on their leaders, may be gauged, for example, in Badr al-Din Tyabji, *Indian Politics and Practice* (Delhi, 1972). The author belonged to a prominent Bombay Muslim family. He wrote: 'On the sensibilities of our Indian Muslims it [i.e. Hindu/Muslim relations] imposes an exacting, almost intolerable, strain: only the strong minded can survive it. ...A continual din of voices of bias, prejudice, hypocrisy and downright falsehood in favour of a sectarian point of view...' (p.204) attending the need to promote Indianization in the face of Hindu extremism and Muslim resentment or apathy. Tyabji deals with the problems of Aligarh University, pp.215-20. For a jaundiced view, see: K.L.Gauba, *Passive Voices: A Penetrating Study of Muslims in India* (Jullundur, 1973). 'The reader will be able to decide...whether the Indian Muslim does not join the mainstream or is successfully kept apart from it.'(p.x.) Gauba derides the Presidency of Dr Zakir Husain as 'a good show-piece in the window'. (p.viii.)

5   Dr Zakir Husain (1897-1969) was a noted educationalist and a staunch admirer of Maulana Azad.

6   Divided opinions on the nature and due mechanisms of Islamic statehood deferred the shaping of the Pakistani Constitution only to have it, at length, abrogated by military coup(s), with its vicissitudes heavily dependent on military attitudes up to the advent of Zia al-Haqq with his strongly conservative views and his distrust of democratic means as any adequate ensuring of a true Islamicity. Are 'Basic Principles' and their implementation in 'non-repugnancy to the Qur'an' safe with the masses as an organ of *Ijma'* (consensus) or must they be vested in '*ulama*' and/or the generals?

7   Fyzee also wrote on Isma'ili Law in particular and numerous articles and pamphlets on Shi'ah Islam in general.

8   The *Da'a'im* of Qadi Nu'man (d. Cairo 974 CE) was edited by Fyzee: Vol. 1 (Cairo, 1951), Vol. 2 (Cairo, 1961). See also his *Compendium of Fatimid Law* (Simla, 1969) pp.xxi- xxvi, and also his article in *The Journal of the Royal Asiatic Society* (London, 1934), pp.1-32. See also *The Muslim World Quarterly*, Vol. L, (1960), pp.30-38 by Bayard Dodge.

9   An interest confided to this writer during Fyzee's second residence at St. John's College, Cambridge. There is a perhaps relevant footnote in MAI p.33 comparing the difficulty presenting itself to Shaikh al-Azhar interpreting St. John, with that of a Christian priest (in this case A.C. Bouquet) handling Islam.

10 Azad's *Autobiographical Narrative*, ed. Humayun Kabir (Bombay, 1959). On Azad, see also: Ian H. Douglas, *Abul Kalam Azad. An Intellectual and Religious Biography*, ed. G. Minault & C.H. Troll (Delhi, 1988) and Kenneth Cragg, *The Pen and the Faith* (London, 1985), pp.14-32.

11 Muhammad Mujeeb, *The Indian Muslims* (New Delhi ed., 1985), pp.441-42.

12 *Tarjuman al-Qur'an*, Vol.1 (Delhi, 1931); Vol.2 (Delhi, 1936).

13   The argument may be thought to forfeit some of its point when it is recalled that the Prophet did so only *en route* to total victory over Mecca and as a tactic to that end, not in the permanent expectation which could only be in view for Muslims in divided India.

14   There was long and anxious debate during the time of the British Raj on the same issue of whether India was then *Dar al-Islam*. Answer had to hinge on what was regarded as crucial to that status – political power or religious liberty only. In 1803 a *Fatwa* was issued by Shah Abdul-Aziz affirming, in Persian, that India was no longer *Dar al-Islam*, since physical power was in the hands of the British. After the failure of the uprising in 1857 Sayyid Ahmad Khan sought to renew Muslims by identifying a veritable *Dar al-Islam* in the full availability of religious rituals etc., despite foreign rule.

15   Having *islam* here as a common noun, not capitalised to distinguish it from the historical actuality of Islam, is a significant usage. Islam is the full and final institutionalising of *islam*, as personal 'submission', but the latter long antedates it and may be validly distinguished from it. Abraham, for example, did not know Islam but he practised *islam* to God.

16   Arthur Jeffery, *Foreign Vocabulary of the Qur'an* (Baroda, 1938). This interesting study of words of non-Arabic origin in the Qur'an had to find a publisher in India, because orthodox Muslims insisted that the Qur'an, being pure Arabic, had no such words. Fyzee had no use for an obscurantism which shielded dogma from evidences.

17   The distinction in Surah 3:7 is of vital importance for exegesis and is the theme of much diverse interpretation. The *muhkamat* are explicit and entirely unambiguous, whereas the *mutashabihat* are, for example, the metaphors used in anthropomorphisms like 'the right hand' of God. The latter afford occasion for freer interpretation against which faith must be on its guard. For the verse itself notes that 'deviants' are fond of them and reserves their real meaning to God alone.

18   The term *Ijtihad* (from the same root as *Jihad*) means 'enterprise' or 'endeavour', and refers in Sunni Islam to initiatives (made only by the duly qualified) which might lead to *Ijma'*, or 'consensus', by which the community might approve what they pioneer. In Shi'ah Islam *Ijtihad* is the guiding activity of the *Mujtahids* acting for the Hidden Imam. The 'gate' (*Bab*) of *Ijtihad* is the crux of the question whether the necessary initiatives have long ago been taken by the Sunni experts and the task of 'consensus' is complete, or whether decisions are still urgent so that the 'gate' must be ever open. For the Shi'ah the 'gate' is within the sole behest of the Imam's spokesmen and Ayatollahs.

19   After disturbances in the Punjab over the claims of the Ahmadiyyah Movement, a Judicial Inquiry, known as the Munir Report, contained an interrogation of 'ulama' in which basic disagreements were revealed in the very definition of Islam. The Report indicated the difficulty of defining, still more of ensuring, the authentic Islam which was the *raison d'être* of the creation of an Islamic state.

20   *Takfir* is the branding of a position as *kufr*, or 'unbelief', with resultant anathema. There are currently radical groups in Islam using the term in their titles to indicate their hostility even to 'conservative' 'ulama', as well as to 'secularisers'.

21 Author of *Our Heritage* (Bombay, 1946), and Editor of Azad's *Memorial Volume* (Bombay, 1959).

22 Aziz Ahmad, *Islamic Modernism in India and Pakistan, 1857-1964* (Oxford, 1967). pp.236-37.

23 The imperative nature of Islam as divine directive is paramount in Isma'il al-Faruqi, Chapter 7, above. Cf. also Fazlur Rahman, *Major Themes of the Qur'an* (Minneapolis, 1980), 'The Qur'an is no treatise about God and His nature: His existence for the Qur'an is strictly functional', p.1.

Chapter 11

1   Raimundo Panikkar, *Myth, Faith and Hermeneutics* (New York, 1970), p.11, (afterwards MFH).

2   Ibid. He finds multi-language 'debilitating' as well as enriching, in that it generates an awareness of how little any language satisfies.

3   Raimundo Panikkar, *Faith and Belief: The Inter-Religious* Dialogue (New York, 1978), p.220.

4   *The Unknown Christ of Hinduism* (London, 1964). 2nd edition (London, 1981), (afterwards UCH).

5   It is interesting to observe how, somehow, the word 'ecumenical' came to be unwittingly monopolised by the Christian purpose with it, in, e.g., the World Council of Churches and 'the Ecumenical Movement'. The United Nations, for example, did not adopt it, though it could have well fitted that world organisation.

6   *The Unknown Christ*, 2nd ed. p.14. The capitalising of 'Man' Panikkar explains, is his attempt to satisfy feminist concern, while refusing to disallow the inclusive meaning: 'humanity' distinguishing 'a man', (male) by lower case 'm'.

7   'The Relation of Christians to their Non-Christian Surroundings,' in ed. Joseph Neuner: *Christian Revelation and World Religions* (London, 1967), p.152, (afterwards CRWR).

8   River imagery figures also in ed. John Hick & Paul. F. Knitter, *The Myth of Christian Uniqueness* (London, 1987). See below.

9   Karl Rahner, the eminent German, Jesuit, theologian (1904-1984) developed the concept of 'anonymous Christians' as a legitimate descriptive of sincere believers in other faiths. It derived from his understanding of Christology and 'God's self-gift' of grace as fulfilling salvific intention towards all mankind whether or not they were cognisant of its reality.

10 There would seem to be an aberration here. Classical Christology, even in its sharpest controversies, has been concerned to understand the divine in the historical. Were divinity 'denied' there would be no mystery to resolve nor could there be a Christ other than in history. To speak of 'limit' here begs the whole meaning of *kenosis* and of Incarnation.

11 Raimundo Panikkar, *The Trinity and the Religious Experience of Man* (London, 1973), p.29, (afterwards TREM).

12 See also: Raimundo Panikkar, *The Vedic Experience* (Berkeley, 1977), pp.747-53.

13 The issue whether to 'call' God can only be 'to address' and not 'to denote', has long engaged theologians. For it has to do with the place of theology in worship and of worship in theology. Can they really be separated since every vocative must be in some way an affirmative? There is a parallel situation in Islam with the Names of God and the precise sense in which they could be used. But used they had to be. Cf. Surah 7:180.

14 Raimundo Panikkar, *Worship and Secular Man* (London, 1973), p.93.

15 He does, however, write that 'the Church brings every true and authentic religion to its fulfilment through a process of death and resurrection which is the true meaning of conversion.' (UCH, p.169) But, if they are 'true and authentic' will they need it? And how should 'fulfilment' be understood?

16 *The Myth* (see note 8) pp.113-14.

17 When Plato in *Timaeus* likened 'the soul of the universe' to the Greek letter 'X', Justin Martyr in his *Apologia*, 1, 60-61, saw it as foreshadowing the Cross of Jesus. 'He (Plato) placed him ('the Son of God') like an 'X' in the universe...not clearly understanding nor realising that it was the form of the Cross, but thinking that it was the letter Chi, said that the power next to God was placed X-wise in the universe.' But while Justin has a Christian 'X', 'X' otherwise is meant as a cypher.

18 See footnote 15, p.115 in *The Myth*. In a different sense, Albert Schweitzer in his *The Quest of the Historical Jesus*, tr. W.Montgomery (London, 1910), p.399, spoke of Jesus coming 'as one unknown' to Christians. His reference was to the allegedly entire discrepancy between Jesus as he had been and the Christ of traditional Christology. Panikkar's 'unknownness' of Jesus among Christians is of a different order, belonging not to historical 'quest' or 'inquest', but to ontology.

19 *Worship and Secular Man*, op.cit., p.68.

20 Cf. Samuel Chew, *The Crescent and the Rose* (New York, 1937), a study of medieval relations between Islam and Christianity.

21 Mahatma Gandhi, in *Young India*, 19 January 1928 and 15 October 1931. Cited by Panikkar in *Christian Revelation and World Religions*, p.182.

Chapter 12

1 The historian Albert Hourani's comment on Arnold Toynbee and *A Study of History*.

2 *Christianity among the Religions of the World* (Oxford, 1958), p.3.

3 Ed. Christian B.Peper, *An Historian's Conscience: The Correspondence of Arnold J.Toynbee & Columba Cary-Elwes, Monk of Ampleforth* (Oxford, 1987). (Later as HC)

4 *Civilization on Trial* (Oxford, 1948), p.94. (Later ConT)

5 Arnold J.Toynbee, *Experiences* (London, 1969), p.165, relating to the Liturgy of Easter Eve, in the Ethiopian Cathedral, Addis Ababa.

6 Perhaps there is an echo of the Qur'an's phrase: *Wa nahnu ilaihi raji'un*, 'and unto Him are we returning', in ConT, Preface 'To Him return we every one'. On the great-uncle Harry, see *Acquaintances* (Oxford, 1967), pp.1-20.

7 Oxford, Vols. i-iii, 1934; iv-vi, 1939; vii-x, 1954, Vols. xi and xii, 1959-61. The summary, by D.C. Somervell, 2 vols, was published with Toynbee's approbation in 1946 and 1955.

8 However, in *Experiences*, p.158f. we do find Toynbee writing: 'Love and conscience may be indicators of the character of ultimate Reality.'

9 There are times when he seems to imply that there is something inherently, i.e., irreversibly, selfish about being a self, though he is strongly critical of Theravada Buddhism in its view that 'self' equals 'selfishness'.

10 An intriguing Muslim study of this very theme of the bias of collectives towards 'injustice' and 'wrong' which Toynbee seems not to have noticed was Muhammad Kamil Husain's *Qaryah Zalimah* (Cairo, 1954), translated into English as *City of Wrong* (Amsterdam, 1958). By that clue it studied the motives instigating the crucifixion of Jesus in Jerusalem. It develops the basic Quranic concept of *Zulm*, or 'perversity' besetting human situation, especially in respect of power.

11 Such, for example, as Al-Muhasibi of Baghdad (781-857) who was the careful 'accountant' of his own soul.

12 'Disproven' in view, for example, of the repeated statement one finds among Muslims today that there has been no authentic Islam since the 'rightly guided Caliphs' between 632 and 661, after whom, under the Umayyads, declension set in.

13 *An Historian's Approach to Religion* (Oxford, 1956), p.110. (Later HAR.)

14 See Oskar K. Rabinowicz, *Arnold Toynbee on Judaism and Zionism, A Critique* (London, 1974).

15 It is clear in the Hebrew Scriptures and in modern Jewish interpretation of them that a close connection exists, in the concept of the *goyim*, between their idolatry and ethnic separatism. Heathenism and race combine. E.g., R. Loewe, *Rationalism, Judaism and Universalism* (London, 1966), p.132.

16 Lamin Sanneh has a fascinating study of the significance of the readiness for multi-language translation characteristic of the Christian possession of Christian Scriptures, in *Translating the Message: The Missionary Impact on Culture* (New York, 1989)

17 It is necessary to say 'combative' here inasmuch as the land was otherwise occupied and could not be had in 'innocence', as Zionist pioneering initially supposed. Nor could such 'existing population' – in its self-understanding – be denied the same philosophy as Zionism, namely the necessity of 'statehood' in the expression, and ensuring, of their identity. Hence the inevitable conflict and the non-innocence.

18 The point is familiar, for example, in Martin Buber's *Two Types of Faith*, trans. N.P. Goldhawk (New York, 1961). Christians have to 'become' such by decision, Jews are 'already there' in covenantal birth-relation with God.

19 Hayy Ibn Yaqzan, 'Alive, Son of Wakeful', according to Muslim legend grew up in total absence of education, nurture, or direction, and arrived by natural sagacity at Islam as the true, rational faith. The corollary of this is that birth 'orients' the human to the Islamic; it is parents, etc. who misguide.

20 Toynbee breaks off, however, before: 'Wherefore, God has highly exalted him . . .' The reason soon becomes apparent.

21 *Christianity among the Religions of the World* (Oxford, 1958), p.107.

22 Ibid. p.21.

23 *A Study of History* Study ix, pp.634-35 It was in 1936. The crucifix in the Abbey is referred to in the correspondence with Columba Cary-Elwes whom Toynbee often visited at Ampleforth when pressures allowed. (See Note 3).

24 The same self-sacrifice was also true of the *bodhisattvas*. In *An Historian's Conscience*, p.199, Toynbee observed: 'a man can still be proud when he expresses his pride through the agency of an institution.' 'Christians do not effectively become humble by transferring their pride to the Church.' Thus, the issue of 'intention' – what Islam calls *niyyah* – is crucial to all efforts to subsume it into something else, whether in negation, martyrdom, or forms of collective commitment that mean to abandon personal considerations of every kind.

25 *A Study of History*, Vol.v, pp.527f.

26 Ibid. Vol.vii. p.443.

27 Ibid. Vol.vii. p.430.

28 Ibid. Vol.vi. pp.276-78.

Chapter 13

1 There is a vast literature on the history of the partition of the sub-continent in 1947 and on the politics of the Muslim League under the leadership of Muhammad Ali Jinnah. There was undoubtedly a deep element of ideology, the urge to proceed upon the age-long principle of Islam that power was the necessary concomitant of Islamic truth and that where power could be had, i.e., in areas of Muslim preponderance of population, it must be attained, in preference to existence in permanent minority status in a united India. That, however, had to be the destiny of those millions of Muslims whom Pakistan could not contain.

But partisan factors, and economic pressures, played their part. As a State founded in the name of a religion Pakistan has been in long and inconclusive debate with itself as to how its Islamicity should be perceived and made good.

2 His doctorate at Princeton, later, concerned the thought and intellectual policy of the Azhar University in Cairo, as evident in its Journal, *Majallat al-Azhar* during the thirties and early forties.

3 London, 1946, (revised edition) Also Lahore, 1943 and 1963.

4 Princeton, 1957.

5 In ed. C.H.Phillips, *Politics and Society in India* (London, 1965): 'The Ulama in Indian Politics,' pp.39-51 (Note p.45).

6 *Faith and Belief* (Princeton, 1979), p.142.

7 The foregoing is summarised from *The Meaning and End of Religion. A New Approach to the Religious Traditions of Mankind* (New York, 1963); *Questions of Religious Truth* (New York, 1967); and *The Faith of Other Men*, enlarged ed. (New York, 1963); and *Belief and History* (Charlottesville, 1977). See also ed. W.G. Oxtoby, *Religious Diversity* (New York, 1976), and Edward J. Hughes, *Wilfred Cantwell Smith, A Theology for the World* (London, 1986).

8 *Towards a World Theology* (London, 1981). Page references are given from this work in brackets when cited.

9 Islam, here, is unique in having a name which is not an 'ism' nor an 'ity', a name integral to its origin and its meaning, a word that can be a common noun, and yielding 'muslim' as the proper denominator of participants.

10 See Muhammad Aziz Lahbabi, *Le Personnalisme Musulman* (Paris, 1964).

11 Martin Buber, *Two Types of Faith, A Study of the Inter-Penetration of Judaism and Christianity*, trans. N.P. Goldhawk (New York, 1951), and *I and Thou*, trans. R. Gregor Smith (New York, 1958). Smith notes that Buber wrote his doctoral dissertation on two Christian thinkers, Nicholas of Cusa and Jacob Böhme.

12 Radhakrishnan (1888-1975) ably mediated between Indian and Western philosophy and religion. See: *The Hindu View of Life* (London, 1927), and *Eastern Religions and Western Thought* (Oxford, 1939).

13 This exclusion of each faith-expression from the other's 'inside-ness' seems to be contrary to the basic assumption of Smith that the essential 'response to transcendence' is all one. If 'the Muslim's ideal of Islam has been an evolving *human* vision' (p.30) why cannot Jew/Christian/Buddhist share it? But can it be shared by exclusion from its particulars? If we 'must admit all that has been operative in peoples' being what they are, as Jew, Muslim, etc., how can we do so without entering into the Scriptures, the rituals, the symbols, the behaviours by which they are themselves? How are we reaching 'a world theology' if we have no passports?

14 Vol.11, 1980, pp.487-505.

15 It is urgent to counter the divisiveness arising from the way fideists in all faiths reserve their Scriptures from 'alien' scrutiny. We can only do so by claiming openness to all as their proper function.

16 Not all scholars have this sensitivity. Lack of it contributes to the defensiveness noted in 15 above.

17 Particularly the analysis of the *raison d'être* of the Islamic State as against a unitary India, and the analysis of the nature of Turkish secular statehood, its logic, its operation and the slow reversion from it.

18 *Al-Fitrah* is 'the faculty of knowing God with which He has in creation endowed or constituted mankind'. This natural faculty of God-awareness is *islam* (Islam) and the word *fitrah* is, therefore, a synonym for that religion. The noun occurs only in Surah 30:30: 'the nature of God on which He natured mankind.'

19 G.W. Choudhury *Islam and the Contemporary World* (London, 1990), p.7. My italics.

20 Turning on the subtleties of *ta'wil* and the authority of the trustees of 'the light of Muhammad' on behalf of 'the Hidden Imam'.

21 Isma'il R. al-Faruqi, *Islam* (Niles, Illinois, 1979). p.68. Not all Muslims would agree.

22 In noting here how the adjectival may be more readily shared than the substantive, we need also to note that Muslims have sometimes distinguished between 'Islamic' and 'Muslim' – using the former to denote what is authentic and the latter what is only approximating to what should be. Thus, for example, one might say that Turkey is a Muslim society while denying that it is Islamic. In this way one might check the vagaries of the adjectival.

23 Muhammad Kamil Husain, *Al-Wadi al-Muqaddas* (Cairo, 1968) Eng. trans. Kenneth Cragg, *The Hallowed Valley* (Cairo, 1977), p.1.

Chapter 14

1   John Bunyan, *Grace Abounding to the Chief of Sinners*, Para. 180. 'I took an opportunity to break my mind to an ancient Christian and told him all my case...I found him, though a good man, a stranger to much combat with the devil. Wherefore, I went to God again as well as I could.'

2   Robert Louis Stevenson, *Virginibus Puerisque and Other Essays* (1924 ed.) p.26.

3   Such volatility is instanced in the writings of Paul Van Buren, who has moved through Barthianism to a radical 'death-of-God' existentialism and back again to a Barthian-style 'Judaicism', which makes categorically absolute the exclusive covenant with Israel. On the last see: *A Theology of the Jewish Christian Reality*, in four Parts (San Francisco, 1980-1988).

4   There is an unhappy ambiguous example of this in the version of the Nicene Creed in the Prayer Book of the Episcopal Church, USA as revised, namely the omission of 'men,' in the clause: '...who for us men and for our salvation came...' The intention is worthy, namely to satisfy the feminists and neatly elide the possible, but unnecessary confinement of 'mankind' to 'males'. But it also tolerates the meaning that the Incarnation relates to 'us present', 'us Americans', 'us believers', rather than to all universally. The confusion is grievous. For in creeds one must – in saying what one means – avoid saying what one does not mean.

5   This issue of human convertibility is discussed more fully in: John R. Stott & Robert T. Coote, *Gospel and Culture*, (Pasadena, 1979), pp. 263-284: 'Conversion and Convertibility.'

6   David Hume, of whom Boswell records: 'he said flatly that the morality of every religion was bad and, I really thought, was not jocular when he said that when he heard a man was religious, he concluded he was a rascal.' ed. C.M. Weis & F.A. Pottle, *Boswell in Extremes, 1776-1778* (New York, 1970), p.15.

7   The preferred phrase in Iris Murdoch, *The Sovereignty of Good* (London, 1970), who disallows the explicitly 'theological' but is eloquently aware of the need for true 'unselfing'.

8   William Cowper, *The Task* (1785), Bk.iii,196-201. Shakespeare, of course, said it better *via* Shylock in: 'Hath not a Jew eyes?'

9   The tradition is found cited in many places. It is traced back to *The Sunan* of Abu 'Isa Muhammad ibn Sawrah al-Tirmidhi, see 3rd edition (Beirut, 1978) (A.H. 1398), Vol.3, p.318.

    The conviction that the 'changing (of evil) in the heart' is 'weaker' than manual action and oral protest lies behind the concept of *taqiyyah* in Shi'ah Islam, i.e., acquiescence in (presently) entrenched evils while not conceding them in the heart, pending the time that will be ripe for coming out into open resistance and – hopefully – effective counter-action.

10   Emily Dickinson, *Collected Poems* (New York, 1890-96). p.183:

> This world is not conclusion:
> A sequel stands beyond,
> Invisible as music, but positive as sound.
> It beckons and it baffles:

> Philosophies don't know,
> And through a riddle at the last
> Sagacity must go . . .

11 W.B. Yeats: 'Wisdom', in *Collected Poems* (London, 1959), p.216.
One might compare William Blake's lines:

> The vision of Christ that thou dost see
> Is my vision's greatest enemy . . .
> Thine is the friend of all mankind,
> Mine speaks in parables to the blind . . .

12 R.S. Thomas' poems dwell often on the theme of the elusiveness of God, the enigma of 'the face', 'its features dissolving in the radiation out of a black hole.' *The Echoes Return Slow*, (London, 1988), p.39. See also *Pieta* (London, 1966), 'In Church'.

13 The word, *sunistesin*, used in Romans 5:8: 'God commends His love towards us in that, while we were yet sinners, Christ died for us', has a rich connotation. 'Commends' is a present tense, about a past event, meaning that the event remains a present proof. *Sunistesin* has the sense of 'to bring out' (by way of evidence), and so 'to establish' and 'to cause to cohere', and so 'to consist in'. It may also be used to bring people together as friends, i.e., 'to introduce'. Used intransitively, it means: 'it stands', as in: 'After further review the decision stands.' Paul uses the same verb in Romans 3:5 in the sense of 'evidencing', and in 16:1, 'recommending' an associate.

INDEX